Lecture Notes in Computer Scie

Commenced Publication in 1973
Founding and Former Series Editors:
Gerhard Goos, Juris Hartmanis, and Jan van Leeuwen

Marco Dorigo   Mauro Birattari
Christian Blum   Anders Lyhne Christensen
Andries P. Engelbrecht   Roderich Groß
Thomas Stützle (Eds.)

Swarm Intelligence

8th International Conference, ANTS 2012
Brussels, Belgium, September 12-14, 2012
Proceedings

 Springer

Volume Editors

Marco Dorigo
Mauro Birattari
Thomas Stützle
Université Libre de Bruxelles
1050 Brussels, Belgium
E-mail: {mdorigo, mbiro, stuetzle}@ulb.ac.be

Christian Blum
Universitat Politècnica de Catalunya
Llenguatges i 08034 Barcelona, Spain
E-mail: cblum@lsi.upc.edu

Anders Lyhne Christensen
Instituto Universitário de Lisboa (ISCTE-IUL)
1649-026 Lisboa, Portugal
E-mail: anders.christensen@iscte.pt

Andries P. Engelbrecht
University of Pretoria
Pretoria 0002, South Africa
E-mail: engel@cs.up.ac.za

Roderich Groß
The University of Sheffield
Sheffield S1 3JD, UK
E-mail: r.gross@sheffield.ac.uk

ISSN 0302-9743   e-ISSN 1611-3349
ISBN 978-3-642-32649-3   e-ISBN 978-3-642-32650-9
DOI 10.1007/978-3-642-32650-9
Springer Heidelberg Dordrecht London New York

Library of Congress Control Number: 2012943942

CR Subject Classification (1998): I.2.6, I.2.8-9, F.2.2, I.2.11, F.1, H.4.2

LNCS Sublibrary: SL 1 – Theoretical Computer Science and General Issues

Typesetting: Camera-ready by author, data conversion by Scientific Publishing Services, Chennai, India

Printed on acid-free paper

Springer is part of Springer Science+Business Media (www.springer.com)

Preface

These proceedings contain the papers presented at ANTS 2012, the 8th International Conference on Swarm Intelligence, held at IRIDIA, Université Libre de Bruxelles, Brussels, Belgium, during September 12–14, 2012. The ANTS series started in 1998 with the First International Workshop on Ant Colony Optimization (ANTS 1998), which attracted more than 50 participants. Since then ANTS, which is held bi-annually, has gradually become an international forum for researchers in the wider field of swarm intelligence. In 2004, this development was acknowledged by the inclusion of the term "Swarm Intelligence" (next to "Ant Colony Optimization") in the conference title. Since 2010, the ANTS conference is officially devoted to the field of swarm intelligence as a whole, without any bias toward specific research directions. This is reflected in the title of the conference: "International Conference on Swarm Intelligence."

This volume contains the best papers selected out of 81 submissions. Of these, 15 were accepted as full-length papers, while 20 were accepted as short papers. This corresponds to an overall acceptance rate of 43%. Also included in this volume are seven extended abstracts.

All the contributions were presented as posters. The full-length papers were also presented orally in a plenary session. Extended versions of the best papers presented at the conference will be published in a special issue of the *Swarm Intelligence* journal.

We take this opportunity to thank the large number of people that were involved in making this conference a success. We express our gratitude to the authors who contributed their work, to the members of the International Program Committee, to the additional referees for their qualified and detailed reviews, and to the staff at IRIDIA for helping with organizational matters. We thank Nigel R. Franks, Vijay Kumar, and Dirk Helbing for their inspiring keynote talks. Finally, we thank AntOptima, ECCAI–the European Coordinating Committee for Artificial Intelligence, the European Research Council, the French Community of Belgium (through the ARC research project META-X), and the Fund for Scientific Research–FNRS for their gracious support.

We hope the reader will find this volume useful both as a reference to current research in swarm intelligence and as a starting point for future work.

July 2012

Marco Dorigo
Mauro Birattari
Christian Blum
Anders Lyhne Christensen
Andries P. Engelbrecht
Roderich Groß
Thomas Stützle

Organization

ANTS 2012 was organized by IRIDIA, Université Libre de Bruxelles, Belgium.

General Chair

Marco Dorigo   Université Libre de Bruxelles, Belgium

Technical Program Chairs

Christian Blum   Universitat Politècnica de Catalunya, Spain
Andries P. Engelbrecht   University of Pretoria, South Africa
Roderich Groß   The University of Sheffield, UK

Publication Chair

Anders Lyhne Christensen   Instituto de Telecomunicações & Instituto
                                Universitário de Lisboa (ISCTE-IUL),
                                Lisbon, Portugal

Organization Chairs

Mauro Birattari   Université Libre de Bruxelles, Belgium
Thomas Stützle   Université Libre de Bruxelles, Belgium

Local Arrangements

Andreagiovanni Reina   Université Libre de Bruxelles, Belgium
Arne Brutschy   Université Libre de Bruxelles, Belgium

Program Committee

Andy Adamatzky   University of the West of England, UK
Abbas Ahmadi   Amirkabir University of Technology, Iran
Daniel Angus   University of Queensland, Australia
Ronald Arkin   Georgia Institute of Technology, USA
Jacob Beal   BBN Technologies, USA
Gerardo Beni   University of California, USA
Spring Berman   Arizona State University, USA

Tim Blackwell	Goldsmiths, University of London, UK
Maria J. Blesa	Universitat Politècnica de Catalunya, Spain
Alfred Bruckstein	Technion–Israel Institute of Technology, Israel
Fernando Buarque	Universidade de Pernambuco, Brazil
Leticia Cagnina	Universidad Nacional de San Luis, Argentina
Emilio Fortunato Campana	Consiglio Nazionale delle Ricerche, Italy
Marco Chiarandini	University of Southern Denmark, Denmark
David Johan Christensen	Technical University of Denmark, Denmark
Maurice Clerc	Independent Consultant, France
Carlos Coello Coello	CINVESTAV-IPN, Mexico
Oscar Cordon	European Centre for Soft Computing, Spain
Iain Couzin	Princeton University, USA
Sanjoy Das	Kansas State University, USA
Kusum Deep	Indian Institute of Technology Roorkee, India
Gianni Di Caro	IDSIA, USI-SUPSI, Switzerland
Luca Di Gaspero	University of Udine, Italy
Karl Doerner	Johannes Kepler Universität Linz, Austria
Leandro Dos Santos Coelho	Pontifical Catholic University of Parana, Brazil
Haibin Duan	Beihang University, China
Frederick Ducatelle	IDSIA, USI-SUPSI, Switzerland
Mohammed El-Abd	American University in Kuwait, Kuwait
Susana Cecilia Esquivel	Universidad Nacional de San Luis, Argentina
Jonathan Fieldsend	Exeter University, UK
Luca Maria Gambardella	IDSIA, USI-SUPSI, Switzerland
Simon Garnier	Princeton University, USA
Veysel Gazi	Istanbul Kemerburgaz University, Turkey
Deborah Gordon	Stanford University, USA
Frédéric Guinand	Université du Havre, France
Walter Gutjahr	Universität Wien, Austria
Saman Halgamuge	University of Melbourne, Australia
Heiko Hamann	Karl-Franzens-Universität Graz, Austria
Julia Handl	The University of Manchester, UK
Richard Hartl	Universität Wien, Austria
Poul Heegaard	Norwegian University of Science and Technology, Norway
Marde Helbig	Council for Scientific and Industrial Research, South Africa
Ani Hsieh	Drexel University, USA
Thomas Jansen	University College Cork, Ireland
Mark Jelasity	University of Szeged, Hungary
Yaochu Jin	University of Surrey, UK
Serge Kernbach	Universität Stuttgart, Germany
Joshua Knowles	The University of Manchester, UK
Oliver Korb	Cambridge Crystallographic Data Centre, UK
Xiaodong Li	RMIT University, Australia
Manuel López-Ibáñez	Université Libre de Bruxelles, Belgium

Vito Trianni	ISTC, CNR, Roma, Italy
Elio Tuci	Aberystwyth University, UK
Willem S. van Heerden	University of Pretoria, South Africa
Richard T. Vaughan	Simon Fraser University, Canada
Mario Ventresca	University of Toronto, Canada
Michael Vrahatis	University of Patras, Greece
Alan Winfield	University of the West of England, UK
Carsten Witt	Technical University of Denmark, Denmark
Xiao-Feng Xie	Carnegie Mellon University, USA
Daniela Zaharie	West University of Timisoara, Romania

Additional Referees

Alexandre Campo	Université Libre de Bruxelles, Belgium
Cyrille Bertelle	University of Le Havre, France
Nikolaus Correll	University of Colorado Boulder, USA
Melvin Gauci	The University of Sheffield, UK
Carlos Gershenson	IIMAS, UNAM, Mexico
Jane Hillston	The University of Edinburgh, UK
Jerome Le Ny	École Polytechnique de Montréal, Canada
Joel Lehman	University of Central Florida, USA
Wenguo Liu	Bristol Robotics Lab, UK
Yan Meng	Stevens Institute of Technology, USA
Mac Schwager	Boston University, USA
Valerio Sperati	ISTC, CNR, Rome, Italy
Lovekesh Vig	Jawaharlal Nehru University, New Delhi, India

Table of Contents

Short Papers

Extended Abstracts

A Particle Swarm Embedding Algorithm for Nonlinear Dimensionality Reduction

Oliver Kramer

University of Oldenburg, Germany
oliver.kramer@uni-oldenburg.de

Abstract. To cope with high-dimensional data dimensionality reduction has become an increasingly important problem class. In this paper we propose an iterative particle swarm embedding algorithm (PSEA) that learns embeddings of low-dimensional representations for high-dimensional input patterns. The iterative method seeks for the best latent position with a particle swarm-inspired approach. The construction can be accelerated with k-d-trees. The quality of the embedding is evaluated with the nearest neighbor data space reconstruction error, and a co-ranking matrix based measure. Experimental studies show that PSEA achieves competitive or even better embeddings like the related methods locally linear embedding, and ISOMAP.

1 Introduction

The world is high-dimensional. Efficient and robust dimensionality reduction (DR) methods are required to process high-dimensional patterns, e.g., for visualization or post processing with symbolic algorithms. With increasing data sets DR becomes an important problem class in machine learning, and a variety of methods has been introduced. Surprisingly, not many swarm-based algorithms for DR are known. DR methods compute a mapping from high-dimensional data space to a latent space of lower dimensionality. Latents point in this space should preserve the topological characteristics of their high-dimensional pendants like neighborhood and distance relations.

In this work we present a novel iterative swarm-inspired approach for DR tasks, a popular problem class in machine learning. First, this paper combines the iterative construction of solutions with particle swarm movement equations. Second, it shows that particle swarm optimization (PSO) approaches can be efficient methods for data mining tasks. PSO is inspired by the movement of swarms in nature like fish schools or flocks of birds, and simulates the movement of candidate solutions using flocking-like equations with locations and velocities [7,17]. The paper is structured as follows. In Section 2 related work is presented. Section 3 introduces the swarm-inspired iterative embedding approach, which is experimentally analyzed and compared to locally linear embedding (LLE) and ISOMAP in Section 4. Conclusions are drawn in Section 5.

M. Dorigo et al. (Eds.): ANTS 2012, LNCS 7461, pp. 1–12, 2012.

2   Related Work

2.1   Dimensionality Reduction

The idea of DR methods is to learn low-dimensional representations of high-dimensional patterns losing as little information as possible. Many DR methods seek for a mapping $\mathbf{F} : \mathbb{R}^d \rightarrow \mathbb{R}^q$ from a high-dimensional data space $\mathbb{R}^d$ to a latent space of lower dimensionality $\mathbb{R}^q$ with $q < d$. Non-parametric dimensionality reduction methods compute a set of low-dimensional representations $\mathbf{X} = (\mathbf{x}_1, \ldots, \mathbf{x}_N) \in \mathbb{R}^{q \times N}$ for N high-dimensional observed patterns $\mathbf{Y} = (\mathbf{y}_1, \ldots, \mathbf{y}_N) \in \mathbb{R}^{d \times N}$.

The decision, which information can be lost, and which has to be preserved in the mapping $\mathbf{F}$ depends on the purpose of the DR process, and the error function defined for the employed method. Many DR methods use an implicit definition of the optimization problem they solve. However, the problem to learn the functional model $\mathbf{F}$ can be a hard optimization problem, because the latent variables $\mathbf{X}$ are unknown. Learning a reconstruction mapping $\mathbf{f} : \mathbb{R}^q \rightarrow \mathbb{R}^d$ back from latent to data space can also be desirable. Some methods learn this mapping automatically. Famous DR methods are PCA [5] that is restricted to linear manifolds. Locally linear embedding (LLE) [16], and ISOMAP [20] are famous for non-linear dimensionality reduction.

2.2   Unsupervised Regression

The framework for unsupervised regression has been introduced by Meinicke [13]. It is based on optimizing latent variables to reconstruct high-dimensional data. Unsupervised regression has first been applied to kernel density regression [14], and later to radial basis function networks (RBFs) [18], Gaussian processes [11], and neural networks [19]. Recently, we fitted nearest neighbor regression to the unsupervised regression framework [9], and introduced extensions w.r.t. robust loss functions [10]. Unsupervised nearest neighbors (UNN) is a fast approach that allows to iteratively construct low-dimensional embeddings in $\mathcal{O}(N^2)$, and has been introduced for latent sorting [9,10]. The approach we introduce in this work extends UNN with a PSO-like mechanism to handle arbitrary latent dimensionalities, i.e., $1 \leq q < d$. An introduction to UNN will be given in Section 3.

2.3   Swarm Intelligence and Unsupervised Learning

In nature systems can be observed, in which comparatively simple units organize in groups. This form of collective and coordinated organization is known as swarm intelligence. The disadvantage of simple behaviors is compensated by their large number, and massive parallelism. Swarms consist of a large number of simple entities that cooperate to act goal-oriented. Natural and artificial system have shown to implement successful solution strategies. To the best of our knowledge no swarm-based methods have yet been proposed for embedding of patterns in low-dimensional latent spaces. But related work in other fields of unsupervised learning with swarm methods has been published, e.g., methods for PSO and ant colony optimization-based clustering. Kao and Cheng [6] have introduced an ACO algorithm for clustering that employs pheromones, and distances between elements as heuristic clustering information. The combination of population-based search and stochastic elements allows to overcome local optima, and find optimal clustering results. Further methods for swarm-based clustering can be found in the book by Abraham *et al.* [1]. O'Neill and Brabazon [15] have introduced a hybrid approach of PSO, and self-organizing maps (SOMs) by Kohonen [8] that control the weights of a SOM employing a PSO-similar update rule. Also ant colony optimization has been employed to improve the topographic SOM mapping [4].

3 Iterative Particle Swarm Embeddings

The iterative particle swarm embedding algorithm is introduced in the following. It is based on K-nearest neighbor regression, and the concept of unsupervised regression.

3.1 Nearest Neighbors

Functional regression models map patterns to continuous labels, i.e., to a subspace of $\mathbb{R}^d$. The problem is to predict output values $\mathbf{y} \in \mathbb{R}^d$ of given input values $\mathbf{x} \in \mathbb{R}^q$ based on sets of N input-output examples $(\mathbf{x}_1, \mathbf{y}_1), \ldots, (\mathbf{x}_N, \mathbf{y}_N)$. The goal is to learn a functional model $\mathbf{f} : \mathbb{R}^q \to \mathbb{R}^d$ known as regression function. We assume a data set consisting of observed pairs $(\mathbf{x}_i, \mathbf{y}_i) \in \mathbf{X} \times \mathbf{Y}$ is given. For a novel pattern $\mathbf{x}'$ K-nearest neighbors (KNN) for regression computes the mean of the function values of its K-nearest patterns:

$$\mathbf{f}_{KNN}(\mathbf{x}') := \frac{1}{K} \sum_{i \in \mathcal{N}_K(\mathbf{x}')} \mathbf{y}_i \qquad (1)$$

with set $\mathcal{N}_K(\mathbf{x}')$ containing the indices of the K-nearest neighbors of $\mathbf{x}'$. The idea of KNN is based on the assumption of locality in data space: In local neighborhoods of $\mathbf{x}$ patterns are expected to have similar label information $\mathbf{f}(\mathbf{x})$ like observed patterns $\mathbf{y}$. Consequently, for an unknown $\mathbf{x}'$ the label must be similar to the labels of the closest patterns, which is modeled by the average of the output value of the K nearest samples. KNN has been proven well in various applications, e.g., in the detection of quasars based on spectroscopic data [3]. We define the output of function $\mathbf{f}_{KNN}$ given the pattern matrix $\mathbf{X}$ as a matrix $\mathbf{f}_{KNN}(\mathbf{X}) = (\mathbf{f}_{KNN}(\mathbf{x}_1), \ldots, \mathbf{f}_{KNN}(\mathbf{x}_N))$, collecting all KNN mappings from patterns in $\mathbf{X}$ to $\mathbb{R}^d$.

3.2 Unsupervised Nearest Neighbors

The idea in unsupervised regression [13] is to reverse the regression approach: we map from latent space to data space, and the latent variables are the free parameters we want to optimize to optimally reconstruct the observed patterns in data space, i.e., the objective is to minimize the data space reconstruction error (DSRE):

$$\text{minimize } E(\mathbf{X}) = \frac{1}{N}\|\mathbf{Y} - \mathbf{f}_{KNN}(\mathbf{X})\|_F^2, \tag{2}$$

with Frobenius norm $\|\cdot\|_F^2$. We define $e(\mathbf{x}, \mathbf{y}, \mathbf{X})$ as the contribution of latent position $\mathbf{x}'$ to the DSRE.

$$e(\mathbf{x}', \mathbf{y}, \mathbf{X}) = \|\mathbf{y} - \mathbf{f}_{KNN}(\mathbf{x}')\|^2 \tag{3}$$

As functional model $\mathbf{f}_{KNN}$ we employ KNN regression. The question comes up how to optimize the functional model. In [9] and [10] we have introduced a latent sorting approach for embedding high-dimensional patterns on a line.

Figure 1(a) illustrates the UNN variant we proposed for sorting high-dimensional data [9,10]. It shows the $\hat{N} + 1$ possible embeddings of a data sample into an existing order of points in latent space (yellow/bright circles). The position of element $\mathbf{x}_3$ results in a lower DSRE (cf. Section 3.2) with $K = 2$ than the

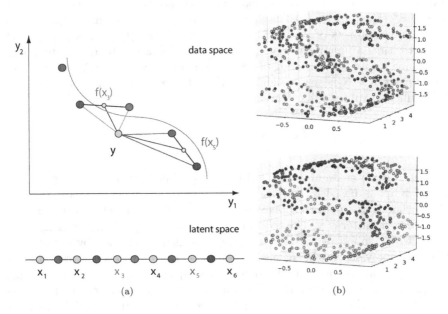

Fig. 1. Left: Illustration of UNN embedding of a low-dimensional point to a fixed latent space topology testing all $\hat{N} + 1$ positions [9]. Right: Example of UNN result of a 3D-S before (upper right) and after embedding (lower right) with UNN and $K = 10$ [9,10].

position of $\mathbf{x}_5$, as the mean of the two nearest neighbors of $\mathbf{x}_3$ is closer to $\mathbf{y}$ than the mean of the two nearest neighbors of $\mathbf{x}_5$. Figure 1(b) shows an example of a UNN embedding of the 3D-S (upper part shows colorization of the *unsorted S*, lower part after UNN embedding), similar colors correspond to neighbored positions in latent space, i.e., a meaningful neighborhood preserving embedding has been computed. In the following, we extend the approach to arbitrary latent dimensionalities, in which the latent variables can be placed in latent space without geometric constraints.

3.3   Particle Swarm Embedding Algorithm

There are two reasons to employ a direct search method to solve the UNN optimization problem. First, the problem is highly multimodal, second, $E(\mathbf{X})$ is not steady, and not differentiable due to the employment of KNN. To illustrate the search for optimal latent positions, we visualize the DSRE space in Figure 2. It shows the DSRE w.r.t. the first pattern $\mathbf{y}_1$ for two neighborhood sizes, i.e., $K = 5$ (left), and $K = 30$ (right) after a run of UNN with $N = 300$. Bright areas represent parts of latent space with low errors, while dark colors represent a large DSRE. The comparison of both figures shows that in case of increasing neighborhood sizes the problem has larger, but less areas with similar fitness. The number of local optima decreases, and the optimization problem becomes easier. In the experimental section we will observe that the variance of the outcome of multiple experiments is smaller for large neighborhood sizes.

The PSEA optimization approach is based on the following two ideas:

1. Iteratively construct a solution (an embedding $\mathbf{X}$) to cope with the large number of free parameters, and
2. perform PSO-like blackbox search steps in each iteration to embed the latent point at an optimal position.

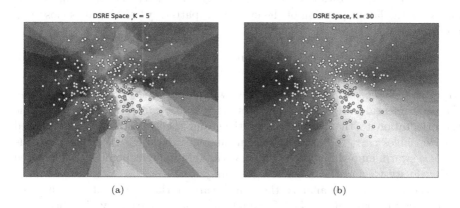

(a)   (b)

Fig. 2. Visualization of DSRE space $e(\cdot, \mathbf{y}_1, \mathbf{X})$ w.r.t. the first pattern $\mathbf{y}_1$ for $K = 5$, and $K = 30$ after a run of UNN with $N = 300$ embedded patterns

Note that the approach does not treat the latent points as swarm, and does not evolve them freely in latent space. As the problem to minimize $E(\mathbf{X})$ scales linearly with the number of patterns N, which may be a very large number in practice, the iterative solution construction is the key concept for efficiently learn the manifold. The approach is described in the following (cf. Algorithm 1.1). In

---

Algorithm 1.1. Particle Swarm Embedding Algorithm

1: **input:** $\mathbf{Y}$, K, κ
2: **repeat**
3:     choose $\mathbf{y} \in \mathbf{Y}$
4:     look for closest pattern $\mathbf{y}^*$ with latent position $\mathbf{x}^*$
5:     **for** $i = 1$ **to** κ **do**
6:         update velocity (cf. Equation 5)
7:         update latent position (cf. Equation 4)
8:         evaluate $E(\mathbf{X})$ or $e(\mathbf{x}', \mathbf{y}, \mathbf{X})$
9:         update best position $\tilde{\mathbf{x}}$
10:     **end for**
11:     embed $\tilde{\mathbf{x}}$
12:     $\mathbf{Y} = \mathbf{Y} \backslash \mathbf{y}$
13: **until** $\mathbf{Y} = \emptyset$

---

each step the pattern that has to be embedded is randomly chosen $\mathbf{y} \in \mathbf{Y}$. In the particle swarm step we seek for the optimal position, where the particle $\mathbf{x}$ should be embedded. For this reason, a loop of PSO-like steps is repeated for κ iterations:

$$\mathbf{x}' = \mathbf{x} + \mathbf{v}' \tag{4}$$

with velocity

$$\mathbf{v}' = \mathbf{v} + c_1 r_1 (\tilde{\mathbf{x}} - \mathbf{x}) + c_2 r_2 (\mathbf{x}^* - \mathbf{x}) \tag{5}$$

Here, $\tilde{\mathbf{x}}$ is the best position w.r.t. the DSRE the latent particle has found so far, and $\mathbf{x}^*$ is the latent position of the embedded pattern $\mathbf{y}^* \in \hat{\mathbf{Y}}$ that is closest to the pattern $\mathbf{y}$ that we want to embed:

$$\mathbf{x}^* = \arg \min_{i=1,\dots,|\hat{\mathbf{Y}}|} \delta(\mathbf{y}, \mathbf{y}_i), \tag{6}$$

with distance measure $\delta(\cdot)$, for which we will employ the Euclidean distance in the experimental part. The parameters $c_1, c_2 \in [0, 1]$ are constants that define the orientation to the best latent particle, and the closest already embedded one. Variables $r_1, r_2 \in [0, 1]$ are uniform random values. Figure 3 illustrates the particle swarm embedding step. The new candidate latent point $\mathbf{x}'$ is generated with velocity $\mathbf{v}'$, and the two scaled vectors.

In the following, we analyze the PSEA variant that takes into account the reconstruction error $e(\cdot, \mathbf{y}, \mathbf{X})$ (cf. Equation 3) of the pattern $\mathbf{y}$ that has to be embedded. A greedy, but slower variant of PSEA is possible that employs the overall DSRE (cf. Equation 2) for each latent position.

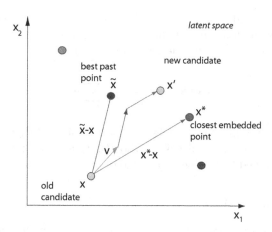

Fig. 3. Illustration of particle swarm embedding: The new candidate latent point $\mathbf{x}'$ is generated with velocity $\mathbf{v}'$, and the two scaled vectors $\tilde{\mathbf{x}} - \mathbf{x}$ and $\mathbf{x}^* - \mathbf{x}$

3.4 Runtime

The embedding has a complexity of $\mathcal{O}(N^2)$, but can be accelerated with k-d-trees [2] in data and latent space. A k-d-tree allows efficient neighborhood queries: not N elements have to be considered, but $O(\log N)$ steps are sufficient to reach the closest pattern. A k-d-tree is a space partitioning data structure for a k-dimensional data space based on axis-aligned splitting planes. The basic k-d-tree cycles through the coordinate axes. Employing k-d-trees in data and latent space allows the PSEA to constructs a solution in $\mathcal{O}(N \log N)$ time, if we assume that the PSO-based search in each step takes constant time. The search for the closest pattern $\mathbf{y}^*$ of $\mathbf{y}$ takes $\mathcal{O}(\log \hat{N})$ (if $\hat{N}$ is the increasing number of embedded patterns when $\mathbf{y}$ is being embedded) employing a k-d-tree in data space. The search for the optimal embedding takes $\kappa \cdot K$-neighborhood computations in latent space, i.e. $\mathcal{O}(\kappa \cdot K \cdot \log \hat{N}) = \mathcal{O}(\log \hat{N})$. Insertion of $\mathbf{x}$ to the latent space k-d-tree, and $\mathbf{y}$ to the data space k-d-tree each take $\mathcal{O}(\log \hat{N})$. Hence, the overall runtime of the approach can be accelerated to $\mathcal{O}(N \log N)$.

4 Experimental Analysis

In this section we analyze the results of the novel PSEA experimentally. To evaluate the quality of the embeddings we employ the DSRE and a co-ranking matrix measure introduced by Lee and Verleysen [12]. It is based on the comparison of ranks (sorting w.r.t. distances from patterns) in data space and latent space. It defines a co-ranking matrix $\mathbf{Q}$ that explicitly states the deviations of ranks in data and latent space, see [12] for a definition of $\mathbf{Q}$. In this matrix rank errors correspond to off-diagonal entries. A point $\mathbf{y}_j$ with lower rank w.r.t. a point $\mathbf{y}_i$

in latent space is called *intrusion*, a higher rank is called *extrusion*. From the co-ranking matrix the following quality measure can be derived that counts the number of proper ranks within a neighborhood of size K:

$$Q_{NX}(K) := \frac{1}{KN} \sum_{k=1}^{K} \sum_{l=1}^{K} q_{kl} \tag{7}$$

This term restricts the measure to neighborhoods of size K. High values for Q_{NX} show that the high-dimensional neighborhood relations are preserved in latent space, a perfect embedding achieves a value of one.

4.1 Neighborhood Sizes

First, we analyze the influence of neighborhood size K on the results of PSEA, LLE and ISOMAP on two test data sets, i.e., *Digits* and *Boston*. For PSEA we choose the following settings. The particle swarm embedding process runs $\kappa = 50$ iterations. The initial velocity is randomly generated with a Gaussian distribution $\mathbf{v}_0 = \mathcal{N}(0,1)$, the initial position starts from the latent position of the closest embedded point $\mathbf{x}_0 = \tilde{\mathbf{x}}$. The constants are both set to $c_1 = c_2 = 0.5$.

Table 1. Comparison of DSRE and E_{NX} with PSEA (mean values of 25 runs with standard deviation), LLE, and ISOMAP on the two test data sets *Digits*, and *Boston*

Digits	PSEA		LLE		ISOMAP	
K	DSRE	E_{NX}	DSRE	E_{NX}	DSRE	E_{NX}
5	**15.87** ± 0.23	**0.47** ± 0.01	24.17	0.25	16.67	0.41
10	**18.77** ± 0.29	**0.42** ± 0.01	19.29	0.41	18.96	**0.42**
15	20.89 ± 0.64	0.40 ± 0.01	*19.98*	*0.44*	**19.52**	**0.47**
30	*24.17* ± 0.48	*0.39* ± 0.01	25.511	0.34	**21.97**	**0.51**
Boston	PSEA		LLE		ISOMAP	
K	DSRE	E_{NX}	DSRE	E_{NX}	DSRE	E_{NX}
5	**29.81** ± 1.86	**0.45** ± 0.01	45.29	0.30	*34.06*	*0.42*
10	**37.35** ± 6.40	**0.43** ± 0.03	62.81	0.29	81.57	0.35
15	*53.59* ± 2.94	*0.40* ± 0.03	69.35	0.20	**44.24**	**0.43**
30	53.03 ± 3.23	041 ± 0.04	*33.32*	*0.55*	**27.69**	**0.66**

Table 1 shows the experimental results w.r.t. the DSRE and E_{NX} for the settings $K = 5, 10, 15$, and 30. Each PSEA experiment has been repeated 25 times. The best results, i.e., low DSRE and high E_{NX} are shown in bold, the second best are shown in italic numbers. The results show that a low DSRE correlates with a high E_{NX}. The DSRE is increasing with the neighborhood size. PSEA achieves the best results of all methods in case of small neighborhood sizes $K = 5$, and $K = 10$ on both data sets. In case of larger neighborhoods ISOMAP shows better results, but PSEA still computes competitive embeddings, and achieves the second best results in half of the cases. LLE and ISOMAP win in performance for larger neighborhoods. The results of LLE are worse than the results of PSEA in three of the four cases, in particular E_{NX} tends to be much worse. Surprising is the bad result of ISOMAP on the *Boston* data set for $K = 10$.

Our experiments with varying data set sizes have shown that ISOMAP, and LLE do not scale well in terms of runtime with an increasing number of patterns. The runtime of the PSEA scales slower with the number of patterns. This can be a major advantage of PSEA over the other methods in large-scale data mining scenarios, one of the most important open problems in machine learning.

4.2 Comparison of Embeddings

In Figure 4 we compare PSEA results employing varying neighborhood sizes. The figures show that reasonable embeddings have been computed for all neighborhood sizes. Similar digits, e.g., the same classes, are mapped to neighbored latent

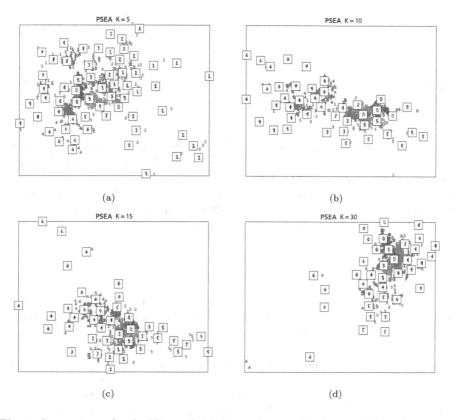

(a)   (b)

(c)   (d)

Fig. 4. Comparison of embeddings of 750 data points, and 6 classes of the *Digits* data set. PSEA results for (a) $K = 5$, and (b) $K = 10$, (c) $K = 15$, and (d) $K = 30$.

areas. The distribution of latent points is broader (and similar to ISOMAP, see Figure 5) for small neighborhood sizes, e.g. $K = 5$, while for larger neighborhoods, e.g. $K = 30$, the whole manifold becomes narrow. For comparison, the figures show that the embedding gets worse for $K = 30$ with outliers. The reason for outliers in case of large neighborhood sizes is that the DSRE function has more plateaus, i.e., areas with the same neighborhoods, and equal or at least similar DSRE values.

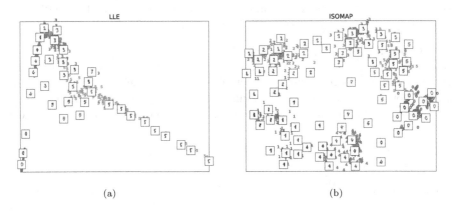

(a)   (b)

Fig. 5. Comparison of embeddings of 750 data points, and 6 classes of the *Digits* data set for (a) LLE, and (b) ISOMAP embeddings with $K = 15$

Figure 5 shows the embeddings of LLE and ISOMAP of the same data set. Both embeddings also separate the classes and fulfill topological requirements like neighborhood preservation. ISOMAP distributes the latent embeddings circularly in latent space, which leads to better shapes than LLE. The plots show that the embeddings of PSEA show similar characteristics like the results of ISOMAP, and distribute the latent points better than LLE.

5   Conclusion

In unsupervised regression the optimization problem of placing latent variables scales with the number of patterns, and becomes impractical for large data sets. In this paper we have introduced a novel optimization approach that is based on the hybridization of iteratively constructing a solution, and PSO-like optimization in each iteration. The proposed method belongs to the first particle swarm approach that allows learning of low-dimensional embeddings from high-dimensional patterns. The results are competitive to embeddings of established methods like ISOMAP, and LLE. The experiments have shown that the PSEA embedding fulfills conditions like neighborhood preservation, and low DSRE.

As extension of the PSEA approach it is reasonable to parallelize the embedding process, and thus allow to learn embeddings of large data sets. Another prospective research direction is to employ further DR criteria for the fitness evaluation of the optimization process like kernel density regression criteria. A promising research direction will be to employ the hybridization of an iterative approach, and PSO optimization for the construction of solutions in related domains.

References

1. Abraham, A., Grosan, C., Ramos, V. (eds.): Swarm Intelligence in Data Mining. SCI, vol. 34. Springer (2006)
2. Bentley, J.L.: Multidimensional binary search trees used for associative searching. Communications of the ACM 18(9), 509–517 (1975)
3. Gieseke, F., Polsterer, K.L., Thom, A., Zinn, P., Bomanns, D., Dettmar, R.-J., Kramer, O., Vahrenhold, J.: Detecting quasars in large-scale astronomical surveys. In: International Conference on Machine Learning and Applications (ICMLA), pp. 352–357 (2010)
4. Herrmann, L., Ultsch, A.: The Architecture of Ant-Based Clustering to Improve Topographic Mapping. In: Dorigo, M., Birattari, M., Blum, C., Clerc, M., Stützle, T., Winfield, A.F.T. (eds.) ANTS 2008. LNCS, vol. 5217, pp. 379–386. Springer, Heidelberg (2008)
5. Jolliffe, I.: Principal component analysis. Springer series in statistics. Springer, New York (1986)
6. Kao, Y., Cheng, K.: An ACO-Based Clustering Algorithm. In: Dorigo, M., Gambardella, L.M., Birattari, M., Martinoli, A., Poli, R., Stützle, T. (eds.) ANTS 2006. LNCS, vol. 4150, pp. 340–347. Springer, Heidelberg (2006)
7. Kennedy, J., Eberhart, R.: Particle swarm optimization. In: Proceedings of IEEE International Conference on Neural Networks, pp. 1942–1948 (1995)
8. Kohonen, T.: Self-Organizing Maps. Springer (2001)
9. Kramer, O.: Dimensionalty reduction by unsupervised nearest neighbor regression. In: International Conference on Machine Learning and Applications (ICMLA), pp. 275–278. IEEE (2011)
10. Kramer, O.: On unsupervised nearest-neighbor regression and robust loss functions. In: International Conference on Artificial Intelligence, pp. 164–170 (2012)
11. Lawrence, N.D.: Probabilistic non-linear principal component analysis with gaussian process latent variable models. Journal of Machine Learning Research 6, 1783–1816 (2005)
12. Lee, J.A., Verleysen, M.: Quality assessment of dimensionality reduction: Rank-based criteria. Neurocomputing 72(7-9), 1431–1443 (2009)
13. Meinicke, P.: Unsupervised Learning in a Generalized Regression Framework. PhD thesis, University of Bielefeld (2000)
14. Meinicke, P., Klanke, S., Memisevic, R., Ritter, H.: Principal surfaces from unsupervised kernel regression. IEEE Transactions on Pattern Analysis and Maching Intelligence 27(9), 1379–1391 (2005)
15. O'Neill, M., Brabazon, A.: Self-organizing swarm (SOSwarm) for financial credit-risk assessment (2008)
16. Roweis, S.T., Saul, L.K.: Nonlinear dimensionality reduction by locally linear embedding. Science 290, 2323–2326 (2000)

17. Shi, Y., Eberhart, R.: A modified particle swarm optimizer. In: Proceedings of the International Conference on Evolutionary Computation, pp. 69–73 (1998)
18. Smola, A.J., Mika, S., Schölkopf, B., Williamson, R.C.: Regularized principal manifolds. Journal of Machine Learning Research 1, 179–209 (2001)
19. Tan, S., Mavrovouniotis, M.: Reducing data dimensionality through optimizing neural network inputs. AIChE Journal 41(6), 1471–1479 (1995)
20. Tenenbaum, J.B., Silva, V.D., Langford, J.C.: A global geometric framework for nonlinear dimensionality reduction. Science 290, 2319–2323 (2000)

ABC-Miner: An Ant-Based Bayesian Classification Algorithm

Khalid M. Salama and Alex A. Freitas

School of Computing, University of Kent, Canterbury, UK
kms39@kent.ac.uk, a.a.freitas@kent.ac.uk

Abstract. Bayesian networks (BNs) are powerful tools for knowledge representation and inference that encode (in)dependencies among random variables. A Bayesian network classifier is a special kind of these networks that aims to compute the posterior probability of each class given an instance of the attributes and predicts the class with the highest posterior probability. Since learning the optimal BN structure from a dataset is $\mathcal{NP}$-hard, heuristic search algorithms need to be applied effectively to build high-quality networks. In this paper, we propose a novel algorithm, called ABC-Miner, for learning the structure of BN classifiers using the Ant Colony Optimization (ACO) meta-heuristic. We describe all the elements necessary to tackle our learning problem using ACO, and experimentally compare the performance of our ant-based Bayesian classification algorithm with other algorithms for learning BN classifiers used in the literature.

1 Introduction

Classification is a data mining task where the goal is to build, from labeled cases, a model (classifier) that can be used to predict the class of unlabeled cases. Learning classifiers from datasets is a central problem in data mining and machine learning research fields. While different approaches for tackling this problem exist, such as decision trees, artificial neural networks and rule list [20], our focus in this paper is on the Bayesian approach for classification.

Naïve-Bayes is the first Bayesian classifier in the literature. Although it is a very simple kind of Bayesian networks that assumes the attributes are independent given the class label, Naïve-Bayes classifiers showed effective predictive performance under the aforementioned assumption [10]. However, since the independency assumption amongst the dataset attributes is not realistic, extended versions were developed to improve the performance of Naïve-Bayes, namely Tree Augmented Naïve-Bayes (TANs), Bayesian networks Augmented Naïve-Bayes (BANs) and General Bayesian Networks (GBNs) [10]. These algorithms consider dependencies between the attributes in the learning process to build more complex and hopefully more accurate BN classifiers. Nonetheless, algorithms used in the literature for building such BNs utilize greedy and deterministic techniques. Since learning the optimal BN structure from a dataset is

M. Dorigo et al. (Eds.): ANTS 2012, LNCS 7461, pp. 13–24, 2012.

$\mathcal{NP}$-hard [5], several stochastic search algorithms can be effectively applied to build high-quality BN classifiers in an acceptable computational time.

Ant Colony Optimization (ACO) [9] is a meta-heuristic for solving combinatorial optimization problems, inspired by observations of the behavior of ant colonies in nature. ACO has been successful in solving several problems, including classification rule induction [13,14,15,18] and general purpose BN construction [2,8,17,21]. However, as far as we know, it has not been used for learning Bayesian network classifiers.

In this paper, we propose a novel ant-based Bayesian classification algorithm, called ABC-Miner, which learns the structure of a BAN with at most k-dependencies from a dataset using ACO technique for optimization. The rest of the paper is organized as follows. In Section 2 a brief overview on Bayesian networks' basic concepts is given as well as a discussion of various Bayesian network classifiers is shown. Section 3 exhibits the related work on the use of ACO algorithms for building BNs in the literature. In Section 4, we introduce our proposed ABC-Miner algorithm and describe each of the elements necessary to tackle our learning problem using the ACO meta-heuristics. After that, section 5 discusses our experimental methodology and results. Finally, we conclude with some general remarks and provide directions for future research in section 6.

2   Bayesian Networks Background

2.1   Overview on Bayesian Networks

Bayesian networks are knowledge representation tools that aim to model dependence and independence relationships amongst random variables [12]. In essence, BNs are used to describe the joint probability distribution of n random variables $\mathbf{X} = \{X_1, X_2, X_3, ..., X_n\}$. A directed acyclic graph (DAG) is used to represent the variables as nodes and statistical dependencies between the variables as edges between the nodes – child nodes (variables) depend on their parent ones. In addition, a set of conditional probability tables (CPTs), one for each variable, is obtained to represent the parameters Θ of the network. The graphical structure of the network along with its parameters specifies a joint probability distribution over the set of variables $\mathbf{X}$ that is formulated in the product form:

$$p(X_1, X_2, ..., X_n) = \prod_{i=1}^{n} p(X_i|\mathbf{Pa}(X_i), \Theta, G) \qquad (1)$$

where $\mathbf{Pa}(X_i)$ are the parents of variable X_i in G (the DAG that represents the structure of the BN).

Learning a Bayesian network from a dataset $\mathbf{D}$ with $\{d^1, d,^2, ..., d^m\}$ instances is decomposed into two phases; learning the network structure, and then learning the parameters of the network. As for parameter learning, it is considered a straightforward process for any given BN structure with specified (in)dependencies between variables. Simply, a conditional probability table (CPT) is computed for each variable with respect to its parent variables. CPT of variable X_i encodes the likelihood of this variable given its parents $\mathbf{Pa}(X_i)$ in the network graph G, and the marginal likelihood of the dataset $\mathbf{D}$ given a structure G is denoted by $P(\mathbf{D}|G)$. The purpose is to find G that maximizes $P(\mathbf{D}|G)$ for a given $\mathbf{D}$, which is the role of BN structure learning phase. The common approach to this problem is to introduce a scoring function, f, that evaluates each G with respect to $\mathbf{D}$, searching for the best network structure according to f. Various scoring metrics are usable for this job [6,12].

A well-known greedy approach for building BN structure is Algorithm B [1]. It starts with an empty DAG (edge-less structure) and at each step it adds the edge with the maximum increase in the scoring metric f, whilst avoiding the inclusion of directed cycles in the graph. The algorithm stops when adding any valid edge does not increase the value of the scoring metric. K2, a metric based on uniform prior scoring, is one of the most used scoring metrics for building and evaluating Bayesian networks [6].

For further information about Bayesian networks, the reader is referred to [11,12], which provide a detailed discussion of the subject.

2.2   Bayesian Networks for Classification

Bayesian network classifiers are a special kind of BNs where the class attribute is treated as a unique variable in the network. The purpose is to compute the probability of each value of the class variable given an instance of the predictor attributes and assign this instance to the class that has the highest posterior probability value. The following are various types of BN classifiers studied in the literature.

- **Naïve-Bayes:** The classifier consists of a simple BN structure that has the class node as the only parent node of all other nodes. This structure assumes that all attributes are independent of each other given the class. In spite of its simplicity, Naïve-Bayes has surprisingly outperformed many sophisticated classifiers over a large number of datasets, especially where the attributes are not strongly correlated [10].
- **Tree Augmented Naïve-Bayes (TAN):** As an extension to Naïve-Bayes, TAN allows a node in a BN to have more than one parent, besides the class variable. This produces a tree-like structure BN. A variation of the Chow-Liu algorithm [3] is the best known method for building TANs. First, it computes the conditional mutual information $I(X, Y|\mathbf{C})$ between each pair of variables X and Y given class variable $\mathbf{C}$. Then it builds a complete undirected graph connecting all the input variables to find the maximum weighted spanning tree from the graph, where the weight of edge $X \to Y$ is annotated with $I(X, Y|\mathbf{C})$. After that, it chooses a root variable and sets the direction of all edges to be outwards of it. Finally, it adds one edge from the class node to each of the other variables, building a TAN classifier.

- **BN Augmented Naïve-Bayes (BAN):** It is an elaborated version of Naïve-Bayes, in which no restrictions (or at most k-dependencies) are enforced on the number of the parents that a node in the network can depend on. In other words, while each node in TAN can have only one parent besides the class node, and in Naïve-Bayes only the class node is allowed to be the parent, each node in BAN can have k of parents (dependencies) besides the class node. Another variation of the Chow-Liu algorithm that is used to build TANs, is utilized to BANs as well [4].
- **General Bayesian Network (GBN):** Unlike the other BN classifier learners, the GBN treats the class variable node as an ordinary node. The idea is to build a general purpose Bayesian network, find the *Markov blanket* of the class node, delete all the other nodes outside it and use the resulting network as a Bayesian classifier. One *Markov blanket* of a node n is the union of the n's parents, n's children, and the parents of n's children.

Friedman et al. provided an excellent study of these algorithms in [10]. A comprehensive investigation and comparisons of these various Bayesian classifiers by Cheng and Greiner are found in [3,4] .

3   ACO Related Work

Ant Colony Optimization has an effective contribution in tackling the classification problem. Ant-Miner [15] is the first ant-based classification algorithm. Several extensions on this algorithm have been introduced in the literature, such as AntMiner+ [13], cAnt-Miner [14], and multi-pheromone Ant-Miner [18]. However, the Ant-Miner algorithm as well as its various versions handles the classification problem by building a list of <**IF**_*Antecedent*_**THEN**_*Class*> classification rules. On the other hand, this paper proposes a new ant-based algorithm that handles classification problems, yet with a different approach; learning a Bayesian network to be used as classifier.

As for the use of ACO for building Bayesian networks, to date, there has been only a few research utilizing such a heuristic in learning BN structure, namely: ACO-B [2], MMACO [16,17], ACO-E [7,8] and CHAINACO - K2ACO [21]. Moreover, none of them has been used for building BN classifiers. As far as we know, our proposed ABC-Miner is the first algorithm to use ACO, or any evolutionary algorithm, in the task of learning Bayesian networks specific for the classification problem.

Campos et al. introduced the first ant-based algorithm for learning Bayesian networks, ACO-B [2], where each ant iteratively constructs a complete Bayesian network from scratch by selecting edges to be added to the network and updates the pheromone on the construction graph according to the quality of the constructed BN. Edge selection is carried out in stochastic fashion, according to the pheromone and the heuristic values associated with the edge. The heuristic function used is the same function used for evaluating the quality of the BN, which is the K2 scoring metric [6].

Pinto et al. used a different local discovery approach for learning BNs in [16,17]. This is hybrid approach, MMACO, based on the local discovery algorithm Max-Min Parents and Children (MMPC) and ant colony optimization (ACO). MMPC is used to construct the skeleton of the Bayesian network and then ACO is used to orientate its edges, thus returning the final structure. Here all the ants are involved in building a single solution by testing several possible edge additions and orientation at the same iteration. BDEu [12] is the function used by MMACO to calculate the heuristics and evaluates the BN quality.

Daly et al. studied learning the structure of a Bayesian network by performing a search through the space of its equivalence classes via extending traditional ACO-based algorithm, ACO-E [7,8]. An equivalence class includes all network structures where changing the orientation (dependency relationship) of one or more edges in a BN obtains the same quality according to a given scoring metric. In which case, not all the edges in an equivalence class of a BN are oriented, since the direction of the dependencies of some edge does not change the quality of the network.

Yanghui et al. proposed two novel ACO approaches for Bayesian network structure learning, CHAINACO and K2ACO [21]. The former is based on a GA algorithm. It consists of two phases; constructing chains (the order of nodes according to dependencies) using ACO instead of GA, then applies K2 to the best ordering found and returns the best structure. K2ACO is also based on another algorithm, K2GA, which only consists of a single phase. The quality of each node ordering chosen by an ant is evaluated by running the K2 search algorithm to construct a BN calculating the score of the network structure found. The best structure returned is that generated by K2 from the best ordering evaluated in this fashion.

Note that the goal of the aforementioned algorithms is to build general purposes BNs. In other words, the selection of the heuristics, quality evaluation metric and other elements of the algorithm are suitable for this aim, but not for building BN classifiers. Hence, in spite of having some similarities, essential aspects of our algorithm are different due to the diversion in the target; our algorithm is only focused on learning BN classifiers. Next we will explore these aspects as we describe our novel Ant-based Bayesian Classifier.

4   A Novel ACO Algorithm for Learning BN Classifiers

4.1   ABC-Miner Algorithm

The overall process of ABC-Miner is illustrated in Algorithm 1. The core element of any ACO-based algorithm is the construction graph that contains the decision components in the search space, with which an ant constructs a candidate solution. As for the problem at hands, the decision components are all the edges $X \rightarrow Y$ where $X \neq Y$ and X, Y belongs to the input attributes of a given training set. These edges represent the variable dependencies in the resulting Bayesian network classifier.

At the beginning of the algorithm, the pheromone amount is initialized for each decision component with the same value. The initial amount of pheromone on each edge is $1/|TotalEdges|$. In addition, the heuristic value for each edge $X \rightarrow Y$ is set using the conditional mutual information, which is computed as follows:

$$I(X, Y|\mathbf{C}) = \sum_{c \in C} p(c) \sum_{x \in X} \sum_{y \in Y} p(x, y|c) \log \frac{p(x, y|c)}{p(x|c)p(y|c)} \qquad (2)$$

where $\mathbf{C}$ is the class variable. $p(x, y|c)$ is the conditional probability of value $x \in X$ and $y \in Y$ given class value c, $p(x|c)$ is the conditional probability of x given c, $p(y|c)$ is the conditional probability of y given c and $p(c)$ is the prior probability of value c in the class variable. Conditional mutual information is a measure of correlation between two random variables given a third one. In our case, we want to lead the ant during the search process to the edges between correlated variables given the class variable, and so we use such a function as heuristic information associated with the selectable edges. Note that the procedure of heuristic calculation is called only once at the beginning and its calculations used throughout the algorithm.

Algorithm 1. Pseudo-code of ABC-Miner

Begin ABC-Miner
$BNC_{gbest} = \phi$; $Q_{gbest} = 0$
$InitializePheromoneAmounts()$;
$InitializeHeuristicValues()$;
$t = 0$;
repeat
    $BNC_{tbest} = \phi$; $Q_{tbest} = 0$;
    for $i = 0 \rightarrow$ colony_size **do**
        $BNC_i = CreateSolution(ant_i)$;
        $Q_i = ComputeQuality(BNC_i)$;
        if $Q_i > Q_{tbest}$ **then**
            $BNC_{tbest} = BNC_i$;
            $Q_i = Q_{tbest}$;
        end if
    end for
    $PerformLocalSearch(BNC_{tbest})$;
    $UpdatePheromone(BNC_{tbest})$;
    if $Q_{tbest} > Q_{gbest}$ **then**
        $BNC_{gbest} = BNC_{tbest}$;
    end if
    $t = t + 1$;
until $t =$ max_itrations **or** $Convergence()$
return BNC_{gbest};
End

The outline of the algorithm is as follows. In essence, each ant_i in the colony creates a candidate solution BNC_i, i. e. a Bayesian network classifier. Then the quality of the constructed solution is evaluated. The best solution BNC_{tbest} produced in the colony is selected to undergo local search before the ant updates the pheromone trail according to the quality of its solution Q_{tbest}. After that, we compare the iteration best solution BNC_{tbest} with the global best solution BNC_{gbest} to keep track of the best solution found so far. This set of steps is considered an iteration of the *repeat − until* loop and is repeated until the same solution is generated for a number of consecutive trials specified by the `conv_iterations` parameter (indicating convergence) or until `max_iterations` is reached. The values of `conv_iterations`, `max_iterations` and `colony_size` are user-specified thresholds. In our experiments (see section 5), we used 10, 500 and 5 for each of these parameters respectively.

4.2 Solution Creation

Instead of having the user selecting the optimum maximum number of dependencies that a variable in the BN can have (at most k parents for each node), this selection is carried out by the ants in ABC-Miner. Prior to solution creation, the ant selects the maximum number of dependencies (k) as a criterion for the currently constructed BN classifier. This selection of k value is done probabilistically from a list of available numbers. The user only specifies `max_parents` parameter (that we set to 3 in our experiments), and all the integer values from 1 to this parameter are available for the ant to use in the BN classifier construction. The various values of the k are treated as decision components as well. More precisely, the ant updates the pheromone on the value k of the maximum number of parents after solution creation according to the quality of this solution, which used value k as a criterion in the BN classifier construction. This pheromone amount represents the selection probability of this value by subsequent ants, leading to convergence on an optimal value of k dependencies. Algorithm 2 shows the outline of the solution creation procedure.

Algorithm 2. Pseudo-code of Solution Creation Procedure

Begin CreateSolution()
$BNC_i \leftarrow$ {Naïve-Bayes structure};
$k = ant_i.SelectMaxParents()$;
while $GetValidEdges() <> \phi$ **do**
    $\{i \rightarrow j\} = ant_i.SelectEdgeProbablistically()$;
    $BNC_i = BNC_i \cup \{i \rightarrow j\}$;
    $RemoveInvalidEdges(BNC_i, k)$;
end while
$BNC_i.LearnParameters()$;
return BNC_i;
End

Each ant starts with the network structure of the Naïve-Bayes classifier, i. e. a BN in which all the variables have only the class variable as a parent. From that point, it starts to expand this Naïve-Bayes network into a Bayesian Augmented Naïve-Bayes (BAN) by adding edges to the network. The selection of the edges is performed according to the following probabilistic state transition formula:

$$P_{ij} = \frac{[\tau_{ij}(t)]^{\alpha} \cdot [\eta_{ij}]^{\beta}}{\sum_{a}^{I} \sum_{b}^{J} [\tau_{ab}(t)]^{\alpha} \cdot [\eta_{ab}]^{\beta}} \tag{3}$$

In this equation, P_{ij} is the probability of selecting the edge $i \rightarrow j$, $\tau_{ij}(t)$ is the amount of pheromone associated with edge $i \rightarrow j$ at iteration t and η_{ij} is the heuristic information for edge $i \rightarrow j$ computed using conditional mutual information (equation 2). The edge $a \rightarrow b$ represents a valid selection in the available edges. The exponents α and β are used to adjust the relative emphases of the pheromone (τ) and heuristic information (η), respectively. Note that edges available for selection are directed, i. e. $i \rightarrow j \neq j \rightarrow i$.

ABC-Miner adapts the "ants with personality" approach, proposed by the author in [18]. Each ant_i is allowed to have its own *personality* by allowing it to have its own values of the α_i and β_i parameters. In other words, some ants will give more importance to pheromone amount, while others will give more importance to heuristic information. The α_i and β_i parameters are each independently drawn from a Gaussian distribution centered at 2 with a standard deviation of 1. This approach aims to advance exploration and improve search diversity in the colony.

An edge $i \rightarrow j$ is valid to be added in the BN classifier being constructed if the following two criteria are justified: 1) its inclusion does not create a directed cycle, 2) the limit of k parents (chosen by the current ant) for the child variable j is not violated by the inclusion of the edge. After the ant adds a valid edge to the BN classifier, all the invalid edges are eliminated from the construction graph. The ant keeps adding edges to the current solution until no valid edges are available. When the structure of BNC_i is finished, the parameters Θ are learnt by calculating the CPT for each variable, according to the network structure, producing a complete solution. Afterward, the quality of the BN classifier is evaluated, and all the edges become available again for the next ant to construct another candidate solution.

4.3   Quality Evaluation and Pheromone Update

Unlike the traditional Bayesian networks, the target of our algorithm is to build an effective BN in terms of predictive power with respect to a specific class attribute. In other words, BN learning algorithms aim to maximize a scoring function that seeks a structure that best represents the dependencies between all the attributes of a given dataset. This structure should fit the knowledge representation and inference purposes of a BN, which treats all the variables in the same way, without distinguishing between the predictor and the class attributes. On the other hand, the purpose of learning a BN classifier is to build a structure that can calculate the probability of a class value given an instance of the input predictor variables, and predict the class value with the highest probability to label the instance.

Therefore, using traditional scoring functions to evaluate the quality of a BN classifier should not fit the purpose of building a classifier [10]. According to this reasoning, we evaluate the quality of the constructed network directly as a classifier, where the predictive efficiency is the main concern. We use the *accuracy*, a conventional measure of predictive performance, to evaluate the constructed BN model, computed as follows:

$$Accuracy = \frac{|Correctly\_Classified\_Cases|}{|Validation\_Set|} \qquad (4)$$

The best BN classifier BNC_{tbest} constructed amongst the ants in the colony undergoes local search, which aims to improve the predictive accuracy of the classifier. The local search operates as follows. It temporarily removes one edge at a time in a reverse order (removing last the edge that was added to the network first). If the quality of the BN classifier improves, this edge is removed permanently from the network, otherwise it is added once again. Then we proceed to the next edge. This procedure continues until all the edges are tested to be removed from the BN classifier and the BN classifier with the highest quality – with respect to classification accuracy – is obtained.

After BNC_{tbest} is optimized via local search, pheromone levels are increased on decision components (edges) in the construction graph included in the structure of the constructed BN classifier, using the following formula:

$$\tau_{ij}(t+1) = \tau_{ij}(t) + \tau_{ij}(t).Q_{tbest}(t) \qquad (5)$$

To simulate pheromone evaporation, normalization is then applied as in [15]; each τ_{ij} is divided over the total pheromone amounts in the construction graph. Note that pheromone update is carried out for the decision components representing the number of dependencies used for building the BN classifier structure as well.

5   Experimental Methodology and Results

The performance of ABC-Miner was evaluated using 15 public-domain datasets from the UCI (University of California at Irvine) dataset repository [19]. Datasets containing continuous attributes were discretized in a pre-possessing step, using the C4.5-Disc [20] algorithm. The main characteristics of the datasets are shown in Table 1. We compare the predictive accuracy of our proposed ant-based algorithm with three other widely used algorithms for learning Bayesian classifiers. In our experiment, we used Weka [20] implementations for these algorithms. Table 2 presents the main characteristics of the used algorithms.

The experiments were carried out using 10-fold cross validation procedure. In essence, a dataset is divided into 10 mutually exclusive partitions, were each time a different partition is used as the test set and the other 9 partitions are used

Table 1. Description of Datasets Used in Experimental Results

Dataset	Size	Attributes	Classes
balance scale	625	4	3
breast cancer (wisconsin)	286	9	2
car evaluation	1,728	6	4
contraceptive method choice	1,473	9	3
statlog credit (australian)	690	14	2
statlog credit (german)	1,000	20	2
dermatology	366	33	6
hayes-roth	160	4	3
heart (cleveland)	303	12	3
iris	150	4	3
monks	432	6	2
nursey	12,960	8	5
soybean	307	35	19
tic-tac-to	958	9	2
voting records	435	16	2

Table 2. Summary of the BN Classifier Learning Algorithms Used in the Experiments

Algorithm	Type	Search Strategy	Optimization
Naïve-Bayes	Deterministic	-	-
TAN	Deterministic	Finding Max. Spanning Tree	Cond. Mutual Info.
GBN	Deterministic	Greedy Hill Climbing	K2 Function
ABC-Miner	Stochastic	Ant Colony Optimization	Predictive Accuracy

as the training set. The results (accuracy rate on the test set) are then averaged and reported in Table 3 as the accuracy rate of the classifier. Since ABC-Miner is a stochastic algorithm, we run it 10 times – using a different random seed to initialize the search each time – for each cross-validation fold. In the case of the deterministic algorithms, each is run just once for each fold.

Table 3 reports the mean and the standard error of predictive accuracy values obtained by 10-fold cross validation for the 15 datasets, where the highest accuracy for each dataset is shown in bold face. As shown, ABC-Miner has achieved the highest predictive accuracy amongst all algorithms in 12 datasets (with 2 ties), while Naïve-Bayes achieved the highest accuracy in 3 datasets (with 2 ties), TAN in 2 datasets (both are ties) and finally GBN in 4 datasets (with 3 ties).

Ranking the algorithms in descending order of accuracy for each dataset and taking the average ranking for each algorithm across all 15 datasets, ABC-Miner obtained a value of 1.6, which is the best predictive accuracy average

Table 3. Predictive Accuracy % (*mean ± standard error*) Results

Dataset	Naïve-Bayes	TAN	GBN	ABC-Miner
bcw	92.1 ± 0.9	**95.4 ± 0.9**	93.8 ± 0.9	**95.4 ± 0.6**
car	85.3 ± 0.9	93.6 ± 0.6	86.2 ± 0.9	**97.2 ± 0.3**
cmc	52.2 ± 1.2	49.8 ± 1.2	49.8 ± 1.2	**67.3 ± 0.6**
crd-a	77.5 ± 1.2	85.1 ± 0.9	85.7 ± 0.9	**87.3 ± 0.6**
crd-g	**75.6 ± 0.9**	73.7 ± 1.2	**75.6 ± 1.2**	69.5 ± 0.9
drm	96.2 ± 0.6	97.8 ± 0.9	97.2 ± 0.6	**99.1 ± 0.3**
hay	80.0 ± 2.8	67.9 ± 3.1	**83.1 ± 2.5**	80.0 ± 3.1
hrt-c	56.7 ± 2.2	58.8 ± 2.5	56.7 ± 2.2	**73.3 ± 0.9**
iris	**96.2 ± 1.5**	94.2 ± 1.8	92.9 ± 1.8	**96.2 ± 0.9**
monk	**61.6 ± 0.6**	58.8 ± 0.6	**61.6 ± 0.9**	51.9 ± 0.9
nurs	90.1 ± 0.9	94.3 ± 0.9	90.1 ± 0.9	**97.0 ± 0.9**
park	84.5 ± 2.5	91.7 ± 2.2	84.5 ± 2.5	**94.2 ± 2.8**
pima	75.4 ± 1.2	**77.8 ± 1.5**	**77.8 ± 1.5**	**77.8 ± 1.5**
ttt	70.3 ± 0.3	76.6 ± 0.6	70.3 ± 0.3	**86.4 ± 0.6**
vot	90.3 ± 0.6	92.1 ± 0.4	90.3 ± 0.6	**94.6 ± 0.9**

rank amongst all algorithms. On the other hand Naïve-Bayes, TAN and GBN have obtained 3.1, 2.5, 2.8 in predictive accuracy average rank respectively. Note that the lower the average rank, the better the performance of the algorithm.

Statistical test according to the non-parametric Friedman test with the Holm's post-hoc test was performed on the average rankings. Comparing to Naïve-Bayes and GBN, ABC-Miner is statistically better with a significance level of 5% as the tests obtained p - values of 0.0018 and 0.013 respectively. Comparing to TAN, ABC-Miner is statistically better with a significance level of 10% as the tests obtained p -value of 0.077.

6 Concluding Remarks

In this paper, we introduced a novel ant-based algorithm for learning Bayesian network classifiers. Empirical results showed that our proposed ABC-Miner significantly out performs the well-known Naïve-Bayes, TAN, and GBN algorithms in term predictive accuracy. Moreover, the automatic selection of the maximum number of k-parents value makes ABC-Miner more adaptive and autonomous than conventional algorithms for learning BN classifiers. As a future work, we would like to explore the effect of using different scoring functions for computing the heuristic value used by ABC-Miner, as well as other scoring functions to evaluate the quality of a constructed BN classifier. Another direction is to explore different methods of choosing the value of k parents for building a network structure for the Bayesian classifier.

References

1. Buntine, W.: Theory refinement on Bayesian networks. In: 17th Conference on Uncertainty in Artificial Intelligence, pp. 52–60. Morgan Kaufmann (1991)
2. De Campos, L.M., Gámez, J.A., Puerta, J.M.: Learning Bayesian network by ant colony optimisation. Mathware and Soft Computing, 251–268 (2002)
3. Cheng, J., Greiner, R.: Comparing Bayesian network classifiers. In: 15th Annual Conference on Uncertainty in Artificial Intelligence, pp. 101–108 (1999)
4. Cheng, J., Greiner, R.: Learning Bayesian Belief Network Classifiers: Algorithms and System. In: 14th Biennial Conference: Advances in Artificial Intelligence, pp. 141–151 (2001)
5. Chickering, D., Geiger, M., Heckerman, D.: Learning Bayesian networks is NP-complete. Advanced Technologies Division, Microsoft Corporation, Redmond, WA, Technical Report (1994)
6. Cooper, G.F., Herskovits, E.: A Bayesian method for the induction of probabilistic networks from data. Machine Learning Journal, 309–348 (1992)
7. Daly, R., Shen, Q., Aitken, S.: Using ant colony optimization in learning Bayesian network equivalence classes. In: Proceedings of UKCI, pp. 111–118 (2006)
8. Daly, R., Shen, Q.: Learning Bayesian network equivalence classes with ant colony optimization. Journal of Artificial Intelligence Research, 391–447 (2009)
9. Dorigo, M., Stützle, T.: Ant Colony Optimization. MIT Press (2004)
10. Friedman, N., Geiger, D., Goldszmidt, M.: Bayesian Network Classifiers. Machine Learning Journal, 131–161 (1997)
11. Friedman, N., Goldszmidt, M.: Learning Bayesian networks with local structure. Learning in Graphical Models, pp. 421–460. Kluwer, Norwell (1998)
12. Heckerman, D., Geiger, D., Chickering, D.M.: Learning Bayesian networks: the combination of knowledge and statistical data. Machine Learning Journal, 197–244 (1995)
13. Martens, D., Backer, M.D., Haesen, R., Vanthienen, J., Snoeck, M., Baesens, B.: Classification with ant colony optimization. In: IEEE TEC, pp. 651–665 (2007)
14. Otero, F.E.B., Freitas, A.A., Johnson, C.G.: cAnt-Miner: An Ant Colony Classification Algorithm to Cope with Continuous Attributes. In: Dorigo, M., Birattari, M., Blum, C., Clerc, M., Stützle, T., Winfield, A.F.T. (eds.) ANTS 2008. LNCS, vol. 5217, pp. 48–59. Springer, Heidelberg (2008)
15. Parpinelli, R.S., Lopes, H.S., Freitas, A.: Data mining with an ant colony optimization algorithm. In: IEEE TEC, pp. 321–332 (2002)
16. Pinto, P.C., Nägele, A., Dejori, M., Runkler, T.A., Costa, J.M.: Learning of Bayesian networks by a local discovery ant colony algorithm. In: IEEE World Congress on Computational Intelligence, pp. 2741–2748 (2008)
17. Pinto, P.C., Nägele, A., Dejori, M., Runkler, T.A., Costa, J.M.: Using a Local Discovery Ant Algorithm for Bayesian Network Structure Learning. In: IEEE TEC, pp. 767–779 (2009)
18. Salama, K.M., Abdelbar, A.M., Freitas, A.A.: Multiple pheromone types and other extensions to the Ant-Miner classification rule discovery algorithm. Swarm Intelligence Journal, 149–182 (2011)
19. UCI Repository of Machine Learning Databases, http://archive.ics.uci.edu/ml/index.html (retrieved October 2011)
20. Witten, H., Frank, E.: Data Mining: Practical Machine Learning Tools and Techniques, 2nd edn. Morgan Kauffman (2005)
21. Yanghui, W., McCall, J., Corne, D.: Two novel Ant Colony Optimization approaches for Bayesian network structure learning. In: IEEE World Congress on Evolutionary Computation, pp. 1–7 (2010)

Analysing Robot Swarm Decision-Making with Bio-PEPA

Mieke Massink[1], Manuele Brambilla[2], Diego Latella[1],
Marco Dorigo[2], and Mauro Birattari[2]

[1] Istituto di Scienza e Tecnologie dell'Informazione 'A. Faedo' (ISTI),
CNR Pisa, Italy
{massink,latella}@isti.cnr.it
[2] IRIDIA, Université Libre de Bruxelles, Brussels, Belgium
{mbrambil,mdorigo,mbiro}@ulb.ac.be

Abstract. We present a novel method to analyse swarm robotics systems based on Bio-PEPA. Bio-PEPA is a process algebraic language originally developed to analyse biochemical systems. Its main advantage is that it allows different kinds of analyses of a swarm robotics system starting from a single description. In general, to carry out different kinds of analysis, it is necessary to develop multiple models, raising issues of mutual consistency. With Bio-PEPA, instead, it is possible to perform stochastic simulation, fluid flow analysis and statistical model checking based on the same system specification. This reduces the complexity of the analysis and ensures consistency between analysis results. Bio-PEPA is well suited for swarm robotics systems, because it lends itself well to modelling distributed scalable systems and their space-time characteristics. We demonstrate the validity of Bio-PEPA by modelling collective decision-making in a swarm robotics system and we evaluate the result of different analyses.

1 Introduction

Swarm robotics is a novel approach to multi-robots systems. Swarm robotics systems (SRSs) are composed by tens or hundreds of robots which cooperate to perform a task, without a centralized controller or global knowledge. The goal of swarm robotics is to develop systems that are robust, scalable and flexible [7].

Analysing large and complex SRSs using physics-based simulations or directly with robots is often difficult and time consuming. For this reason, a common way to study these systems is by using models [16]. Models allow the developer to abstract from the complexity of a system and its implementation details and focus on the aspects that are relevant for the analysis. Different approaches are available to model a SRS. *Macroscopic modelling* [16] is commonly used for describing the collective behaviour of a system. Another approach, namely *microscopic modelling* [8], focuses instead on the behaviour of individual robots. Finally, *model checking* has been used to verify formal properties of a SRS [13]. These approaches allow a developer to obtain different "views" of the system

M. Dorigo et al. (Eds.): ANTS 2012, LNCS 7461, pp. 25–36, 2012.

behaviour. However, for each of these views, a different model is necessary. Producing different models greatly increases the complexity of the analysis process. Moreover, when dealing with different models, the issue of mutual consistency must be addressed.

In this paper we present a novel approach to model SRSs based on Bio-PEPA [6] which allows to obtain different consistent views of a system from the same formal specification. Bio-PEPA is a process algebraic language for biochemical and distributed systems. It has also been used[1] to analyse emergency egress [18] and crowd dynamics [19] which are systems characterized by a high number of individuals and lack of a centralized controller, aspects common also to SRSs. Bio-PEPA is well suited to analyse and develop SRSs; it provides for a clear specification at the microscopic level while providing also primitives for spatial description (e.g. *locations*) and for composition of individual robots (e.g *cooperation* operator). Moreover, Bio-PEPA allows to easily define *species*, which can be used to characterize groups of robots with specific attributes and actions; for instance, they can be used to differentiate between groups of robots performing different tasks at the same location. We use Bio-PEPA to develop a formal specification and analyse a collective decision-making behaviour which has been extensively studied in [21,22]. The case study consists of a swarm of robots that have to collectively identify the shortest path between two possible choices. We validate our results against those presented in [21].

The outline of the paper is as follows. In Section 2, we present related work. In Section 3, we give a brief presentation of Bio-PEPA. In Section 4, we present the case study and its Bio-PEPA specification. In Section 5, we present and validate our results. Some conclusions are drawn in Section 6.

2   Related Work

The most common approaches to modelling in swarm robotics are based on microscopic and macroscopic models. The main advantage of microscopic modelling is that it allows to study in detail the robot-to-robot and robot-to-environment interactions that are the key components of any SRS. Microscopic modelling, through stochastic simulation, can be used to analyse a system both in its equilibrium and far-from-equilibrium states. An example of a microscopic model of a SRS can be found in [11]. Macroscopic modelling, instead, considers only the swarm and its time evolution, ignoring the individual behaviour of the robots composing it. For this reason, it can be used to analyse systems composed by thousands of robots using fluid flow (Ordinary Differential Equations) approximation. Macroscopic modelling provides an important technique to address equilibrium analysis, but is focussed on the average behaviour of the system, abstracting from local stochastic fluctuations. A review on macroscopic modelling in swarm robotics can be found in [16]. A comparison between the microscopic and macroscopic models of a swarm robotics system is presented in [17].

---

[1] See http://www.biopepa.org for a complete list of publications.

A further way to model a SRS models is through mathematical logic. Models developed through mathematical logic can be used to formally verify given properties of a SRS by *automated* model checking (e.g. [2]). Up to now this approach has not been explored extensively in swarm robotics. Examples of model checking in swarm robotics can be found in [13,3].

To perform stochastic simulation, fluid flow (ODE) approximation and model checking different models of a system are necessary. Our approach, instead, requires only a single Bio-PEPA specification permitting different kinds of system analyses.

3   Bio-PEPA

Bio-PEPA [6] is a process algebraic language that originally was developed for the stochastic analysis of biochemical systems. Bio-PEPA specifications consist of two main kinds of components. The first kind is called the *"species"* component, specifying the behaviour of individual entities. The second kind is the *model component*, specifying the interactions between the various species. In the context of this paper, the individual entities are the robots, and the model component defines how they interact.

The syntax of Bio-PEPA components is defined as:

$$S ::= (\alpha, \kappa) \text{ op } S \mid S + S \mid C \quad \text{with op} = \downarrow \mid \uparrow \mid \oplus \mid \ominus \mid \odot \quad \text{and } P ::= P \bowtie_{\mathcal{L}} P \mid S(x)$$

where S is a *species component* and P is a *model component*.

The *prefix combinator* "op" in the prefix term (α, κ) op S represents the impact that action α has on species S. Specifically, $\downarrow$ indicates that the number of entities of species S reduces when α occurs, and $\uparrow$ indicates that this number increases. The amount of the change is defined by the coefficient κ. This coefficient captures the multiples of an entity involved in an occurring action. We will see an example of its use in the next section. The default value of κ is 1, in which case we simply write α instead of (α, κ). Action durations are assumed to be random variables with negative exponential distributions, characterised by their *rates*. The rate of action α is defined by a so called functional rate or kinetics rate. Action rates are defined in the context section of a Bio-PEPA specification.

The symbol $\oplus$ denotes an *activator*, $\ominus$ an *inhibitor* and $\odot$ a generic *modifier*, all of which play a role in an action without being produced or consumed and have a defined meaning in the biochemical context. The operator "+" expresses the choice between possible actions, and the constant C is defined by the equation $C=S$. The process $P \bowtie_{\mathcal{L}} Q$ denotes synchronisation between components P and Q, the set $\mathcal{L}$ determines those actions on which the components P and Q are forced to synchronise. The shorthand $P \bowtie^{*} Q$ denotes synchronisation on all actions that P and Q have in common. In $S(x)$, the parameter $x \in \mathbb{R}$ represents the initial amount of the species. A Bio-PEPA *system* with *locations* consists of a set of species components, a model component, and a context containing definitions of locations, functional/kinetics rates, parameters, etc.. The prefix term (α, κ) op $S@l$ is used to specify that the action is performed by S in location l.

Bio-PEPA is given a formal operational semantics [6] which is based on Continuous Time Markov Chains (CTMCs). It is supported by a suite of software tools which automatically process Bio-PEPA models and generate internal representations suitable for different types of analysis [6,4]. These tools include mappings from Bio-PEPA to differential equations (ODE) supporting a fluid flow approximation [10], stochastic simulation models [9], CTMCs with levels [5] and PRISM models [15] amenable to statistical model checking. Consistency of the analyses is supported by a rich theory including process algebra, and the relationships between CTMCs and ODE.

4   Collective Decision-Making: A Bio-PEPA Specification

In this paper, we analyse a collective decision-making system originally proposed by Montes de Oca et al. [21]. The task of the robots is to transport objects from a *start* area to a *goal* area. The objects to transport are too heavy for a single robot, thus the robots have to form groups of three in order to transport a single object. There are two possible paths between the start and the goal area and the robots can choose between the two. This is similar to what ants do in the well known double bridge experiment with the difference that ants use pheromones while in our setup robots use voting.

Each individual robot has a preferred path. When a group of three robots is formed in the start area, the robots choose the path that is preferred by the majority of them. The chosen path becomes the preferred one for all the robots in the group. More details are given in Sections 4.1. An analysis of the system is presented in Montes de Oca et al. [21] and in Scheidler [22].

This collective decision-making system is a good benchmark for testing Bio-PEPA since it displays two important aspects of swarm robotics: cooperation and space-time characteristics. Cooperation can be direct and indirect: the robots cooperate directly to transport the objects, and indirectly to select a path via the dynamics of their preferences. Space-time characteristics are displayed in the voting process itself, as it involves only the robots that are in the start area at a given time, and in the fact that the collective decision-making process depends on the time taken to navigate over the two different paths.

4.1   The Bio-PEPA Specification

In the remaining part of this section we present the Bio-PEPA specification of the system. The full specification can be found in the supplementary material [20]. As shown in Fig. 1, the system is described by eight Bio-PEPA *locations*: two boundary locations, start and goal; two choice locations, A and B, where the robots decide which path to take; and two locations for each path, L1 and L2 for the long path and S1 and S2 for the short one. We also define a set of Bio-PEPA *species* to specify the behaviour of the robots. For example in start we distinguish two species of robots: those that last time returned via the short path, denoted as *Robo_start_fromS*, and those that returned via the long path,

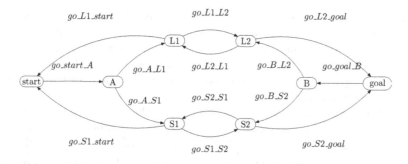

Fig. 1. Locations and transitions of robots in the Bio-PEPA specification

denoted as *Robo_start_fromL*. In the sequel we will refer to these two groups also as the *S-population* and the *L-population*, respectively. Similarly, other locations contain populations of teams of robots that move in the direction from the start area to the goal area and those that move in the opposite direction. For example, in location S1 we can have *Teams_S1_StoG* and *Teams_S1_GtoS*, where *StoG* denotes the direction from the start area to the goal area and *GtoS* the opposite direction.

The Bio-PEPA fragment below specifies the behaviour of a robot. Robots leave the start area in groups of three. Each group is randomly composed by either three robots from the S-population, three from the L-population or two from S and one from L or two from L and one from S. These combinations are modelled as four different actions: *allS*, *allL*, *S2L1* and *S1L2*. In Bio-PEPA the formation of teams of robots is modelled by the coefficient that indicates how many entities are involved in an action. For example, upon action *allS* three robots of the S-population leave start (indicated by $(allS, 3)\downarrow$), to form an additional *team* of robots in choice point A (indicated by $(allS, 1)\uparrow$ in *Teams_A_S*) which is ready to take the short path when the team continues its journey towards the goal area (population *Teams_A_S@A*). Since action *allS* is shared between the species components *Robo_start_fromS* and *Teams_A_S* this movement occurs simultaneously with the rate of action *allS* that will be defined later on.

$$\begin{aligned}
Robo\_start\_fromS = \ &(allS, 3)\downarrow Robo\_start\_fromS@start+ \\
&(S2L1, 2)\downarrow Robo\_start\_fromS@start+ \\
&(S1L2, 1)\downarrow Robo\_start\_fromS@start+ \\
&(go\_S1\_start, 3)\uparrow Robo\_start\_fromS@start;
\end{aligned}$$

$$\begin{aligned}
Teams\_A\_S = \ &(allS, 1)\uparrow Teams\_A\_S@A+ \\
&(S2L1, 1)\uparrow Teams\_A\_S@A+ \\
&go\_A\_S1\downarrow Teams\_A\_S@A;
\end{aligned}$$

In a similar way, upon action *S2L1*, which is present in three components (*Robo_start_fromS*, *Teams_A_S* and *Robo_start_fromL*, the latter is not shown), all three components synchronize, resulting in two robots from the S-population and one from the L-population leaving the start area and forming at the same time 1 new team in choice point A in the population $Teams\_A\_S$. The synchronization pattern of the components is given by the model component shown later on. The excerpt above only shows the behaviour of teams voting for the short path. The behaviour of those voting for the long path is similar and omitted for reasons of space. For the same reason also the behaviour of teams moving between different locations is not shown.

The actions denoting groups of robots leaving the start area need to occur with appropriate rates. For example, a group of three robots all from the S-population has a probability of $\frac{(RSS)}{(RSS)+(RSL)} * \frac{(RSS-1)}{(RSS-1)+(RSL)} * \frac{(RSS-2)}{(RSS-2)+(RSL)}$ times the rate of leaving the start area, where RSL (RSS resp.) abbreviates $Robo\_start\_fromL@start$ ($Robo\_start\_fromS@start$ resp.). A similar probability can be defined for a group of three from the L-population.

When considering mixed groups also the order in which the elements are extracted from the population in the start area is of influence. This is particularly true when relatively small populations of robots are considered. For example, the probability to extract two robots from the S-population in the start area and then one from the L-population is:

$$pSSL = \frac{(RSS)}{(RSS)+(RSL)} * \frac{(RSS-1)}{(RSS-1)+(RSL)} * \frac{(RSL)}{(RSS-2)+(RSL)}$$

Similarly we define probabilities for $pSLS$, $pLSS$, $pLLS$, $pLSL$ and $pSLL$. The rates of actions $S2L1$ and $S1L2$ can now be defined as $(pSSL+pSLS+pLSS)*$ move and $(pSLL+pLSL+pLLS)*$ move, respectively. Note that the sum of these six probabilities and the probability of the combination of three S or three L is 1. So the total rate at which groups of robots leave the start area is constant and given by the parameter 'move'. The rate at which groups move from A to $S1$ and to $L1$ is also dependent on the number of groups present in A and are $walk\_normal * Teams\_A\_S@A$ and $walk\_normal * Teams\_A\_L@A$, respectively. The rate parameter $walk\_normal$ specifies the time it takes a group of robots to move from choice-point A to the first section of a path.

Finally, the overall system definition shows the initial size of robot populations in each location. The overall robot behaviour is defined using multi-part synchronization on shared actions:

$$Robo\_start\_fromS@start(SS) \bowtie Robo\_start\_fromL@start(SL) \bowtie$$
$$Teams\_A\_S@A(0) \bowtie Teams\_A\_L@A(0) \bowtie$$
$$Teams\_S1\_StoG@S1(0) \bowtie Teams\_S1\_GtoS@S1(0) \bowtie$$
$$Teams\_S2\_StoG@S2(0) \bowtie Teams\_S2\_GtoS@S2(0) \bowtie$$
$$Teams\_L1\_StoG@L1(0) \bowtie Teams\_L1\_GtoS@L1(0) \bowtie$$
$$Teams\_L2\_StoG@L2(0) \bowtie Teams\_L2\_GtoS@L2(0) \bowtie$$
$$Teams\_goal\_fromS@goal(0) \bowtie Teams\_goal\_fromL@goal(0) \bowtie$$
$$Teams\_B\_fromS@B(0) \bowtie Teams\_B\_fromL@B(0)$$

where the number SS in $Robo\_start\_fromS@start(SS)$ (resp. SL) is the initial size of the robot S (resp. L)-population present in the start area (@start). There is a further issue to consider which is the way to model the length of the paths. This can be done in two ways. The first is to model each path by two sections, as illustrated above, and vary the time it takes teams to traverse these sections by choosing a different rate for the movement between sections on the short and the long path. However, as also discussed in [21], this model has the disadvantage that the duration of path traversal is essentially modelled by a short series of exponential distributions which in general approximates the average duration well, but not the variability. It therefore does not reflect very well realistic robot behaviour. An alternative is to choose the same rate for each section and to vary the number of sections on each path to model their difference in length. This way the traversal time of a path is modelled by a sequence of say m exponentially distributed random variables with rate λ, also known as an Erlang distribution, using the well-known method of stages [12] (p. 119).[2] We model the two paths of the environment with 8 S-sections and 15 L-sections. Each section takes, on average, ten time units to traverse. This is modelled in the system by defining the rate $walk\_normal = 0.1$. Considering also the movements from the choice points to the path and those from the path to the start area and the goal area, in this way the short path takes on average 100 time units to traverse, and the long one 170. This is comparable to the latency periods used in [21] (end of Section 4). Other free variables of the model not provided in [21] have been selected by us.

5   Analysis

For the analysis in this section we consider a Bio-PEPA voting specification with a population of 32 robots. In [21] the analysis results make reference to the number of teams, k, that are active in the system at any time. We specify this in Bio-PEPA by making sure that at any time at least min_start robots are in the start area, corresponding to $k = (32 - min\_start)/3$.[3] We furthermore consider the following parameters for the specification: $N = 32$, of which initially $SS = 16$ and $SL = 16$, $move = 0.28$, $walk\_normal = 0.1$.

In the following we illustrate three different forms of analysis of the same Bio-PEPA specification and validate their results with those from the literature [21].

5.1   Stochastic Simulation

The first kind of analysis uses stochastic simulation to check the average number of active teams in the system over time for different assumptions on the minimal number of robots that remain in the start area. Fig. 2 presents two stochastic simulation results (average over 10 simulation runs) for $min\_start = 5$

---

[2] For m going to infinite, an Erlang distribution $[m, \lambda]$ converges to a normal distribution with mean m/λ and variance m/λ^2. So, in general, the larger m is, the better the Erlang distribution $[m, \lambda]$ approximates a normal distribution.

[3] In Bio-PEPA, one can make use of a predefined function H which takes a rate as argument. If the rate is zero, H returns zero, otherwise it returns 1. To guarantee a minimum number, min_start, in the start area, the rate of, e.g., action $S2L1$ can then be defined as: $S2L1 = (pSSL+pSLS+pLSS)*move*H((RSS+RSL)-min\_start)$.

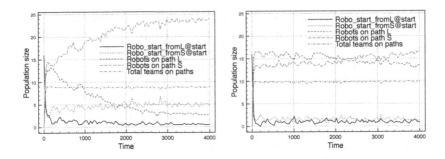

Fig. 2. Number of active teams for $min\_start = 5$ (left) and $min\_start = 2$ (right)

(Fig. 2 left) and $min\_start = 2$ (Fig. 2 right). The figure shows that the number of active teams on the paths quickly increases to 9 (resp. 10) and then stabilizes at that level. This means that the rate at which robots leave the start area, i.e. $move = 0.28$, is sufficiently high to quickly reach a situation with the desired number of active teams. This makes it possible to compare the results of this analysis with the results obtained with the physics-based simulation and Monte Carlo simulation as reported in [21] which will be discussed later on. The figures show the number of robots on the paths and in the start area and the total number of teams on the paths.

5.2   Statistical Model Checking

Another way to analyse the system is via statistical model checking provided, for example, by the model-checker PRISM [15]. In particular, the Bio-PEPA specification can be exported automatically [4] to the PRISM input language. The PRISM specification can be found in the supplementary material [20]. Statistical model checking is an analysis method in which a logical formula, formalizing a particular property of the system, can be automatically checked against a set of randomly generated simulation runs of a model of the system via statistical analysis. For example, if we denote convergence on the short path by the shorthand "Convergence_on_S", and convergence on the long path by "Convergence_on_L", the statement "what is the probability that the system did not converge on the long path until it converges on the short path" can be expressed in the Continuous Stochastic temporal Logic (CSL) [1,2] as:

$$P =? \; [!\,\text{``}Convergence\_on\_L\text{''} \; U \; \text{``}Convergence\_on\_S\text{''}] \qquad (1)$$

where $P =?$ is used to compute a probability, ! stands for negation and U reads as "until". "Convergence_on_S" can be defined as the situation in which all the 32 robots are either in a team on the short path or in the S-population in the start area or at the goal area. "Convergence_on_L" can be defined similarly, but requiring that the above sum is equal to 0 instead of 32.

In a similar way, the model can be analysed to obtain the expected number of team formations and the expected time until convergence. For the number of team formations, one needs to count the number of times the actions 'go_A_S1' and 'go_A_L1' occur until convergence happens. Let us assume that the variable *teams* accumulates the number of teams formed until convergence, and the variable *total_time* the total time that passed until convergence in the various simulation runs[4]. The question "what is the expected number of teams formed until eventually convergence has taken place on the short or the long path" can then be answered by statistical model checking with the logical reward formula:

$$R\{\text{"teams"}\} =? \; [F \; (\text{"_Convergence_on_S"} | \text{"_Convergence_on_L"})] \quad (2)$$

where F reads as "eventually", | denotes logical disjunction and $R =?$ is used to compute the expected value, commonly called 'reward', of specific events. A similar analysis using the same formula, but substituting *teams* with *total_time*, gives the expected time until convergence. The following analyses have been based on 100 random samples and a confidence level of 99%, except where explicitly indicated. In the figures the confidence intervals are shown as error-bars.

Figure 3 (a), (b) and (c) show the result of statistical model checking of the above formulas for models that only differ in the number of active teams k, where $k = \{1, 2, ..., 10\}$. In particular, Fig. 3(a) shows the probability of convergence on the short path (i.e. Formula (1)). The data are compared to those obtained via physics-based simulation and Monte Carlo simulation of the same case-study reported in [21]. The latter are close to the results obtained with the Bio-PEPA specification and well within the error-margins. Fig. 3(b) shows results on the expected number of team formations until convergence on the short or long path (i.e. Formula (2)) using 1000 samples. The data correspond very well for k from 1 to 7, but diverge for higher values of k perhaps caused by strong stochastic fluctuations due to the small number of robots present in the start location. Fig. 3(c) shows the expected convergence time. No data from the literature concerning this aspect is available for comparison. The total model-checking time to produce the data in Fig. 3(a) was ca. 10 minutes, those in Fig. 3(b) ca. 48 minutes and those in Fig. 3(c) ca. 5 minutes. Due to space limits we limit our analysis to the shown properties. However, other interesting properties of the system could be analysed this way. For example it can be shown that for any value of k from 1 to 10 the probability that convergence occurs is equal to 1.

5.3   Fluid Flow Analysis

The third kind of analysis is a fluid flow approximation or numerical analysis of the ODE underlying the Bio-PEPA specification. Based on the Bio-PEPA syntax, the underlying ODE model can be generated automatically and in a systematic way [10] using the Bio-PEPA tool suite [4]. This provides yet another view on the behavioural aspects of the system. One can, for example, explore numerically the sensitivity of the system to initial values and discover stationary

---

[4] In terms of Markov theory such 'counting' is defined by *reward structures* In statistical model checking these numbers are used in the statistical analysis of the generated simulation runs.

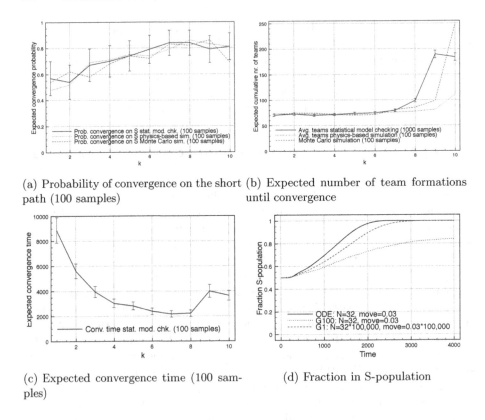

(a) Probability of convergence on the short path (100 samples)

(b) Expected number of team formations until convergence

(c) Expected convergence time (100 samples)

(d) Fraction in S-population

Fig. 3. Results with Erlang distribution of path length

points and other aspects related to stability analysis. As an example, here we show the relation between stochastic simulation and fluid approximation results.

In Fig. 3(d) a fluid flow analysis (ODE) is shown of the total fraction of robots in the S-population over time, i.e. both those present in the start area and those in the teams[5]. Clearly, the fluid approximation predicts that the system converges in 100% of the cases to the short path. Stochastic simulation over 100 independent runs (G100) shows that such convergence happens only in 85% of the cases, which corresponds to what we found with statistical model checking for a comparable value of k (see Fig. 3(a)). The difference can be explained by the larger effect of stochastic fluctuations when the population is small. The probability that the system 'accidentally' converges on the long path is then relatively high. For large populations such a probability tends to zero, as stochastic simulation trajectories start to approximate the deterministic ODE solution when the specification satisfies certain scaling conditions (see [14]). This phenomenon

---

[5] To guarantee continuity of the ODE model the H-function has been removed and replaced by setting $move = 0.03$ to approximate a scenario in which $k = 7$.

can be observed in Fig. 3(d) from the curve labelled G1. This insight provides a way to interpret results obtained with fluid approximation.

6   Conclusions

Bio-PEPA [6] is a process algebraic language originally developed for the stochastic modelling and analysis of biochemical systems. In this paper we used Bio-PEPA to specify and analyse a robot swarm decision-making behaviour, originally presented in [21]. We showed that with Bio-PEPA issues relevant to SRS modelling can be addressed at the microscopic level. Among these issues are: robot team-formation, voting, certain spatial and temporal aspects, species of robots with particular behavioural characteristics, and direct and indirect inter-action. The main advantage is that a single microscopic Bio-PEPA specification of the system lends itself to a variety of analyses methods such as stochastic simulation, fluid flow (ODE) approximation and statistical (stochastic) model checking. This provides an efficient way to obtain different views of the system behaviour, while *preserving their mutual consistency*. The results were shown to be largely comparable with those obtained in [21] via physics-based simulation and Monte Carlo simulation of the same case study. A limit of Bio-PEPA is its limited capability to tackle sophisticated spatial and temporal concepts. In future work, we plan to address this and develop facilities to further explore non-linear behavioural aspects using numerical techniques. Our goal is to extend Bio-PEPA to ease the modelling and analysis process of SRS. We believe that this could facilitate the more widespread uptake of modelling and analysis in swarm robotics.

Acknowledgements. The research leading to the results presented in this pa-per has received funding from the European Research Council under the Eu-ropean Union's Seventh Framework Programme (FP7/2007-2013) / ERC grant agreement n 246939, and by the EU project ASCENS, 257414. Manuele Bram-billa, Mauro Birattari and Marco Dorigo acknowledge support from the F.R.S.-FNRS of Belgium's Wallonia-Brussels Federation. The authors would like to thank Stephen Gilmore and Alan Clark (Edinburgh University) for their help with the Bio-PEPA tool suite and templates.

References

1. Aziz, A., Sanwal, K., Singhal, V., Brayton, R.: Model checking Continuous Time Markov Chains. ACM Transactions on Computational Logic 1(1), 162–170 (2000)
2. Baier, C., Katoen, J.-P., Hermanns, H.: Approximate Symbolic Model Checking of Continuous-Time Markov Chains (Extended Abstract). In: Baeten, J.C.M., Mauw, S. (eds.) CONCUR 1999. LNCS, vol. 1664, pp. 146–162. Springer, Heidelberg (1999)
3. Brambilla, M., Pinciroli, C., Birattari, M., Dorigo, M.: Property-driven design for swarm robotics. In: Proceedings of 11th International Conference on Autonomous Agents and Multiagent Systems, AAMAS 2012. IFAAMAS (in press, 2012)

4. Ciocchetta, F., Duguid, A., Gilmore, S., Guerriero, M.L., Hillston, J.: The Bio-PEPA Tool Suite. In: Proc. of the 6th Int. Conf. on Quantitative Evaluation of Systems (QEST 2009), pp. 309–310. IEEE Computer Society, Washington, DC (2009)
5. Ciocchetta, F., Hillston, J.: Bio-PEPA: An extension of the process algebra PEPA for biochemical networks. ENTCS 194(3), 103–117 (2008)
6. Ciocchetta, F., Hillston, J.: Bio-PEPA: A framework for the modelling and analysis of biological systems. TCS 410(33-34), 3065–3084 (2009)
7. Şahin, E.: Swarm Robotics: From Sources of Inspiration to Domains of Application. In: Şahin, E., Spears, W.M. (eds.) Swarm Robotics 2004. LNCS, vol. 3342, pp. 10–20. Springer, Heidelberg (2005)
8. Dixon, C., Winfield, A., Fisher, M.: Towards Temporal Verification of Emergent Behaviours in Swarm Robotic Systems. In: Groß, R., Alboul, L., Melhuish, C., Witkowski, M., Prescott, T.J., Penders, J. (eds.) TAROS 2011. LNCS, vol. 6856, pp. 336–347. Springer, Heidelberg (2011)
9. Gillespie, D.T.: Exact stochastic simulation of coupled chemical reactions. The Journal of Physical Chemistry 81(25), 2340–2361 (1977)
10. Hillston, J.: Fluid flow approximation of PEPA models. In: Proceedings of the 2th International Conference on Quantitative Evaluation of SysTems (QEST 2005), pp. 33–43. IEEE Computer Society, Washington, DC (2005)
11. Ijspeert, A., Martinoli, A., Billard, A., Gambardella, L.M.: Collaboration through the exploitation of local interactions in autonomous collective robotics: The stick pulling experiment. Autonomous Robots 11, 149–171 (2001)
12. Kleinrock, L.: Queueing Systems. Theory, vol. 1. Wiley, New York (1975)
13. Konur, S., Dixon, C., Fisher, M.: Analysing robot swarm behaviour via probabilistic model checking. Robotics and Autonomous Systems 60(2), 199–213 (2012)
14. Kurtz, T.: Solutions of ordinary differential equations as limits of pure jump Markov processes. Journal of Applied Probability 7, 49–58 (1970)
15. Kwiatkowska, M., Norman, G., Parker, D.: PRISM 4.0: Verification of Probabilistic Real-Time Systems. In: Gopalakrishnan, G., Qadeer, S. (eds.) CAV 2011. LNCS, vol. 6806, pp. 585–591. Springer, Heidelberg (2011)
16. Lerman, K., Martinoli, A., Galstyan, A.: A Review of Probabilistic Macroscopic Models for Swarm Robotic Systems. In: Şahin, E., Spears, W.M. (eds.) Swarm Robotics 2004. LNCS, vol. 3342, pp. 143–152. Springer, Heidelberg (2005)
17. Martinoli, A., Easton, K., Agassounon, W.: Modeling swarm robotic systems: a case study in collaborative distributed manipulation. The International Journal of Robotics Research 23(4-5), 415–436 (2004)
18. Massink, M., Latella, D., Bracciali, A., Harrison, M., Hillston, J.: Scalable context-dependent analysis of emergency egress models. Formal Aspects of Computing 24(2), 267–302 (2012)
19. Massink, M., Latella, D., Bracciali, A., Hillston, J.: Modelling Non-linear Crowd Dynamics in Bio-PEPA. In: Giannakopoulou, D., Orejas, F. (eds.) FASE 2011. LNCS, vol. 6603, pp. 96–110. Springer, Heidelberg (2011)
20. Massink, M., Brambilla, M., Latella, D., Dorigo, M., Birattari, M.: Analysing robot swarm decision-making with Bio-PEPA: Complete data (2012), Supplementary information page at http://iridia.ulb.ac.be/supp/IridiaSupp2012-012/
21. Montes de Oca, M.A., Ferrante, E., Scheidler, A., Pinciroli, C., Birattari, M., Dorigo, M.: Majority-rule opinion dynamics with differential latency: A mechanism for self-organized collective decision-making. Swarm Intelligence 5(3-4), 305–327 (2011)
22. Scheidler, A.: Dynamics of majority rule with differential latencies. Phys. Rev. E 83, 031116 (2011)

Automatic Generation of Multi-objective ACO Algorithms for the Bi-objective Knapsack

Leonardo C.T. Bezerra, Manuel López-Ibáñez, and Thomas Stützle

IRIDIA, Université Libre de Bruxelles, Brussels, Belgium
leonardo@iridia.ulb.ac.be, {manuel.lopez-ibanez,stuetzle}@ulb.ac.be

Abstract. Multi-objective ant colony optimization (MOACO) algorithms have shown promising results for various multi-objective problems, but they also offer a large number of possible design choices. Often, exploring all possible configurations is practically infeasible. Recently, the automatic configuration of a MOACO framework was explored and was shown to result in new state-of-the-art MOACO algorithms for the bi-objective traveling salesman problem. In this paper, we apply this approach to the bi-objective bidimensional knapsack problem (bBKP) to prove its generality and power. As a first step, we tune and improve the performance of four MOACO algorithms that have been earlier proposed for the bBKP. In a second step, we configure the full MOACO framework and show that the automatically configured MOACO framework outperforms all previous MOACO algorithms for the bBKP as well as their improved variants.

1 Introduction

Multi-objective ant colony optimization (MOACO) algorithms have been applied to multi-objective combinatorial optimization problems (MCOPs) since more than 10 years [7,3,1,10,12,9]. The interest in MOACO algorithms may be explained by the practical relevance of multi-objective problems and by the positive results that have been achieved with these algorithms. The available MOACO algorithms provide a large number of different design choices that allow the instantiation of a huge number of structurally different MOACO algorithms. Recently, López-Ibáñez and Stützle [13] proposed a MOACO framework that implements most of those design possibilities. The automatic configuration tool *Iterated F-race* (I/F-Race) [2,11] was used to automatically generate MOACO algorithms for the bi-objective traveling salesman problem (bTSP). The authors showed that the automatic configuration of a generic MOACO framework produced better results than the MOACO algorithms from the literature used to build the framework. In this paper, we continue the investigation of the effectiveness of this approach by extending the MOACO framework to deal with the bi-objective bidimensional knapsack problem (bBKP).

The bBKP is a popular benchmark problem in multi-objective optimization [16,14]. Moreover, four different MOACO algorithms have been proposed for the bBKP [1]. The bBKP has also some properties that make it interesting

M. Dorigo et al. (Eds.): ANTS 2012, LNCS 7461, pp. 37–48, 2012.
© Springer-Verlag Berlin Heidelberg 2012

for further exploring the possibilities of the automatic design of MOACO algorithms from a flexible framework. In particular, the representation of solutions is different from the TSP, pheromone information is represented by a vector instead of a matrix, and the structure of the solution space is quite different from the TSP.

This paper shows that the proposed method for the automatic design of MOACO algorithms also works for the bBKP. The proposed method is able to generate, with little effort from the human designer, MOACO algorithms that are clearly better than those proposed earlier for the bBKP, even after tuning the ACO settings of the MOACO algorithms from the literature and improving significantly their performance.

2 The Bi-objective Bidimensional Knapsack Problem

In an MCOP, the quality of solutions is evaluated based on a D-dimensional objective vector. Given two different candidate solutions x_1 and x_2 of a maximization problem, the Pareto dominance relation states that x_1 *dominates* x_2 iff $\forall d = 1, \ldots, D \ f^d(x_1) \geq f^d(x_2)$, and $\exists j \in \{1, \ldots, D\}$ such that $f^d(x_1) > f^d(x_2)$. The goal in MCOPs that are tackled according to Pareto dominance is to identify the Pareto-optimal set, i.e., the solutions that are *nondominated* w.r.t. all feasible solutions. Since most of such MCOPs are NP-hard, this goal is typically relaxed towards finding an as good as possible approximation to the Pareto set.

In this paper, we tackle the bBKP, which is a widely used bi-objective benchmark problem [16,14]. The bBKP is a special case of the general multi-objective multidimensional knapsack problem (moMKP), which is formalized as follows:

$$\max \ f^d(x) = \sum_{i=1}^{n} p_i^d x_i \quad d = 1, \ldots, D \qquad \text{s.t.} \quad \sum_{i=1}^{n} w_i^j x_i \leq W_j \quad j = 1, \ldots, m$$

where each item i has D profits and m costs, f^d is the d-th component of the D-dimensional objective vector f, n is the number of items, p_i^d is the d-th profit of item i, w_i^j is the j-th cost of item i, W_j is the j-th capacity of the knapsack, and x_i is a decision variable in $\{0, 1\}$ that controls whether item i is included in the knapsack ($x_i = 1$) or not ($x_i = 0$). The set of feasible solutions is $X \subseteq \{0, 1\}^n$. The bBKP is a special case of the moMKP where $D = m = 2$.

3 ACO Algorithms for the bBKP

When applying ACO to the single-objective multidimensional knapsack problem, the pheromone information is defined as a vector, where each component τ_i gives the desirability of adding item i to the knapsack. Each ant k constructs a solution by adding, at each step, item i to the knapsack with a probability p_i

$$p_i = \begin{cases} \dfrac{\tau_i^\alpha \cdot \eta_i^\beta}{\sum_{j \in N^k} \tau_j^\alpha \cdot \eta_j^\beta} & \forall i \in N^k, \\ 0 & \text{otherwise,} \end{cases} \qquad (1)$$

where η_i is a heuristic estimation of the benefit of adding item i, and N^k is a set of candidate items. After each step, the item added to the current solution and those items that do not fit anymore in the remaining capacity of the knapsack are removed from the candidate set. The solution construction stops when the candidate set is empty. After the constructed solutions are evaluated, the pheromone information is updated in two steps. First, pheromone values are evaporated, that is, decreased by a factor ρ. Second, the pheromone values corresponding to items present in the best solutions are updated by depositing an amount of pheromone $\Delta\tau$, thus increasing the probability that newly constructed solutions contain those items. Alaya et al. [1] proposed four different algorithms that extend the ACO metaheuristic to the bBKP.

mACO$_1$ has one pheromone vector for each objective, that is, τ^1 and τ^2. Ants are divided in three groups $\lambda \in \{0, 0.5, 1\}$ according to the weight λ they use for aggregating the two pheromone vectors when constructing solutions. The solution construction uses *random aggregation*, that is, at each step the pheromone information to be used is chosen as τ^1 with a probability $(1 - \lambda)$, and as τ^2, otherwise. This means that ants using $\lambda = 0$ or $\lambda = 1$ use only τ^1 or τ^2, respectively. The heuristic information is aggregated by means of *weighted sum aggregation*, that is, $\eta = (1 - \lambda) \cdot \eta^1 + \lambda \cdot \eta^2$, where η^1 and η^2 are the heuristic information corresponding to each objective.

The pheromone update method used by mACO$_1$ is a particular case for $\lambda \in \{0, 0.5, 1\}$ of a method called *best-of-objective-per-weight* (BOW) [13]. In BOW, those solutions generated with the same weight λ are kept in the same list. For the lists of $\lambda \notin \{0, 1\}$, the best solution according to each objective updates the pheromone vector of the corresponding objective. For the list of $\lambda = 0$, only the best solution according to the first objective updates τ^1, whereas for the list of $\lambda = 1$, only the best solution according to the second objective updates τ^2.

Finally, mACO$_1$ uses a particular pheromone deposit. Given the best solution constructed in the current iteration and the best-so-far solution according to objective d (s_{ib}^d and s_{bf}^d, respectively), the amount of pheromone deposited is given by $\Delta\tau^d = \frac{1}{1 + f^d(s_{bf}^d) - f^d(s_{ib}^d)}$. We refer to this method as *fobj-mACO*.

mACO$_2$ is identical to mACO$_1$ except for how the multiple pheromone vectors are aggregated. Instead of a random aggregation, mACO$_2$ uses a weighted sum aggregation, that is, $\tau = (1 - \lambda) \cdot \tau^1 + \lambda \cdot \tau^2$.

mACO$_3$ uses only a single pheromone vector. The heuristic information is also a single vector, which is statically computed at the start of the algorithm as $\eta_i = \eta_i^1 + \eta_i^2$. Pheromone information is updated using all nondominated solutions found since the start of the algorithm, that is, the best-so-far archive. Every solution component is rewarded a constant $\Delta\tau = 1$ only once per iteration, regardless of how many times it is present on different solutions.

mACO$_4$ follows mACO$_1$: one pheromone vector per objective, which are aggregated by weighted random aggregation; BOW pheromone update, and pheromone deposit is *fobj-mACO*. However, there is only one weight $\lambda = 0.5$, and one heuristic vector defined as in mACO$_3$.

Algorithm 1. MOACO framework

1: **for** each colony $c \in \{1, \ldots, N^{\text{col}}\}$ **do**
2:    InitializePheromoneInformation()
3:    $\Lambda_c := \text{MultiColonyWeights}()$
4:    InitializeHeuristicInformation()
5: $A^{\text{bf}} := \emptyset$
6: $iter := 0$
7: **while** not termination criteria met **do**
8:    $A^{iter} := \emptyset$
9:    **for** each colony $c \in \{1, \ldots, N^{\text{col}}\}$ **do**
10:       **for** each ant $k \in \{1, \ldots, N^{\text{a}}\}$ **do**
11:          $\lambda := \text{NextWeight}(\Lambda_c, k, iter)$
12:          $\tau := \begin{cases} \text{Aggregation}(\lambda, \{\tau_c^1, \tau_c^2\}) & \text{if multiple } [\tau] \\ \tau_c & \text{if single } [\tau] \end{cases}$
13:          $\eta := \begin{cases} \text{Aggregation}(\lambda, \{\eta^1, \eta^2\}) & \text{if multiple } [\eta] \\ \eta & \text{if single } [\eta] \end{cases}$
14:          $s := \text{ConstructSolution}(\tau, \eta)$
15:          $A^{iter} := \text{RemoveDominated}(A^{iter} \cup \{s\})$
16:    $A^{\text{bf}} := \text{RemoveDominated}(A^{\text{bf}} \cup A^{iter})$
17:    $A^{\text{upd}} := \text{ChooseUpdateSet}(A^{iter}, A^{\text{bf}})$
18:    **for** each colony $c \in \{1, \ldots, N^{\text{col}}\}$ **do**
19:       $A_c^{\text{upd}} := \text{MultiColonyUpdate}(A^{\text{upd}})$
20:       PheromoneUpdate($A_c^{\text{upd}}, N^{\text{upd}}$)
21:    $iter := iter + 1$
22: **Output:** A^{bf}

The mACO algorithms can be instantiated as described above by our MOACO framework [13]. We have confirmed this approach is equivalent to the original [1].

4   A Flexible MOACO Framework for the bBKP

In this paper, we extend the flexible MOACO framework proposed for the bTSP by López-Ibáñez and Stützle [13] to also tackle the bBKP and we automatically instantiate MOACO algorithms. The MOACO framework is able to replicate most MOACO designs proposed in the literature and can generate new MOACO designs by combining components in novel ways. However, its application to the bBKP requires extending it concerning the solution representation and other problem-specific features. Here, we briefly summarize the high-level structure of the framework and its components (see [13] for further details).

The high-level algorithmic scheme of the MOACO framework is given in Algorithm 1. The MOACO framework is a multi-colony algorithm, where each colony c of ants has its own pheromone information and its own set of weights Λ_c for possibly aggregating information. The assignment of weights to colonies is defined by MOACO component MultiColonyWeights. Within each colony, each ant constructs a solution according to pheromone information τ and heuristic information η. Either τ or η may be the result of aggregation. That is, if the pheromone information consists of multiple pheromone vectors, one for each objective, these are aggregated into a single pheromone vector τ by means of MOACO component Aggregation (line 12), using a particular weight λ. If multiple heuristic vectors are used, they are aggregated in a similar way. Which weight is used by each ant may depend on the set of weights of each colony, the particular ant, and the particular iteration. The different possibilities are encapsulated by MOACO component NextWeight (line 11). Once all ants have constructed a solution, the resulting iteration-best archive of nondominated solutions (A^{iter}) is merged into the best-so-far archive (A^{bf}) (line 16). After this step, the pheromone information of each colony is updated in two steps. First, the set of solutions for update (either A^{iter} or A^{bf}), is partitioned among colonies according to component MultiColonyUpdate (line 19). Next, a number of solutions from each set is used to update the pheromone information of each colony in a way defined by component PheromoneUpdate (line 20). The algorithm stops when a termination criterion is met, typically a maximum number of iterations or a time limit, and returns the best-so-far archive.

The flexibility of the MOACO framework is given by the alternative definitions of the algorithmic components that specify the key steps in the algorithm. Defining these components in particular ways allows the framework to replicate most of the MOACO algorithms in the literature. A summary of the available alternatives is given in Table 1. The complete description of all components and their alternatives can be found in the original publication [13]. For brevity, we restrict ourselves here to the new extensions implemented for the bBKP.

Following [13], we use $\mathcal{MAX}$-$\mathcal{MIN}$ Ant System ($\mathcal{MMAS}$) [15] as the underlying ACO algorithm that defines details such as the pheromone deposit $\Delta\tau$, and maximum and minimum pheromone levels ($\tau_{\max}$ and $\tau_{\min}$). Here, we have adapted $\mathcal{MMAS}$ to the bBKP, but making more flexible the definition of $\Delta\tau$, $\tau_{\max}$ and $\tau_{\min}$ to be able to replicate faithfully the original mACO algorithms for the bBKP. The alternatives implemented for the definition of the pheromone deposit ($\Delta\tau$) are:

fobj, that is, $\Delta\tau^d = f^d(s)$, where τ^d is the pheromone information corresponding to objective d. If only one pheromone vector is used instead of multiple, then $\Delta\tau = f^1(s) + f^2(s)$. This method is the one used in the original $\mathcal{MMAS}$.

constant, that is, $\Delta\tau^d = 1 - \frac{r^d(s)-1}{N^{upd}}$, where $r^d(s)$ is the rank of solution s ordered according to objective d and N^{upd} is the number of solutions used to update τ^d. This method is inspired by rank-based ant system [5].

fobj-mACO, this is the method used in mACO$_1$, mACO$_2$ and mACO$_4$.

MACS, that is, $\Delta\tau = f^1(s) \cdot f^2(s)$, which is adapted from MACS [3].

For the definition of the pheromone levels we consider two possibilities. The first is the **default** setting of $\mathcal{MMAS}$, which uses $\tau_{\max} = \frac{\max^{iter}(\Delta\tau)}{\rho}$, where $\max^{iter}(\Delta\tau)$ is the maximum amount of pheromone deposited at iteration $iter$ for a single pheromone component, and $\tau_{\min} = \frac{\tau_{\max}}{\nu \cdot n}$, where $\nu \in \mathbb{R}^+$ is a parameter ($\nu = 2$ in $\mathcal{MMAS}$). The second is the **value** setting, where $\tau_{\max}$ and $\tau_{\min}$

Table 1. Algorithmic components of the MOACO framework

Component	Domain	Description
$[\tau]$	{ single, multiple }	Num. pheromone vectors
$[\eta]$	{ single, multiple }	Num. heuristic vectors
N^{weights}	$\mathbb{N}^+$	Number of weights
Aggregation	weighted sum, weighted product, random	How weights are used to aggregate multiple $[\tau]$ or $[\eta]$
NextWeight	one weight per iteration (1wpi), all weights per iteration (awpi)	How weights are used at each iteration
PheromoneUpdate	nondominated solutions (ND), best-of-objective (BO), best-of-objective-per-weight (BOW)	Which solutions are selected to update the pheromone information
N^{upd}	$\mathbb{N}^+$	Num. solutions that update each $[\tau]$
ChooseUpdateSet	best-so-far (BSF), iteration-best (IB), mixed	Whether the solutions used for update are taken from A^{bf}, A^{iter} or using both alternately
The following components have an effect only when using multiple colonies.		
N^{col}	$\mathbb{N}^+$	Number of colonies
MultiColonyWeights	same ($\cap_{100\%}$), overlapping ($\cap_{50\%}$), disjoint ($\cap_{0\%}$	Whether colonies share all, 50% or no weights.
MultiColonyUpdate	{ origin, region }	How solutions are assigned to colonies
New components added in this work for the bBKP.		
$\tau_{\max}$ method	{ default, value }	Method for calculating $\tau_{\max}$
$\tau_{\min}$ method	{ default, value }	Method for calculating $\tau_{\min}$
$\Delta\tau$	{ constant, fobj-mACO, fobj, MACS }	Method for calculating $\Delta\tau$
η_i	{ $\frac{\text{profit}}{\text{cost}}$, $\frac{\sum \text{profits}}{\text{cost}}$, $\frac{\text{profit}}{\sum \text{costs}}$ }	Heuristic information used

are set to two different constant values $\tau_{\max} > \tau_{\min}$. A **value** setting is used in all mACO algorithms.

In addition, we have implemented three alternatives for the heuristic information. For a given objective d and item i, the heuristic information can be either profit divided by cost ($\eta 1_i^d$), which is the one used in the mACO algorithms [1], sum profits divided by cost ($\eta 2_i^d$), or profit divided by sum costs ($\eta 3_i^d$) [14], that is,

$$\eta 1_i^d = \frac{p_i^d}{w_i^d} \qquad \eta 2_i^d = \frac{\sum_{k=1}^D p_i^k}{w_i^d} \qquad \eta 3_i^d = \frac{p_i^d}{\sum_{l=1}^m w_i^l} \qquad (2)$$

5 Experimental Setup

Our experiments are divided in two stages. In a first stage, we automatically configure the ACO settings of the mACO algorithms and compare the resulting configurations with the original settings. This is done to avoid a bias by possibly poor ACO parameter settings of the mACO algorithms. In the second stage, we compare the best configurations with an algorithm automatically instantiated from the MOACO framework.

As the automatic algorithm configuration tool, we use I/F-Race [2,11]. The input of I/F-Race is a definition of the parameter space, which may contain categorical and numerical parameters, and a set of training instances. I/F-Race was originally designed for single-objective algorithms, but it has been extended to handle the multi-objective case by using the hypervolume quality measure [13] (I_H). The hypervolume is a well-known quality measure in multi-objective optimization [17]. It computes for each approximation set, the volume in the objective space weakly dominated by the approximation set and bounded by a reference point; hence, the larger the hypervolume the better. We use the hypervolume (concretely, the implementation provided by Fonseca et al. [8]) not only in combination with I/F-Race, but also to compare the various MOACO algorithms.

For the application of I/F-Race, we create a training set of 100 randomly generated instances of the bBKP, following the method proposed by Zitzler and Thiele [16]. These instances have random sizes in the range $n \in \{100, \ldots, 750\}$. For comparing the algorithms, we generate a different test set of 50 bBKP instances for each size $n \in \{100, 250, 500, 750\}$. We include in our test set also the four instances by Zitzler and Thiele [16] of sizes $n \in \{100, 250, 500, 750\}$, called ZTZ instances. All algorithms are implemented in C and all experiments are run on a single core of Intel Xeon E5410 CPUs, running at 2.33GHz with 6MB of cache size under Cluster Rocks Linux version 4.2.1/CentOS 4.

The mACO algorithms were originally run with different termination criteria, that is, a different number of iterations, for each variant [1]. To replicate the original mACO experiments, we consider four different computation time limits in our experiments, which correspond to the mean time taken by each of the four mACO variants measured across 25 independent runs on the four ZTZ instances using the corresponding number of iterations (see Table 2). Then, we compute a formula that approximates the computation time obtained for each termination criterion. The four resulting termination criteria are given in Table 2, sorted from the shortest to the longest time.

Table 2. Termination criteria used in our experiments

	$TIME_1$	$TIME_2$	$TIME_3$	$TIME_4$
Time (s)	$0.00001 \cdot n^2$	$0.00003 \cdot n^2$	$0.0001 \cdot n^2$	$0.001 \cdot n^2$
Equivalent to	9000 solutions of mACO$_2$	3000 solutions of mACO$_1$	30000 solutions of mACO$_3$	300000 solutions of mACO$_4$

Comparisons are conducted using empirical attainment functions (EAFs), boxplots of the hypervolume (I^H) and the unary additive epsilon ($I^{\epsilon+}$) indicators [17], and the Friedman non-parametrical test. In the paper, only few representative results are given; for the complete set of results and the test and training instances we generated, we refer to the supplementary material [4].

6   Experimental Analysis

6.1   Improving the ACO Settings of the mACO Algorithms

In the first stage of our analysis, we automatically configure the ACO settings of the four mACO variants. The parameter space given to I/F-Race is shown in Table 3. Parameter a_f is a surrogate parameter of the total number of ants, which is given by $N^a = a_f \cdot (0.12 \cdot n + 36)$. N^a is rounded to the closest smaller number divisible by three, because mACO$_1$ and mACO$_2$ divide the ants into three groups. We apply I/F-Race with a budget of 5 000 independent runs in the tuning phase for each mACO algorithm and for each termination criterion TIME$_i$. Here, the mACO algorithms use their original heuristic information $\eta 1$ [1]. The resulting 16 configurations of mACO are provided as supplementary material [4]. Here, we focus on the configurations obtained when using TIME$_4$, which are shown in Table 4.

We compare all algorithms (original and tuned versions) in terms of the hypervolume. We run all algorithms for all four termination criteria 10 independent times on each of the 200 randomly generated bBKP instances (50 instances per instance size $n \in \{100, 250, 500, 750\}$). We normalize the objective values per instance to the interval $[1, 2]$, with 1 corresponding to the maximum value and 2 to the minimum, and compute the hypervolume using the reference point $(2.1, 2.1)$. To analyze the results, we apply the Friedman test, and its associated post-hoc test for multiple comparisons [6], using the median hypervolume obtained by

Table 3. Parameter space for tuning the ACO settings of the mACO algorithms

Parameter	α	β	ρ	q_0	a_f	$\tau_{\max}$ method	$\tau_{\min}$ method
Domain	$\{0, \ldots, 10\}$	$\{0, \ldots, 15\}$	$[0.01, 1]$	$[0, 0.99]$	$\{1, \ldots, 30\}$	$\{default, value\}$ $value \in [6, 100]$	$\{default, value\}$ $value \in [0.01, 6]$ $\nu \in [1.5, 15]$

Table 4. Settings chosen by *irace* for mACO$_i$-tuned under TIME$_4$

Variant	α $\{0, ..., 10\}$	β $\{0, ..., 15\}$	ρ $[0.01, 1]$	q_0 $[0, 0.99]$	τ_{max} method $\{default, value\}$	τ_{min} method $\{default, value\}$	a_f $\{1, ..., 30\}$
mACO$_1$-tuned	8	1	0.03	0.03	$value = 65$	$value = 0.33$	27
mACO$_2$-tuned	3	1	0.07	0.10	$default$	$default, \nu = 6$	26
mACO$_3$-tuned	3	1	0.08	0.18	$value = 49$	$value = 0.34$	2
mACO$_4$-tuned	2	1	0.19	0.19	$default$	$default, \nu = 8$	5

each algorithm on each instance as values, the instances as the blocking factor and the different mACO algorithms as the treatment factor. In all cases, the Friedman test rejects the null hypothesis of equal performance at a significance level of 0.05. Those algorithms whose ranks differ by more than the critical difference are considered to be significantly different. Table 5 summarizes the results of applying this statistical analysis for each termination criterion. Ranks obtained by each algorithm are shown in parenthesis. The minimum significant rank difference is displayed between parenthesis on the header of each column. The best algorithm and those that are not significantly different from the best are marked in boldface.

From Table 5, we observe that $mACO_2$-tuned is the best performing algorithm for all different $TIME_i$, whereas $mACO_4$ performs the worst. This seems to contradict the results reported by Alaya et al. [1], which considered $mACO_4$ as the best performing variant. The different results are explained because, in their case, $mACO_4$ constructed 100 times more solutions than $mACO_2$, which roughly requires 100 times more computational time (Table 2). By contrast, we compare algorithms using the same computation time limit.

The main conclusion we take from these results is that each tuned mACO algorithm clearly outperforms its corresponding original version for each stopping criterion. Hence, we use these tuned variants for comparing against the automatically generated MOACO algorithm in the next section.

Table 5. Friedman test results for I_H obtained by the mACO algorithms

Rank	I_H **TIME**$_1$ (32.957)	I_H **TIME**$_2$ (31.793)	I_H **TIME**$_3$ (35.433)	I_H **TIME**$_4$ (40.745)
1	**mACO$_2$-tuned (293)**	**mACO$_2$-tuned (208)**	**mACO$_2$-tuned (220)**	**mACO$_2$-tuned (227)**
2	**mACO$_1$-tuned (319)**	mACO$_1$-tuned (402)	mACO$_1$-tuned (380)	mACO$_1$-tuned (373)
3	mACO$_2$ (591)	mACO$_2$ (610)	mACO$_2$ (644)	mACO$_3$-tuned (757)
4	mACO$_4$-tuned (958)	mACO$_3$-tuned (973)	mACO$_1$ (987)	mACO$_2$ (779)
5	mACO$_3$-tuned (1005)	mACO$_1$ (1036)	mACO$_3$-tuned (1040)	mACO$_4$-tuned (1076)
6	mACO$_3$ (1202)	mACO$_4$-tuned (1087)	mACO$_4$-tuned (1073)	mACO$_1$ (1238)
7	mACO$_1$ (1268)	mACO$_3$ (1301)	mACO$_3$ (1287)	mACO$_3$ (1282)
8	mACO$_4$ (1564)	mACO$_4$ (1583)	mACO$_4$ (1569)	mACO$_4$ (1468)

6.2   Automatically Generating MOACO Algorithms for the bBKP

In this second stage of our analysis, we automatically configure all parameters of the MOACO framework. In particular, for the parameters specific to the underlying ACO algorithms, we use the same parameter space as for the mACO algorithms (Table 3). For the multi-objective components, we consider all alternatives described in Table 1, plus the following ranges: $N^{col} \in \{1, 2, 5\}$ and $N^{upd} \in \{1, \ldots, 10\}$. Since N^a, the number of ants, has to be divisible by N^{col}, and the result be divisible by $N^{weights}$ (when $awpi$ is used), N^a was always rounded to the largest smaller number divisible by 10. The weights are defined as, $N^{weights} \in \{0.2, 5, N^a\}$, when $N^{col} = 2$, and $N^{weights} \in \{0.5, 2, N^a\}$, when $N^{col} = 5$. For single colony versions, only two values were allowed: 0.2 and 0.5.

As in the previous section, we apply I/F-Race four times, once for each stopping criterion. The budget of each run of I/F-Race is 5 000 runs of the MOACO framework. The four resulting configurations are given as supplementary material [4]. Here, we focus on the configuration obtained for TIME$_4$ (Table 6).

The analysis of the AutoMOACO configurations shows several commonalities. First, heuristic $\eta 3$ is always chosen, which is different from the one used in the mACO algorithms. Second, the parameter β is always close to the maximum value allowed, thus giving very high importance to the heuristic information. Third, the parameter value of q_0 is also high. This together with the high value of the parameter β implies that most of the items are chosen greedily. Fourth, the number of ants is always very large. For example, 1000 ants are used for instance size 750. As a result, the number of iterations executed by the MOACO algorithm in the given time limits is rather small. It reaches from at most two iterations for the shortest time limits (TIME$_1$ and TIME$_2$) to about 60 to 85 iterations for the larger time limit (TIME$_4$). In the first case, if very few iterations are executed, the algorithm actually behaves as a greedy construction procedure that performs multiple scalarizations of the bi-objective problem. For the longer time limits, we confirmed that excluding the pheromone information (that is, setting $\alpha = 0$) makes the performance become significantly worse (see supplementary material [4]). This implies that for the larger computation time limits, despite the low number of iterations, the ACO component is effective.

Finally, we compare the performance obtained by the automatically configured MOACO algorithms and the mACO algorithms. Given the high impact of using heuristic information $\eta 3$, we repeated the tuning of each of the mACO variants as described above, but this time leaving open also the choice of the heuristic information. In the following comparison, we consider only the original and the two tuned variants of mACO$_2$, which are the best mACO variants for

Table 6. Parameter settings chosen by I/F-Race for AutoMOACO: TIME$_4$

Parameter α	β	ρ	q_0	a_f	$\tau_{\max}$	$\tau_{\min}$	N^{col}	N^{weights}	MCWeights	NextWeight	MCUpdate
Value 1	12	0.12	0.57	8	83	2.49	5	N^{a}	$\cap_{50\%}$	*awpi*	*origin*

Parameter N^{upd}	Selection	Ref.	$\Delta\tau$	$[\tau]$	$[\eta]$	$[\tau]$-Aggreg.	$[\eta]$-Aggreg.	Heuristic
Value 10	BO	BSF	*constant*	*multiple*	*multiple*	*product*	*sum*	$\eta 3$

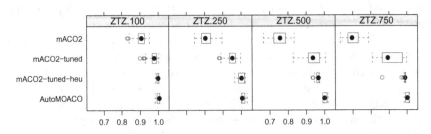

Fig. 1. Boxplots of the I_H indicator for several MOACO algorithms with TIME$_4$

Table 7. Friedman test results for I_H for various MOACO algorithms

Rank	I_H **TIME**$_1$ (14.74)	I_H **TIME**$_2$ (11.416)	I_H **TIME**$_3$ (7.635)	I_H **TIME**$_4$ (5.987)
1	**AutoMOACO (236)**	**AutoMOACO (228)**	**AutoMOACO (212)**	**AutoMOACO (204)**
2	mACO$_2$-tuned-heu (365)	mACO$_2$-tuned-heu (373)	mACO$_2$-tuned-heu (388)	mACO$_2$-tuned-heu (399)
3	mACO$_2$-tuned (611)	mACO$_2$-tuned (599)	mACO$_2$-tuned (600)	mACO$_2$-tuned (597)
4	mACO$_2$ (688)	mACO$_2$ (800)	mACO$_2$ (800)	mACO$_2$ (800)

each of the time limits. In Fig. 1 we show boxplots of the hypervolume distribution for the algorithm automatically instantiated from the MOACO framework (AutoMOACO), the original mACO$_2$, mACO$_2$ tuned with $\eta 1$ and mACO$_2$ tuned leaving open the choice of the heuristic information (mACO$_2$-tuned-heu). The instances shown are the four ZTZ instances. Finally, Table 7 gives the results of the Friedman test, which is applied as described in Section 6.1. Clearly, the AutoMOACO algorithm is the top performer, outperforming significantly the other variants. For complete results, we again refer to the supplementary material [4].

7 Conclusions and Future Work

We have extended the MOACO framework [13] to the bBKP and automatically generated MOACO algorithms. The results reported here for the bBKP confirm the previous conclusions obtained in the bTSP, that is, the automatically configured MOACO algorithms outperform the MOACO algorithms from the literature, even after the ACO parameters of the latter have been tuned with the same effort. Interestingly, the MOACO algorithm tuned for very short time limit is rather a repeated stochastic greedy construction procedure than an ACO algorithm. Although this result may seem counter-intuitive at first, it is, however, a strength of automatic configuration procedures, because they are not biased towards our expectations. The fact that the resulting algorithm is better than the MOACO algorithms proposed in the literature, indicates that the automatic design works as desired, that is, it provides a high-performing algorithm for the given termination criterion. For higher computation time limits, the ACO component of the finally configured algorithm works and contributes to its high performance.

Future work should extend the MOACO framework, and apply the proposed automatic design method, to new problems in order to further confirm the above conclusions. The method is not restricted to MOACO algorithms, and, hence, extensions to other metaheuristics are possible.

Acknowledgments. The research leading to the results presented in this paper has received funding from the European Research Council under the European Union's Seventh Framework Programme (FP7/2007-2013) / ERC grant agreement n° 246939, and from the Meta-X project from the Scientific Research Directorate of the French Community of Belgium. Leonardo C. T. Bezerra, Manuel López-Ibáñez and Thomas Stützle acknowledge support from the Belgian F.R.S.-FNRS, of which they are a FRIA doctoral fellow, a postdoctoral researcher and a research associate, respectively.

References

1. Alaya, I., Solnon, C., Ghédira, K.: Ant colony optimization for multi-objective optimization problems. In: ICTAI 2007, vol. 1, pp. 450–457. IEEE Computer Society Press, Los Alamitos (2007)
2. Balaprakash, P., Birattari, M., Stützle, T.: Improvement Strategies for the F-Race Algorithm: Sampling Design and Iterative Refinement. In: Bartz-Beielstein, T., Blesa Aguilera, M.J., Blum, C., Naujoks, B., Roli, A., Rudolph, G., Sampels, M. (eds.) HCI/ICCV 2007. LNCS, vol. 4771, pp. 108–122. Springer, Heidelberg (2007)
3. Barán, B., Schaerer, M.: A multiobjective ant colony system for vehicle routing problem with time windows. In: Proceedings of the Twenty-first IASTED Intern. Conf. on Appl. Informat., Insbruck, Austria, pp. 97–102 (2003)
4. Bezerra, L.C.T., López-Ibáñez, M., Stützle, T.: Automatic Generation of MOACO Algorithms for the Biobjective Bidimensional Knapsack Problem: Supplementary material (2012), http://iridia.ulb.ac.be/supp/IridiaSupp2012-008/
5. Bullnheimer, B., Hartl, R., Strauss, C.: A new rank-based version of the Ant System: A computational study. Cen. Eur. J. for Oper. Res. and Econ. 7(1), 25–38 (1999)
6. Conover, W.J.: Practical Nonparametric Statistics, 3rd edn. John Wiley & Sons, New York (1999)
7. Doerner, K.F., Hartl, R.F., Reimann, M.: Are Competants more competent for problem solving? The case of a multiple objective transportation problem. Cen. Eur. J. for Oper. Res. and Econ. 11(2), 115–141 (2003)
8. Fonseca, C.M., Paquete, L., López-Ibáñez, M.: An improved dimension-sweep algorithm for the hypervolume indicator. In: CEC 2006, pp. 1157–1163. IEEE Press, Piscataway (2006)
9. García-Martínez, C., Cordón, O., Herrera, F.: A taxonomy and an empirical analysis of multiple objective ant colony optimization algorithms for the bi-criteria TSP. Eur. J. of Oper. Res. 180(1), 116–148 (2007)
10. Iredi, S., Merkle, D., Middendorf, M.: Bi-Criterion Optimization with Multi Colony Ant Algorithms. In: Zitzler, E., Deb, K., Thiele, L., Coello Coello, C.A., Corne, D.W. (eds.) EMO 2001. LNCS, vol. 1993, pp. 359–372. Springer, Heidelberg (2001)
11. López-Ibáñez, M., Dubois-Lacoste, J., Stützle, T., Birattari, M.: The irace package, iterated race for automatic algorithm configuration. Tech. Rep. TR/IRIDIA/2011-004, IRIDIA, Université Libre de Bruxelles, Belgium (2011)
12. López-Ibáñez, M., Stützle, T.: The impact of design choices of multi-objective ant colony optimization algorithms on performance: An experimental study on the biobjective TSP. In: Pelikan, M., Branke, J. (eds.) GECCO 2010, pp. 71–78. ACM press, New York (2010)
13. López-Ibáñez, M., Stützle, T.: The automatic design of multi-objective ant colony optimization algorithms. IEEE Trans. on Evol. Comput. (in press, 2012)
14. Lust, T., Teghem, J.: The multiobjective multidimensional knapsack problem: a survey and a new approach. Arxiv preprint arXiv:1007.4063 (2010)
15. Stützle, T., Hoos, H.H.: $\mathcal{MAX} - \mathcal{MIN}$ Ant System. Future Generat. Comput. Systems 16(8), 889–914 (2000)
16. Zitzler, E., Thiele, L.: Multiobjective evolutionary algorithms: A comparative case study and the strength Pareto evolutionary algorithm. IEEE Trans. on Evol. Comput. 3(4), 257–271 (1999)
17. Zitzler, E., Thiele, L., Laumanns, M., Fonseca, C.M., Grunert da Fonseca, V.: Performance assessment of multiobjective optimizers: an analysis and review. IEEE Trans. on Evol. Comput. 7(2), 117–132 (2003)

Bare Bones Particle Swarms with Jumps

Mohammad Majid al-Rifaie and Tim Blackwell

Goldsmiths, University of London, New Cross, London, UK
{m.majid,tim.blackwell}@gold.ac.uk

Abstract. Bare Bones PSO was proposed by Kennedy as a model of
PSO dynamics. Dependence on velocity is replaced by sampling from
a Gaussian distribution. Although Kennedy's original formulation is not
competitive to standard PSO, the addition of a component-wise jumping
mechanism, and a tuning of the standard deviation, can produce a comparable optimisation algorithm. This algorithm, Bare Bones with Jumps,
exists in a variety of formulations. Two particular models are empirically
examined in this paper and comparisons are made to canonical PSO and
standard Bare Bones.

1 Introduction

There has been many attempts to understand the behaviour of the swarms
in Particle Swarm Optimisation algorithm (PSO). This proved to be difficult
due the presence of many moving parts (e.g. the effects of various parameters on the trajectory of the particle, particles' oscillation around constantly
changing centres, the effects of swarm topology on its performance, etc.). A
number of theoretical studies have tried to understand the dynamics of PSO,
mainly concentrating on particle trajectories, swarm equilibria and formal convergence to local optima proofs [1,2,3]. In 2003, in one such attempt, Kennedy
[4] proposed a minimised version of PSO – Bare Bones (BB) swarm optimisation – where the velocity update is eliminated. In this paper, after briefly
describing BB, the Bare Bones with Jumps (BBJ1) algorithm [5] is presented
alongside a second model, BBJ2. The performance of the newly introduced algorithms are compared against a standard PSO (which is taken here to be the
Clerc and Kennedy (CK) [1] formulation), as well as Bare Bones (BB) swarm
optimisation.

2 Bare Bones Swarm

It is known that particles converge to a weighted average between their personal best and neighbourhood best positions [6], but in order to understand
the behaviour of particles and identify the similarity it has with other stochastic
population-based optimiser, Kennedy [4] proposed a modified algorithm without

M. Dorigo et al. (Eds.): ANTS 2012, LNCS 7461, pp. 49–60, 2012.

the velocity formula in the update equation. The standard Bare Bones swarm (BB) has the following update formula:

$$x_{id} = g + \sigma_{id} N(0,1) \tag{1}$$

$$g = \frac{1}{2}(g_{id} + p_{id}) \tag{2}$$

$$\sigma_{id} = |g_{id} - p_{id}| \tag{3}$$

where $N(0,1)$ is the Gaussian distribution between 0 and 1; g_i is the best informer in the neighbourhood of particle i and p_{id} is the personal best position of particle i in dimension d.

In the next section, two new variants of this minimised algorithm are presented. The main differences are: a component-wise jumping method, and the presence of an implicit scale parameter that multiplies the standard deviation of the sampling distribution.

3   Bare Bones with Jumps

Bare Bones swarm can be generalised [5] so that the search focus g (centre of the search volume at stagnation) and the search spread σ can each be chosen from local or global neighbourhoods. This idea is embodied in the following rules:

$$g_i = BEST(p_i \in N_i) \tag{4}$$

$$\delta_{id} = |p_{i-1\,d} - p_{i+1\,d}| \quad \text{--local\quad neighbouthood} \tag{5}$$

$$\delta_{id} = |g_{id} - p_{id}| \quad \text{--global neighbourhood} \tag{6}$$

$$x_{id} = g_{id} + \alpha\delta_{id} N(0,1) \tag{7}$$

where α is an arbitrary number and N_i denotes the search neighbourhood of particle i. N_i, the μ-neighbourhood can be global, or any local structure. The separation factor δ_i which controls search concentration, can be taken from a local or a global informer neighbourhood (the σ-neighbourhood). Theoretically, it is shown that for the sphere function, there is a critical value, $\alpha_c = 0.65$, such that, for $\alpha > \alpha_c$ the swarm resists collapse. Fastest convergence occurs at the critical value, but larger values promote exploration [5]. The Bare Bones with Jumps algorithm, Algorithm 1, includes a probabilistic jumping mechanism: a particle may jump uniformly in any dimension with probability p_J. This can be viewed as a partial re-initialisation (since in general not every component undergoes a jump) or, alternatively, as a tail broadening mechanism, allowing further search in areas where the Gaussian distribution tails are thin.

The investigations reported in [5] propose that a small jump probability $p_J = 0.01$ enhances performance over standard test set of 30D problems. This paper proposes a second Bare Bones with Jumps algorithm, model 2 (BBJ2), with an altered search spread component, and a smaller jump probability ($p_J = 0.001$):

$$x_{id} = g_i + \alpha\delta_{id} N(0,1) \tag{8}$$

$$\delta_{id} = |g_i - x_{id}| \tag{9}$$

Algorithm 1. Bare Bones with Jumps Models 1 and 2

$r \sim U(0,1)$
if $(\ r < p_J\ )$
    $x_{id} = U\left(-X_d, X_d\right)$
else
    $x_{id} = g_i + \alpha \delta_{id} N(0,1)$

This algorithm utilises the difference between the neighbourhood best with the current position (in $|g_i - x_{id}|$, Equation 9) rather than the difference between either the left and right neighbours' bests (in local neighbourhood; see Equation 5) or the particle's personal best and the neighbourhood best (in global neighbourhood; see Equation 7). The reason behind proposing this alternation is to increase the influence of the current positions of the particles in the update equation on the assumption that this might offer a wider search capability.

In the next section, a set of experiments is designed to compare the performance of the algorithms referred to in this paper followed by some statistical analysis.

4 Experiments

The aim of this set of experiments is to compare the performance of the new BBJ variant, BBJ2, to BBJ1 and Bare Bones swarm (BB) and standard PSO (CK) [1]. The effect of the jumping mechanism is isolated by running experiments on BBJ2 without jumps (BBNJ), which is simply accomplished by setting p_J to zero. In order to determine the quality of each algorithm, three performance measures are used (accuracy, efficiency and reliability which are presented next, in section 4.1).

4.1 Performance Measures

Three different performance measures [7] are used in the experiments conducted in this paper. These performance measures are accuracy, reliability and efficiency.

Accuracy of the swarms is defined by the quality of the best position in terms of its closeness to the optimum position. If knowledge about the optimum position is known *a priori* (which is the case here), the following would define the accuracy:

$$\text{Accuracy} = \left| f\left(p_g^t\right) - f\left(x_{opt}\right) \right| \tag{10}$$

where p_g^t is the best position at time t and x_{opt} is the position of the known optimum solution.

If no information exists about the optimum solution, the fitness of the best position will be the accuracy of the swarm.

Another measure used is reliability which is the percentage of trials where swarms converge with a specified accuracy; this is defined by:

$$\text{Reliability} = \frac{n'}{n} \times 100 \tag{11}$$

where n is the total number of trials in the experiment and n' is the number of successful trials.

Finally, efficiency is the number of iterations or objective function evaluations needed to converge with a specified accuracy (i.e. 10^{-8}):

$$\text{Efficiency} = \frac{1}{n} \sum_{i=0}^{n} FEs \qquad (12)$$

where n is the total number of trials and FEs is the number of function evaluations before convergence.

4.2   Experiment Setup

The algorithms used are tested over a number of benchmarking functions from Jones et al. [8] and De Jong [9] test suite, preserving different dimensionality and modality (see Tables I and II in [10]). The first two functions (Sphere/Parabola and Schwefel 1.2) have a single minimum and are unimodal functions; Generalised Rosenbrock for dimension D, where $D > 3$, is multimodal; Generalised Schwefel 2.6, Generalized Rastrigin, Ackley, Generalized Griewank, Penalised Function P8 and Penalised Function P16 are complex high-dimensional multimodal problems with many local minima and a single global optimum; Six-hump Camel-back, Goldstein-Price, Shekel 5, 7 and 10 are lower-dimensional multimodal problems with fewer local minima. Goldstein-Price, Shekel 5, 7 and 10 have one global optimum and Six-hump Camel-back has two global optima symmetric about the origin. In order not to initialise the particles on or near a region in the search space known to have the global optimum, *region scaling* technique is used [11], which makes sure particles are initialised at a corner of the search space where there are no optimal solutions. The experiments are conducted with a population of 50 particles in global and local neighbourhoods independently. However, the halting criterion for this experiment is either to reach the optima (with function errors less than 10^{-8}) or to exceed the $300,000$ function evaluations (FEs). There are 30 independent runs for each benchmarking function and results are averaged over these independent trials.

4.3   BB, PSO and BBJ Parameter Values

Bare Bones enjoys the luxury of having no adjustable parameters. The parameters defined by Bratton [12] were used for the CK trials. α was set to 0.75 for both BBJ models, and, following the recommendations in [5] p_J was fixed at 0.01 for BBJ1. Preliminary experiments suggested that BBJ2 performs better with a smaller p_J and a value of 0.001 was used in the following. A global μ neighbourhood is used for BBJ in every experiment.

4.4   Results

In this experiment two types of σ-neighbourhoods (global and local) are tested. The results are shown in the following tables and figures:

- Global neighbourhood:
  - Table 1a reflects the accuracy of each algorithm over each function and the reliability of each algorithm averaged over all benchmarks in global neighbourhood. Table 1b highlights any significant difference in the accuracy of the algorithms over each function.
  - Table 2a shows the efficiency of each algorithm over each benchmark. Table 2b underlines any existing significant difference between any two algorithms over the benchmarks in the global neighbourhood.
  - Figure 1 shows the plots for the accuracy and efficiency measures.
- Local neighbourhood:
  - Table 3 displays the results using the same measures (accuracy and reliability) as Tables 1 but in the local neighbourhood topology.
  - Table 4 displays the results using the same measure (efficiency) as Table 2 but in a local neighbourhood topology.
  - Figure 2 shows the plots for the accuracy and efficiency measures.

Observing the reliability of the algorithms both in global and local neighbourhoods (see the last rows of Tables 1a and 3a), shows that on average BB is the least reliable algorithm. This finding does not come as a surprise as BB was proposed for understanding PSO rather than being deployed for optimisation purposes; the result of this experiment confirms this view empirically. Among other algorithms, BBJ2 shows the most reliable performance in both local and global neighbourhood. Additionally, BBJ2 shows better reliability in global vs. local neighbourhood, which is not always the expectation (as global neighbourhood is usually criticised for its premature convergence [13]. CK and BBJ1 show contradicting results in different neighbourhoods: BBJ1 is more reliable than CK in the global neighbourhood, but less reliable in the local neighbourhood.

In terms of the accuracy of the algorithms in the global neighbourhood (see Table 1b), BB shows significantly worse accuracy. When there exists convergence, in most cases, BBJ1 and BBJ2 outperform CK significantly. Over all benchmarks, BBJ1 and BBJ2 do not outperform each other significantly (except in f_{11}). As for the efficiency of the algorithms in the global neighbourhood (see Table 2), when there exists a significant difference BBJ2 outperform all algorithms over all benchmarks significantly. The second best algorithm is BBJ1.

In the local neighbourhood (see Table 3), compared to other algorithms, BB and BBJ1, are significantly worse in terms of accuracy. When functions with convergence are considered, BBJ2 outperform other algorithms. In terms of efficiency in the local neighbourhood (see Table 4b), CK is outperformed by BB in most significant cases. Observing functions with successful convergence, BBJ1 and BBJ2 are the least and the most efficient algorithms respectively.

In order to investigate the role of jumping in BBJ2, this mechanism is removed in a control algorithm – BBJ2 with No Jumps (BBNJ) – which uses the same parameters and update equations as BBJ2 but with $p_J = 0$. This algorithm, in terms of efficiency, outperforms BBJ2 in local neighbourhood in all 3 significant cases; however in global neighbourhood, BBNJ is outperformed by BBJ2 in all 4 significant cases. In terms of accuracy, both in global and local neighbourhood,

Table 1. Accuracy Details; Global Neighbourhood

(a) Accuracy± Standard Error is shown with two decimal places after 30 trials of 300,000 function evaluations. Total number of convergence of each algorithm over the benchmarks can be found in the last row.

Fn	CK	BB	BBJ1	BBJ2	BBNJ
f_1	0.0 ±0.0	0.0 ±0.0	0.0 ±0.0	0.0 ±0.0	4.14E-05±4.13E-05
f_2	0.0 ±0.0	6.34E+03±4.69E+02	8.51E-04±7.86E-04	0.0 ±0.0	2.72E+03±5.03E+02
f_3	9.14E+00±3.18E+00	5.86E+01±1.80E+01	1.08E+01±4.47E+00	1.28E-06±6.09E-07	6.18E+00±2.80E+00
f_4	3.60E+03±8.50E+01	3.46E+03±2.29E+01	8.32E-02±1.43E-02	0.0 ±0.0	4.61E+03±9.40E+01
f_5	6.33E+01±2.57E+00	1.59E+02±4.93E+00	9.93E-03±3.37E-03	0.0 ±0.0	3.47E+02±9.56E+00
f_6	1.17E+00±1.95E-01	1.92E+01±8.43E-02	2.07E-05±1.69E-05	0.0 ±0.0	1.98E+01±1.39E-02
f_7	2.88E-02±6.13E-03	9.40E-02±3.39E-02	4.42E-02±7.18E-03	3.37E-02±6.43E-03	4.64E+00±2.18E+00
f_8	6.22E-02±2.03E-02	4.16E+00±1.36E+00	0.0 ±0.0	0.0 ±0.0	6.44E+00±2.40E+00
f_9	3.00E-02±1.44E-02	4.13E+00±3.23E+00	0.0 ±0.0	0.0 ±0.0	3.66E+01±1.92E+01
f_{10}	0.0 ±0.0	0.0 ±0.0	0.0 ±0.0	0.0 ±0.0	2.72E-02±2.72E-02
f_{11}	0.0 ±0.0	4.86E+01±7.37E+00	1.89E+01±6.36E+00	4.32E+01±7.50	5.67E+01±6.52E+00
f_{12}	1.85E+00±4.97E-01	5.05E+00±0.00E+00	5.05E+00±7.38E-17	5.05E+00±1.13E-16	5.05E+00±9.99E-17
f_{13}	2.39E+00±5.95E-01	5.27E+00±3.01E-17	5.35E+00±7.92E-02	5.27E+00±8.52E-17	5.27E+00±1.35E-16
f_{14}	1.11E+00±4.68E-01	5.36E+00±6.02E-17	5.36E+00±9.03E-17	5.36E+00±9.52E-17	5.47E+00±1.11E-01
Σ	(180)	(99)	(198)	(268)	(93)
	42.68%	23.57%	47.14%	63.81%	22.14%

(b) Based on TukeyHSD Test, if the difference between each pair of algorithms is significant, the pairs are marked. X–o shows that the left algorithm is significantly better than the right one; and o–X shows that the right one is significantly better than the left algorithm.

Fn	BBJ1-BB	BBJ2-BB	CK-BB	BBJ2-BBJ1	CK-BBJ1	CK-BBJ2	BBNJ-BBJ2
f_1	–	–	–	–	–	–	–
f_2	X – o	X – o	X – o	–	–	–	o – X
f_3	X – o	X – o	X – o	–	–	–	o – X
f_4	X – o	X – o	–	–	o – X	o – X	o – X
f_5	X – o	X – o	X – o	–	o – X	o – X	o – X
f_6	X – o	X – o	X – o	–	o – X	o – X	o – X
f_7	–	–	–	–	–	–	o – X
f_8	X – o	X – o	X – o	–	–	–	o – X
f_9	–	–	–	–	–	–	–
f_{10}	–	–	–	–	–	–	–
f_{11}	X – o	–	X – o	o – X	–	X – o	–
f_{12}	–	–	X – o	–	X – o	X – o	–
f_{13}	–	–	X – o	–	X – o	X – o	–
f_{14}	–	–	X – o	–	X – o	X – o	–

Table 2. Efficiency Details; Global Neighbourhood

(a) Mean FEs (±standard error) is shown with two decimal places after 30 trials of 300,000 function evaluations.

Fn	CK	BB	BBJ1	BBJ2	BBNJ
f_1	23224±194	12262±164	13270±148	22685±119	14454±244
f_2	–	160358±2920	89637±575	191064±1290	–
f_3	–	–	–	276020±7039	213310±7324
f_4	–	–	–	63399±3805	–
f_5	–	124701±12900	124701±12900	54825±3182	–
f_6	–	41811±870	37004±318	47486±2226	–
f_7	22786±259	11518±136	13807±335	24006±259	14036±833
f_8	44735±567	20194±1701	15013±285	33627±744	21554±383
f_9	49228±1309	39656±3719	18855±981	31147±720	26835±563
f_{10}	1458±17	516±4	551±5	3515±37	534±8
f_{11}	5876±397	61199±11951	663±10	3929±39	649±10
f_{12}	–	–	–	–	–
f_{13}	–	–	–	–	–
f_{14}	–	–	–	–	–

(b) Based on TukeyHSD Test, if the difference between each pair of algorithms is significant, the pairs are marked. X–o shows that the left algorithm is significantly better than the right one; and o–X shows that the right one is significantly better than the left algorithm.

Fn	BBJ1-BB	BBJ2-BB	CK-BB	BBJ2-BBJ1	CK-BBJ1	CK-BBJ2	BBNJ-BBJ2
f_1	X – o	X – o	–	–	o – X	o – X	o – X
f_2	NP	NP	NP	X – o	o – X	o – X	NP
f_3	NP	NP	NP	NP	NP	NP	o – X
f_4	NP	NP	NP	NP	NP	NP	NP
f_5	NP	NP	NP	X – o	NP	NP	NP
f_6	NP	NP	NP	X – o	o – X	o – X	NP
f_7	X – o	X – o	–	–	o – X	o – X	–
f_8	X – o	X – o	–	–	o – X	o – X	o – X
f_9	–	X – o	–	X – o	–	–	o – X
f_{10}	X – o	X – o	o – X	–	o – X	o – X	–
f_{11}	o – X	–	–	X – o	X – o	–	–
f_{12}	NP	NP	NP	NP	NP	NP	NP
f_{13}	NP	NP	NP	NP	NP	NP	NP
f_{14}	NP	NP	NP	NP	NP	NP	NP

Table 3. Accuracy Details; Local Neighbourhood

(a) Accuracy ± Standard Error is shown with two decimal places after 30 trials of 300,000 function evaluations. Total number of convergence of each algorithm over each benchmark is shown in brackets after the accuracy and standard error. Total number of convergence of each algorithm over the benchmarks can be found in the last row.

Fn	CK	BB	BBJ1	BBJ2	BBNJ
f_1	0.0 ±0.0	0.0 ±0.0	0.0 ±0.0	0.0 ±0.0	9.57E-09±1.14E-10
f_2	7.84E-02±1.09E-02	9.66E+01±8.68E+00	3.93E+02±4.38E+01	1.87E-01±3.02E-02	2.55E-01±2.02E-01
f_3	1.33E+01±3.73E+00	1.27E+01±5.50E-01	2.88E+01±3.20E+00	2.59E+01±5.73E+00	2.99E+01±6.02E+00
f_4	4.14E+03±7.11E+01	3.26E+03±3.10E+01	1.92E+03±6.89E+01	0.0 ±0.0	4.03E+03±4.77E+01
f_5	5.87E+01±1.88E+00	2.46E+01±3.04E+00	9.22E+01±4.47E+00	0.0 ±0.0	2.85E+02±6.11E+00
f_6	0.0 ±0.0	1.96E+01±2.24E-02	1.89E-06±1.55E-06	0.0 ±0.0	1.98E+01±1.27E-02
f_7	1.07E-03±6.10E-04	1.41E-05±1.04E-05	2.48E-04±2.46E-04	1.19E-02±2.96E-03	1.95E-02±4.65E-03
f_8	0.0 ±0.0	2.76E-02±1.92E-02	0.0 ±0.0	0.0 ±0.0	7.01E-01±2.69E-01
f_9	0.0 ±0.0	5.27E-02±5.27E-02	3.62E-07±2.84E-07	0.0 ±0.0	2.05E-01±6.39E-02
f_{10}	0.0 ±0.0	8.16E-02±4.55E-02	0.0 ±0.0	0.0 ±0.0	5.84E-09±5.17E-10
f_{11}	0.0 ±0.0	7.92E+01±2.71E+01	1.27E-05±1.27E-05	2.79E+01±7.03E+00	4.86E+01±7.37E+00
f_{12}	3.70E-06±1.27E-07	5.05E+00±0.00E+00	5.05E+00±0.00E+00	5.05E+00±4.26E-17	5.05E+00±1.13E-16
f_{13}	1.22E-04±0.00E+00	5.27E+00±0.00E+00	5.10E+00±1.76E-01	5.27E+00±0.00E+00	5.27E+00±4.26E-17
f_{14}	1.26E-04±1.12E-16	5.36E+00±5.22E-17	5.18E+00±1.79E-01	5.36E+00±1.09E-16	5.36E+00±6.02E-17
Σ	(208)	(145)	(199)	(241)	(108)
	49.52%	34.52%	47.38%	57.38%	25.71%

(b) Based on TukeyHSD Test, if the difference between each pair of algorithms is significant, the pairs are marked. X–o shows that the left algorithm is significantly better than the right one; and o–X shows that the right one is significantly better than the left algorithm.

Fn	BBJ1-BB	BBJ2-BB	CK-BB	BBJ2-BBJ1	CK-BBJ1	CK-BBJ2	BBNJ-BBJ2
f_1	–	–	–	–	–	–	–
f_2	o – X	X – o	X – o	X – o	X – o	–	–
f_3	o – X	–	–	–	X – o	–	–
f_4	X – o	X – o	o – X	X – o	o – X	o – X	o – X
f_5	o – X	X – o	o – X	X – o	X – o	o – X	o – X
f_6	X – o	X – o	X – o	–	–	–	o – X
f_7	–	o – X	–	o – X	–	X – o	–
f_8	–	–	–	–	–	–	o – X
f_9	–	–	–	–	–	–	o – X
f_{10}	–	–	–	–	–	–	–
f_{11}	X – o	–	X – o	–	–	–	o – X
f_{12}	–	–	X – o	–	X – o	X – o	–
f_{13}	–	–	X – o	–	X – o	X – o	–
f_{14}	–	–	X – o	–	X – o	X – o	–

Table 4. Efficiency Details; Local Neighbourhood

(a) Mean FEs ±Standard Error is shown with two decimal places after 30 trials of 300,000 function evaluations.

Fn	CK	BB	BBJ1	BBJ2	BBNJ
f_1	47589±97	98383±327	67968±213	73090±196	49574±260
f_2	–	–	–	–	–
f_3	–	–	–	–	–
f_4	–	–	–	139118±3975	–
f_5	–	–	–	134816±2801	–
f_6	–	189139±4687	175902±944	118098±389	–
f_7	84612±4962	146979±4494	72048±332	95680±4051	49970±396
f_8	79067±765	121186±1035	69658±489	103658±1287	68597±1434
f_9	61328±374	122631±853	75080±392	86281±480	71144±1217
f_{10}	5389±100	1891±31	2161±161	4935±53	1716±31
f_{11}	46300±2012	9030±2367	2536±75	5063±51	2891±184
f_{12}	–	–	–	8895±0	–
f_{13}	–	–	–	–	–
f_{14}	–	–	–	–	–

(b) Based on TukeyHSD Test, if the difference between each pair of algorithms is significant, the pairs are marked. X–o shows that the left algorithm is significantly better than the right one; and o–X shows that the right one is significantly better than the left algorithm.

Fn	BBJ1-BB	BBJ2-BB	CK-BB	BBJ2-BBJ1	CK-BBJ1	CK-BBJ2	BBNJ-BBJ2
f_1	o – X	o – X	o – X	X – o	X – o	o – X	X – o
f_2	NP	NP	NP	NP	NP	NP	NP
f_3	NP	NP	NP	NP	NP	NP	NP
f_4	NP	NP	NP	NP	NP	NP	NP
f_5	NP	NP	NP	NP	NP	NP	NP
f_6	NP	NP	NP	X – o	X – o	X – o	NP
f_7	o – X	–	–	X – o	X – o	–	X – o
f_8	o – X	X – o	o – X	X – o	X – o	o – X	–
f_9	o – X	o – X	o – X	X – o	X – o	o – X	X – o
f_{10}	X – o	X – o	–	–	o – X	o – X	–
f_{11}	X – o	X – o	X – o	–	–	–	–
f_{12}	NP	NP	NP	NP	NP	NP	NP
f_{13}	NP	NP	NP	NP	NP	NP	NP
f_{14}	NP	NP	NP	NP	NP	NP	NP

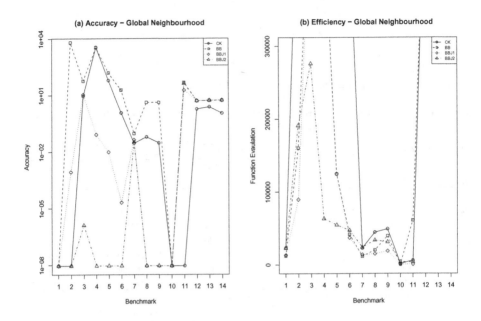

Fig. 1. Accuracy and efficiency in global neighbourhood

whenever there is a difference, BBJ2 outperforms BBNJ in the entire cases, 12 of which are significantly better. Also in terms of reliability, BBNJ is the least reliable algorithm.

4.5 Discussion

More experiments are needed in order to form a concrete theoretical idea as to why BBJ2 outperforms the other algorithms. The initial thought behind this outperformance is the reliance on the difference between the particles' current positions and their neighbourhood best position. This effectively eliminates the direct influence of the particles' personal bests from the update equations. On the other hand, in the rest of the algorithms (used in this paper), each particle's personal best leaves a direct impact on the update equations. This presence of many influencing factors – which is one of the reasons why understanding PSO is complicated – in the update process might be counter-productive.

BB and BBJ, in contrast to CK, are distinguished by the absence of particle position information in the update rule. Search always begins at a point determined by particle informers g or g_i and the extent of the search is determined by informer separation, $|p_i - g_i|$ or $|p_{i-1} - p_{i-1}|$. A trial position $x_i \sim g_i + \sigma_i N(0, 1)$ is ignored if an informer p_i is not bettered. The particle, figuratively speaking, returns to p_i after a single trial at search centre g_i. On the other hand, BBJ2 retains information of an unsuccessful attempt since search spread is determined by the difference between x_i and g_i. This provides a convergence inhibition

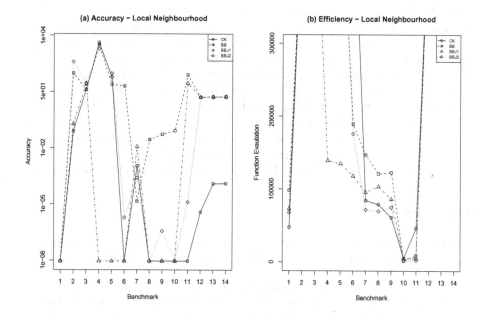

Fig. 2. Accuracy and efficiency in local neighbourhood

mechanism: informers will crowd together as the swarm converges, with a consequent decrease, for BBJ1, in diversity. However in BBJ2, a trial position x_i may lie beyond the informer group. This will lead to a broader search at the next iteration since $\delta^{BBJ2} = |g_i - x_i|$.

Finally, we note the significance of jumping: the probability of jumping in one or more dimensions is $1 - (1 - p_J)^D = 0.03$ (30 dimensions, $p_J = 0.001$). Even this small figure appears to be enough for enhanced performance. A law of diminishing returns applies since excessive jumping slows convergence. The fact that jumping appears to be less necessary in BBJ2 than in BBJ1 is perhaps attributable to the greater search diversity inherent in the formation of δ. The efficacy of tail broadening for distribution based swarm optimisers has already been observed in a study of Lèvy bare bones [14]. We remark that tail broadening is a more subtle effect than re-initialisation. The latter is equivalent to jumping in each of the D dimensions, occurring with only a very small probability ($prob = p_J^D$) in the BBJ models.

5 Conclusion

This paper briefly describes Bare Bones swarm optimisation which was proposed to provide better understanding of the behaviour of particle swarm algorithms. Although this algorithm does not intend to enhance the optimisation capability of standard PSO of Clerc-Kennedy (CK), the other variations (Bare Bones with

Jumps Model 1 & 2) explained and introduced respectively in this paper offer promising results. The algorithms used in this paper are compared against each other using three performance measures (i.e. accuracy, efficiency and reliability). Using these measures, it is shown that in terms of accuracy, when benchmarks with successful convergence are considered, the accuracy of BBJ2 compared to all other algorithms is significantly better. Additionally, BBJ2 is empirically shown to be *both* the most efficient and the most reliable algorithm in both local and global σ neighbourhoods. A brief discussion is also presented with the possible reasons which might boost the outperformance of BBJ2 compared to other algorithms, and an experiment is conducted to demonstrate that despite the very small jump probability of BBJ2, this mechanism plays a crucial role.

References

1. Clerc, M., Kennedy, J.: The particle swarm-explosion, stability, and convergence in amultidimensional complex space. IEEE Transactions on Evolutionary Computation 6(1), 58–73 (2002)
2. Yang, Y., Kamel, M.: Clustering ensemble using swarm intelligence. In: Proceedings of the 2003 IEEE Swarm Intelligence Symposium, SIS 2003, pp. 65–71. IEEE (2003)
3. van den Bergh, F., Engelbrecht, A.P.: A study of particle swarm optimization particle trajectories. Information Sciences 176(8), 937–971 (2006)
4. Kennedy, J.: Bare bones particle swarms. In: Proceedings of Swarm Intelligence Symposium (SIS 2003), pp. 80–87. IEEE (2003)
5. Blackwell, T.: A study of collapse in bare bones particle swarm optimisation. IEEE Transactions on Evolutionary Computing (99) (2012)
6. Trelea, I.C.: The particle swarm optimization algorithm: convergence analysis and parameter selection. Information Processing Letters 85(6), 317–325 (2003)
7. Engelbrecht, A.P.: Fundamentals of Computational Swarm Intelligence. Wiley (2006)
8. Jones, D.R., Perttunen, C.D., Stuckman, B.E.: Lipschitzian optimization without the lipschitz constant. J. Optim. Theory Appl. 79(1), 157–181 (1993)
9. Jong, K.A.D.: An analysis of the behavior of a class of genetic adaptive systems. PhD thesis, University of Michigan, Ann Arbor, MI, USA (1975)
10. al-Rifaie, M.M., Bishop, M., Blackwell, T.: Resource allocation and dispensation impact of stochastic diffusion search on differential evolution algorithm. In: Nature Inspired Cooperative Strategies for Optimisation (NICSO 2011). Springer (2011)
11. Gehlhaar, D., Fogel, D.: Tuning evolutionary programming for conformationally flexible molecular docking. In: Evolutionary Programming V: Proc. of the Fifth Annual Conference on Evolutionary Programming, pp. 419–429 (1996)
12. Bratton, D., Kennedy, J.: Defining a standard for particle swarm optimization. In: Proc. of the Swarm Intelligence Symposium, Honolulu, Hawaii, USA, pp. 120–127. IEEE (2007)
13. Clerc, M.: From theory to practice in particle swarm optimization. In: Handbook of Swarm Intelligence, pp. 3–36 (2010)
14. Richer, T., Blackwell, T.: The lévy particle swarm. In: IEEE Congress on Evolutionary Computation, pp. 3150–3157 (2006)

Hybrid Algorithms for the Minimum-Weight Rooted Arborescence Problem

Sergi Mateo[1], Christian Blum[1], Pascal Fua[2], and Engin Türetgen[2]

[1] ALBCOM Research Group, Universitat Politécnica de Catalunya, Barcelona, Spain
sergi.mateo.bellido@est.fib.upc.edu, cblum@lsi.upc.edu
[2] Computer Vision Lab, Ecole Polytechnique Fédérale de Lausanne, Switzerland
{pascal.fua@,engin.turetken}@epfl.ch

Abstract. Minimum-weight arborescence problems have recently enjoyed an increased attention due to their relation to imporant problems in computer vision. A prominent example is the automated reconstruction of consistent tree structures from noisy images. In this paper, we first propose a heuristic for tackling the minimum-weight rooted arborescence problem. Moreover, we propose an ant colony optimization algorithm. Both approaches are strongly based on dynamic programming, and can therefore be regarded as hybrid techniques. An extensive experimental evaluation shows that both algorithms generally improve over an exisiting heuristic from the literature.

1 Introduction

The minimum-weight rooted arborescence (MWRA) problem, which is considered in this work, is a generalization of the problem proposed by Venkata Rao and Sridharan in [10]. It can technically be described as follows. Given is a directed acyclic graph $G = (V, A)$ with integer weights on the arcs, that is, for each $a \in A$ exists a corresponding weight $w(a) \in \mathbb{Z}$. Moreover, a vertex $v_r \in V$ is designated as the *root node*. Let $\mathcal{A}$ be the set of all arborescences in G that are rooted in v_r. In this context, note that an arborescence is a directed, rooted tree in which all arcs point away from the root vertex (see also [9]). Moreover, note that $\mathcal{A}$ contains all arborescences, not only the ones with maximal size. The objective function value (that is, the weight) $f(T)$ of an arboresence $T \in \mathcal{A}$ is defined as follows:

$$f(T) := \sum_{a \in T} w(a) \ . \tag{1}$$

The goal of the MWRA problem is to find an arboresence $T^* \in \mathcal{A}$ such that the weight of T^* is smaller or equal to all other arborescences in $\mathcal{A}$. In other words, the goal is to minimize objective function $f(\cdot)$. An example of the MWRA problem is shown in Figure 1.

The differences to the problem proposed in [10] are as follows. The authors of [10] require the root v_r to have only one single outgoing arc. Moreover, numbering the vertices from 1 to $|V|$, the given acyclic graph G is restricted to contain

M. Dorigo et al. (Eds.): ANTS 2012, LNCS 7461, pp. 61–72, 2012.
© Springer-Verlag Berlin Heidelberg 2012

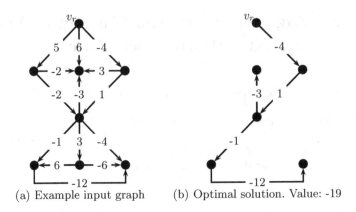

(a) Example input graph   (b) Optimal solution. Value: -19

Fig. 1. (a) shows an input DAG with eight vertices and 14 arcs. The uppermost vertex is the root vertex v_r. (b) shows the optimal solution, that is, the arborescence rooted in v_r which has the minimum weight among all arborescence rooted in v_r that can be found in the input graph.

only arcs $a_{i,j}$ such that $i < j$. These restrictions do not apply to the MWRA problem. Nevertheless, as a generalization of the problem proposed in [10], the MWRA problem is NP-hard. Concerning existing work, the literature only offers the heuristic proposed in [10], which can also be applied to the more general MWRA problem.

The definition of the MWRA problem as outlined above is inspired by a novel method which was recently proposed in [8] for the automated reconstruction of consistent tree structures from noisy images, which is an important problem, for example, in Neuroscience. Tree-like structures, such as dendritic, vascular, or bronchial networks, are pervasive in biological systems. Examples are 2D retinal fundus images and 3D optical micrographs of neurons. The approach proposed in [8] builds a set of candidate arborescences over many different subsets of points likely to belong to the optimal delineation and then chooses the best one according to a global objective function that combines image evidence with geometric priors (see Figure 2 for an example). The solution of the MWRA problem (with additional hard and soft constraints) plays an important role in this process. Therefore, developing better algorithms for the MWRA problem may help in composing better techniques for the problem of the automated reconstruction of consistent tree structures from noisy images.

The contribution of this work is as follows. First, a new heuristic for the MWRA problem is presented which is based on the deterministic construction of an arborescence of maximal size, and the subsequent application of dynamic programming for finding the best solution within this constructed arborescence. The second contribution is to be found in the application of ant colony optimization (ACO) [4] to the MWRA problem. As both the heuristic and the ACO approach are based on a sub-ordinate dynamic programming procedure, both

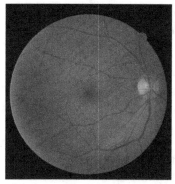
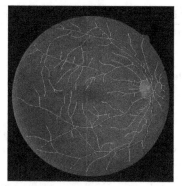

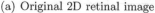

(a) Original 2D retinal image   (b) Reconstruction of the vascular structure

Fig. 2. (a) shows a 2D image of the retina of a human eye. The problem consists in the automatic reconstruction (or delineation) of the vascular structure. (b) shows the reconstruction of the vascular structure as produced by the algorithm proposed in [8].

algorithms can be seen as hybrid (meta-)heuristics [3]. An extensive experimental evalution of both algorithms shows their superiority to the only exisiting heuristic proposed in [10].

The outline of this paper is as follows. Section 2 is dedicated to the new heuristic proposed in this work. Furthermore, in Section 3 our ant colony optimization approach is outlined. Finally, an extensive experimental study is described in Section 4 and conclusions as well as an outlook to future work is given in Section 5.

2   A New Heuristic Approach

In the following we describe a new heuristic approach for solving the MWRA problem. First, starting from root vertex v_r, an arborescence T' of maximal size in G is constructed as outlined in lines 2–9 of Algorithm 1. Second, a dynamic programming (DP) algorithm is applied to T' in order to obtain the minimum-weight arborescence T that is contained in T' and rooted in v_r. The DP algorithm from [1] is used for this purpose. Given an undirected tree $T = (V_T, E_T)$ with vertex and/or edge weights, and any integer number $k \in [0, |V_T| - 1]$, this DP algorithm provides—among all trees with exactly k edges in T—the minimum-weight tree T^*. The first step of the DP algorithm consists in artificially converting the input tree T into a rooted arborescence. Therefore, the DP algorithm can directly be applied to arborescences. Morever, as a side product, the DP algorithm also provides the minimum-weight arborescences for all l with $0 \leq l \leq k$, as well as the minimum-weight arborescences rooted in v_r for all l with $0 \leq l \leq k$. Therefore, given an arborescence of maximal size T', which has $t \leq |V| - 1$ arcs (where V is the vertex set of the input graph G), the DP algorithm is applied with $k = t$. Then, among all the minimum-weight

Algorithm 1. Heuristic DP-HEUR for the MWRA problem

1: **input:** a DAG $G = (V, A)$, and a root node v_r
2: $T' := (V' = \{v_r\}, A' = \emptyset)$
3: $A_{\text{pos}} := \{a = (v_i, v_j) \in A \mid v_i \in V', v_j \notin V'\}$
4: **while** $A_{\text{pos}} \neq \emptyset$ **do**
5:    $a^* = (v_i, v_j) := \text{argmin}\{w(a) \mid a \in A_{\text{pos}}\}$
6:    $A' := A' \cup \{a^*\}$
7:    $V' := V' \cup \{v_j\}$
8:    $A_{\text{pos}} := \{a = (v_i, v_j) \in A \mid v_i \in V', v_j \notin V'\}$
9: **end while**
10: $T := \text{Dynamic\_Programming}(T', k = |V| - 1)$
11: **output:** arborescence T

arborescences rooted in v_r for $l \leq t$, the one with minimum weight is chosen as the output of the DP algorithm. In this way, the DP algorithm is able to generate the minimum-weight arborescence T (rooted in v_r) which can be found in arborescence T'. The heuristic described above is henceforth labelled DP-HEUR.

3   Ant Colony Optimization for the MWRA Problem

The ant colony optimization (ACO) approach for the MWRA problem which is described in the following is a $\mathcal{MAX}$–$\mathcal{MIN}$ Ant System ($MMAS$) [6] implemented in the Hyper-Cube Framework (HCF) [2]. The algorithm, whose pseudo-code can be found in Algorithm 2, works roughly as follows. At each iteration, a number of n_a solutions to the problem is probabilistically constructed based both on pheromone and heuristic information. Each solution construction consists of a first phase in which a rooted arborescence of maximal size T' in input graph G is probabilistically constructed, starting from the root vertex v_r. Moreover, in a second phase, the minimum-weight arborescence T rooted in v_r which exists in T' is obtained by dynamic programming. The second algorithmic component which is executed at each iteration is the pheromone update. Hereby, some of the constructed solutions—that is, the iteration-best solution T^{ib}, the restart-best solution T^{rb}, and the best-so-far solution T^{bs}—are used for a modification of the pheromone values. This is done with the goal of focusing the search over time on high-quality areas of the search space. Just like any other $MMAS$ algorithm, our approach employs restarts consisting of a re-initialization of the pheromone values. Restarts are controlled by the so-called convergence factor (cf) and a Boolean control variable called bs_update. The main functions of our approach are outlined in detail in the following.

Construct_Arborescence_Of_Maximal_Size(G, v_r): This function constructs a solution in the way which is shown in lines 2–9 of Algorithm 1. The only difference is in the choice of the next arc to be added to the current arborescence T' at each step (line 5 of Algorithm 1). Instead of deterministically choosing from A_{pos} the arc which has the smallest weight value, the choice is done probabilistically,

---

Algorithm 2. Ant Colony Optimization for the MWRA Problem

1: **input:** a DAG $G = (V, A)$, and a root node v_r
2: $T^{bs} := (\{v_r\}, \emptyset)$, $T^{rb} := (\{v_r\}, \emptyset)$, $cf := 0$, $bs\_update :=$ **false**
3: $\tau_a := 0.5$ for all $a \in A$
4: **while** termination conditions not met **do**
5:   **for** $i = 1, \cdots, n_a$ **do**
6:     $T' :=$ Construct_Arborescence_Of_Maximal_Size(G, v_r)
7:     $T_i :=$ Dynamic_Programming$(T', k = |V| - 1)$
8:   **end for**
9:   $T^{ib} := \mathrm{argmin}\{f(T_i) \mid T_1, \ldots, T_{n_a}\}$
10: **if** $T^{ib} < T^{rb}$ **then** $T^{rb} := T^{ib}$
11: **if** $T^{ib} < T^{bs}$ **then** $T^{bs} := T^{ib}$
12: ApplyPheromoneUpdate$(cf, bs\_update, T, T^{ib}, T^{rb}, T^{bs})$
13: $cf :=$ ComputeConvergenceFactor(T)
14: **if** $cf > 0.99$ **then**
15:    **if** $bs\_update =$ **true then**
16:      $\tau_a := 0.5$ for all $a \in A$
17:      $T^{rb} := (\{v_r\}, \emptyset)$
18:      $bs\_update :=$ **false**
19:    **else**
20:      $bs\_update :=$ **true**
21:    **end if**
22: **end if**
23: **end while**
24: **output:** T^{bs}, the best solution found by the algorithm

---

based on pheromone and heuristic information. The pheromone model T that is used for this purpose contains a pheromone value τ_a for each arc $a \in A$. The heuristic information $\eta(a)$ of an arc a is computed as follows. First, let

$$w_{\max} := \max\{w(a) \mid a \in A\}. \tag{2}$$

Based on this maximal weight of all arcs in G, the heuristic information is defined as follows:

$$\eta(a) := w_{\max} + 1 - w(a) \tag{3}$$

In this way, the heuristic information of all arcs is a positive number. Moreover, the arc with minimal weight will have the heighest value concerning the heuristic information. Given an arborescence T', and the non-empty set of arcs A_{pos} that may be used for extending T', the probability for choosing arc $a \in A_{\mathrm{pos}}$ is defined as follows:

$$\mathbf{p}(a \mid T') := \frac{\tau_a \cdot \eta(a)}{\sum_{\hat{a} \in A_{\mathrm{pos}}} \tau_{\hat{a}} \cdot \eta(\hat{a})} \tag{4}$$

However, instead of choosing an arc from A_{pos} always in a probabilistic way, the following scheme is applied at each construction step. First, a value $r \in [0, 1]$ is chosen uniformly at random. Second, r is compared to a so-called *determinism*

Table 1. Setting of κ_{ib}, κ_{rb}, κ_{bs}, and ρ depending on the convergence factor cf and the Boolean control variable bs_update

	bs_update = FALSE				bs_update
	$cf < 0.4$	$cf \in [0.4, 0.6)$	$cf \in [0.6, 0.8)$	$cf \geq 0.8$	= TRUE
κ_{ib}	1	2/3	1/3	0	0
κ_{rb}	0	1/3	2/3	1	0
κ_{bs}	0	0	0	0	1
ρ	0.1	0.1	0.1	0.1	0.1

rate $\delta \in [0, 1]$, which is a fixed parameter of the algorithm. If $r \leq \delta$, arc $a^* \in A_{\text{pos}}$ is chosen to be the one with the maximum probability, that is:

$$a^* := \text{argmax}\{\mathbf{p}(a \mid T') \mid a \in A_{\text{pos}}\} \tag{5}$$

Otherwise, that is, when $r > \delta$, arc $a^* \in A_{\text{pos}}$ is chosen probabilistically according to the probability values.

ApplyPheromoneUpdate(cf,bs_update,T,T^{ib},T^{rb},T^{bs}): The pheromone update is performed in the same way as in all $\mathcal{MMAS}$ algorithms implemented in the HCF. The three solutions T^{ib}, T^{rb}, and T^{bs} (as described at the beginning of this section) are used for the pheromone update. The influence of these three solutions on the pheromone update is determined by the current value of the convergence factor cf, which is defined later. Each pheromone value $\tau_a \in T$ is updated as follows:

$$\tau_a := \tau_a + \rho \cdot (\xi_a - \tau_a) \ , \tag{6}$$

where

$$\xi_a := \kappa_{ib} \cdot \Delta(T^{ib}, a) + \kappa_{rb} \cdot \Delta(T^{rb}, a) + \kappa_{bs} \cdot \Delta(T^{bs}, a) \ , \tag{7}$$

where κ_{ib} is the weight of solution T^{ib}, κ_{rb} the one of solution T^{rb}, and κ_{bs} the one of solution T^{bs}. Moreover, $\Delta(T, a)$ evaluates to 1 if and only if arc a is a component of arborescence T. Otherwise, the function evaluates to 0. Note also that the three weights must be chosen such that $\kappa_{ib} + \kappa_{rb} + \kappa_{bs} = 1$. After the application of Equation 6, pheromone values that exceed $\tau_{\text{max}} = 0.99$ are set back to τ_{max}, and pheromone values that have fallen below $\tau_{\text{min}} = 0.01$ are set back to τ_{min}. This prevents the algorithm from reaching a state of complete convergence. Finally, note that the exact values of the weights depends on the convergence factor cf and on the value of the Boolean control variable bs_update. The standard schedule as shown in Table 1 has been adopted for our algorithm.

ComputeConvergenceFactor(T): The convergence factor cf is computed on the basis of the pheromone values:

$$cf := 2 \left(\left(\frac{\sum\limits_{\tau_a \in T} \max\{\tau_{\text{max}} - \tau_a, \tau_a - \tau_{\text{min}}\}}{|T| \cdot (\tau_{\text{max}} - \tau_{\text{min}})} \right) - 0.5 \right)$$

This results in $cf = 0$ when all pheromone values are set to 0.5. On the other side, when all pheromone values have either value τ_{min} or τ_{max}, then $cf = 1$. In all other cases, cf has a value in $(0, 1)$. This completes the description of all components of the proposed algorithm, which is henceforth labelled ACO.

4   Experimental Evaluation

The algorithms proposed in this work—that is, DP-HEUR and ACO—were implemented in ANSI C++ using GCC 4.4 for compiling the software. Moreover, we reimplemented the heuristic proposed in [10]. As mentioned in the introduction, this heuristic—henceforth labelled VENSRI—is the only existing algorithm which can directly be applied to the MWRA problem. All three algorithms were experimentally evaluated on a cluster of PCs equipped with Intel Xeon X3350 processors with 2667 MHz and 8 Gigabyte of memory. In the following, we first describe the set of benchmark instances that have been used to test the three algorithms. Afterwards, the experimental results are described in detail.

4.1   Benchmark Instances

Due to the lack of a publicly availabe set of benchmark instances, a benchmark set was generated. The construction of each DAG $G(V, A)$ from this benchmark set was based on a pre-defined number of vertices (n) and a pre-defined number of arcs (m). First, a random arborescence T with n vertices was generated. The root node of T is called v_r. Each one of the remaining $m-n+1$ arcs was generated by randomly choosing two vertices v_i and v_j, and adding the corresponding arc $a = (v_i, v_j)$ to T. In this context, $a = (v_i, v_j)$ may be added to T, if and only if by its addition no directed cycle is produced, and neither (v_i, v_j) nor (v_j, v_i) form already part of the graph. In order to generate a diverse set of benchmark instances we considered $n \in \{20, 50, 100, 500, 1000, 5000\}$ and $m \in \{2n, 4n, 6n\}$. A total of 10 problem instances was generated for each combination of n and m. This resulted in a total of 180 problem instances. The arc weights for all instances were chosen uniformly at random from $[-100, 100]$.

4.2   Results

The three algorithms considered for the comparison were applied exactly once to each of the 180 problem instances of the benchmark set. Although ACO is a stochastic search algorithm, this is a valid choice, because results are averaged over groups of instances that were generated with the same parameters. ACO was applied with $n_a = 10$—that is, 10 solution constructions per iteration—, with a determinism rate of $\delta = 0.9$, and with a stopping criterion of 10.000 solution evaluations per run. Table 2 presents the results of each algorithm averaged over the 10 instances for each combination of n and m (as indicated in the first two table columns). Four table columns are used for presenting the results of each algorithm. The column with heading **value** provides the average of the objective

Table 2. Experimental results. ACO is compared to the heuristic proposed in this work (DP-HEUR), and the algorithm from [10] (VENSRI).

n	m	DP-HEUR				VENSRI				ACO				
		value	std	size	time (s)	value	std	size	time (s)	value	std	size	evals	time (s)
20	2n	-524.50	(134.16)	12.60	< 0.01	-569.10	(156.69)	14.90	< 0.01	-605.20	(162.61)	14.30	394.80	1.10
	4n	-831.60	(230.68)	15.90	< 0.01	-806.30	(108.14)	17.40	< 0.01	-996.60	(153.12)	17.30	5243.80	1.13
	6n	-1031.10	(197.50)	17.70	< 0.01	-947.10	(151.05)	17.80	< 0.01	-1196.50	(151.63)	17.90	2666.20	1.26
50	2n	-1246.30	(273.88)	33.60	< 0.01	-1476.70	(295.11)	38.50	< 0.01	-1571.00	(288.52)	38.90	4635.00	4.41
	4n	-1912.30	(432.79)	39.70	< 0.01	-1812.30	(208.43)	43.80	< 0.01	-2404.60	(312.18)	43.40	7093.40	4.86
	6n	-2372.70	(368.03)	43.60	< 0.01	-2166.10	(307.75)	45.70	< 0.01	-2884.90	(251.08)	44.70	7474.40	5.00
100	2n	-2523.10	(442.91)	67.10	< 0.01	-2828.70	(409.73)	76.20	0.01	-3130.40	(445.62)	75.00	5714.70	19.21
	4n	-3903.00	(659.69)	82.30	< 0.01	-3871.70	(305.29)	89.90	0.02	-4955.90	(321.75)	88.90	8204.40	17.68
	6n	-4819.40	(582.18)	87.30	< 0.01	-4059.70	(374.22)	93.10	0.02	-5782.70	(391.22)	90.60	7642.70	18.14
500	2n	-12404.50	(1308.74)	348.90	0.06	-14085.50	(608.59)	398.70	2.12	-15489.00	(637.26)	378.00	8536.60	460.25
	4n	-18321.80	(2222.19)	402.00	0.06	-17256.00	(703.46)	449.20	2.28	-22644.80	(1537.49)	437.90	8902.20	675.37
	6n	-22386.60	(2202.23)	434.90	0.06	-18896.40	(739.65)	471.60	2.38	-27279.50	(446.92)	458.10	8620.70	688.30
1000	2n	-24493.80	(1577.30)	671.60	0.23	-26995.80	(995.40)	770.10	17.40	-29915.40	(1268.64)	742.90	9451.90	3016.34
	4n	-37715.40	(3030.59)	811.80	0.23	-34317.50	(1461.89)	905.10	18.69	-45489.80	(1463.91)	876.80	8332.50	4948.00
	6n	-45280.10	(2376.76)	875.00	0.27	-36790.50	(846.78)	941.40	19.41	-54352.10	(1001.77)	920.00	7409.30	4726.81
5000	2n	-119122.90	(4980.74)	3371.60	5.23	-135333.80	(2296.56)	3921.10	2440.70	-146081.80	(2377.79)	3758.50	8532.80	174329.90
	4n	-177605.60	(7388.53)	4045.10	6.42	-163385.60	(2153.92)	4550.00	2585.65	-216564.20	(4425.38)	4372.50	8592.40	321099.20
	6n	-217112.00	(12667.37)	4325.60	7.29	-171483.70	(2839.81)	4707.20	2679.99	-258965.20	(3947.91)	4566.70	8176.80	354718.90

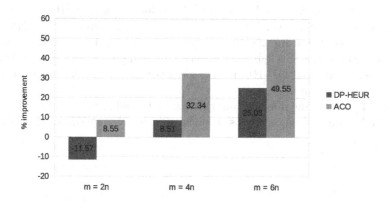

Fig. 3. Average improvement (in %) of ACO and DP-HEUR over VENSRI. Positive values correspond to an improvement, while negative values indicate that the respective algorithm is inferior to VENSRI. The improvement is shown for the three different arc-densities that are considered in the benchmark set, that is, $m = 2n$, $m = 4n$, and $m = 6n$.

function values of the best solutions found by the respective algorithm for the 10 instances of each combination of n and m. The second column (with heading **std**) contains the corresponding standard deviation. The third column (with heading **size**) indicates the average size (in terms of the number or arcs) of the best solutions found by the respective algorithm.[1] Finally, the fourth column (with heading **time (s)**) contains the average compution time (in seconds). For all three algorithms, the computation time indicates the time of the algorithm termination. In the case of ACO, an additional table column (with heading **evals**) indicates at which solution evaluation, on average, the best solution of a run was found. Finally, for each combination of n and m, the result of the best-performing algorithm is indicated in bold font.

The results allow to make the following observations. First, ACO is for all combinations of n and m the best-performing algorithm. Averaged over all problem instances ACO obtains an improvement of 31.9% over VENSRI. Figure 3 shows the average improvement of ACO over VENSRI for three groups of input instances concerning the different arc-densities. It is interesting to observe that the advantage of ACO over VENSRI seems to grow when the arc-density increases. On the downside, these improvements are obtained at the cost of a significantly increased computation time. Concerning heuristic DP-HEUR, we can observe that it improves in all 12 combinations of n and m where $m \in \{4n, 6n\}$ over VENSRI. Interestingly, however, DP-HEUR is inferior to VENSRI for all combinations with $m = 2n$. In other words, DP-HEUR seems to be inferior to VENSRI when rather sparse input graphs are concerned, whereas the opposite is the case for more

---

[1] Remember that solutions—that is, arborescences—may have any number of arcs between 0 and $|V| - 1$, where $|V|$ is the number of the input DAG $G = (V, A)$.

dense input graphs. Averaged over all problem instances, DP-HEUR obtains an improvement of 8.87% over VENSRI. The average improvement of DP-HEUR over VENSRI is shown for the three groups of input instances concerning the different arc-densities in Figure 3. Concerning a comparison of the computation times, we can state that DP-HEUR has a clear advantage over VENSRI especially for large-size problem instances.

Figure 4 presents the information which is contained in the columns of Table 2 that have headings **size** and **evals**. Concerning the average size of the solutions

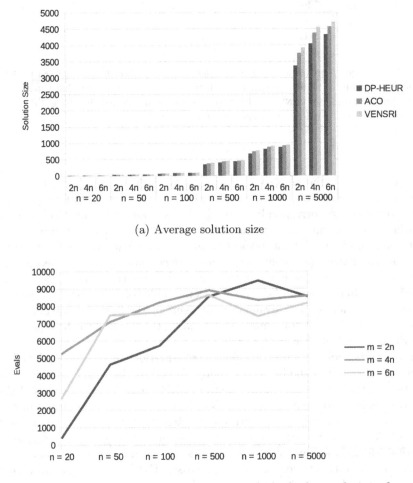

(a) Average solution size

(b) Average number of solution evaluations at which the best solution of an ACO run is found

Fig. 4. (a) shows, for each combination of n and m, information about the average size—in terms of the number of arcs—of the solutions produced by DP-HEUR, ACO, and VENSRI. (b) shows for each combination of n and m the average number of solution evaluations at which the best solution of a run of ACO is found.

produced by the three algorithms (as shown in Figure 4(a)) it is interesting to observe that the solutions produced by DP-HEUR consistently seem to be the smallest ones, while the solutions produced by VENSRI seem generally to be the largest ones. The size of the solutions produced by ACO is generally inbetween these two extremes. We currently have no explanation for this aspect, which certainly deserves further examination.

Finally, Figure 4(b) presents the average number of solution evaluations at which the best solution of a run of ACO is found. Not surprisingly, when large graphs are concerned, significantly more solution evaluations are necessary for reaching the best solutions than when rather small graphs are tackled. Concerning a comparison between the groups of graphs characterized by different arc-densities, it can be observed that when rather small graphs are concerned ACO seems to faster in obtaining good solutions for sparse graphs. However, when the size of the input graph grows, this difference disappears.

5   Conclusions and Future Work

In this work we have proposed a heuristic and an ant colony optimization approach for the minimum-weight rooted arboresence problem. Both algorithms make use of dynamic programming as sub-ordinate procedure. Therefore, they may be regarded as hybrid algorithms. The experimental results show that both approaches improve (on average) over an existing heuristic from the literature. Interestingly, the advantage of the proposed algorithm over the existing heuristic grows with increasing arc-density of the input graph.

Concerning future work, we plan to apply both approaches to other types of problem instances. For example, we plan to generate problem instances in which the number of arcs with negative weights is significantly higher than the number of arcs with positive weights, or vice versa. Moreover, we plan to implement an integer programming model for the tackled problem—in the line of the model proposed in [5] for a related problem—and to solve the model with an efficient integer programming solver. In [7] we already proposed an extension of this model for the problem of reconstructing tree structures.

Acknowledgments. This work was supported by grant TIN2007-66523 (FORMALISM) of the Spanish government.

References

1. Blum, C.: Revisiting dynamic programming for finding optimal subtrees in trees. European Journal of Operational Research 177(1), 102–114 (2007)
2. Blum, C., Dorigo, M.: The hyper-cube framework for ant colony optimization. IEEE Transactions on Systems, Man and Cybernetics – Part B 34(2), 1161–1172 (2004)
3. Blum, C., Puchinger, J., Raidl, G., Roli, A.: Hybrid metaheuristics in combinatorial optimization: A survey. Applied Soft Computing 11(6), 4135–4151 (2011)

4. Dorigo, M., Stützle, T.: Ant Colony Optimization. MIT Press, Cambridge (2004)
5. Duhamel, C., Gouveia, L., Moura, P., Souza, M.: Models and heuristics for a minimum arborescence problem. Networks 51(1), 34–47 (2008)
6. Stützle, T., Hoos, H.H.: $\mathcal{MAX} - \mathcal{MIN}$ Ant System. Future Generation Computer Systems 16(8), 889–914 (2000)
7. Türetken, E., Benmansour, F., Fua, P.: Automated reconstruction of tree structures using path classifiers and mixed integer programming. In: Proceedings of CVPR 2012 – 25th IEEE Conference on Computer Vision and Pattern Recognition. IEEE Press (in press, 2012)
8. Türetken, E., González, G., Blum, C., Fua, P.: Automated reconstruction of dendritic and axonal trees by global optimization with geometric priors. Neuroinformatics 9(2-3), 279–302 (2011)
9. Tutte, W.T.: Graph Theory. Cambridge University Press, Cambridge (2001)
10. Venkata Rao, V., Sridharan, R.: Minimum-weight rooted not-necessarily-spanning arborescence problem. Networks 39(2), 77–87 (2002)

Improving the cAnt-Miner$_{\text{PB}}$ Classification Algorithm

Matthew Medland, Fernando E.B. Otero, and Alex A. Freitas

School of Computing, University of Kent, Canterbury, UK
{mm443,f.e.b.otero,a.a.freitas}@kent.ac.uk

Abstract. Ant Colony Optimisation (ACO) has been successfully applied to the classification task of data mining in the form of Ant-Miner. A new extension of Ant-Miner, called cAnt-Miner$_{\text{PB}}$, uses the ACO procedure in a different fashion. The main difference is that the search in cAnt-Miner$_{\text{PB}}$ is optimised to find the best list of rules, whereas in Ant-Miner the search is optimised to find the best individual rule at each step of the sequential covering, producing a list of best rules. We aim to improve cAnt-Miner$_{\text{PB}}$ in two ways, firstly by dynamically finding the rule quality function which is used while the rules are being pruned, and secondly improving the rule-list quality function which is used to guide the search. We have found that changing the rule quality function has little effect on the overall performance, but that by improving the rule-list quality function we can positively affect the discovered lists of rules.

1 Introduction

Data mining is the automatic search for useful, usable, and preferably interesting patterns in data [3,13]. These patterns are used by anyone with an interest in what their data holds—e.g., businessmen or scientists. There are multiple data mining tasks, of which classification is the most studied.

The classification task seeks to create a model that places objects (examples) into groups. A class value (group name) is then assigned by analysing common traits (attributes' values) between objects of that class. Classification problems can therefore be viewed as optimisation problems, where the intended outcome is to find the best model that represents the predictive relationships in the data. There are many different ways to represent these models, such as 'black-box' models produced by support vector machines (SVM) and artificial neural networks, which are difficult to interpret, and 'white-box' decision tree and classification rule models, which are more readily interpreted [11]. 'White-box' methods have the advantage of being easier to comprehend, and so they are used to provide further understanding of the data. This enhanced understanding leads to a greater degree of trust in the models produced and enables decision makers to make the best possible decisions.

Ant Colony Optimization (ACO) algorithms have successfully been applied to the classification task in the form of Ant-Miner [2,10]. Ant-Miner seeks to extract a list of classification rules of the form *IF antecedent THEN consequent*

M. Dorigo et al. (Eds.): ANTS 2012, LNCS 7461, pp. 73–84, 2012.

from a data set, where the antecedent is composed by predictor attribute-value conditions, and the consequent corresponds to the class value to be predicted.

Several extensions of Ant-Miner have been proposed in the literature and have been reviewed in [8]. The majority of these extensions maintain the overall structure of the algorithm—i.e., the algorithm employs an ACO-based procedure to create individual rules which are joined to create a complete classification model (list of rules). This strategy to produce a list of classification rules is known as sequential covering (or separate-and-conquer), where each rule is discovered individually. An improved strategy has recently been proposed in the cAnt-Miner$_{PB}$ algorithm [9], where an ACO-based procedure is used not to construct individual rules, but a full list of rules. One of the main differences between the cAnt-Miner$_{PB}$ and Ant-Miner algorithms is that in cAnt-Miner$_{PB}$ the search is performed and optimised to find the best list of rules, whereas in Ant-Miner (and its extensions) the search is performed and optimised to find the best individual rule at each step of the sequential covering, resulting in the list of best rules. In other words, in cAnt-Miner$_{PB}$ the search is governed by the quality of a candidate list of rules, while in Ant-Miner the search is guided by the quality of an individual rule.

One of the main components of Ant-Miner is the rule quality function used to guide the search. The use of different rule quality functions in sequential covering algorithms has been studied in [5,7] and in Ant-Miner algorithm in [12]. Improving the rule quality function of sequential covering algorithms tends to improve the overall performance of the algorithm. Although the search in cAnt-Miner$_{PB}$ is guided by the quality of a list of rules, the algorithm uses a rule quality function to prune (i.e., remove irrelevant terms) from a candidate rule. Therefore, there are two quality functions involved in the search for the best list of rules in cAnt-Miner$_{PB}$: the rule quality function used during pruning and the rule-list quality function used to guide the search (i.e., update pheromones).

In this paper we propose to improve the search of the cAnt-Miner$_{PB}$ algorithm by (1) allowing the algorithm to dynamically choose a rule quality evaluation function for a candidate rule and (2) using a new rule-list quality function to guide the search. The extension (1) is possible since the rule quality function has a smaller role in cAnt-Miner$_{PB}$—it is only used during pruning—and it is not used as a criterion to compare different rules. A dynamic rule quality function selection would not be possible in Ant-Miner, as the rule quality function needs to be consistent throughout to ensure that the algorithm is comparing like-to-like. The extension (2) aims at preventing overfitting—the case where the list of rules is too tailored to the training set and has poor generalisation performance. We evaluate the effect of these extensions using 14 data sets from the UCI Machine Learning repository [4] in terms of both predictive accuracy and size of the discovered classification model.

The remainder of this paper is organised as follows. In Section 2 we discuss the differences in the search strategy of Ant-Miner and cAnt-Miner$_{PB}$ algorithms. In Section 3 we discuss our proposed improvements to cAnt-Miner$_{PB}$. Then we present and discuss our results in Section 4. Section 5 then concludes this paper.

2   Background

Separate-and-conquer, also known as sequential covering, classification algorithms are data mining algorithms that employ two steps to create a classification model. First, the algorithm classifies part of the dataset (conquer) and then removes the classified data from the dataset (separate). This process is repeated until the number of unclassified examples falls below a set threshold. At each stage, the data which is classified depends on the classification rule chosen, and which classification rule is chosen depends on the quality of possible rules. To calculate this, a rule quality function is used and it is this function which determines the success of most sequential covering algorithms. There are multiple aspects of a rule which can affect its quality. For example, a rule may never misclassify an example (high consistency) but only cover a small subset of examples (low coverage). Deciding which rule quality function to use always has the problem of finding an effective trade-off between consistency and coverage.

The Ant-Miner algorithm follows a sequential covering strategy using an ACO procedure to create individual rules. First, a construction graph is created where each node is a value for a given attribute, with every attribute-value pair from the data set represented. Each ant then moves from a start node (with an empty rule) and stochastically chooses a vertex with a probability based upon the pheromone value and a heuristic value. The visited vertex is a rule term as a [attribute, value] pair. The ant will continue to add new terms until either all attributes have been used or adding another would decrease the number of covered examples below a predefined threshold. After a rule has been created, a pruning algorithm removes irrelevant terms from the newly created rule. Once every ant in the colony has traversed the graph, the best rule based on a quality function is selected and the pheromone levels are adjusted. The pheromone on the terms included in the best rule increase and the pheromone on the others (unused terms) decrease. After a rule has been created by the ACO procedure, all of the examples which it covers are removed from the data set and the next rule is created. The algorithm finishes once the training set has less than a predefined number of training examples remaining and the list of best rules is returned as the discovered classification model. Most of the proposed extensions of Ant-Miner follow this same strategy to create a list of rules [8].

cAnt-Miner$_{\text{PB}}$ is an ACO classification algorithm that employs a different search strategy than Ant-Miner. Rather than searching for the list of best rules as Ant-Miner does, cAnt-Miner$_{\text{PB}}$ instead searches for the best list of rules. This change may sound minor, but it has a dramatic effect on the algorithm. In Ant-Miner each ant creates an individual rule, whereas in cAnt-Miner$_{\text{PB}}$ each ant creates an entire list of rules. Once the best candidate list of rules has been created, the pheromones are updated which affects the lists that will be created in the future iterations. The best list of rules chosen throughout the execution of the algorithm is returned as the discovered classification model.

The high-level pseudocode of cAnt-Miner$_{\text{PB}}$ is presented in Figure 1. At each iteration, an ant in the colony starts with an empty list and the full training set. An ant then creates a rule, prunes the rule using the rule quality function,

Input: training examples
Output: best discovered list of rules
1. $InitialisePheromones()$;
2. $list_{gb} \leftarrow \{\}$;
3. $m \leftarrow 0$;
4. **while** m < maximum iterations **and** not stagnation **do**
5. $list_{ib} \leftarrow \{\}$;
6.   **for** n $\leftarrow$ 1 **to** colony_size **do**
7. $examples \leftarrow$ *all training examples*;
8. $list_n \leftarrow \{\}$;
9.   **while** $|examples|$ > maximum uncovered **do**
10. $ComputeHeuristicInformation(examples)$;
11. $rule \leftarrow CreateRule(examples)$;
12. $Prune(rule)$;
13. $examples \leftarrow examples - Covered(rule, examples)$;
14. $list_n \leftarrow list_n + rule$;
15.   **end while**
16.   **if** $Quality(list_n) > Quality(list_{ib})$ **then**
17. $list_{ib} \leftarrow list_n$;
18.   **end if**
19.   **end for**
20. $UpdatePheromones(list_{ib})$;
21.   **if** $Quality(list_{ib}) > Quality(list_{gb})$ **then**
22. $list_{gb} \leftarrow list_{ib}$;
23.   **end if**
24. $m \leftarrow m + 1$;
25. **end while**
26. **return** $list_{gb}$;

Fig. 1. High-level pseudocode of the cAnt-Miner_PB algorithm [9]

and removes all of the covered examples from the training set. The ant then repeats these steps until the number of remaining examples lies below a predefined threshold. It is important to note that at no point are rules compared to each other, and that the only time the rule quality function is used is during the pruning stage. The list of rules created by the ant is then compared to the current best list of rules and if it is better than the current best, it replaces it as the current best. Once all ants in the colony have finished creating candidate list of rules, the pheromones are updated. This entire process repeats until either the maximum number of iterations has been reached or until the algorithm converges.

There is a clear difference in the search strategy between Ant-Miner (and its extensions) and cAnt-Miner_PB algorithms. The search in Ant-Miner is guided by the quality of the individual rules, as in (traditional) sequential covering algorithms. The best rule found is always used, regardless of how it affects the list of rules. The search in cAnt-Miner_PB algorithm, however, is not concerned by the quality of the individual rules as long as the quality of the complete list of rules is improving, since the entire list is created at once and the best list is chosen to guide the search. Therefore, the rule quality function has a smaller role—only used to decide whether or not to prune a rule—and the rule-list quality function guides the search.

3   Proposed Improvements to cAnt-Miner_PB

This paper presents two extensions of the cAnt-Miner_PB algorithm in order to improve the search for the best list of rules. The first extension consists of allowing the algorithm to dynamically choose the rule quality function to be used during the pruning procedure (per rule fashion), where different rules can be pruned using different rule quality functions. As has been previously studied [5,7,12], rule quality functions have different bias and capture different aspects of the rule (e.g., some might favour consistency over coverage). The second extension consists of using a pessimistic error rate rule-list quality function to evaluate a candidate list of rules and, consequently, to guide the search.

3.1   Dynamically Choosing Rule Evaluation Functions

In cAnt-Miner_PB, ants find routes through a fully connected graph of all possible rule terms (attribute-value pairs) in order to construct rules. Our initial approach to dynamically choose the rule quality function was based around adding extra vertices to the construction graph containing the candidate rule terms to represent the available rule quality functions, resulting in one large graph. This simple approach had the benefits that it was an easy concept to grasp and it fits very nicely into cAnt-Miner_PB with very few modifications to the existing algorithm. However, we have found that using this approach, the same rules can be created by the pruning procedure but with different rule quality functions. This affected the convergence of the algorithm, since the choices of the rule quality functions were not unique and, consequently, there was no selective pressure towards a particular rule quality function. This meant that the algorithm would rarely converge.

These results led us to realise that the convergence tests had to purely rely upon the terms selected to create the rules. To enable this behaviour, we used two separate construction graphs: one purely consisting of different rule quality functions, and the other consisting of rule terms. When creating a rule, an ant will first visit the rule quality functions graph to select an evaluation function, and then visit the rule terms graph to create the rule.

This process can be implemented adding only a few lines to the algorithm presented in Figure 1. The first addition would be the creation of a rule quality functions graph and initialise its pheromones (line 1). Next, each ant would choose the rule quality function before creating a rule (line 11), and then store the rule quality for later use in the pruning stage (line 12). The selection of the rule quality function is only based on pheromone levels, no heuristic information is used. Once the iteration-best list of rules has been determined, the two pheromone matrices would be updated (line 20) to reflect the chosen rule quality functions as well as the list of rule terms used in the list of rules.

Though the rule quality functions and rule terms graphs are independent, the pheromones in cAnt-Miner_PB are retained in sequence. In other words, the first rule being chosen in a list has a list of pheromones which is saved and updated across iterations, as does the second and so forth. This means that the first rule

```
IF petal-width <= 0.8 THEN Iris-setosa USING F-measure function
IF petal-width > 1.75 THEN Iris-virginica USING Error-based function
IF sepal-length <= 6.15 THEN Iris-versicolor USING M-Estimate function
IF <empty> THEN Iris-virginica
```

Fig. 2. An example of a list of rules with associated rule quality functions. The default rule (with an empty antecedent) does not have a function associated.

is now converging to the list of terms, which was affected by the choice of the rule quality function, both of which may be vastly different to the terms and quality function used by the second rule. Convergence is only determined by analysing the rule terms graph, since different rule quality functions can lead to the same rule and the choice of the rule quality function does not affect the quality of the list of rules (as long as they produce the same rules). Figure 2 presents an example of a list of rules with associated rule quality functions.

In order for our dynamic rule quality function selection process to be of any use we needed a wide selection of different rule quality functions. We have selected previously used rule quality functions described in [7,12], as well as the original rule quality function used in cAnt-Miner$_{PB}$ (Sensitivity × Specificity) and a rule quality function based on C4.5's error-based measure [11, p. 41]. The chosen functions can be found in Table 1. For the parametric quality functions, we have used their default parameter values [7] (shown in the 'Parameter' column in Table 1). In the function definitions we make use of a series of shorthands to condense the formulae. These are defined as below:

TP The number of examples covered by the rule that belong to the class predicted by the rule (true positives).
FP The number of examples covered by the rule that do not belong to the class predicted by the rule (false positives).
TN The number of examples not covered by the rule that do not belong to the class predicted by the rule (true negatives).
FN The number of examples not covered by the rule that belong to the class predicted by the rule (false negatives).
S The total number of training examples (TP + FP + TN + FN).

3.2 Error-Based Rule-List Function

After a candidate list of rules is created in cAnt-Miner$_{PB}$, its quality is measured in terms of predictive accuracy in the training set. It is expected that a list of rules that perform well in the training set will also perform well in the test set (the set of unseen examples). However, the use of the predicted accuracy can lead to overfitting—the case where the list of rules created is too tailored to the training set and does not generalise well, i.e., it has a lower predictive accuracy in the test set. In order to mitigate the possibility of overfitting, we propose the

Table 1. The rule quality functions used in the dynamic selection process

Function Name	Parameter	Formula
Accuracy	-	$\frac{TP+TN}{TP+FP+TN+FN}$
Confidence + Coverage	-	$\frac{TP}{TP+FP} + \frac{TP}{S}$
Cost Measure	$c = 0.437$	$(c \cdot TP) - ((1-c) \cdot FP)$
F-measure	$\beta = 0.5$	$\frac{(1+\beta^2) \cdot \frac{TP}{TP+FN} \cdot \frac{TP}{TP+FP}}{\beta^2 \cdot \frac{TP}{TP+FN} + \frac{TP}{TP+FP}}$
Jaccard	-	$\frac{TP}{TP+FP+FN}$
Klösgen	$\omega = 0.4323$	$\left(\frac{TP+FP}{S}\right)^{\omega} \cdot \left(\frac{TP}{TP+FP} - \frac{TP+FN}{S}\right)$
M-Estimate	$m = 22.466$	$\frac{TP+m \cdot \frac{TP}{S}}{TP+FP+m}$
C4.5's Error-based function*	-	$U_{CF}(FP, TP+FP)$
Relative Cost Measure	$cr = 0.342$	$(cr \cdot recall) - ((1-cr) \cdot \frac{FP}{FP+TN})$
Sensitivity × Specificity	-	$\frac{TP}{TP+FN} \cdot \frac{TN}{TN+FP}$

*The U_{CF} function corresponds to the upper limit of the probability of an error (FP) over the examples covered by a rule ($TP + FP$). More details can be found in [11, p. 41]

use of a function based on C4.5's pessimistic error rate (U_{CF}) to measure the quality of a candidate list of rules, given by

$$1 - \frac{\sum_{r=1}^{L}(TP_r + FP_r) \cdot U_{CF}(FP_r, TP_r + FP_r)}{S}, \tag{1}$$

where FP_r and TP_r are the number of false positives and true positives of the r-th rule, respectively, L is the number of rules in the candidate list and S is the number of training examples. According to (1), the quality of a list of rules corresponds to 1 minus the sum of the predicted errors (the number of examples classified by a rule times its associated U_{CF} error rate [11, p. 41]) of the rules divided by the number of examples in the training set—the lower the sum of predicted errors, the higher the quality of the list.

4   Results

In order to evaluate the proposed extensions of the cAnt-Miner_PB algorithm, we have selected 14 datasets from the UCI Machine Learning repository [4]. Table 2 presents a summary of the data sets used in our experiments. We have

Table 2. Summary of the data sets used in the experiments

Data set	# Attributes		# Classes	# Examples
	Nominal	Continuous		
balance-scale	4	0	3	625
breast-l	9	0	2	286
breast-w	0	30	2	569
credit-a	8	6	2	690
dermatology	33	1	6	366
glass	0	9	7	214
heart-c	6	7	5	303
hepatitis	13	6	2	155
ionosphere	0	34	2	351
iris	0	4	3	150
liver-disorders	0	6	2	345
parkinsons	0	22	2	195
wine	0	13	3	178
zoo	16	0	7	101

evaluated four different variations of cAnt-Miner$_{PB}$: the original cAnt-Miner$_{PB}$; the cAnt-Miner$_{PB}$ with the proposed dynamic rule quality function selection (denoted with a '[D]' marking); the cAnt-Miner$_{PB}$ with the proposed error-based rule-list quality function (denoted with a '[E]' marking); and cAnt-Miner$_{PB}$ with both dynamic rule quality function selection and error-based list quality function (denoted with a '[D+E]' marking). We carried out a tenfold cross-validation procedure and the cAnt-Miner$_{PB}$ default parameters were used [9]: *colony size* of 5, *maximum number of iterations* of 500 and *evaporation factor* of 0.90 (i.e., the evaporation rate is equal to $1 - factor$, therefore the pheromone values are decreased by 10% during evaporation). Since cAnt-Miner$_{PB}$ is a stochastic algorithm, it was run 10 times for each of the cross-validation folds.

The results of our experiments are presented in Table 3, for predictive accuracy, and Table 4, for the size of the discovered model (measured as the total number of terms in the list of rules). A value on those tables corresponds to the average value measured over the tenfold cross-validation. Table 5 presents the results of the non-parametric Friedman statistical test with the post-hoc Hommel's test [1,6]. The information presented in Table 5 corresponds to the average rank (first column), where the lower the rank the better the algorithm's performance, and the adjusted p_{Homm} value. Statistically significant differences among the algorithm with the highest rank (the control '(c)' algorithm) are determined by the p_{Homm} value: if the p value is less than 0.1, the difference in the rank is statistically significant at the $\alpha = 0.1$ level; if the p value is less than 0.05, the difference in the rank is statistically significant at the $\alpha = 0.05$ level.

Table 3. Average predictive accuracy (*average ± standard error*) measured over tenfold cross-validation. The highest predictive accuracy for a given data set is shown in bold.

	cAM$_{PB}$	cAM$_{PB}$ [E]	cAM$_{PB}$ [D]	cAM$_{PB}$ [D+E]
balance-scale	**76.83 ± 0.24**	76.26 ± 0.29	76.69 ± 0.17	76.28 ± 0.21
breast-l	72.32 ± 0.31	**75.27 ± 0.35**	70.59 ± 0.42	73.77 ± 0.36
breast-w	94.29 ± 0.16	94.34 ± 0.16	94.09 ± 0.33	**94.60 ± 0.20**
credit-a	85.68 ± 0.15	**86.10 ± 0.23**	85.19 ± 0.31	85.77 ± 0.22
dermatology	**92.46 ± 0.31**	92.40 ± 0.40	91.72 ± 0.35	91.97 ± 0.28
glass	**73.94 ± 0.49**	73.11 ± 0.61	72.73 ± 0.65	73.52 ± 0.42
heart-c	**55.50 ± 0.37**	55.21 ± 0.41	54.57 ± 0.63	54.83 ± 0.62
hepatitis	78.78 ± 0.43	78.55 ± 0.66	**79.50 ± 0.61**	78.83 ± 0.55
ionosphere	89.65 ± 0.31	89.95 ± 0.23	89.32 ± 0.30	**90.58 ± 0.45**
iris	93.24 ± 0.20	93.13 ± 0.26	94.33 ± 0.25	**94.47 ± 0.14**
liver-disorders	66.72 ± 0.40	66.71 ± 0.41	67.10 ± 0.49	**67.98 ± 0.53**
parkinsons	86.98 ± 0.65	**88.42 ± 0.50**	87.88 ± 0.29	87.72 ± 0.55
wine	93.57 ± 0.32	94.51 ± 0.31	94.18 ± 0.56	**95.04 ± 0.33**
zoo	88.59 ± 0.50	88.67 ± 0.26	**89.19 ± 0.41**	88.57 ± 0.49

Table 4. Average number of terms (*average ± standard error*) measured over tenfold cross-validation. The lowest number of terms for a given data set is shown in bold.

	cAM$_{PB}$	cAM$_{PB}$ [E]	cAM$_{PB}$ [D]	cAM$_{PB}$ [D+E]
balance-scale	**12.64 ± 0.03**	12.66 ± 0.05	15.45 ± 0.16	14.32 ± 0.13
breast-l	19.15 ± 0.40	**8.65 ± 0.17**	34.65 ± 0.82	11.85 ± 0.62
breast-w	8.55 ± 0.12	**8.03 ± 0.19**	11.90 ± 0.21	9.50 ± 0.28
credit-a	17.54 ± 0.32	**13.71 ± 0.38**	35.53 ± 0.74	25.23 ± 0.64
dermatology	44.47 ± 0.63	43.93 ± 0.63	42.39 ± 0.66	**41.89 ± 0.57**
glass	10.73 ± 0.14	**9.99 ± 0.15**	13.24 ± 0.25	12.61 ± 0.22
heart-c	27.65 ± 0.58	**25.10 ± 0.57**	38.66 ± 0.68	29.90 ± 0.71
hepatitis	10.87 ± 0.17	**10.36 ± 0.40**	12.71 ± 0.43	11.47 ± 0.20
ionosphere	11.04 ± 0.17	**9.96 ± 0.25**	15.35 ± 0.38	11.38 ± 0.32
iris	4.92 ± 0.08	4.17 ± 0.13	5.04 ± 0.11	**4.13 ± 0.05**
liver-disorders	11.78 ± 0.08	**11.49 ± 0.12**	29.66 ± 0.30	23.70 ± 0.50
parkinsons	7.02 ± 0.11	**5.96 ± 0.08**	7.94 ± 0.15	7.00 ± 0.15
wine	4.75 ± 0.08	**3.83 ± 0.07**	5.66 ± 0.14	4.42 ± 0.07
zoo	**6.70 ± 0.09**	7.12 ± 0.10	6.97 ± 0.10	7.41 ± 0.19

The use of the dynamic rule quality function selection combined with the error-based rule-list quality function (cAnt-Miner$_{PB}$ [D+E]) led to an overall improvement in predictive accuracy and achieved the highest average rank, although the differences are not statistically significant according to the Friedman test. The use of the error-based rule-list quality (cAnt-Miner$_{PB}$ [E]) had a similar predictive accuracy to the original cAnt-Miner$_{PB}$, achieving a similar

Table 5. Statistical test results according to the non-parametric Friedman test with the Hommel's post-hoc test. Statistically significant differences at the $\alpha = 0.1$ level are tabulated in bold and differences at the $\alpha = 0.05$ level are underlined.

Configuration	Average Rank	Adjusted p_{Homm}
(i) Predictive Accuracy		
cAnt-Miner$_{PB}$ [D+E] (c)	2.07	–
cAnt-Miner$_{PB}$ [E]	2.43	0.4642
cAnt-Miner$_{PB}$	2.57	0.4642
cAnt-Miner$_{PB}$ [D]	2.93	0.2369
(ii) Model Size		
cAnt-Miner$_{PB}$ [E] (c)	1.43	–
cAnt-Miner$_{PB}$	2.29	**0.0789**
cAnt-Miner$_{PB}$ [D+E]	2.57	**0.0383**
cAnt-Miner$_{PB}$ [D]	3.71	**8.4E-6**

average rank. The use of the dynamic rule quality function (cAnt-Miner$_{PB}$ [D]) has not led to an improvement in predictive accuracy, achieving the lowest average rank. In terms of the discovered model size, the use of the error-based rule-list quality (cAnt-Miner$_{PB}$ [E]) led to a statistically significant improvement in the size of the discovered lists, reducing the average number of terms in the lists. The use of the dynamic rule quality function selection (cAnt-Miner$_{PB}$ [D] and cAnt-Miner$_{PB}$ [D+E]) resulted in longer lists and achieved the lowest rank.

The error-based rule-list function has shown significant improvement in terms of the size of the discovered lists of rules, without a drop in accuracy. This is a very useful finding as the cAnt-Miner$_{PB}$ algorithm suffered from increased list size, which now can be avoiding by the use of the new error-based rule-list function. The dynamic rule quality function selection, however, has shown no significant gain in accuracy while performing much worse in terms of size.

During the experiments using the dynamic rule quality function selection we monitored which rule quality functions were being chosen. The frequency of each rule quality function being chosen per dataset can be found in Figure 3. The top image (Figure 3a) shows the results when using the dynamic search alongside the traditional predictive accuracy rule-list function, whereas the bottom image (Figure 3b) shows the results when the proposed error-based rule-list function was used. In Figure 3a, it appears that four rule quality functions were being used more often quite consistently, except in the case of the zoo dataset, suggesting that the use of these functions can lead to improvements in the accuracy during training and potentially overfitting. In Figure 3b, however, the pattern is much less clear and no rule quality function stands out.

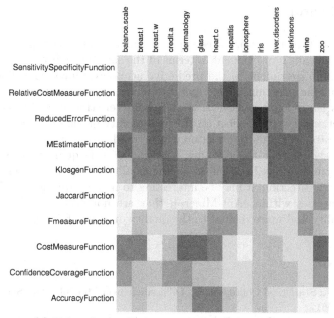

(a) Using the predictive accuracy rule-list function.

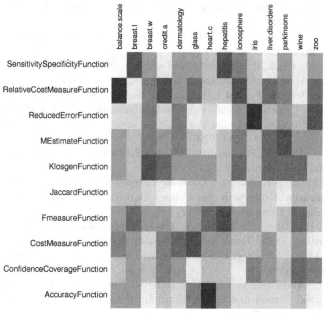

(b) Using the error-based rule-list function.

Fig. 3. Heatmaps showing the frequency at which different rule quality functions were chosen per dataset—the darker the colour the more often the rule quality function was used

5   Conclusion

We have found that the error-based rule-list evaluation function produces a statistically significant improvement in terms of the size of the discovered lists, and that there is no detriment to the predictive accuracy. Our second finding was that the dynamic selection of rule quality functions did not yield any improvements. This leads us to believe that the characteristics of an individual rule quality function have little effect on the final quality of the discovered lists, and that any sensible rule quality function can be used.

We have shown that the dynamic selection of rule quality function (used purely for pruning) has little effect on the quality of the lists, therefore as a future research direction, it may be interesting to investigate the use of different pruning strategies within cAnt-Miner$_{PB}$ that are not necessary dependent on the rule quality and more related to the quality of a list of rules.

References

1. Demšar, J.: Statistical Comparisons of Classifiers over Multiple Data Sets. JMLR 7, 1–30 (2006)
2. Dorigo, M., Stüzle, T.: Ant Colony Optimization. The MIT Press (2004)
3. Fayyad, U., Piatetsky-Shapiro, G., Smith, P.: From data mining to knowledge discovery: an overview. In: Advances in Knowledge Discovery & Data Mining, pp. 1–34. MIT Press (1996)
4. Frank, A., Asuncion, A.: UCI Machine Learning Repository (2010), http://archive.ics.uci.edu/ml
5. Fürnkranz, J., Flach, P.: ROC 'n' Rule Learning—Towards a Better Understanding of Covering Algorithms. Machine Learning 58, 39–77 (2005)
6. García, S., Herrera, F.: An Extension on 'Statistical Comparisons of Classifiers over Multiple Data Sets' for all Pairwise Comparisons. JMLR 9, 2677–2694 (2008)
7. Janssen, F., Fürnkranz, J.: On the quest for optimal rule learning heuristics. Machine Learning 78, 343–379 (2010)
8. Martens, D., Baesens, B., Fawcett, T.: Editorial survey: swarm intelligence for data mining. Machine Learning 82, 1–42 (2011)
9. Otero, F., Freitas, A., Johnson, C.: A New Sequential Covering Strategy for Inducing Classification Rules with Ant Colony Algorithms. To Appear in IEEE Trans. on Evolutionary Computation (2012)
10. Parpinelli, R., Lopes, H., Freitas, A.: Data Mining with an Ant Colony Optimization Algorithm. IEEE Trans. on Evolutionary Computation 6(4), 321–332 (2002)
11. Quinlan, J.R.: C4.5: Programs for Machine Learning. Kaufmann Publishers Inc., San Francisco (1993)
12. Salama, K., Abdelbar, A.: Exploring Different Rule Quality Evaluation Functions in ACO-based Classification Algorithms. In: IEEE Symposium on Swarm Intelligence (SIS), pp. 1–8 (2011)
13. Witten, I., Frank, E., Hall, M.: Data Mining: Practical Machine Learning Tools and Techniques, 3rd edn. Morgan Kaufmann (2011)

Introducing Novelty Search
in Evolutionary Swarm Robotics

Jorge Gomes[1,3], Paulo Urbano[1], and Anders Lyhne Christensen[2,3]

[1] LabMAg, Faculdade de Ciências da Universidade de Lisboa, Portugal
[2] Instituto Universitário de Lisboa (ISCTE-IUL), Lisboa, Portugal
[3] Instituto de Telecomunicações, Lisboa, Portugal
{jgomes,pub}@di.fc.ul.pt, anders.christensen@iscte.pt

Abstract. Novelty search is a recent and promising evolutionary technique. The main idea behind it is to reward novel solutions instead of progress towards a fixed goal, in order to avoid premature convergence and deception. In this paper, we use novelty search together with NEAT, to evolve neuro-controllers for a swarm of simulated robots that should perform an aggregation task. In the past, novelty search has been applied to single robot systems. We demonstrate that novelty search can be applied successfully to multirobot systems, and we discuss the challenges introduced when moving from a single robot setup to a multirobot setup. Our results show that novelty search can outperform the fitness-based evolution in swarm robotic systems, finding (i) a more diverse set of successful solutions to an aggregation task, (ii) solutions with higher fitness scores earlier in the evolutionary runs, and (iii) simpler solutions in terms of the topological complexity of the evolved neural networks.

1 Introduction

Novelty search [10] is a divergent evolutionary technique. In traditional evolutionary computation, candidate solutions are scored by an objective function that has been derived directly from the task or problem for which a solution is sought. Novelty search does not drive the evolutionary process toward a fixed goal. In novelty search, candidate solutions are scored based on how different they are from solutions seen so far and the evolutionary process is therefore continuously driven towards novelty. As a result, novelty search has the potential to overcome deception [4]. Deception can be a challenging problem in evolutionary computation and occurs when the evolutionary process converges prematurely to a local optimum because the objective function fails to reward the intermediate steps needed to achieve the final goal. Lehman and Stanley [10] have shown that, although novelty search does not pursue a goal directly, it may be able to find the goal faster and more consistently than traditional fitness-based evolution. Novelty search has also proven to be able to find a greater diversity of solutions to a problem than traditional fitness-based evolution [11].

Novelty search has been successfully applied to many domains, including non-collective evolutionary robotics in tasks such as maze navigation [10,13], T-maze

M. Dorigo et al. (Eds.): ANTS 2012, LNCS 7461, pp. 85–96, 2012.

tasks that require lifetime learning [14], biped walking [10], and the deceptive tartarus problem [3]. There are many motivations behind the use of evolutionary techniques for the design of a control system for a robot [5]. In a multirobot domain in particular, the dynamical interactions among robots and the environment make it difficult to hand-design a control system for the robots that yields the desired macroscopic swarm behaviours. However, artificial evolution has been shown capable of exploiting these dynamic features and synthesise self-organised behaviours [18].

In this paper, we use novelty search to evolve neural controllers for swarm robotic systems, where fitness-based evolutionary approaches has been previously used. Our motivation for applying novelty search to swarm robotic systems is their high level of complexity, resulting from the intricate dynamics between many interacting units. As the complexity of a task or a system increases, artificial evolution is more likely to get affected by deception [19], and novelty search has been shown capable of overcoming deception [10]. The drive of novelty search towards behavioural diversity is also valuable because it can generate a diversity of solutions in a single evolutionary run, as opposed to fitness-based evolution, in which a particular run often converges to a single solution.

There are many works that describe the evolution of robot swarms with neuroevolution methods that optimise only the weights of the neural network. However, the evolution of the network topology along with the weights has proved to be beneficial in other domains [19,16]. In this paper, we use NEAT (NeuroEvolution of Augmenting Topologies) [17] to evolve the neural controllers used by the robots in a swarm. NEAT is a method that evolves both the network topology and weights, allowing solutions to become gradually more complex as they become better [17]. The use of novelty search together with NEAT is motivated by the complexifying nature of NEAT, which imposes some order in the exploration of the behaviour space, because simple controllers are explored before moving on to more complex ones.

We use an aggregation task for the experiments in this study. In this task, the robots should move around in an environment to search for each other and ultimately form a single aggregate. Aggregation is of particular interest since it stands as a prerequisite for other forms of cooperation in swarm robotics systems [18]. This task has been used in previous works in evolutionary swarm robotics [2,18,1]. In our experiments, the domain was made challenging by increasing the size of the arena and by reducing the sensors capabilities, compared to the previous studies on aggregation in robots.

2   Background

In this section, we review the related work on aggregation in evolutionary robotics, the NEAT neuroevolution method used in our experiments, and the novelty search method.

2.1 Evolution of Aggregation Behaviours

Several works describe the evolution of aggregation behaviours in swarms of robots, where neural networks with fixed topologies are evolved via evolutionary algorithms guided by fitness. Baldassarre et al. [2] successfully evolved controllers for a swarm of robots to aggregate and move towards a light source in a clustered formation. Trianni et al. [18] describe the evolution of a swarm of simple robots to perform aggregation in a square arena. In this experiment, two different behaviours were evolved: a *static clustering* which forms compact and stable aggregates and a *dynamic clustering* which creates loose but moving aggregates. Bahgeçi et al. [1] used a similar experimental setup as [18], and studied how some parameters of the evolutionary methods affect the performance and the scalability of the behaviours in swarm robotic systems.

In these studies, the robots used directional sound sensors and sound signalling to identify other robots in the environment. Sound signalling enabled robots to follow sound gradients in order to aggregate. In fact, these works show that neural networks without any hidden neurons are sufficient to successfully solve the task. In our work, we make the aggregation task more challenging: we remove the sound gradient, decrease the range of the sensors, and increase the size of the arena. These modifications increase the difficulty of the task and may require quite different strategies for aggregation because it is harder for the robots to find each other [15].

2.2 NEAT

NEAT [17] is a neuroevolution method that optimises both the weighting parameters and the structure of artificial neural networks. It begins the evolution with a population of small, simple networks and complexifies the network topology into diverse species over generations, potentially leading to increasingly sophisticated behaviour. A key feature in NEAT is its distinctive approach to maintaining a healthy diversity of growing structures simultaneously. Unique historical markings are assigned to each new structural component. During crossover, genes with the same historical markings are aligned, producing valid offspring efficiently, without having to rely on complex topological comparisons. Speciation in NEAT protects new structural innovations by reducing competition between differing networks, giving time for newer and more complex structures to have their weights optimised. Networks are assigned to species based on the extent to which they share historical markings. Complexification is thus supported by both historical markings and speciation, allowing NEAT to establish high-level features early in evolution and then later elaborate on them. In effect, NEAT searches for a compact, appropriate network topology by incrementally complexifying existing structures.

2.3 Novelty Search

In novelty search [10], individuals in an evolving population are selected based exclusively on how different their behaviour is when compared to the other behaviours discovered so far. Implementing novelty search requires little change to any evolutionary algorithm aside from replacing the fitness function with a domain dependent novelty metric. This metric measures how different an individual is from the other individuals with respect to their behaviour. The use of a novelty measure creates a constant pressure to evolve individuals with novel behaviour features.

The novelty of a newly generated individual is computed with respect to the behaviours of an archive of past individuals and to the current population, giving a comprehensive sample of where the search has been and where it currently is. However, the archive does not contain all of the behaviours previously explored, in order to minimise the impact in the algorithm's computational complexity. The archive is initially empty, and behaviours are added to it if they are significantly different from the ones already there, i.e., if their novelty is above some threshold. The purpose of the archive is to allow the penalisation of future individuals that exhibit previously explored behaviours.

The novelty metric characterises how far away the new individual is from the rest of the population and its predecessors in behaviour space, determining the sparseness at any point in that space. A simple measure of sparseness at a point is the average distance to the k-nearest neighbours of that point, where k is a fixed parameter empirically determined. The sparseness ρ at point x is given by

$$\rho(x) = \frac{1}{k} \sum_{i=1}^{k} dist(x, \mu_i) \tag{1}$$

where μ_i the ith-nearest neighbour of x with respect to the distance metric $dist$, which is a domain-dependent measure of behavioural difference between two individuals in the search space. Candidates from more sparse regions of the behaviour space thus receive higher novelty scores, guiding the search towards what is new, with no other explicit objective.

3   Aggregation Experiments

In this section, we apply novelty search to the aggregation task and compare it with fitness-based evolution. Three experiments were performed using different novelty measures: one highly correlated with the fitness function, an alternative measure only weakly correlated, and finally a combination of the two. In each experiment, the performance of novelty search was compared to the performance of traditional fitness-based evolution. NEAT with random selection is used as a baseline for performance comparisons.

3.1   Experimental Setup

The simulated environment is modelled in a customised version of the Simbad 3d Robot Simulator [7]. The environment is a 5 m by 5 m square arena bounded by walls. The robots are modelled based on the the e-puck educational robot [12], but do not strictly follow its specification. Each simulated robot has 8 IR sensors evenly distributed around its chassis for the detection of obstacles (walls or other robots) within a range of 10 cm, and 8 sensors dedicated to the detection of other robots within 25 cm range. An additional sensor calculates the percentage of nearby robots, relative to the size of the swarm, within a radius of 25 cm.

The swarm is homogeneous and the controllers of the robots are time recurrent neural networks. For fitness-based evolution, we used the NEAT implementation available in the Encog 3.0.1 library [6]. For novelty search, we extended the same NEAT implementation following the description and parameters in [10], with a k value of 15 and a dynamic archive threshold [9]. This dynamic threshold ensures a constant and reasonable flow of individuals to the archive, at an average rate of 2 individuals per generation. The NEAT parameters were the same in both evolutionary methods: the crossover rate was 25%, the mutation rate 10%, the population size 200, and each evolution runs for 250 generations. The rest of the parameters were the default of the Encog implementation.

To evaluate each controller, 10 simulations are run with it, varying the number of robots and their starting positions and orientations. The starting positions and orientations are random but ensure a minimum distance between the robots. The group size varies from 3 to 10, with each controller being run at least once with every group size. Each simulation lasts for 500 s of simulated time.

The fitness function that evaluates each simulation is based on the average distance to the centre of mass, also used in [18]. The average distance is sampled throughout the simulation at regular intervals of 10 s. The samples are then combined in a single fitness value using a weighted average, with linearly more weight towards the end of the simulation. The fitness F of a simulation with T time steps and N robots is defined as:

$$F = 1 - \frac{1}{\sum \frac{t}{T}} \sum_{t=1}^{T} \frac{t}{T} \sum_{i=1}^{N} \frac{dist(\mathbf{R}_t, \mathbf{r}_{i_t})}{N} \qquad (2)$$

where $\mathbf{R}_t$ is the centre of mass at each instant, and $\mathbf{r}_{i_t}$ is the position of each robot. The fitness values obtained in each of the 10 simulations are combined in a single value using the harmonic mean, which gives more weight to the lower values, as advocated in [1].

As mentioned above, the novelty measure characterises the distance between one controller and the others in behaviour space. We use the Euclidian distance between vectors that represent the level of aggregation along time. These vectors are built by measuring behaviour features at regular intervals throughout the simulation (every 10 s). We devised three ways of measuring the group behaviour, which will be explained in the next sections. As 10 simulations are conducted to evaluate each controller, its behaviour vector is the average of the vectors obtained in each of the simulations. In order to compare novelty search with the fitness-based evolution, the controllers evolved by novelty search were also evaluated with the fitness function F. It is important to note that the fitness scores did not have any influence in the novelty search experiments.

3.2   The First Experiment

The first behaviour measure uses the same metric as the fitness function; a vector is built with the average distance to centre of mass, sampled throughout the simulation. Considering a simulation with N robots and T temporal samples, the behaviour vector $\mathbf{b_{cm}}$ that characterises a controller is given by:

$$\mathbf{b_{cm}} = \frac{1}{N}\left[\sum_{i=1}^{N} dist(\mathbf{R}_1, \mathbf{r}_{i_1}), \cdots, \sum_{i=1}^{N} dist(\mathbf{R}_T, \mathbf{r}_{i_T})\right] . \tag{3}$$

In our experiments, the sampling rate was 10 s and the simulation time 500 s, resulting in a behaviour vector of length 50.

The fitness scores of the highest scoring individuals evolved using novelty search and fitness driven evolution, respectively, are listed in Table 1. There is not a significant difference between the fitness of the controllers evolved in these experiments, but both methods are significantly better than the random evolution (Student's t-test with p-value < 0.05). If we look at the behaviours of the best controllers evolved by both methods, significant differences are found, despite the similar fitness values. In the fitness-based evolution, the highest scoring controllers were always very similar, displaying only one distinctive behaviour: the robots explore the environment in large circles, and form static clusters when they encounter one another. If the cluster is small, the robots abandon it after a while and start exploring again.

Novelty search, on the other hand, found several distinct high-scoring controllers that could perform the aggregation task: (1) The robots go straight forward until they hit the wall, and then, depending on the impact angle, they stay there for a while or start moving along the wall until they find other robots; (2) Similar to (1), but when they meet each other they continue to follow the wall until they hit a corner, aggregating there; (3) Similar to the behaviour evolved by fitness, but without splitting the small clusters; (4) Similar to (3) but navigating in the environment only in straight trajectories instead of curves. It is important to note that each evolutionary run of novelty search could evolve several different solutions, finding many (if not all) of the solutions described above and variants of them.

The main difference between the behaviours was that novelty search evolved controllers that exploited the wall to achieve better solutions, while in the fitness-based evolution robots always avoided navigating near the walls. Our hypothesis is that learning to navigate along the walls requires going against the

Table 1. Highest fitness found with each evolutionary method. The values were obtained with 10 runs for each experiment. Individuals with fitness value over 0.8 are considered to be solutions to the task. Note that in practice the minimum fitness value is not 0, since an initial random population has an average fitness of around 0.6.

Evolutionary Setup	Average	Max.	Min.
Fitness-based NEAT	0.863	0.892	0.826
NEAT with novelty search	0.864	0.906	0.828
NEAT with random selection	0.725	0.752	0.706

fitness gradient. If the robots go towards the walls, they will often end up in different ones, and staying there will result in a low fitness because the centre of mass will be in the centre of the arena, far from the robots. On the other hand, avoiding the walls results in better fitness because they will be on average closer to the centre. If the fitness evolution misses the stepping stone of being close to the walls, it will hardly be able to reach behaviours that require the use of walls to achieve aggregation. This is an important result because it demonstrates that the fitness function is preventing the evolution of certain types of solutions.

To confirm our hypothesis, we analysed the behaviour space explored in novelty search and in fitness evolution. To facilitate this analysis, all the individuals evolved in fitness evolution were also evaluated with the same behaviour measure that was used in novelty search. Since each behaviour description is a long vector, we applied a dimensionality reduction method in order to visualise the behaviour space. We used a Kohonen self-organising map [8], a type of neural network trained using unsupervised learning to produce a two-dimensional discretisation of the input space of the training samples, preserving the topological relations. The map was trained with all the behaviours found both in novelty search and in fitness evolution, and then the behaviours found by each method were mapped individually to the trained map. The resulting maps can be seen in Figure 1.

As it can be seen in the maps, the fitness-based evolution avoids the zones where the average distance to the centre of mass rises beyond the initial value, preventing the evolution of good solutions that might require traits found only in those behaviour zones. The evolution is much more focused in behaviours that express a monotonic fall of the average distance to the centre of mass, which is consistent with the observable performances of the best controllers. On the other hand, novelty search is not subject to this fitness pressure, and can therefore explore and discover a wide range of solutions to the task.

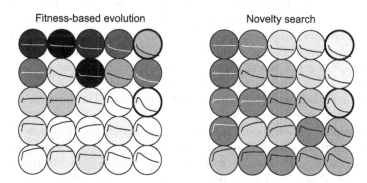

Fig. 1. Kohonen maps representing the explored behaviour space in fitness evolution (left) and in novelty search (right). Each circle is a neuron that is characterised by the vector depicted by the line inside (the average distance to the centre of mass over time). Each behaviour vector is mapped to the most similar neuron. The darker the background of a neuron is, the more behaviours were mapped to it. The neurons corresponding to the best behaviours have a bold circle.

3.3   The Alternative Novelty Measure

We devised a new behaviour description, based on the metric used in [1], in order to determine how the novelty measure influences the evolved solutions. The new description consists of measuring the number of robot clusters along the simulation. Two robots belong to the same cluster if the distance between them is less than 30 cm. Applying this iteratively we can obtain the number of clusters. The number of samples was the same as in our previous experiments (50). The behaviour vector $\mathbf{b_{cl}}$ is described by:

$$\mathbf{b_{cl}} = \frac{1}{N} \left[clustersCount(1), \cdots, clustersCount(T) \right] \ . \tag{4}$$

The best fitness found in each evolutionary run was 0.83 on average, which is significantly lower (p-value < 0.05) than the novelty search with the centre of mass behaviour measure (0.864 on average). This might be explained by the use of a novelty measure that is less related to the fitness function. But again, we have to look at the evolved behaviours to determine the significant differences. The following distinct successful behaviours were evolved: (1) The robots go towards walls, navigate along it and when they find another one, they form a single file, keeping a fixed distance; (2) They navigate in circles in the environment, forming a static cluster when they meet each other; (3) Similar to (2), but they randomly abandon their respective clusters; (4) They navigate in circles and when two robots meet at some distance, one tries to follow the other. When robots collide, they form a cluster and remain aggregated.

Most behaviours were quite different from the ones found in the previous experiment. The reason the previous experiment did not find these behaviours (and vice-versa) is conflation (see [10]). Conflation occurs when individuals with distinct observable behaviours have very similar behaviour descriptions. The consequence is that an individual with a distinct observable behaviour might not be considered novel by the novelty measure, thus eventually disappearing from the population. Conflation can represent both an advantage because it reduces the search space, and a disadvantage, when different successful solutions or important stepping stones are dismissed. In our experiments, what happens is that the centre of mass novelty measure is conflating some solutions that are not conflated in the clusters measure and vice-versa, thus evolving different solutions in both the experiments.

Two examples of behaviours that can be conflated are shown in Figure 2. When the centre of mass measure is used, for example, the clustering of the robots is irrelevant. The search will therefore avoid behaviours that have an already explored centre of mass progression but differ in the clustering of the robots, possibly bypassing interesting solutions. This effect can also be seen in the evolved behaviours: with the centre of mass measure, there were more solutions that exploited the use of the walls, because navigating near them has a great impact in that novelty measure; while with the number of clusters measure, the solutions focused on the interactions between the agents and clusters, including following each other and leaving the cluster.

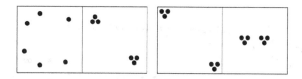

Fig. 2. An illustration of conflation in the centre of mass measure (left) and in the number of clusters measure (right). In both cases, if the robots evolved from the left configuration to the right, that change would not be captured by the respective behaviour description, despite potentially being relevant.

3.4 Combining Novelty Measures

In order to reduce conflation, we setup a new experiment with a richer behaviour description, by combining the novelty measures proposed in the two previous experiments. To combine the two behaviour descriptions presented before in Equations 3 and 4, we simply concatenate the two vectors. But as the novelty measure is based on the Euclidean distance between the vectors, caution must be displayed to ensure that both components have similar contributions to this distance. Namely, we want the vectors to have the same length and the items in the vectors to have the same range, which can be achieved by normalising each of the components. The new behaviour description $\mathbf{b_{comb}}$ is thus defined as:

$$\mathbf{b_{comb}} = (\mathbf{b_{cm}}, \mathbf{b_{cl}}) \ . \tag{5}$$

The fitness performance of the search with this new measure was improved, evolving individuals with high fitness scores much sooner than in the other experiments, as seen in Figure 3. The fitness values in novelty search were higher than fitness-based evolution until generation 150. It is also interesting to look at the explored behaviour space (Figure 4). We can see that there was a greater diversity of solutions, exploring many combinations of the progression of the number of clusters and the distance to the centre of mass. Observing the best controllers in action, we notice that this combined measure evolved all the behaviours that were generated using the previous two measures independently.

To determine why novelty search with the combined measure was faster than fitness-based evolution in finding good individuals, we evaluated the network complexity of the solutions. On average, novelty search finds the first good individual (with fitness value over 0.8) at the generation 33 with a network of 1 hidden neuron and 39 links, while the fitness evolution finds the first good individual at the generation 83 with a network of 4 hidden neurons and 44 links. Looking at the early solutions found by novelty search, we discovered that in some cases they are the ones that the fitness-based evolution could not evolve at all (behaviours that used the wall). In other cases, they were apparently the same solutions that the fitness-based evolution would find in later generations with more complex networks. Due to the incremental nature of NEAT, more complex networks take more generations to evolve. If fitness starts to converge to more complex structures, it takes more time to evolve effective controllers.

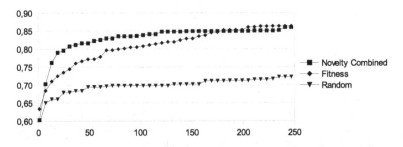

Fig. 3. Fitness value of the best individual found so far in each generation. The values are averaged over 10 evolutionary runs for each experiment. Individuals with fitness value over 0.8 are considered to be solutions to the task. The evolution was tested with more generations but there is no change in the fitness values after the 250th generation.

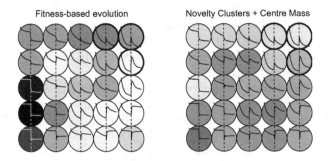

Fig. 4. The explored behaviour space in novelty search with the combined novelty measure and in the fitness-based evolution. In each neuron, the left half is the number of clusters measure and the right half is the centre of mass. The darker the neuron background is, the more behaviours were mapped to it. Neurons with the best behaviours have a bold circle.

4   Discussion

Our experiments revealed that novelty search could outperform fitness-based evolution in respect to the fitness values of the evolved individuals. Other works have shown that novelty search can perform better than fitness-based evolution in deceptive tasks, but fails to be better as the task gets less deceptive [10,13]. Our results suggest that the task is not notably deceptive, as fitness evolution can always find high-scoring solutions. Still, novelty search managed to outperform the fitness-based evolution.

Looking beyond the fitness of the solutions, we showed that the diversity found by novelty search can produce many different solutions to the same task. This can be used to provide a range of different solutions to the experimenter that is using the evolutionary process. This is especially relevant in the swarm robotics domain, because there are many behaviour possibilities and non-obvious relations between the agents that might be revealed. Another advantage of novelty search was that it found solutions with simpler neural networks than the ones found by fitness evolution, confirming the results reported in [10].

The Kohonen maps proved to be useful in the visualisation of the behaviour search space. They allow the understanding of the behaviour zones that were explored by novelty search and the zones where the fitness-based evolution gets stuck. We verified that controllers mapped to different neurons typically have different observable behaviours. This suggests that analysing the differences in the behaviour vectors might be a way of automatically identifying distinct solutions.

The biggest challenge in using novelty search in the domain of swarm robotics was the definition of the novelty measure. Our experiments suggest that conflation can be a serious issue when evolving collective behaviours with novelty search. While in single robot systems, conflation can be mitigated by describing the full behaviour of the robot, for example its position in space over time [10], in swarm robotics that is not possible. Describing the behaviour of all the robots individually would open the search space too much. It would also introduce scalability issues, for example if the number of robots varies or if the swarm is very large. It is necessary to devise measures that evaluate the swarm as whole. Conflation is essential to cope with the greater diversity of collective behaviours, but caution must be displayed in order not to conflate aspects of the swarm that are relevant to the solution. Our last experiment showed that by combining different novelty measures, we can reduce conflation and improve the performance of novelty search. This combination can simply be the concatenation of the behaviour vectors associated with each measure, which was effective in our case.

5   Conclusion

This study showed that novelty search is a promising technique for evolving controllers for swarm robotic systems. Compared to the fitness-based evolution, novelty search could find a greater diversity of solutions, solutions with higher fitness earlier in the evolution, and solutions based on simpler neural networks. We studied the impact of the novelty measure in the evolved behaviours and showed how conflation can be mitigated by combining different novelty measures. In future research, we will use other novelty search variants that combine the fitness value and the novelty measure [3,9] to investigate if our results can be further improved. We will also use novelty search to evolve controllers for other swarm robotics tasks, to evaluate if the results presented in this paper generalise.

Acknowledgments. This work was supported by FCT project PEst-OE/EEI/ LA-0008/2011.

References

1. Bahgeçi, E., Şahin, E.: Evolving aggregation behaviors for swarm robotic systems: A systematic case study. In: Swarm Intelligence Symposium, pp. 333–340. IEEE, New York (2005)

2. Baldassarre, G., Nolfi, S., Parisi, D.: Evolving mobile robots able to display collective behaviors. Artificial Life 9(3), 255–268 (2003)
3. Cuccu, G., Gomez, F.: When Novelty Is Not Enough. In: Di Chio, C., Cagnoni, S., Cotta, C., Ebner, M., Ekárt, A., Esparcia-Alcázar, A.I., Merelo, J.J., Neri, F., Preuss, M., Richter, H., Togelius, J., Yannakakis, G.N. (eds.) EvoApplications 2011, Part I. LNCS, vol. 6624, pp. 234–243. Springer, Heidelberg (2011)
4. Goldberg, D.E.: Simple genetic algorithms and the minimal, deceptive problem. In: Genetic Algorithms and Simulated Annealing. Research Notes in Artificial Intelligence, pp. 74–88. Pitman Publishing, London (1987)
5. Harvey, I., Husbands, P., Cliff, D., et al.: Issues in evolutionary robotics. In: Second Int. Conf. on Simulation of Adaptive Behavior, pp. 364–373. MIT Press, Cambridge (1993)
6. Heaton, J.: Programming Neural Networks with Encog3 in Java. Heaton Research, Chesterfield (2011)
7. Hugues, L., Bredeche, N.: Simbad: An Autonomous Robot Simulation Package for Education and Research. In: Nolfi, S., Baldassarre, G., Calabretta, R., Hallam, J.C.T., Marocco, D., Meyer, J.-A., Miglino, O., Parisi, D. (eds.) SAB 2006. LNCS (LNAI), vol. 4095, pp. 831–842. Springer, Heidelberg (2006)
8. Kohonen, T.: The self-organizing map. Proc. of the IEEE 78(9), 1464–1480 (1990)
9. Lehman, J., Stanley, K.O.: Revising the evolutionary computation abstraction: minimal criteria novelty search. In: Genetic and Evolutionary Computation Conf., pp. 103–110. ACM, New York (2010)
10. Lehman, J., Stanley, K.O.: Abandoning objectives: Evolution through the search for novelty alone. Evolutionary Computation 19(2), 189–223 (2011)
11. Lehman, J., Stanley, K.O.: Evolving a diversity of virtual creatures through novelty search and local competition. In: Genetic and Evolutionary Computation Conf., pp. 211–218. ACM, New York (2011)
12. Mondada, F., Bonani, M., Raemy, X., Pugh, J., Cianci, C., Klaptocz, A., Magnenat, S., Zufferey, J.C., Floreano, D., Martinoli, A.: The e-puck, a robot designed for education in engineering. In: 9th Conf. on Autonomous Robot Systems and Competitions, pp. 59–65. IPCB, Castelo Branco (2009)
13. Mouret, J.: Novelty-based multiobjectivization. New Horizons in Evolutionary Robotics, pp. 139–154. Springer, Berlin (2011)
14. Risi, S., Vanderbleek, S.D., Hughes, C.E., Stanley, K.O.: How novelty search escapes the deceptive trap of learning to learn. In: Genetic and Evolutionary Computation Conf., pp. 153–160. ACM, New York (2009)
15. Soysal, O., Bahgeçi, E., Şahin, E.: Aggregation in swarm robotic systems: Evolution and probabilistic control. Turkish Journal of Electrical Eng. 15(2), 199–225 (2007)
16. Stanley, K.O.: Efficient Evolution of Neural Networks Through Complexification. Ph.D. thesis, Dep. of Computer Sciences, The University of Texas, Austin (2004)
17. Stanley, K.O., Miikkulainen, R.: Evolving neural network through augmenting topologies. Evolutionary Computation 10(2), 99–127 (2002)
18. Trianni, V., Groß, R., Labella, T.H., Şahin, E., Dorigo, M.: Evolving Aggregation Behaviors in a Swarm of Robots. In: Banzhaf, W., Ziegler, J., Christaller, T., Dittrich, P., Kim, J.T. (eds.) ECAL 2003. LNCS (LNAI), vol. 2801, pp. 865–874. Springer, Heidelberg (2003)
19. Whitley, L.D.: Fundamental principles of deception in genetic search. In: Foundations of Genetic Algorithms, pp. 221–241. Morgan Kaufmann, San Mateo (1991)

Measuring Diversity in the Cooperative Particle Swarm Optimizer

Adiel Ismail[1,2] and Andries P. Engelbrecht[2]

[1] Department of Computer Science, University of the Western Cape, South Africa
aismail@uwc.ac.za
[2] Department of Computer Science, University of Pretoria, South Africa
engel@cs.up.ac.za

Abstract. Diversity is an important aspect of population-based search algorithms such as particle swarm optimizers (PSO) since it influences their performance. Diversity is closely linked to the exploration-exploitation tradeoff. High diversity facilitates exploration, which is usually required during the initial iterations of the optimization algorithm. A low diversity is indicative of exploitation of a small area of the search space, desired during the latter part of the optimization process. The success of the Cooperative Particle Swarm Optimizer (CPSO), a variant of PSO which has outperformed the basic PSO on numerous multi-modal functions, has been ascribed to its increased diversity. Although numerous population diversity measures have been proposed for the basic PSO, not all can be readily applied to the CPSO. This paper proposes a measurement of diversity for the CPSO which is compared with three other diversity measures to establish the most appropriate diversity measure for CPSO. The proposed diversity measure is applied to the CPSO on a few well known test functions and compared with the diversity of the basic global best PSO with the objective to justify the claim that the CPSO increases diversity. The paper also investigates whether diversity increases with an increase in the number of subswarms of the CPSO.

1 Introduction

Particle swarm optimization (PSO) is an effective and efficient population based stochastic optimization approach which was originally developed by Eberhart and Kennedy [3]. The basic PSO exhibits good performance on well-known test functions, but tends to converge prematurely on strongly multi-modal test functions [8]. One of the causes of premature convergence in the basic PSO is poor swarm diversity [11]. Numerous diversity measures have been developed for PSO [1], [9], [11], [13] with each approach having numerous variations. Some diversity measures are sensitive to outliers which may result in the diversity not to accurately reflect the search behavior of the swarm with regards to exploration and exploitation.

Diversity has also been used to guide the search in PSO. Several diversity guided PSOs have been developed such as the Attractive-Repulsive PSO

M. Dorigo et al. (Eds.): ANTS 2012, LNCS 7461, pp. 97–108, 2012.

(ARPSO) [11], the modified ARPSO of Pant *et al* [10] and the diversity guided PSO of Cui and Ju [2] amongst others. The accuracy of the diversity measure can therefore influence the performance of the diversity guided PSOs.

The Cooperative Particle Swarm Optimizer (CPSO), a variant of the PSO, differs from the basic PSO in that values for different components of the solution vector are stored in different subswarms. The diversity measures of PSO referred to above cannot readily be applied to CPSO due to the subswarms solving only a section of the original optimization problem. It is not always clear how subswarms which contain partial solution vectors should be treated in the diversity measures.

This paper proposes an alternative measure of diversity for the CPSO and investigates how the proposed method compares with three other diversity measures. The claim that CPSO improves diversity is tested by comparing the diversity of the CPSO with the diversity of the PSO on 9 well-known test problems. This paper also investigates whether the diversity increases with an increase in the number of subswarms of the CPSO.

The rest of the paper is organized as follows: Section 2 provides an overview of PSO and CPSO. Section 3 presents a brief overview of diversity measures. The diversity measures for CPSO are presented in section 4. The experiments and their results are presented and discussed in section 5. The paper is concluded in section 6.

2   Overview of PSO and CPSO

2.1   PSO

PSO is a nature-based stochastic optimization algorithm that emulates the swarm behaviors of bird flocks [7]. PSO consists of a swarm of particles where the position of each particle of the swarm represents a potential solution to the optimization problem. PSO searches for an optimum solution by merely drawing the position of each particle in the swarm toward its own historical best position and toward the position of the historical best particle in a defined neighborhood [6]. The position and velocity of each particle are updated over time. Each particle is viewed as a point in D-dimensional space and has a fitness. The best position in a defined neighbourhood is the position yielding the best fitness. The position and velocity of particle i are denoted by $\mathbf{x}_i$ and $\mathbf{v}_i$, respectively. The best position of particle i since the start of optimization is referred to as the personal best position and is represented as $\mathbf{y}_i$ and 'pbest' its corresponding fitness. The best position of all personal best positions in the entire swarm is represented by $\hat{\mathbf{y}}$ with 'gbest' as its corresponding fitness. This PSO is known as the global best PSO. The position and velocity are updated as follows:

$$v_i^d(t+1) = w \cdot v_i^d(t) + c_1 \cdot r_1^d(t) \cdot (y_i^d(t) - x_i^d(t)) + c_2 \cdot r_2^d(t) \cdot (\hat{y}^d(t) - x_i^d(t)) \quad (1)$$

$$x_i^d(t+1) = x_i^d(t) + v_i^d(t+1) \quad (2)$$

where $d = 1, 2, ..., n$, $i = 1, 2, ..., S$, and S is the size of the swarm; w is the inertia weight with $0 \leq w < 1$; constants c_1 and c_2 are called *acceleration coefficients*; $\mathbf{r}_1$ and $\mathbf{r}_2$ are two vectors containing random numbers uniformly distributed in $(0, 1)$; and t denotes the iteration number. The second and third terms in equation (1) are respectively referred to as the cognitive and the social components.

2.2 Cooperative Particle Swarm Optimizer (CPSO)

In PSO, a position vector of a particle serves as a complete solution vector for the optimization problem. In CPSO the solution vector of the optimization problem is split into K components with each component optimized in a separate subswarm. This CPSO is denoted as CPSO-S_K. If $K = n$, then each subswarm consists of 1-dimensional particles. This special case is denoted by CPSO-S. A particle in a subswarm represents only part of the complete solution vector and its fitness cannot be calculated in isolation from the other subswarms. All swarms will have to share their information, i.e. cooperate, to form a complete solution vector [14]. To represent the n-dimensional solution a context vector is required. One way of constructing a context vector is to simply concatenate the global best positions from all K subswarms, arranged in the order 1 to K.

The rest of the discussion focuses on the CPSO-S, but it is easily applicable to CPSO-S_K. The fitness of particle i in subswarm j is equal to the function value after applying the objective function to a temporarily updated context vector where the j-th component of the context vector has been replaced with the position of particle i in subswarm j, but only for the duration of the fitness calculation. Note, that for the evaluation of the fitness of particle i in subswarm j, all components of the context vector except component j retained the global best positions of the other $(n-1)$ subswarms.

The algorithm for the CPSO-S as defined in [14] appears in Algorithm 1, where R_j, $R_j.\mathbf{x}_i$, $R_j.\mathbf{v}_i$ and $R_j.\mathbf{y}_i$ refer, respectively, to subswarm j and the position, velocity and personal best position of particle i in subswarm j. The global best particle in subswarm j is denoted by $R_j.\hat{\mathbf{y}}$. The context vector is defined as $(R_1.\hat{\mathbf{y}}, R_2.\hat{\mathbf{y}}, ..., R_n.\hat{\mathbf{y}})$. The operator $\mathbf{b}(j, z)$ replaces the j-th component of the context vector with z to produce $(R_1.\hat{\mathbf{y}}, R_2.\hat{\mathbf{y}}, ..., R_{j-1}.\hat{\mathbf{y}}, z, R_{j+1}.\hat{\mathbf{y}}, ..., R_n.\hat{\mathbf{y}})$.

3 Diversity Measures

Population diversity can be used to monitor swarm behaviour, i.e. the degree of convergence or divergence [16]. It is therefor important that a measurement of population diversity provide accurate information about the swarm's behaviour, with regards to exploration and exploitation. However, not all diversity measures accurately reflect such information as a result of the diversity measures' sensitivity to outliers [9].

3.1 Characteristics of Diversity Measure

Given a PSO with an initial high diversity and a sequence of global best solutions $\{\hat{\mathbf{y}}_t\}_{t=0}^{K}$, then the PSO is said to converge to point $\mathbf{p}$, a weighted average of the

---

Algorithm 1. The CPSO algorithm

Create and initialize n one-dimensional PSOs: $R_j, j \in [1..n]$
repeat
    for each swarm $j \in [1..n]$
        for each particle $i \in [1..s]$
            if $f(\mathbf{b}(j, R_j.\mathbf{x}_i)) < f(\mathbf{b}(j, R_j.\mathbf{y}_i))$
                then $R_j.\mathbf{y}_i = R_j.\mathbf{x}_i$
            if $f(\mathbf{b}(j, R_j.\mathbf{y}_i)) < f(\mathbf{b}(j, R_j.\hat{\mathbf{y}}))$
                then $R_j.\hat{\mathbf{y}} = R_j.\mathbf{y}_i$
        endfor
        Update all particles in R_j using equations (1) and (2)
    endfor
until stopping condition is true

---

global best and personal best positions, if $\lim_{(t \to +\infty)} \hat{\mathbf{y}}_t = \mathbf{p}$, where t denotes time step [15]. In this case the diversity of the swarm at time step t approaches zero as t approaches infinity. Under these conditions an accurate measure of diversity should reflect an average decrease proportional with time to a value that approaches zero [9].

3.2 Diversity Measures for PSO

Olorunda and Engelbrecht [9] investigated a number of diversity measures which included (a) the swarm diameter and swarm radius, (b) the average distance around the swarm center, (c) the normalized average distance around the swarm center, (d) the average of the average distance around all particles in the swarm, and (e) swarm coherence (defined as the swarm center divided by the average speed of all particles in the swarm). Olorunda and Engelbrecht concluded that the average distance around the swarm center is a more robust measure than the other diversity measures in the presence of outliers. The 'average distance around the swarm center' is defined as,

$$\text{diversity}_1(R) = \frac{1}{S} \cdot \sum_{i=1}^{S} \sqrt{\sum_{j=1}^{n} (x_i^j - \bar{x}^j)^2} \tag{3}$$

with

$$\bar{x}^j = \frac{1}{S} \sum_{i=1}^{S} x_i^j \tag{4}$$

where R denotes the swarm, S is the size of the swarm, n is the dimensionality of the optimization problem, x_i^j is the value of dimension j of particle i, and $\bar{x}^j$ is the average value for dimension j over all particles.

The diversity formula in equation (3) is used in the experiments of this study to calculate the diversity of the PSO. A normalized version of the average distance around the swarm center was successfully used to guide the search in Attractive-Repulsive PSO (ARPSO) developed in [11].

Shi and Eberhart [13] defined several population diversity measures based on a particle's (a) position, (b) velocity and (c) cognitive term. Position diversity is measured using either an element-wise or a dimension-wise approach. A simple example indicated that element-wise diversity could not differentiate between two vastly different diversity situations. Results in [13] also confirmed that the element-wise approach could not provide accurate information about the distribution of particles. Dimension-wise diversity has a clearer geometric interpretation than the element-wise diversity measure, while velocity diversity provides dynamic information of particles and measures the distribution of the current velocities of the particles. The formula for cognitive diversity measurement is similar to the position diversity measurement except that all references to the particle's current position are replaced with its personal best position.

In the knowledge-based cooperative particle swarm optimizer (KCPSO) of Jie et al [5], a distinction is made between diversity of a subswarm and diversity of the entire swarm. Jie et al describes the distribution of the particles locally in a subswarm using a formula similar to equation (3). The diversity of the entire swarm in KCPSO is calculated using a formula similar to that in equation (3) except that, (a) all references to a particle's current position are replaced with the particle's personal best position, (b) the average of all particles in the entire swarm is replaced with the average of all personal best positions, and (c) the diversity is normalized by dividing the diversity by the distance of the longest diagonal in the search space. The diversity measure of Jie et al [5] uses only the personal best position of a subswarm, while ignoring all other particles in each subswarm. This approach may not accurately reflect the diversity of the subswarm.

4   Diversity Measures for CPSO

The 'average distance around the swarm center', as a proven robust diversity measure, is applied in this paper to calculate the diversity of the CPSO, unless stated otherwise. Applying this formula to the CPSO poses a problem, since the formula assumes that each particle in the swarm is a complete solution vector. This is not the case in the CPSO. Each particle in a subswarm represents only a part of a solution vector. To address this problem four methods, denoted by CPSO-Div 1 to CPSO-Div 4, are used to calculate the diversity of the CPSO.

The approach that generates solution vectors for fitness evaluation in CPSO is also used in the first method, i.e. CPSO-Div 1, to generate solution vectors which are subsequently used to calculate the diversity of the CPSO. CPSO uses the method outlined in section 2.2 to calculate a fitness value for each particle in each subswarm. This approach generates a solution vector for each particle in each CPSO subswarm. Since there are n subswarms, each of size m, the total number of particles in all subswarms is equal to $m \times n$. Hence, the total number of complete solution vectors generated during each iteration of the CPSO algorithm is $m \times n$. These solution vectors will subsequently be used to calculate the population diversity of CPSO. In the implementation of the proposed diversity measure the diversity of the CPSO is calculated immediately before the end of each iteration. In this approach the formula in equation (3) is applied to all $m \times n$ solution vectors. Note, as the swarm converges, $(x_i^j - \bar{x}^j)^2 \to 0$ for all dimensions j for all particles i, the diversity measure, CPSO-Div 1, reduces to zero with time.

The second method does not use complete solution vectors and the diversity is calculated based on the particles in each subswarm. This method uses the dimension-wise definition based on the L_1 norm in [13]. The center $\bar{x}$ of the entire swarm is computed. Then an n-dimensional vector is computed as follows: For each dimension of the n-dimensional vector, corresponding to a subswarm, the average of the absolute difference between each particle in the subswarm and corresponding dimension of the swarm center is calculated. The average of all dimensions of the computed vector is subsequently returned as the diversity of the CPSO. This approach is referred to as CPSO-Div 2, computed using,

$$\text{diversity}_2(R) = \frac{1}{n} \cdot \sum_{j=1}^{n} \left(\frac{1}{S} \cdot \sum_{i=1}^{S} |x_i^j - \bar{x}^j| \right) \tag{5}$$

Note, as the swarm converges $|x_i^j - \bar{x}^j| \to 0$ for all dimensions j for all particles i. Although the diversity measure, CPSO-Div 2, reduces to zero with time the actual solution vectors used for evaluation of fitness are not taken into account when calculating the diversity. Since the diversity is not directly based on the solution vectors of the CPSO, CPSO-Div 2 may inaccurately reflect the diversity of the swarm.

In the third method, instead of using a context vector which consists of the global best particles from each of the subswarms, all possible combinations of all particles in all subswarms are used to form n-dimensional solution vectors. The solution vectors can be generated using n nested for-loops, with each for-loop associated with one of the n subswarms consisting of 1-dimensional particles. The value of the running variable of each for-loop indexes a particle in the specific subswarm whose position is copied to the corresponding component of the solution vector. This approach will be referred to as CPSO-Div 3.

The fourth method called CPSO-Div 4 corresponds to the approach proposed by Jie *et al* in section 3. Diversity is calculated based on the personal best positions and not on the current positions of the particles. This approach is reminiscent of the normalized average distance around the swarm center, except that the pool of current positions is replaced with the pool of personal best positions. As the swarm converges, $(y_i^j - \bar{y}^j)^2 \to 0$ for all dimensions i of all particles j, resulting in the diversity measure, CPSO-Div 4, to reduce to zero with time.

5   Experiments and Results

The objective of this section is to describe and report on the experiments performed in this paper. For this purpose, section 5.1 describes the experiments and defines the test functions and its parameters, while section 5.2 reports the results of the experiments.

5.1   Experimental Procedure

The goal of this paper is to answer the following research questions:

1. Which diversity measures are appropriate for CPSO?
2. Which diversity measure is the best to use for CPSO?
3. Does CPSO increase diversity compared to global best PSO?
4. Does diversity increase with an increase in the number of subswarms?

To answer questions (1) and (2) the four diversity measures in section 4 were applied to the 9 well-known optimization test problems defined in table 1. The dimension of the test functions was set to five, since a relatively large value for the dimension makes the application of CPSO-Div 3 infeasible as pointed out in section 4.

To answer question (3) the diversity values produced by the best diversity measure approach as identified by question (2) are compared with the diversity values of the global best PSO. The dimension of the test functions was set to 30.

To answer question (4) the diversity of a few CPSO variants is investigated. The best diversity measure as identified by question (2) was then used to calculate the diversity of the CPSO-S_K where K varies from 3 to 30, i.e. $K = 3, 6, 10, 15, 30$. The dimension of the test functions was set to 30.

In the experiments the size of each subswarm for the five dimensional test functions was set to 10 and the CPSO was executed for a total of 10000 function evaluations or 200 (=10000/(5 (number of subswarms) × 10 (number of particles)) iterations. For the 30 dimensional test functions the size of each subswarm was set to 20 and all variants of the CPSO were executed for 200000 function evaluations, bearing in mind that the CPSO-S require 600 (= number of subswarms (30) × number of particles (20)) function evaluations per iteration. The CPSO-S_2, CPSO-S_3, CPSO-S_5 and CPSO-S_{10} require respectively 40, 60, 100 and 200 function evaluations per iteration. Results plotted are averages calculated over 30 simulations.

The inertia weight, w, and acceleration coefficients c_1 and c_2 were set as suggested by Shi and Eberhart [4] to 0.72, 1.49 and 1.49, respectively, for both the global best PSO and all the CPSO variants.

The Sphere function is unimodal, while the remaining test functions are multimodal. In general, to prevent n one dimensional searches on separable test functions, functions are rotated. In this paper the Griewank test function was rotated. For rotation, Salomon's method [12] was used to construct an n-dimensional orthogonal matrix which was then left multiplied by the particle's position vector. The resulting vector was used to determine a particle's fitness.

5.2   Experimental Results

Investigating Research Question 1: The average diversity values calculated over 30 simulations for each of the four diversity measures as defined in section 4

Table 1. Definitions and parameters of test functions

Function (where $D = 30$)	Domain	Name
$f_1(\mathbf{x}) = \sum_{i=1}^{D} x_i^2$	$[-100, 100]^D$	Sphere
$f_2(\mathbf{x}) = \sum_{i=1}^{\frac{D}{2}} 100(x_{2i} - x_{2i-1}^2)^2 + (1 - x_{2i-1})^2$	$[-10, 10]^D$	Rosenbrock
$f_3(\mathbf{x}) = -20 \cdot \exp\left(-0.2 \cdot \sqrt{\frac{1}{D} \sum_{i=1}^{n} x_i^2}\right)$ $- \exp\left(\frac{1}{n} \sum_{i=1}^{D} \cos(2\pi x_i)\right) + 20 + e$	$[-32, 32]^D$	Ackley
$f_4(\mathbf{x}) = \frac{1}{4000} \sum_{i=1}^{D} x_i^2 - \prod_{i=1}^{D} \cos(\frac{x_i}{\sqrt{i}}) + 1$	$[-600, 600]^D$	Griewank
$f_5(\mathbf{x}) = \sum_{i=1}^{D}(x_i^2 - 10\cos(2\pi x_i) + 10)$	$[-5.12, 5.12]^D$	Rastrigin
$f_6(\mathbf{x}) = \sum_{i=1}^{D}(y_i^2 - 10\cos(2\pi y_i) + 10)$ where $y_i = \begin{cases} x_i & \text{if } \|x_i\| < \frac{1}{2} \\ \frac{round(2x_i)}{2} & \text{if } \|x_i\| \geq \frac{1}{2} \end{cases}$	$[-5.12, 5.12]^D$	Non-continuous Rastrigin
$f_7(\mathbf{x}) = -\sum_{i=1}^{D} x_i \sin\left(\sqrt{\|x_i\|}\right)$	$[-500, 500]^D$	Schwefel
$f_8(\mathbf{x}) = \frac{1}{4000} \sum_{i=1}^{D} x_i^2 - \prod_{i=1}^{D} \cos(\frac{x_i}{\sqrt{i}}) + 1$ $\mathbf{y} = M * \mathbf{x}$	$[-600, 600]^D$	Rotated Griewank
$f_9(\mathbf{x}) = \frac{\pi}{D}(10\sin^2(\pi \cdot y_i)$ $+ \sum_{i=1}^{D-1}(y_i - 1)^2 \cdot (1 + 10\sin^2(\pi \cdot y_{i+1}))$ $+(y_D - 1)^2) + \sum_{i=1}^{D} u(x, 10, 100, 4)$ where $y_i = 1 + \frac{1}{4}(x_i + 1)$, $u(x, a, k, m) = \begin{cases} k(x_i - a)^m, & \text{if } x_i > a \\ 0, & \text{if } -a \leq x_i \leq a \\ k(-x_i - a)^m & \text{if } x_i < -a \end{cases}$	$[-50, 50]^D$	Generalized Penalized function

on the five-dimensional test functions are plotted in figure 1. Firstly, an important observation is that all the diversity measures of CPSO-S decrease towards zero on all functions. Secondly, plots in figure 1 indicate that the rate of reduction is the same. All four diversity measures satisfy the criteria as indicated in section 4. Although the CPSO-Div 3 maintained the highest average diversity its applicability to functions with higher dimensions is infeasible as indicated in section 4. Hence, the plots in figure 1 indicate that the remaining diversity measures are all appropriate for CPSO-S, except CPSO-Div 3 for high dimensional functions.

Investigating Research Question 2: From subfigures (a) to (i) in figure 1, CPSO-Div 3 maintained the highest average diversity for each iteration except for the Griewank (f_4) function. CPSO-Div 4 generally maintained a high diversity except on the Sphere and Ackley functions, where the diversity was the smallest of all the diversity methods for a larger part of the duration of optimization. CPSO-Div 1 and CPSO-Div 2 maintained identical diversities for functions f_1 and f_3 to f_8, while CPSO-Div 1 exceeded the diversity values reached by CPSO-Div 2 midway through optimization on function f_2. Although the CPSO-Div 3 maintained the highest average diversity its applicability to functions with higher dimensions is infeasible as indicated in section 4. Hence, the plots in figure 1 indicate that the remaining diversity measures are all appropriate for CPSO. The best diversity measure(s) on higher dimensional test functions are CPSO-Div 1 and CPSO-Div 2, with CPSO-Div 1 achieving slightly better diversity than CPSO-Div 2 on the Rosenbrock function (f_2). The best diversity measure for CPSO based on diversity plots of the test functions in this paper is CPSO-Div 1.

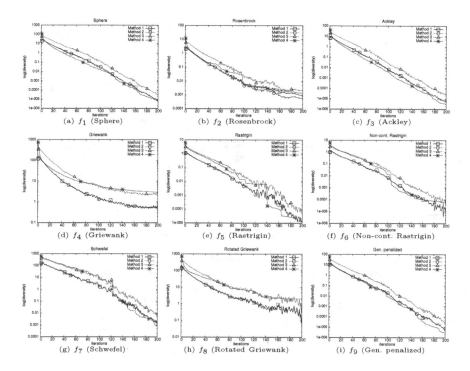

Fig. 1. Plots of average diversity for each of the four diversity methods for 5D functions

Investigating Research Question 3: The diversity of the global best PSO and the CPSO-S on the 30 dimensional test functions listed in table 1 was also investigated. CPSO-Div 1 as the best diversity approach for CPSO was used to calculate the diversity of the CPSO-S, while the diversity of the PSO was calculated using equation 3. Figure 3 contains plots of the average diversity for each of the 9 test functions. CPSO-S maintained a higher average diversity than global best PSO throughout the optimization process except for the Rosenbrock function (f_2), where the low diversity maintained by the CPSO-S can be ascribed to the CPSO-S converging much quicker than the global best PSO. From the plots it is clear that CPSO-S generally maintained a higher average diversity than global best PSO. This proves the claim that CPSO-S (or CPSO) maintains a higher diversity than the global best PSO.

Investigating Research Question 4: The effect of an increased number of swarms in CPSO on diversity was also investigated. CPSO-Div 1 was used to calculate the diversity of the CPSO-S_K where K varies from 3 to 30, i.e. $K = 3, 6, 10, 15, 30$. The experiments were performed on the test functions listed in table 1 with dimension 30. Plots of the average diversity for each of the 9 test functions appear in figure 3. The plots indicate that an increase in number of swarms generally resulted in an increase in diversity except for the Rosenbrock

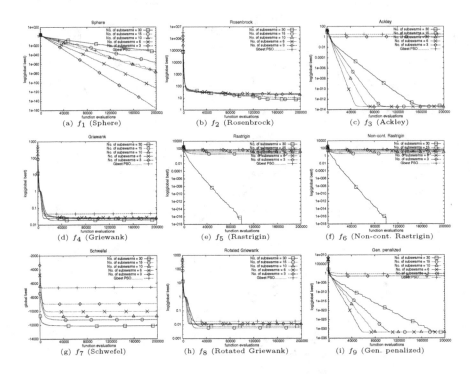

Fig. 2. Plots of average global best for subswarms of different sizes for 30D functions

function (f_2) where the opposite is observed. As shown in figure 3(b) the CPSO-S and CPSO-S$_{15}$ converged quickly to the minimum indicating excellent exploitation which resulted in lower diversity on the Rosenbrock function (f_2), while the other CPSO variants were still exploring the search space thus reflecting a larger diversity. The same behaviour is also observed in figure 3(d) on the Griewank function (f_4). In figure 3(e) the CPSO-S and CPSO-S$_{15}$ maintained a high diversity while exploring the search space and managed to find the optimum, while all other CPSO variants converged prematurely as reflected in figure 2(e). In figure 2(e) the premature convergence to local optima by all CPSO-S variants, except CPSO-S and CPSO-S$_{15}$, lead to a lower diversity of the swarm. For the Rastrigin function (f_5) the low diversity maintained by the CPSO-S - with the largest number of subswarms - can be ascribed to quicker convergence which is experienced earlier than all other CPSO variants. The plots indicate that an increase in the number of subswarms results in an increased diversity.

A comparison of plots in figures 2 and 3 also indicates that an increase in diversity, increased performance of the CPSO as reflected for functions f_4 to f_8 functions, while the increased diversity of the CPSO-S resulted in slower convergence on functions f_1. However, the decreasing graphs in figures 2(a) and (i) indicate that with increased optimization time the optima could be found by

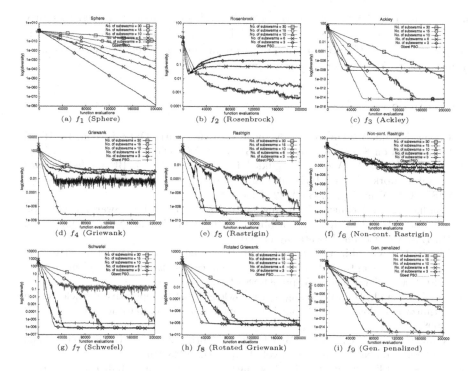

Fig. 3. Plots of average diversity of the CPSO-S$_K$ for $K = 3, 6, 10, 15, 30$ (30D test functions)

the CPSO-S on these two functions. Thus, increased diversity generally improves performance of the CPSO-S.

6 Conclusion

This paper proposed an alternative measure of diversity for the CPSO and compared the proposed method with 3 other diversity measures. The best diversity measure of the four approaches was identified and used to compare the diversity of the CPSO-S with the diversity of the global best PSO to test the claim that CPSO improves diversity. This paper also investigated whether diversity increases with an increase in the number of subswarms of the CPSO. Application of the four diversity measures to nine well-known test functions indicated that the diversity measure, which is based on solution vectors generated by using all possible combinations of particles in all subswarms, maintained the highest diversity during optimization. This approach becomes infeasible for objective functions with a relatively large dimension and large swarm size. According to the diversity plots the proposed diversity measure which is based on the same context vector used for fitness evaluations in CPSO managed to maintain a diversity which is at least as good as the diversity of the dimension-wise approach proposed in [13]. Results of experiments also indicated that the higher diversity maintained by the CPSO-S on multi-modal functions lead to improved solutions compared to other CPSO variants and that in general diversity increased with an increase in the number of subswarms of CPSO.

References

1. Cheng, S., Shi, Y.: Diversity Control in Particle Swarm Optimization. In: IEEE Symposium on Swarm Intelligence (SIS), pp. 1–9 (2011)
2. Cui, Y., Ju, S.-G.: A diversity guided PSO combined with BP for feedforward neural networks. In: 3rd International Congress on Image and Signal Processing, CISP 2010, Yantai, pp. 1538–1542 (2010)
3. Eberhart, R.C., Kennedy, J.: A New Optimizer Using Particle Swarm Theory. In: 6th International Symposium on Micro Machine and Human Science, pp. 39–43. IEEE Service Center, Piscataway (1995)
4. Eberhart, R.C., Shi, Y.: Comparing inertia weights and constriction factors in particle swarm optimization. In: IEEE Congress on Evolutionary Computation (CEC 2000), San Diego, CA, pp. 84–88 (2000)
5. Jie, J., Zeng, J., Han, C., Wang, Q.: Knowledge-based cooperative particle swarm optimization. Journal of Applied Mathematics and Computation 205, 861–873 (2008)
6. Kennedy, J., Eberhart, R.C.: Particle Swarm Optimization. In: IEEE International Conference on Neural Networks, vol. 4, pp. 1942–1948 (1995)
7. Kennedy, J.F., Kennedy, J., Eberhart, R.C.: Swarm Intelligence. Morgan Kaufmann Publishers (2001)
8. Liang, J.J., Qin, A.K., Suganthan, P.N., Baskar, S.: Comprehensive Learning Particle Swarm Optimizer for Global Optimization of Multimodal Functions. IEEE Trans. Evol. Comput. 10(3) (June 2006)
9. Olorunda, O., Engelbrecht, A.P.: Measuring Exploration/Exploitation in Particle Swarms using Swarm Diversity. In: IEEE World Congress on Computational Intelligence (CEC 2008), pp. 1128–1134 (2008)
10. Pant, M., Radha, T., Singh, V.P.: A Simple Diversity Guided Particle Swarm Optimization. In: IEEE Congress on Evolutionary Computation (CEC 2007), pp. 3294–3299 (2007)
11. Riget, J., Vesterstrøm, J.S.: A Diversity-Guided Particle Swarm Optimizer - the ARPSO, Technical report, EVALife, Denmark (2002)
12. Salomon, R.: Reevaluating genetic algorithm performance under coordinate rotation of benchmark functions. BioSystems 39, 263–278 (1996)
13. Shi, Y., Eberhart, R.: Population diversity of particle swarms. In: Congress on Evolutionary Computation (CEC 2008), pp. 1063–1067 (2008)
14. Van den Bergh, F., Engelbrecht, A.P.: A Cooperative Approach to Particle Swarm Optimization. IEEE Transactions on Evolutionary Computation 8(3), 225–239 (2004)
15. Van den Bergh, F.: An analysis of particle swarm optimizers. PhD Thesis, Department of Computer Science, University of Pretoria (2002)
16. Zhan, Z., Zhang, J., Li, Y., Chung, H.S.: Adaptive Particle Swarm Optimization. IEEE Transactions on Systems, Man and Cybernetics - Part B: Cybernetics 139(6), 1362–1381 (2009)

Multi-armed Bandit Formulation of the Task Partitioning Problem in Swarm Robotics

Giovanni Pini, Arne Brutschy, Gianpiero Francesca,
Marco Dorigo, and Mauro Birattari

IRIDIA, Université Libre de Bruxelles, Brussels, Belgium
{gpini,arne.brutschy,gianpiero.francesca,mdorigo,mbiro}@ulb.ac.be

Abstract. Task partitioning is a way of organizing work consisting in the decomposition of a task into smaller sub-tasks that can be tackled separately. Task partitioning can be beneficial in terms of reduction of physical interference, increase of efficiency, higher parallelism, and exploitation of specialization. However, task partitioning also entails costs in terms of coordination efforts and overheads that can reduce its benefits. It is therefore important to decide when to make use of task partitioning. In this paper we show that such a decision can be formulated as a multi-armed bandit problem. This is advantageous since the theoretical properties of the multi-armed bandit problem are well understood and several algorithms have been proposed for tackling it. We carry out our study in simulation, using a swarm robotics foraging scenario as a testbed. We test an ad-hoc algorithm and two algorithms proposed in the literature for multi-armed bandit problems. The results confirm that the problem of selecting whether to partition a task can be formulated as a multi-armed bandit problem and tackled with existing algorithms.

1 Introduction

Task partitioning refers to the act of dividing a task into a sequence of sub-tasks that can be tackled separately [9]. Many social insects, such as ants, bees, and wasps employ task partitioning for organizing their work. The benefits that insects draw from task partitioning are many: decrease of physical interference between individuals, higher exploitation of specialization, higher parallelism and efficiency in performing tasks [17]. Swarms of robots could benefit from task partitioning in the same ways. However, task partitioning also entails costs that are mainly a consequence of the coordination required to link different sub-tasks one to another. Therefore, task partitioning should be employed only when the benefits overcome the costs. In the rest of the paper, we will refer to the problem of selecting whether to employ task partitioning as the *task partitioning problem*.

In a previous work, we proposed a method that allows the robots to choose when to employ task partitioning, on the basis of the costs involved [16]. In this paper, we extend the work by reformulating the task partitioning problem as a multi-armed bandit problem [3]. The multi-armed bandit problem consists in repeatedly selecting actions to be performed in order to maximize a reward

M. Dorigo et al. (Eds.): ANTS 2012, LNCS 7461, pp. 109–120, 2012.

that depends on the actions taken. In terms of the multi-armed bandit, the task partitioning problem can be reformulated as the problem of choosing between partitioning the overall task and performing it as an unpartitioned task, with the goal of minimizing the resulting costs. Each robot tackles the multi-armed bandit problem independently of the other robots: it selects its actions on the basis of its individual estimate of the costs. The advantage of formulating the task partitioning problem as a multi-armed bandit stems from the fact that the latter is widely studied in statistics. Consequently, its theoretical properties are well understood and, most importantly, one can select among several existing algorithms, without the need of implementing ad-hoc solutions every time. The approach presented in this paper can be used to solve the task partitioning problem in situations in which the robots can measure or estimate the costs associated to employing task partitioning.

Multi-armed bandit problems are characterized by a tradeoff between *exploitation* and *exploration*. A balance has to be found between "exploring the environment to find profitable actions" [2] and "taking the empirically best action as often as possible" [2]. Also in the task partitioning problem there is such a tradeoff. Task partitioning should be exploited as much as possible, if the expected resulting costs are low. However, changes in the environment can affect costs. Therefore, the option of using task partitioning should be reconsidered in time, in order to detect such changes.

The rest of the paper is organized as follows. In Section 2 we review the existing work on task partitioning in swarm robotics. In Section 3 we describe the specific problem tackled in this work and present the three algorithms that we consider for tackling the problem. In Section 4 we briefly describe the experimental setup and the tools used to carry out the research. In Section 5 we present and comment the results of the experiments. Finally, in Section 6 we summarize the contribution of the work and we describe directions for future research.

2   Related Work

The biology literature is rich in studies devoted to task partitioning. In particular, task partitioning has been observed in social insects in the organization of tasks such as material transportation, nest excavation, and waste removal [17]. Swarm robotics draws inspiration from the world of social insects in the implementation of robotic systems composed of a large number of relatively simple cooperating robots [5]. The tasks performed by swarms of robots have often a counterpart in the world of social insects. As social insects draw benefits from task partitioning, it is interesting to study the application of task partitioning to swarms of robots performing similar tasks.

While in biology the body of literature on task partitioning is large, few works in swarm robotics have been devoted to this topic. In the majority of the works, the focus is on the use of task partitioning as a means for reducing physical interference. In [7], a foraging task is partitioned into sub-tasks developing in separate areas, each one assigned a-priori to a different robot. A similar work is presented in [14], with the difference that in this case the areas are not assigned statically and several robots can share the same working area. In [18], a swarm of robots has to forage for objects. Objects are progressively moved towards the nest by different robots, each working in an area of a given radius. The study shows that the higher the number of robots, the smaller the working area radius should be. The work as been extended to allow for a dynamical regulation of the working areas size [10] and to relocate the working areas depending on the objects distribution in the environment [11]. In [12], a swarm of robots has to perform foraging in an environment composed of several corridors. The authors show that task partitioning improves performance when the corridors are too narrow for two robots traveling in opposite directions to pass at the same time.

In a previous work we studied task partitioning in a foraging task and proposed a simple method that allows a swarm of robots to tackle the task partitioning problem [8]. In a follow up research the method has been extended to explicitly take into account costs linked to task-partitioning [16].

3   Problem Description and Methodology

We study the task partitioning problem: how to choose whether to partition a given task, or to perform it as a whole, unpartitioned task. When task partitioning is employed, the given task is partitioned into a sequence of sub-tasks. In this paper, we focus on the case in which there are two sub-tasks. The sub-tasks are linked by an interface of finite capacity. The output of the first sub-task can be stored at the interface and be subsequently used as the input for the second sub-task. In this paper we use a swarm robotics foraging scenario as testbed.

Figure 1 provides a schematic representation of the environment and the problem we study in this work. In the foraging scenario, the robots repeat an object retrieval task: harvesting an object from the *source*, and storing it at the *nest*. The environment is composed of two areas, one containing the source and the other containing the nest, separated by a *cache*. The robots cannot cross the cache, but they can use it to transfer objects from one area to the other. A *corridor* links the two areas and allows the robots to reach one from the other.

In the setup described, using the cache allows the robots to partition the object retrieval task into two sub-tasks: the first consists in harvesting an object from the source and drop it in the cache, the second in picking up an object from the cache and storing it at the nest. Therefore, the cache acts as an interface between sub-tasks. Conversely, the use of the corridor allows the robots to perform object retrieval as an unpartitioned task: a robot can directly reach the source from the nest and the other way around, harvesting and storing objects.

Each robot chooses whether to employ task partitioning in two situations, represented by a question mark in Fig. 1. First, after taking an object from the source, a robot decides whether to use the cache to DROP the object, or to use the corridor and STORE the object at the nest. Second, after storing an object in the nest, a robot decides whether to PICK UP an object from the cache, or to use the corridor and HARVEST an object from the source.

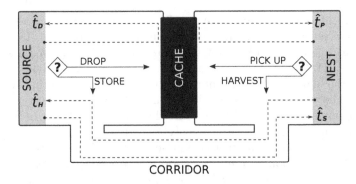

Fig. 1. Representation of the studied foraging problem. Foraging consists in harvesting objects from the source and storing them at the nest. Robots choose between using task partitioning (i.e., use the cache) or not (i.e., use the corridor) in two cases, marked with "?" in the figure. After taking an object from the source, a robot chooses between STORE it at the nest or DROP it at the cache. Upon storing an object in the nest, a robot chooses between PICK UP the next at the cache or HARVEST one from the source. The dashed arrows represent cost estimates $\hat{t}_i$ that the robot associates to each action.

In this work, we show that the task partitioning problem can be formulated as a multi-armed bandit problem. In the multi-armed bandit problem, the goal is to maximize a reward. If the dual problem of minimizing costs is tackled, algorithms and techniques for the bandit problem can be employed for the task partitioning problem as well. The nature of the costs depends on the specific task and on the characteristics of the environment. Typically costs are represented by resources needed to perform the task. Examples are: energy, time required to complete a task, or materials employed. In the foraging scenario studied in this paper, the goal is to maximize the number of objects delivered to the nest. This can be done by maximizing the throughput; we therefore express costs in terms of time.

Each robot keeps a cost estimate for each of the possible four actions: i) HARVEST an object from the source (using the corridor), ii) PICK UP an object from the cache, iii) DROP an object in the cache, and iv) STORE an object in the nest (using the corridor). Each estimate $\hat{t}_i$ is computed as:

$$\hat{t}_i \leftarrow (1 - \alpha)\,\hat{t}_i + \alpha\,t_M \,, \tag{1}$$

where $\alpha \in (0, 1]$ is a weight factor. t_M is the measure of the time taken by the last action performed by the robot, its meaning depending on the specific estimate being updated (refer to the dashed arrows in Fig. 1). When estimating the cost $\hat{t}_H$ of HARVESTING an object from the source, t_M measures the time from the moment an object is stored in the nest till the moment a new object is harvested from the source. Analogously, when estimating the cost $\hat{t}_S$ of STORING an object in the nest, t_M denotes the time measured from the moment an object is taken from the source to the moment it is deposited in the nest. When estimating the cost $\hat{t}_D$ of DROPPING objects in the cache, t_M measures the time from the moment an object is taken from the source, to the moment the following one is taken from the source, after dropping the first in the cache. Analogously, for the cost $\hat{t}_P$ of PICKING UP, t_M accounts for the time between two objects being stored in the nest, with the second one taken from the cache. These estimates are used by the robots to decide between using the cache or the corridor.

In this work we compare three algorithms, used by the robots to make this decision. The first is an *ad-hoc* algorithm that we proposed in a previous work [16]. Using the ad-hoc algorithm, after taking an object from the source, a robot has a probability P_p of DROPPING it in the cache:

$$
P_p = \begin{cases} \left[1 + e^{-S((\hat{t}_H + \hat{t}_S)/(\hat{t}_P + \hat{t}_D)-1)}\right]^{-1}, & \text{if } \hat{t}_H + \hat{t}_S > (\hat{t}_P + \hat{t}_D) \\ \left[1 + e^{-S(1-(\hat{t}_P + \hat{t}_D)/(\hat{t}_H + \hat{t}_S))}\right]^{-1}, & \text{if } \hat{t}_H + \hat{t}_S \leq (\hat{t}_P + \hat{t}_D) \end{cases}, \qquad (2)
$$

where S is a steepness factor. The higher its value, the higher the degree of exploitation of the algorithm. Analogously, after delivering an object to the nest, a robot has the same probability P_p of PICKING UP the following one from the cache. Thus, the object retrieval task is performed as a partitioned task with a probability of P_p and performed as an unpartitioned task with a probability $1 - P_p$.

We compare the ad-hoc algorithm with two other algorithms that have been previously proposed in the literature to tackle multi-armed bandit problems. The first of the two, which we will refer to as *UCB*, is a modified version of the UCB1 policy presented in [2] that, in turn, is derived from the index-based policy described in [1]. Using UCB, after taking an object from the source, a robot DROPS it in the cache if:

$$
\hat{t}_D - \gamma\sqrt{\frac{2\ln(n_D + n_S)}{n_D}} < \hat{t}_S - \gamma\sqrt{\frac{2\ln(n_D + n_S)}{n_S}}, \qquad (3)
$$

otherwise it takes the corridor to STORE the object in the nest. n_D is the number of times that the robot selected the cache for DROPPING an object, n_S the number of times the robot used the corridor for STORING an object in the nest. γ is a parameter that allows to tune the degree of exploration of the algorithm: the higher the value, the higher the exploration. An analogous formula is used to choose between PICKING UP an object from the cache or HARVEST it from the source using the corridor.

The third algorithm studied in this work, is the *ε-greedy* algorithm, a simple algorithm widely employed in reinforcement learning [19]. With the ε-greedy algorithm, the action perceived as the less costly is selected with a probability $1 - \varepsilon$, otherwise a random action is selected. ε defines the degree of exploration of the algorithm: the higher the value, the higher the exploration.

Notice the difference between the ad-hoc algorithm and the other two. In the former, no distinction is made between the two decision points: both at the nest and at the source there is the same probability P_p of employing task partitioning.

In the UCB and the ε-greedy algorithms, the robots discriminate between the two cases when making their choice.

For all the algorithms, a *give up* mechanism allows the robots to abandon the choice of using the cache. Without this mechanism, deadlocks could occur in two cases. The first case happens if all the robots are trying to drop objects in the cache and the cache is full. The second case happens if all the robots are trying to pick up objects from the cache, and the cache is empty. Giving up is implemented using a timeout: the robot measures the time it has been trying to access the cache, and abandons its choice when the time reaches a given threshold. Details about how the threshold is computed can be found in the online supplementary material [15]. When a robot gives up, its current waiting time updates the respective estimate $\hat{t}_D$ or $\hat{t}_P$ using Equation 1.

4   Experimental Setup

This section briefly describes the experimental tools and the environment in which we run the experiments presented in the paper. A more detailed description can be found in [16], of which the research presented here is a follow up.

All the experiments presented in this work have been carried out in simulation using *ARGoS* [13], a simulator developed within the *Swarmanoid*[1] project [6]. We simulate the *e-puck*[2], a small wheeled robot that has been used in many studies in swarm robotics. As the e-puck does not have the capability of grasping objects, we abstract this process by using a device called *Task Allocation Module (TAM)* [4]. Each TAM is a small booth in which an e-puck can enter. In the experiments, we simulate the TAM and its basic functionalities: two RGB LEDs that can be perceived by the e-pucks and a light barrier that can detect the presence of a robot within the TAM. In the experiments presented in this article, we implement the source, the nest, and the cache using TAMs.

The experiments take place in the environment represented in Fig. 2. The source is located at the top-left, the nest at the top-right, and the cache between the source and the nest. The nest and the source are implemented using four TAMs on one side; the cache is implemented with eight TAMs, four on each side, organized in pairs facing opposite directions[3]. The corridor links the areas containing the source and the nest.

We perform the experiments in two environments, called short-corridor and long-corridor environments. In both environments, the source is 1.5 m away from the nest. The environments differ in terms of the total length of the corridor: 5.0 m in the short-corridor and 7.5 m in the long-corridor environment. We also impose a cache processing time Π that the robots have to spend in the cache when dropping or picking up an object. The length of the corridor and the value of Π determine whether it is more advantageous to perform the object retrieval

---

[1] http://www.swarmanoid.org

[2] http://www.e-puck.org

[3] A video showing the behavior of the cache can be found in the online supplementary material at the following url: http://iridia.ulb.ac.be/supp/IridiaSupp2012-005/

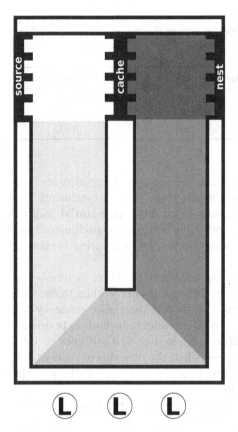

Fig. 2. Representation of the experimental environment. Nest, source and cache are implemented using TAMs. The different ground colors are used by the robots for localization in the arena. Light sources, marked with "L", provide directional information. The short-corridor and long-corridor environments differ in the total length of the corridor.

task as unpartitioned task, or to partition it into two sub-tasks. By changing the value of Π, we can tune the relation between the performance obtained by using the cache and the one obtained by using the corridor. Consequently, we can also define how advantageous it is to employ task partitioning.

5   Experiments and Results

We run all the experiments in both the short-corridor and long-corridor environments, with swarms of 10 and 20 robots. Every experiment lasts 10 simulated hours. At the beginning of each experiment, half of the swarm is positioned in the area containing the source and the other half in the area containing the nest. The value of α, used for computing the time estimates in Equation 1, has been set to 0.5. Notice that, in order to reduce the parameter space, we do not tune the value of α with systematic experiments. We select this value of α since low values are likely to render the algorithms poor in reacting to changes, while high values increase sensitivity to noise. The values of the cost estimates are initialized randomly: $\hat{t}_H$ and $\hat{t}_S$ are uniformly sampled in the interval $[40, 80]$, $\hat{t}_P$ and $\hat{t}_D$ in $[20, 40]$.

Table 1. Selected parameters for the exploiting and exploring versions of the three algorithms

Algorithm	parameter	exploiting version	exploring version
ad-hoc	S	6.0	1.0
UCB	γ	100	1000
ε-greedy	ε	0.01	0.11

We run two sets of experiments. The goal of the first set of experiments is to select the parameters for each algorithm. Details about these experiments and the complete results can be found in the online supplementary material. Following these experiments, we selected two parameters settings for each algorithm, one corresponding to an *exploring* version and one to an *exploiting* version of the algorithm.

In the second set of experiments, the goal is to test whether, by employing the different algorithms, the robots are able to choose properly when to use task partitioning and when not to. Additionally, we test if the choice made by the robot adapts to variations occurring in the environment. In each experiment, the value of the cache interfacing time Π is initialized to 0, it switches to 160 s after 2.5 hours, and then it switches back to 0 when the experiment reaches half of its duration. The robots are expected to choose between the cache and the corridor and to adapt their choice in time.

Figure 3 reports the results of the experiments, for a swarm composed of 20 robots, in the long-corridor environment. Plots on the same row refer to the same algorithm (from top to bottom: ad-hoc, UCB, ε-greedy). The plots in the left column report the results for the exploiting version of the corresponding algorithm, the ones on the right for the exploring version. Each box reports the percentage of usage of the cache in the 30 minutes preceding the time reported on the X axis. The grey horizontal lines report the optimal cache usage, that changes depending on the value of Π. The grey slanted lines report percentages of cache usage that lead to a performance of at least 95% of the optimal. Performance is measured as average total number of objects retrieved at the end of the experiment. To determine the optimal way of using the cache, we performed experiments in which some of the robots were forced to always use the cache. For each value of Π and the two swarm sizes, we exhaustively tested all the possible values of the number of robots forced to use the cache and recorded the corresponding performance. The performance of the different algorithms is reported in Fig. 4. The optimal performance and the performance of an algorithm randomly selecting between cache and corridor are also reported for reference.

A comparison between the two versions of each algorithm highlights the trade-off between exploration and exploitation, typical in multi-armed bandit problems. When the exploiting versions of the algorithms are employed, the robots can select when to use the cache and when to use the corridor, but are unable to detect changes occurring in the environment. This can be seen in the near

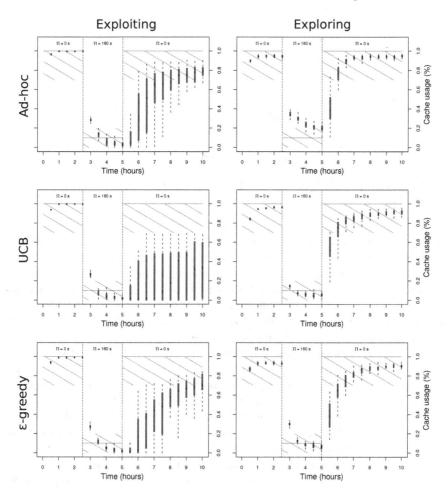

Fig. 3. Percentage of usage of the cache for the ad-hoc (first row), the UCB (second row), and the ε-greedy (third row) algorithm. In each row, the plot on the left reports the results for the exploiting version, the one on the right for the exploring version of the corresponding algorithm. We report the results obtained in the long-corridor environment, with a swarm composed of 20 robots. The cache interfacing time Π is initialized to 0. After 2.5 hours of experiment, the value is changed to 160 seconds, and returns to 0 at half experiment. Vertical dashed lines mark the moments in which the value of Π changes. Each box reports the percentage of usage (over 25 experimental runs) of the cache in the 30 minutes preceding the time reported on the X axis. The grey horizontal line reports the cache usage that maximizes the number of objects retrieved, which varies with the value of Π. The grey slanted lines report percentages of cache usage that lead to a number of objects retrieved that is at least 95% of the maximum.

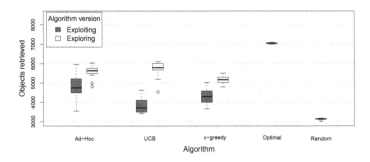

Fig. 4. Total number of objects retrieved by a swarm of 20 robots in the long-corridor environment

optimal behavior in the first half of the experiment, which degrades in the second half. Notice that the first change in the value of Π is detected also when employing the exploiting version of the algorithms. The reason is that initially the cache is selected often by the robots. Consequently, they can detect changes in Π independently of the version of the algorithm being employed. Detecting the opposite transition in the value of Π is harder and it only happens when the exploring version of the algorithms is employed.

The overall results (see online supplementary material) indicate that, in general, the algorithms perform better, more consistently, and with higher reactivity to changes, when the swarm is larger. This highlights that cooperation is required in order to render task partitioning effective. When the robots are many, it is more likely that robots are present on both sides of the cache, which is critical in order to exploit the cache properly. The length of the corridor seems to have little effect on the behavior of algorithms.

The results confirm that the task partitioning problem can be formulated as a multi-armed bandit problem. General algorithms for tackling bandit problems, such as the UCB and the ε-greedy, can be successfully employed to tackle the task partitioning problem, with results comparable with those of an ad-hoc algorithm. In particular the ε-greedy is a suitable candidate, since it is simple and its only parameter is easy to understand and tune manually.

6   Conclusions

In this paper, we studied the problem of choosing whether to tackle a task as a whole, or to partition it into a sequence of two sub-tasks. We show that the problem can be formulated as a multi-armed bandit problem. This is advantageous since the problem is well studied and understood, and its theoretical properties are known. Most importantly, several algorithms have been proposed in the literature for tackling the problem. This allows one to select an algorithm knowing its strengths and weaknesses and apply it to task partitioning problems without the need of designing ad-hoc solutions each time. The approach can be applied to situations in which costs can be measured or estimated by the robots. We pointed out that the tradeoff between exploration and exploitation, typical of multi-armed bandit problems, also arises in the task partitioning problem. This tradeoff has to be taken into account when choosing an algorithm and its parameters. Directions for future work aim at investigating more complex cases with more than two sub-tasks, as well as cases in which the location of the sub-tasks interface is not predefined, but must be decided by the robots autonomously. Additionally, in this work each robot tackles the task partitioning problem individually. As future work, we also plan to enhance the system with explicit communication. The robots could exchange information about the environment and compute cost estimates also on the basis of the information received.

Acknowledgements. The research leading to the results presented in this paper has received funding from the European Research Council under the European Union's Seventh Framework Programme (FP7/2007-2013) / ERC grant agreement n° 246939. Marco Dorigo, Mauro Birattari, and Arne Brutschy acknowledge support from the Belgian F.R.S.–FNRS. Giovanni Pini acknowledges support from Université Libre de Bruxelles through the "Fonds David & Alice Van Buuren".

References

1. Agrawal, R.: Sample mean based index policies with $O(\log n)$ regret for the multi-armed bandit problem. Advances in Applied Probability 27, 1054–1078 (1995)
2. Auer, P., Cesa-Bianchi, N., Fischer, P.: Finite-time analysis of the multiarmed bandit problem. Machine Learning 47(2), 235–256 (2002)
3. Berry, D.A., Fristedt, B.: Bandit problems: Sequential allocation of experiments. Chapman & Hall, London (1985)
4. Brutschy, A., Pini, G., Baiboun, N., Decugnière, A., Birattari, M.: The IRIDIA TAM: A device for task abstraction for the e-puck robot. Tech. Rep. TR/IRIDIA/2010-015, IRIDIA, Université Libre de Bruxelles, Brussels, Belgium (2010)
5. Dorigo, M., Şahin, E.: Guest editorial. Special Issue: Swarm robotics. Autonomous Robots 17(2-3), 111–113 (2004)
6. Dorigo, M., Floreano, D., Gambardella, L.M., Mondada, F., Nolfi, S., Baaboura, T., Birattari, M., Bonani, M., Brambilla, M., Brutschy, A., Burnier, D., Campo, A., Christensen, A.L., Decugnière, A., Caro, G.D., Ducatelle, F., Ferrante, E., Förster, A., Gonzales, J.M., Guzzi, J., Longchamp, V., Magnenat, S., Mathews, N., de Oca, M.M., O'Grady, R., Pinciroli, C., Pini, G., Rétornaz, P., Roberts, J., Sperati, V., Stirling, T., Stranieri, A., Stützle, T., Trianni, V., Tuci, E., Turgut, A.E., Vaussard, F.: Swarmanoid: a novel concept for the study of heterogeneous robotic swarms. IEEE Robotics & Automation Magazine (in press, 2012)
7. Fontan, M.S., Matarić, M.J.: A study of territoriality: The role of critical mass in adaptive task division. In: Maes, P., Matarić, M.J., Meyer, J.A., Pollack, J., Wilson, S. (eds.) From Animals to Animats 4: Proceedings of the Fourth International Conference of Simulation of Adaptive Behavior, pp. 553–561. MIT Press, Cambridge (1996)

8. Frison, M., Tran, N.-L., Baiboun, N., Brutschy, A., Pini, G., Roli, A., Dorigo, M., Birattari, M.: Self-organized Task Partitioning in a Swarm of Robots. In: Dorigo, M., Birattari, M., Di Caro, G.A., Doursat, R., Engelbrecht, A.P., Floreano, D., Gambardella, L.M., Groß, R., Şahin, E., Sayama, H., Stützle, T. (eds.) ANTS 2010. LNCS, vol. 6234, pp. 287–298. Springer, Heidelberg (2010)

9. Jeanne, R.L.: The evolution of the organization of work in social insects. Monitore Zoologico Italiano 20, 119–133 (1986)

10. Lein, A., Vaughan, R.: Adaptive multi-robot bucket brigade foraging. In: Bullock, S., Noble, J., Watson, R., Bedau, M.A. (eds.) Artificial Life XI: Proceedings of the Eleventh International Conference on the Simulation and Synthesis of Living Systems, pp. 337–342. MIT Press, Cambridge (2008)

11. Lein, A., Vaughan, R.T.: Adapting to non-uniform resource distributions in robotic swarm foraging through work-site relocation. In: 2009 IEEE/RSJ International Conference on Intelligent Robots and Systems (IROS 2009), pp. 601–606. IEEE Press, Piscataway (2009)

12. Østergaard, E.H., Sukhatme, G.S., Matarić, M.J.: Emergent bucket brigading: A simple mechanisms for improving performance in multi-robot constrained-space foraging tasks. In: AGENTS 2001: Proceedings of the Fifth International Conference on Autonomous Agents, pp. 29–30. ACM Press, New York (2001)

13. Pinciroli, C., Trianni, V., O'Grady, R., Pini, G., Brutschy, A., Brambilla, M., Mathews, N., Ferrante, E., Di Caro, G.A., Ducatelle, F., Stirling, T., Gutiérrez, A., Gambardella, L.M., Dorigo, M.: ARGoS: A modular, multi-engine simulator for heterogeneous swarm robotics. In: Proceedings of the 2011 IEEE/RSJ International Conference on Intelligent Robots and Systems (IROS 2011), pp. 5027–5034. IEEE Computer Society Press, Los Alamitos (2011)

14. Pini, G., Brutschy, A., Birattari, M., Dorigo, M.: Task Partitioning in Swarms of Robots: Reducing Performance Losses Due to Interference at Shared Resources. In: Cetto, J.A., Filipe, J., Ferrier, J.-L. (eds.) Informatics in Control Automation and Robotics. LNEE, vol. 85, pp. 217–228. Springer, Heidelberg (2011)

15. Pini, G., Brutschy, A., Francesca, G., Dorigo, M., Birattari, M.: Multi-armed bandit formulation of the task partitioning problem in swarm robotics – Online supplementary material (2012), http://iridia.ulb.ac.be/supp/IridiaSupp2012-005/

16. Pini, G., Brutschy, A., Frison, M., Roli, A., Birattari, M., Dorigo, M.: Task partitioning in swarms of robots: An adaptive method for strategy selection. Swarm Intelligence 5(3–4), 283–304 (2011)

17. Ratnieks, F.L.W., Anderson, C.: Task partitioning in insect societies. Insectes Sociaux 46(2), 95–108 (1999)

18. Shell, D.J., Matarić, M.J.: On foraging strategies for large-scale multi-robot systems. In: Proceedings of the 19th IEEE/RSJ International Conference on Intelligent Robots and Systems (IROS), pp. 2717–2723. IEEE Press, Pitscataway (2006)

19. Sutton, R., Barto, A.: Reinforcement learning, an introduction. MIT Press, Cambridge (1998)

Scalability Study of Particle Swarm Optimizers in Dynamic Environments

Barend J. Leonard and Andries P. Engelbrecht

Department of Computer Science,
University of Pretoria, South Africa
{bleonard,engel}@cs.up.ac.za

Abstract. This study investigates the scalability of three particle swarm optimizers (PSO) on dynamic environments. The charged PSO (CPSO), quantum PSO (QPSO) and dynamic heterogeneous PSO (dHPSO) algorithms are evaluated on a number of DF1 and moving peaks benchmark (MPB) environments that differ with respect to the severity and frequency of change. It is shown that dHPSO scales better to high severity and high frequency DF1 environments. For MPB environments, similar scalability results are observed, with dHPSO obtaining the best average results over all test cases. The good performance of dHPSO is ascribed to its ability to explore and exploit the search space more efficiently than CPSO and QPSO.

1 Introduction

Many real-world problems are dynamic in the sense that the search landscape changes over time. Landscape changes can be due to changes in the objective function(s) and/or problem constraints. When such changes occur, a known solution to a problem may no longer be good or valid. A new solution must therefore be found to reflect the landscape changes. This study focusses on single-objective dynamic optimization problems, where only the objective function changes.

Two commonly used benchmarks to generate dynamic optimization problems are the moving peaks benchmark (MPB) [5] and the DF1 function generator [11]. By using these generators, optimization techniques can be evaluated on problems that accurately reflect real-world situations.

The particle swarm optimization (PSO) algorithm [9] is a well known optimization technique. PSO has been successfully applied to a wide variety of problems since its introduction and is known to perform well on static optimization problems. However, PSO faces two obstacles when dynamic problems are considered. The first is a problem referred to as *outdated memory*. The second, more severe problem, is that of *diversity loss*.

In order to solve dynamic problems using PSO, both of the above-mentioned problems must be overcome. Two variants of the PSO algorithm, known as the *charged PSO* (CPSO) and *quantum PSO* (QPSO), were designed to address these problems [2], [3]. Both variants prohibit particles in a swarm to completely converge, thereby ensuring that some particles are always distributed in

M. Dorigo et al. (Eds.): ANTS 2012, LNCS 7461, pp. 121–132, 2012.

the search landscape within a region around the best known solution. Therefore, the distributed particles are able to detect when the optimum moves to a new location within the covered region. In this way, the problem of diversity loss is addressed. Additionally, particles are forced to re-evaluate the function value at their current positions, either periodically or whenever a change in the environment is detected, thereby addressing the problem of outdated memory.

Recently, another variant of PSO, known as *dynamic heterogeneous PSO* (dHPSO), was developed [7]. The dHPSO was first proposed to address the exploration-exploitation trade-off problem on static optimization problems, but it was later shown that dHPSO could also be successfully applied to dynamic problems [10]. The dHPSO allows particles in a swarm to follow different position- and velocity update rules from one another. In addition, the algorithm allows particles to select new update rules from a *behaviour pool* of update rules if the particle stagnates at any time during execution.

This study investigates the scalability of CPSO, QPSO and dHPSO in dynamic environments. Experiments are conducted to show how the performance of the algorithms deteriorate as the severity and frequency of changes in the environment increase.

The rest of this paper is structured as follows: Section 2 gives an overview of the PSO algorithm. Section 3 discusses the problems associated with applying PSO to dynamic function optimization. In addition, the PSO variants that address those problems are explained. The experimental procedure is given in section 4 and the results are discussed in section 5. The study is concluded in section 6.

2 Particle Swarm Optimization

Particle swarm optimization is a stochastic, population-based optimization algorithm [9]. The algorithm maintains a population (or a *swarm*) of candidate solutions (known as *particles*) to some optimization problem. Each particle i has a *position* $\mathbf{x}_i$ and *velocity* $\mathbf{v}_i$ in an n_x-dimensional *search space*. A particle's position $\mathbf{x}_i$ represents the solution proposed by particle i. In addition to its position and velocity, each particle also keeps track of the best position $\mathbf{y}_i$ that it has found during the search process, known as the particle's *personal best position*. The best position $\hat{\mathbf{y}}$ found by the swarm is called the *global best position*.

At every time step, each particle's velocity is updated using

$$\mathbf{v}_i(t+1) = \omega\mathbf{v}_i(t) + c_1\mathbf{r}_1(t)[\mathbf{y}_i(t) - \mathbf{x}_i(t)] + c_2\mathbf{r}_2(t)[\hat{\mathbf{y}}(t) - \mathbf{x}_i(t)] \qquad (1)$$

where ω is the inertia weight [14], c_1 and c_2 are acceleration constants, and $r_{1j}(t)$ and $r_{2j}(t)$ are random values, sampled from $U(0,1)$ in each dimension $j = 1, \ldots, n_x$.

The second and third terms in equation (1) are referred to as the *cognitive component* and the *social component*, respectively.

Once a particle's velocity has been updated, its new position is calculated as

$$\mathbf{x}_i(t+1) = \mathbf{x}_i(t) + \mathbf{v}_i(t+1). \qquad (2)$$

The resulting behaviour is that particles stochastically return to regions of the search space that are known to contain promising solutions.

3 Particle Swarm Optimization in Dynamic Environments

For the purpose of this study, a dynamic environment is a function f whose optima may move around the function domain during the search process. An optimum can move in two distinct ways. Firstly, the position $\mathbf{x}^*$ of an optimum may change in any or all dimensions. Secondly, the value $f(\mathbf{x}^*)$ of the optimum may increase or decrease. Furthermore, the magnitude (or *severity*) and the frequency of changes may vary. The consequences of the changes are that optima may appear or disappear during the search process. In addition, a local optimum may become a global optimum and *vice versa*.

To perform optimization in dynamic environments, the goal is to find the optimum, and then track its movement over time. When considering environments with multiple optima, it may also be necessary to detect when an optimum being tracked is no longer the global optimum. In such a case it the new global optimum must be found and tracked instead. Assuming that environmental changes occur only at known intervals, the PSO algorithm is subject to two problems when applied to dynamic functions: outdated memory and diversity loss.

Outdated memory occurs whenever the environment changes. Recall that each particle in the swarm keeps track of its personal best position $\mathbf{y}_i$. When a change occurs, the value $f(\mathbf{y}_i)$ associated with a particle's personal best may no longer be correct. This could cause particles to be attracted to regions of the search space that used to contain good solutions, but are no longer desirable. To solve the problem of outdated memory, Eberhart and Shi [6] showed that it is sufficient to re-evaluate f at the particles' personal best positions, as well as at the global best position $\hat{\mathbf{y}}$ whenever the environment changes.

A subsequent study by Blackwell and Bentley [2] identified the problem of diversity loss. Diversity loss occurs when the swarm converges on a point in the search space. If the swarm is too highly converged, there is no way to detect optima outside the region where particles are present. Therefore, if an optimum moves or appears outside this small area, the PSO algorithm is unable to find and track it [1], [2], [3]. It was further shown in [2] that particle swarms in this situation are prone to oscillation on a line perpendicular to the true optimum in a phenomenon known as *linear collapse*. To overcome diversity loss, it is necessary to control the diversity of the swarm in some way. That is, either prevent particles from converging, or provide a way for the swarm to diverge if necessary.

Three variants of the PSO algorithm that have been successfully applied to dynamic environments are discussed below.

3.1 PSO with Charged Particles

Blackwell and Bentley [2] proposed the use of *charged particles* to prevent swarm convergence. The approach was later modified by Blackwell and Branke [4].

A charged particle has an electrostatic charge $Q_i > 0$. A particle with no charge is referred to as a *neutral particle*. Swarm convergence is then prevented by introducing a Coulomb repulsion force $\mathbf{a}_i$ in equation (1). The repulsion force acting on a particle i at time t is given by

$$\mathbf{a}_i(t) = \sum_{k \neq i} \frac{Q_i Q_k}{(\delta_{ik}(t))^3} \boldsymbol{\delta}_{ik}(t), \quad p_{core} < \delta_{ik}(t) < p \tag{3}$$

where $\boldsymbol{\delta}_{ik}(t) = \mathbf{x}_i(t) - \mathbf{x}_k(t)$, and $\delta_{ik}(t) = \|\mathbf{x}_i(t) - \mathbf{x}_k(t)\|$. The lower limit p_{core} prevents the repulsion force from becoming too large between particles that are very close to each other. Equation (1) then becomes

$$\mathbf{v}_i(t+1) = \omega \mathbf{v}_i(t) + c_1 \mathbf{r}_1(t)[\mathbf{y}_i(t) - \mathbf{x}_i(t)] + c_2 \mathbf{r}_2(t)[\hat{\mathbf{y}}(t) - \mathbf{x}_i(t)] + \mathbf{a}_i(t). \tag{4}$$

A charged particle i is therefore repelled by all other charged particles $k \neq i$ where $p_{core} < \delta_{ik} < p$.

Outdated memory is addressed by re-evaluating the personal best positions of all particles whenever the environment changes.

By using both charged particles and neutral particles in a single swarm, the neutral particles converge in order to exploit an optimum, while the charged particles remain distributed in a region around the neutral particles. Thus, the problem of diversity loss is solved. However, the computational complexity of this approach is much higher than that of the standard PSO, because of the need to calculate euclidean distances between all pairs of particles at each iteration.

This approach is often referred to as *charged PSO* (CPSO).

3.2   PSO with Quantum Particles

The use of *quantum particles* was proposed by Blackwell and Branke [3]. In this approach, a quantum particle i samples a new position $\mathbf{x}_i(t+1)$ at each time step, such that $\mathbf{x}_i(t+1) \in B(\phi_{cloud})$, where $B(\phi_{cloud})$ is an n_x-dimensional ball with radius ϕ_{cloud} around $\hat{\mathbf{y}}(t)$.

The problem of diversity loss is therefore solved in the same way as charged PSO (by partially preventing swarm convergence), but without the need to calculate euclidean distances between particles.

A re-evaluation strategy is used to address the problem of outdated memory. This variant is known as *Quantum PSO* (QPSO).

3.3   Dynamic Heterogeneous PSO

The dHPSO was introduced by Engelbrecht [7] and was first applied to dynamic environments by Leonard et al. [10].

The dHPSO maintains a collection of position- and velocity update equations. The collection is known as the behaviour pool and velocity- and position updates are grouped together to form behaviours that particles may choose to follow. In addition, particles are monitored for stagnation. When stagnation is detected, the particle in question is forced to randomly select a new behaviour from the behaviour pool. In [7], a particle was deemed to be stagnating whenever its personal best position did not change for ten consecutive iterations.

It was shown in [10] that dHPSO is able to diversify by selecting exploratory behaviours when exploitative behaviours begin to stagnate. In this way, random behaviour selection in dHPSO contributes to addressing the problem of diversity loss.

Leonard et al. [10] further showed that, in order to apply dHPSO to dynamic environments, it is necessary to combine the approach with the periodic re-initialization of a portion of the particles in the swarm. The reason for this is that particles in dHPSO converge and are therefore not capable of detecting changes in the environment. By re-initializing a portion of the particles when a change occurs, the re-initialized particles are able to observe the change. However, for this reason, the current implementation of dHPSO only works on dynamic environments for which the changes occur at known intervals.

To address outdated memory, the personal best positions of all particles are re-evaluated whenever the environment changes.

In Engelbrecht's work [7], the following five behaviours were included in the behaviour pool:

- **Standard PSO behaviour**, where equations (1) and (2) were used. The cognitive acceleration constant c_1 was linearly decreased from 2.5 to 0.5 throughout the search process, while the social acceleration constant c_2 was linearly increased from 0.5 to 2.5. This behaviour promotes exploration during the initial stages of the search process, while promoting exploitation towards the end of the search process.
- **Cognitive PSO behaviour**, where the social acceleration constant c_2 in equation (1) is set to 0.0, so that a particle is only attracted to its own personal best position $\mathbf{y}_i$. This behaviour facilitates exploration by turning the particle that follows this behaviour into an independent hill-climber.
- **Social PSO behaviour**, where the cognitive acceleration constant c_1 in equation (1) is set to 0.0, so that a particle is only attracted to the global best position $\hat{\mathbf{y}}$. This behaviour facilitates exploitation by effectively turning all particles that follow it into a single stochastic hill-climber.
- **Bare bones PSO behaviour**, introduced by Kennedy [8]. The bare bones behaviour after he observed that a single particle, attracted to its personal best position $\mathbf{y}_i$ and the global best position $\hat{\mathbf{y}}$, exploits the point α in the middle along a straight line between these two positions. He further observed that the positions visited by the particle are normally distributed around the point α. In a bare bones PSO, a particle's velocity is not calculated using equation (1), but is sampled from a Gaussian distribution such that

$$v_{ij}(t+1) \sim N\left(\frac{y_{ij}(t) + \hat{y}_j(t)}{2}, \sigma^2\right) \tag{5}$$

where the variance $\sigma^2 = |y_{ij}(t) - \hat{y}_j(t)|$. The position update rule in equation (2) then changes to

$$\mathbf{x}_i(t+1) = \mathbf{v}_i(t+1). \tag{6}$$

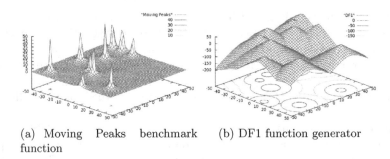

(a) Moving Peaks benchmark function

(b) DF1 function generator

Fig. 1. Example 2-dimensional environments with 10 optima

Initially, this behaviour will promote exploration, because the personal best positions of particles are widely distributed around the search space. As the personal best positions converge, this behaviour will become more exploitative.

- **Modified bare bones PSO behaviour**, which is a slightly modified version of bare bones PSO, also proposed by Kennedy [8]. In this approach, equation (5) is changed to

$$v_{ij}(t+1) = \begin{cases} y_{ij}(t) & \text{if } U(0,1) < 0.5 \\ \varphi & \text{otherwise.} \end{cases} \tag{7}$$

where

$$\varphi \sim N\left(\frac{y_{ij}(t) + \hat{y}_j(t)}{2}, \sigma^2\right). \tag{8}$$

Equation (6) is still used for position updates. This behaviour facilitates better initial exploration and later exploitation than the standard bare bones PSO, because particles exploit their personal best positions 50% of the time.

4   Experimental Procedure

For this study, a number of dynamic environments were generated using the DF1 function generator [11], as well as the Moving Peaks Benchmark (MPB) [5]. Example 2-dimensional environments are shown in figure 1.

All problems and algorithms were implemented using the open source computation intelligence library, CIlib [13].

4.1   Problems

The problems used for this study were generated using the MPB function [5] and the DF1 function generator [11]. Each of the two generators were used to create environments with the change severity settings shown in table 1. The position and height severities were chosen to correspond to percentages of the

Table 1. MPB Severity Parameters

Shift severity	Height Severity	%	Shift severity	Height Severity	%
0.5	0.2	0.5%	20.0	8.0	20.0%
1.0	0.4	1.0%	30.0	12.0	30.0%
2.0	0.8	2.0%	40.0	16.0	40.0%
5.0	2.0	5.0%	50.0	20.0	50.0%
10.0	4.0	10.0%			

range within which they were allowed to move. In addition, all environments were also generated with the following change frequencies: 10, 50, 100, 200 and 500 iterations. Finally, each environment was created in a unimodal and multimodal fashion, with all multimodal environments having 10 optima. This gave rise to 320 unique problems.

For all the environments, optima moved around a 2-dimensional domain in the range $[-50, 50]^2$. The heights of the optima oscillated in the range $[10, 50]$, while the widths and slopes of the peaks and cones were set to a constant value of 5.0. These parameters are the same as those used for dynamic environments in [10], except for the dimensionality. Scalability to higher dimensions will be examined in future studies.

4.2   Algorithms

For this study, the QPSO, CPSO and dHPSO algorithms described in section 3 were tested on a range of dynamic environments. For all experiments, the algorithms ran for 2000 iterations and all reported results are averages over 30 independent samples.

Unless otherwise stated, all chosen parameter values correspond to the parameters used by Leonard *et al.* [10].

Charged PSO: For CPSO, the acceleration constants c_1 and c_2 were both set to 1.496180. The parameter p_{core} was set to 1, while p had a value of 30. The values $\mathbf{y}_i$ and $\hat{\mathbf{y}}$ of all particles were re-evaluated at each change interval.

In [10], 50% of the particles in CPSO were also re-initialized at each change interval. However, since the algorithm maintains swarm diversity throughout the search process, there is no need to include a re-initialization strategy that is designed to re-introduce diversity into converged swarms. Therefore, no re-initialization was performed for CPSO in this study.

Quantum PSO: The acceleration constants c_1 and c_2 were both set to 1.496180. The radius ϕ_{cloud} was set to 30. At each change interval, the values of $\mathbf{y}_i$ and $\hat{\mathbf{y}}$, were re-evaluated for all particles.

No re-initialization of particles was performed for QPSO in this study for the same reason explained in section 4.2.

Dynamic Heterogeneous PSO: For this study, the behaviour pool was populated with the same five behaviours that were used in [7] and [10]. However, one change was made to the initialization of dHPSO swarms in this study:

The cognitive PSO behaviour in the previous studies suffered from immediate stagnation in the first ten iterations of the search process. The reason for this is that particle velocities were initialized to 0.0, and that particles' initial personal best positions $\mathbf{y}_i(0)$ and their initial positions $\mathbf{x}_i(0)$ were the same. This resulted in a zero attraction force on particles with zero velocity (cognitive particles are only attracted towards their own personal best positions). Because of the stagnation detection in dHPSO, those particles would, however, change their behaviours after the first ten iterations and would gain velocity as new attraction forces were introduced.

To prevent the immediate stagnation of cognitive particles, the personal best positions of all particles in the swarm were initialized randomly in the range $[-50, 50]^2$ for this study. Doing so meant that the cognitive components of all particles were initially a random point within the search domain. However, since the personal best positions of particles are updated after each iteration, any inferior personal best positions that may have resulted from random initialization only persisted for one iteration. In addition, cognitive particles gained initial velocity, solving the problem of immediate stagnation.

4.3   Measurements

To quantify the performance of the different algorithms with respect to the quality of the solutions found, the *collective mean error* [12] was recorded. The collective mean error at iteration t is the average of all *actual error* measurements that have been recorded up to iteration t since the beginning of the search process. The actual error is taken as the difference between the global best fitness $f(\hat{\mathbf{y}})$ and the global maximum value (assuming a maximization problem).

Since the aim of this study is to investigate the ability of algorithms to find good solutions in environments with varying change severities and change frequencies, no other performance criteria are reported. However, the actual error measurements and the diversity of swarms will likely provide further insight into how swarms are affected by environmental changes. Those measurements were therefore recorded to be studied in future work.

5   Results and Discussion

The scalability results of dHPSO are reported in table 2. For comparison with other algorithms, figures 2 and 3 illustrate the scalability trends for DF1 environments and MPB environments, respectively.

For unimodal DF1 environments, all algorithms showed a decrease in performance as the severity and frequency of changes increased, as was expected. Initially, QPSO mostly obtained the lowest collective mean error, but at

Table 2. DHPSO Collective Mean Errors

Multimodal DF1	Frequency (iterations)				
Severity (%)	10	50	100	200	500
0.5	1.57±0.29	0.87±0.36	0.63±0.44	0.67±0.64	0.57±0.52
1	2.03±0.24	1.18±0.42	0.99±0.4	0.59±0.29	0.85±0.76
2	3.08±0.27	1.50±0.23	1.29±0.33	0.95±0.34	0.69±0.56
5	5.46±0.18	2.39±0.3	1.58±0.36	1.09±0.4	0.94±0.56
10	6.72±0.28	2.87±0.29	1.98±0.39	1.56±0.43	1.14±0.68
20	7.89±0.35	3.34±0.38	2.28±0.44	1.40±0.46	0.95±0.56
30	7.30±0.29	2.98±0.49	2.13±0.39	1.45±0.36	0.99±0.45
40	8.51±0.3	3.99±0.49	2.90±0.49	2.30±0.54	1.85±1.07
50	6.45±0.26	3.15±0.34	2.45±0.34	1.92±0.33	0.92±0.51

Unimodal DF1	Frequency (iterations)				
Severity (%)	10	50	100	200	500
0.5	0.5±0.04	0.41±0.04	0.29±0.05	0.21±0.05	0.13±0.04
1	0.84±0.05	0.6±0.05	0.43±0.11	0.26±0.04	0.15±0.04
2	1.51±0.07	0.83±0.05	0.58±0.10	0.32±0.41	0.18±0.04
5	2.86±0.12	1.13±0.12	0.69±0.07	0.33±0.06	0.2±0.05
10	4.09±0.11	1.22±0.14	0.74±0.11	0.35±0.04	0.22±0.05
20	4.8±0.07	1.13±0.05	0.7±0.10	0.42±0.05	0.25±0.05
30	5.04±0.2	1.11±0.09	0.75±0.09	0.47±0.07	0.2±0.04
40	5.74±0.25	1.23±0.11	0.84±0.08	0.54±0.07	0.31±0.05
50	5.25±0.26	1.17±0.10	0.75±0.07	0.54±0.07	0.32±0.05

Multimodal MPB	Frequency (iterations)				
Severity (%)	10	50	100	200	500
0.5	2.28±1.82	2.4±1.68	2.15±1.47	1.92±1.62	2.45±1.96
1	2.09±2.01	2.19±1.79	2.12±1.77	2.53±2.03	2.28±2.11
2	3.41±2.20	1.68±1.73	2.97±1.84	2.46±1.95	2.55±3.5
5	2.98±1.89	2.01±1.71	2.45±1.85	2.89±1.95	2.12±2.12
10	2.8±2.04	2.44±2.28	1.99±1.41	2.18±1.97	1.94±2.11
20	2.78±2.07	1.93±1.67	2.31±1.90	2.02±1.69	1.9±1.75
30	3.24±1.85	2.24±1.87	2.62±1.98	2.19±1.92	2.62±1.94
40	2.96±2.02	2.12±1.75	1.94±1.54	2.26±2.28	2.4±1.83
50	2.64±2.08	1.96±1.60	2.18±1.86	2.65±1.86	2.06±1.43

Unimodal MPB	Frequency (iterations)				
Severity (%)	10	50	100	200	500
0.5	0.21±0.04	0.21±0.05	0.2±0.05	0.19±0.06	0.22±0.04
1	0.21±0.05	0.2±0.05	0.2±0.06	0.2±0.05	0.21±0.06
2	0.24±0.06	0.22±0.04	0.21±0.04	0.2±0.05	0.21±0.03
5	0.22±0.05	0.19±0.07	0.2±0.06	0.21±0.04	0.21±0.05
10	0.23±0.06	0.2±0.05	0.21±0.05	0.22±0.04	0.2±0.05
20	0.22±0.06	0.2±0.05	0.2±0.05	0.2±0.06	0.19±0.04
30	0.21±0.05	0.2±0.05	0.21±0.07	0.21±0.05	0.21±0.03
40	0.19±0.04	0.18±0.04	0.2±0.04	0.2±0.04	0.21±0.04
50	0.23±0.06	0.2±0.04	0.21±0.04	0.23±0.04	0.23±0.05

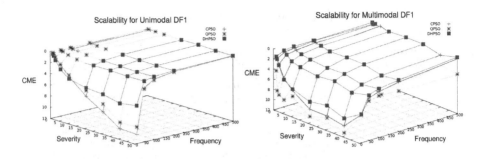

Fig. 2. DF1 Environments Severity Results

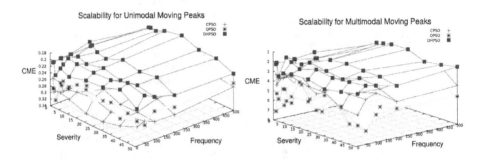

Fig. 3. MPB Environments Severity Results

higher severities, dHPSO showed lower errors over all frequencies. The dHPSO algorithm also showed a better scalability to high severity changes at high frequencies.

The inferior performance of dHPSO on low severity unimodal DF1 problems can be attributed to the fast convergent behaviour of dHPSO, as shown in [10], when compared to CPSO and QPSO. When changes in the environment occur, dHPSO needs time to diverge in order to exploit the moved optimum. Since the neutral particles of CPSO and QPSO take longer to converge, they are in a better position to locate the shifted optimum. However, as the severity increase, CPSO and QPSO begin to struggle. Leonard *et al.* [10] suggested that the inability of charged and quantum particles to converge may prevent them from thoroughly exploring the search space. The results presented here support their suggestion. The re-initialized particles of dHPSO are capable of converging on solutions and may therefore begin to exploit a shifted optimum even before the rest of the particles have diverged.

For multimodal DF1 problems, dHPSO obtained a lower error in almost all test cases. Again, all algorithms showed a decrease in performance as the severity and frequency of changes increased. The lower collective mean error of dHPSO on low severity multimodal DF1 environments is attributed to the algorithm's superior exploration abilities, as shown in [10]. In unimodal environments, the exploring particles in dHPSO served little purpose, because the optimum was still close to its previous position. However, in the case of multimodal functions, it is likely that new optima appear elsewhere in the search space. The re-initialized particles of dHPSO are then better equipped to find and exploit these new optima than the charged or quantum particles in the other algorithms.

Figure 3 shows that dHPSO produced lower collective mean errors in all test cases on MPB environments. In both the unimodal and multimodal cases, all algorithms showed a less pronounced effect as the severity and change frequency increased. The peaks in MPB environments are much narrower that the cones in DF1 and are therefore difficult to locate. Once CPSO or QPSO has located a shifted peak, additional time is required for the neutral particles to diverge. The diverging process in dHPSO is much quicker, because particles are able to switch to exploratory behaviours independently from the re-initialized particles. The neutral particles in CPSO and QPSO will only diverge once a better solution has been found elsewhere in the search space. Figure 3 shows a correlation between the frequency and severity of changes in that the performance of the algorithms decrease as both the frequency and severity increase. However, when only the severity or only the frequency of changes increased, all three algorithms showed similar performance across all test cases, with the exception of very high severities and very high frequencies. Again, the difference in performance between the two environments is attributed to the different shapes of the search landscapes.

6   Conclusion and Future Work

This study investigated the scalability of three particle swarm optimization (PSO) algorithms on dynamic optimization problems. The charged PSO (CPSO), quantum PSO (QPSO) and dynamic heterogeneous PSO (dHPSO) algorithms were tested on a variety of functions, generated with the moving peaks benchmark (MPB) and the DF1 function generator.

It was shown that dHPSO scales better to high severities and frequencies of changes on DF 1 environments. When considering MPB environments, the algorithms showed similar scalability results, but dHPSO obtained the best average results in all test cases. The bad performance of CPSO and QPSO was attributed to the inability of charged and quantum particles to exploit viable solutions. Charged and quantum particles can only explore, while the neutral particles must first diverge and reach an optimum before exploitation can take place. In the case of dHPSO, the exploring particles may change their behaviour to become exploiting particles. The only cases where CPSO and QPSO performed well was on low severity DF 1 environments. In these cases, the environment changes occurred within the range of the neutral particles and the shape of the search landscape allowed the neutral particles to easily locate the shifted optimum. The observed differences in performance between DF 1 and MPB environments were caused by the different shapes of the functions.

Future studies will investigate the scalability of the algorithms to higher dimensional problems and also consider the effects on swarm diversity. Self-adaptive models, where the stagnation detection of dHPSO is replaced with probabilistic selection of behaviours, based on their past performance should also be compared to the standard dHPSO in order to observe the effect that different selection schemes have on the algorithm's performance. Finally, the effect of including different behaviours in the behaviour pool might also produce interesting studies.

References

1. Blackwell, T.: Particle swarms and population diversity. Soft Computing – A Fusion of Foundations, Methodologies and Applications 9(11), 793–802 (2005)
2. Blackwell, T., Bentley, P.: Dynamic search with charged swarms. In: Proceedings of the Genetic and Evolutionary Computation Conference, pp. 19–26 (2002)
3. Blackwell, T., Branke, J.: Multi-swarm Optimization in Dynamic Environments. In: Raidl, G.R., Cagnoni, S., Branke, J., Corne, D.W., Drechsler, R., Jin, Y., Johnson, C.G., Machado, P., Marchiori, E., Rothlauf, F., Smith, G.D., Squillero, G. (eds.) EvoWorkshops 2004. LNCS, vol. 3005, pp. 489–500. Springer, Heidelberg (2004)
4. Blackwell, T., Branke, J.: Multiswarms, exclusion, and anti-convergence in dynamic environments. IEEE Transactions on Evolutionary Computation 10(4), 459–472 (2006)
5. Branke, J.: Memory enhanced evolutionary algorithms for changing optimization problems. In: Proceedings of the IEEE Congress on Evolutionary Computation, vol. 3. IEEE (1999)
6. Eberhart, R., Shi, Y.: Tracking and optimizing dynamic systems with particle swarms. In: Proceedings of the IEEE Congress on Evolutionary Computation, vol. 1, pp. 94–100. IEEE (2001)
7. Engelbrecht, A.P.: Heterogeneous Particle Swarm Optimization. In: Dorigo, M., Birattari, M., Di Caro, G.A., Doursat, R., Engelbrecht, A.P., Floreano, D., Gambardella, L.M., Groß, R., Şahin, E., Sayama, H., Stützle, T. (eds.) ANTS 2010. LNCS, vol. 6234, pp. 191–202. Springer, Heidelberg (2010)
8. Kennedy, J.: Bare bones particle swarms. In: Proceedings of the IEEE Swarm Intelligence Symposium, pp. 80–87. IEEE (2003)
9. Kennedy, J., Eberhart, R.: Particle swarm optimization. In: Proceedings of the IEEE International Conference on Neural Networks, vol. 4, pp. 1942–1948 (1995)
10. Leonard, B., Engelbrecht, A., van Wyk, A.: Heterogeneous particle swarms in dynamic environments. In: Proceedings of the IEEE Swarm Intelligence Symposium, pp. 1–8. IEEE (2011)
11. Morrison, R., De Jong, K.: A test problem generator for non-stationary environments. In: Proceedings of the IEEE Congress on Evolutionary Computation, vol. 3, IEEE (1999)
12. Morrison, R.: Performance measurement in dynamic environments. In: GECCO Workshop on Evolutionary Algorithms for Dynamic Optimization Problems, pp. 5–8 (2003)
13. Pamparà, G., Engelbrecht, A., Cloete, T.: Cilib: A collaborative framework for computational intelligence algorithms – part i. In: Proceedings of the International Joint Conference on Neural Networks, pp. 1750–1757. IEEE (2008)
14. Shi, Y., Eberhart, R.: A modified particle swarm optimizer. In: Proceedings of the IEEE Congress on Evolutionary Computation, pp. 69–73. IEEE (2002)

Self-reconfigurable Modular e-pucks

Lachlan Murray[1], Jon Timmis[1,2], and Andy Tyrrell[1]

[1] Department of Electronics, University of York, UK
[2] Department of Computer Science, University of York, UK
{ljm505,jt517,amt}@ohm.york.ac.uk

Abstract. We present the design of a new structural extension for the e-puck mobile robot. The extension may be used to transform what is a swarm robotics platform into a self-reconfigurable modular robotic system. As a proof of concept, we present an algorithm for controlling the collective locomotion of a group of e-pucks that are equipped with the extension. Our approach proves itself to be an effective method of coordinating the movement of a group of physically connected e-pucks. Furthermore, the system shows robustness in its ability to self-reconfigure and self-assemble following a disruption which alters the group's structure.

1 Introduction

Swarm robotics and self-reconfigurable modular robotics are two closely related areas within the larger field of autonomous mobile robotics. Swarm robotics concerns the study of how a collection of relatively simple embodied agents may coordinate their behaviour in a distributed and self-organising manner, whilst relying exclusively on local sensing and communication [17]. Modular robotic systems are also composed of several relatively simple units, however, unlike robotic swarms, the individuals in a modular robotic system may physically connect with one another to form larger robotic structures. An advantage of such systems is that by varying the connectivity of neighbouring units, structures may dynamically transform their morphology to suit their task or environment [19].

The field of swarm robotics is currently far more accessible than that of modular robotics. As is reflected in the availability of both types of hardware. Several swarm robotic platforms are available to buy or have been released as open hardware projects [14,13,9,3,11,2]. In contrast, the authors are not aware of any modular robots that are available commercially, and know of only a single open source project [21]. This may, at least partially, be attributed to the differing complexity of the required hardware. Swarm robots are purposefully simple units, whereas modular robots, although simple in comparison to the structures that they may form, require complex electrical and mechanical hardware to facilitate the processes of docking, reconfiguration and inter-robot communication.

To help redress the balance between the two fields and encourage research into modular robotic systems, here we present a low-cost, low-technology extension that may be used to transform an existing swarm robotics platform into a modular robotic system. Our chosen platform is the e-puck robot [14]. As an open

M. Dorigo et al. (Eds.): ANTS 2012, LNCS 7461, pp. 133–144, 2012.

hardware project, the e-puck robot is a highly flexible platform. Over recent years a number of extensions have been developed, including an omnidirectional vision turret, a range-bearing board [7], colour LEDs, a ZigBee radio module [1], and even an embedded Linux implementation [12].

In this paper we describe a purely structural extension that allows each equipped e-puck to physically connect with up to four other modules through passive magnetic docking interfaces. The extension may serve as a low-cost and accessible platform for research into the control of 2-dimensional modular robotic systems. As a proof of concept, we present an algorithm for coordinating the motion of a collection of physically connected e-puck robots and observe that our approach is not only amenable to the task, but exhibits robust behaviour in the face of perturbations that disrupt the arrangement of the robots.

The remainder of this paper is structured as follows. In section 2 we provide a short review of existing modular robotics hardware. In section 3 we describe the design of our extension. In section 4 we introduce a proof of concept control algorithm. In section 5 we present results of some preliminary experiments utilising our modular extension. Finally, in section 6 we present our conclusions.

2   Self-reconfigurable Modular Robotics

In 2007, Yim et al. produced a review of the state of the art in modular robotics [19]. The review includes a 'taxonomy of architectures' which classifies platforms as either: *chain*, *lattice*, *mobile*, or if they combine elements of more than one of the previous three, *hybrid*. Platforms may further be classified according to the number of degrees of freedom that the individual units posses, the number of dimensions in which structures can be formed and the method by which they reconfigure themselves, which may be described as *deterministic* or *stochastic*.

In chain-based architectures modules are connected to one another in series but may branch to form tree like structures or fold and reconnect to form loops. The *CKBot* is one such example. Each of the cube shaped modules possess only a single degree of freedom, but as a collective have been shown demonstrate a wide range of movements, notably, including the ability to self-repair following a high impact event that breaks the system into multiple sub-structures [20]. The open source *Molecubes* platform is another example, similar to our goal, the platform was designed to encourage research into modular robotics [21].

Lattice architectures are more restrictive than chain-based systems, with modules only able to occupy discrete positions within a conceptual grid. The *Miche* [4] and subsequent *Smart Pebble* systems [5] are two examples of lattice architectures. Envisaged as a test bed for future systems of *programmable matter*, these small, immobile, cube shaped modules may self-assemble with the help an external stocastic force, for example a vibrating table. Once assembled in a densely packed arrangement, a distributed strategy of self-*disassembly* is used to 'sculpt' the desired object from the robotic substrate.

In a mobile architecture, as well being able to form collective robotic structures, modules are able to move freely around their environment as individuals.

The *s-bot* platform [15], developed as part of the Swarm-bot project, and the robots of the succeeding Swarmanoid project represent the best example of a mobile self-reconfigurable robotic system. The individual robots can physically connect to one another using grippers. Although unable to create structures as complex as those produced by other modular robotic systems, the platforms have been used to developed several distributed control strategies for tackling tasks such as self-assembly [6] and collective recovery [16].

The term "hybrid" is commonly used to describe systems which combine elements from both chain and lattice based architectures. Recently, a new type of hybrid has emerged which also shares some of the properties of mobile architectures. The *Sambot* platform [18], and the robots being developed by the SYMBRION and REPLICATOR projects [10] are two good examples of such mobile-hybrids. Like the Swarm-bot and Swarmanoid projects, the individual robots are independently mobile. However, unlike the s-bot and its derivatives, the modules are also designed to be capable of forming complex 3D structures.

3 Modular e-puck Extension

In this section we present the design of our *modular e-puck extension*. The extension may be used to transform the existing e-puck platform into what can be described as a hybrid *mobile-lattice* modular robotic system. Robots equipped with the extension remain independently mobile, but through passive magnetic docking interfaces may physically connect with other modules within a 2D grid.

As shown in figure 1a, the extension consists of three parts: a circular base plate which sits directly on top of the e-puck, a central frame which rests on top of the base plate, and a second circular plate which sits on top of the frame.

To ensure that there is enough room to clear the selector switch on the default extension board, and to allow access to the reset button, the base plate is positioned on top of three 15*mm* hexagonal spacers. A small overhang on the base plate allows the inner ring of the central frame to rest on the base plate without being permanently attached. This lip allows the frame to rotate unhindered around the central axis of the e-puck. To enable separate modules to connect with one another, two magnets are fitted on each internal edge of the central frame, with opposing poles facing outwards. The strength and positioning of the magnets were chosen such that if connected modules coordinate their motion they will remain attached, but if they do not, they will break apart. Therefore ensuring that the extension provides a suitable platform for investigating both collective behaviour and self-reconfiguration. Screws which pass through the two circular plates secure the extension to the epuck and an arrow shaped window in the top plate allows the current heading of the robot to be easily recognised.

To date, four prototype modules have been produced. The three structural parts of the extension were fabricated using a MakerBot 3D printer. The complete set of parts required to construct a single extension are displayed in figure 1b, we estimate the total cost to be around €5 per unit. Figure 1c shows a potential arrangement of four e-pucks equipped with the fully assembled extension.

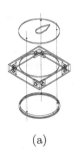 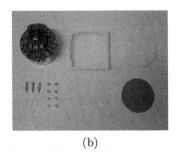 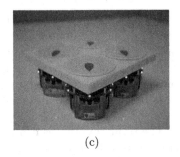

(a)   (b)   (c)

Fig. 1. A schematic of the main structural components of the modular e-puck extension (a) and photographs of unassembled (b) and assembled prototypes (c)

4   Collective Locomotion

In this section we present an algorithm for controlling the collective locomotion of a group of e-pucks that are physically connected using the modular e-puck extension. Through a behaviour-based approach every robot in the group is motivated to move forward, to align with its neighbours and to avoid obstacles. The summation of these three objectives determines the speed of the robot's motors. Regardless of their position within the larger structure, each robot runs the same controller and exchanges information only via local communication.

As a collective, the robots are able to exhibit continuous coordinated motion within an enclosed arena, whilst at the same time demonstrating robustness to perturbations in the overall structure. Following the removal of one or more modules from a group, whether deliberate or accidental, the system is able to self-reconfigure and re-form either the original structure, or an entirely new one. This process of self-assembly is not pre-programmed but emerges due to a combination factors including: the design of the structural extension, the design of the locomotion controller, and the nature of the robot's environment.

The two primary objectives of the controller, to align with neighbouring robots and to avoid obstacles, both make use of the e-puck's infrared (IR) sensors. The arrangement of the eight sensors on a single e-puck is shown in figure 2a. The obstacle avoidance behaviour uses the IR sensors for proximity detection whilst, with the help of the *LibIrcom* library [8], the alignment behaviour uses them for short-range communication.

The alignment behaviour is based upon the same principle of exchanging relative bearings as both the *LibIrcom* library's 'synchronize' example, and the alignment technique described in [7]. We begin this section by describing this method of alignment, from this point on referred to as *static synchronisation*, due to the fact that the robots remain stationary throughout. We identify some problems with this approach when considering non-stationary alignment and whilst introducing a new alignment behaviour propose some solutions. Following which we introduce the obstacle avoidance behaviour and describe how the two parts are combined with a forward bias to produce the desired overall locomotion.

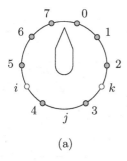
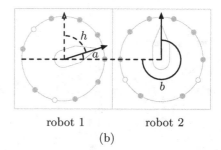

robot 1   robot 2

(a)   (b)

Fig. 2. The positioning of the infrared sensors on board an e-puck robot (a) and the mechanism for exchanging relative bearings between two modules (b)

4.1 Static Synchronisation

The static synchronisation example shows how, by exchanging relative bearings, a group of stationary robots may converge to and maintain a common heading.

Every robot broadcasts its ID and listens for the IDs of others. Based upon the sensor at which a message is received, robots are able to estimate the position of their neighbours as an angle relative to their own heading. For every ID that a robot receives, a message is sent to the corresponding neighbour, notifying it of the angle at which it was detected. As shown in figure 2b, using the angle at which robot 2 was detected (a), and the angle at which robot 2 detected robot 1 (b), robot 1 may calculate the relative heading of robot 2 as $h = a + \pi - b$. The relative heading of each of a robot's neighbours is used to incrementally update the robot's own desired heading, which consequently determines whether a robot should turn left, turn right, or remain stationary at each control cycle.

The approach is effective at synchronising the alignment of stationary robots, but we observe two problems which make it unsuitable for the alignment of mobile robots connected using the modular e-puck extension. Both problems are a consequence of the arrangement of the IR sensors on board the e-puck robot.

Firstly, because the angle between neighbouring sensors ranges from around 30° to 60°, unless two sensors are perfectly aligned, the estimate of angles a and b is often inaccurate. Although the static synchronisation approach incorporates mechanisms for reducing this uncertainty, it is still present. As is evident in the behaviour of the robots, which continuously switch between turning left and right, even once the robots have converged to approximately the same heading.

The second problem is a result of the large gaps between sensors 2, 3, 4 and 5. When two robots are physically connected, the close proximity of the modules and the gaps between the sensors can create blind spots in some orientations (marked i, j and k in figure 2a). As a result of these blind spots, in certain configurations the time taken to converge to a common heading is increased.

The two problems are further highlighted in figure 3. When sending messages via infrared, it is possible to estimate the distance between the sending and receiving sensors by measuring the intensity of the light received. Figure 3a maps the intensity of the infrared signal for messages sent between two robots

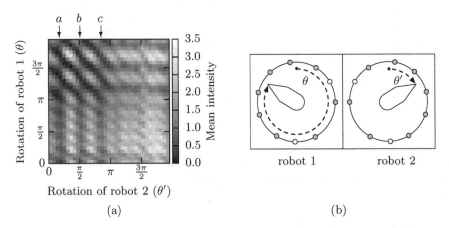

Fig. 3. A map of the intensity of the IR messages sent between two modules at various orientations (a) and a diagram of the setup used to gather the data (b)

arranged at various orientations. The setup used to gather this data is shown in figure 3b where robot 1 is the receiving module and robot 2 is the sender. The intensity of the signal associated with five received messages was recorded at 10° intervals for every 1296 (36 × 36) possible configurations of the two robots. Where no message was received within a certain time limit an intensity of 0 was assigned. The mean value of the five measurements is plotted. It can be noted from figure 3a that, due to the distribution of the sensors, when the two robots are facing each other (bottom right) the intensity of the received signals is high, but when two robots are facing away from each other (top left) the intensity is often low. A high intensity value indicates that the sending and receiving sensors are closely aligned, so when two robots are facing each other the measurement of angle a and b is likely to be more accurate than when they are facing away.

4.2 Alignment

We now present an alternative approach to alignment which aims to tackle the problems identified in the previous section by making use of the information available in figure 3a. Building upon the static synchronisation approach, robots still broadcast their IDs and track the relative orientation of their neighbours, but as well as making use of the content and direction of the messages they receive, the intensity of the signals also influences their behaviour.

In figure 3a the lines at $x = a$, $x = b$ and $x = c$ correspond respectively to the configurations at which the blind spots i, j and k of robot 2 are directly aligned with robot 1. As shown in figure 3a, the intensity values of the messages received along and adjacent to the lines a, b and c are low. It is possible to make use of this fact to infer when the blind spot of a robot is aligned with its neighbour, and hence to determine the position of the neighbour more accurately. Specifically, as shown in figure 4a we may infer that the blind spot k of robot 1 is facing robot 2,

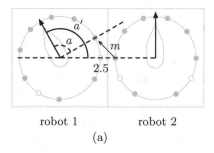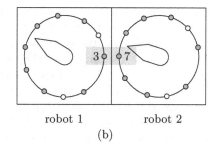

robot 1	robot 2	robot 1	robot 2
	(a)		(b)

Fig. 4. Diagrams showing the strategy for correcting misalignment using 'virtual' sensors (a) and alignment based upon paired sensors (b)

when the message m received at sensor 2 reports a low intensity. Whilst it is true that sensor 2 will also report low intensity values when the point between sensors 1 and 2 is aligned with robot 2, because this gap is smaller, these values will never drop as far they do in blind spot k.

A similar inference can be applied to blind spot i and its relation to sensor 5. Notionally then we may define two *virtual* sensors '2.5' and '4.5' which lie between sensors 2-3 and 4-5 respectively. As shown in figure 4a if a message is detected at sensor 2.5, rather than assume it to have originated from a point at an angle a, we may more accurately assume that it originated from an angle a' half way between sensors 2 and 3. Note that it is not possible to define a virtual sensor '3.5' which lies between sensors 3 and 4 because from the perspective of these sensors the blind spots i, j and k are indistinguishable.

It should be noted that, using intensity values alone, it is difficult for a robot to differentiate between the scenarios in which its own blind spot is facing its neighbour, its neighbour's blind spot is facing it, or both blind spots are facing each other. This is not a major concern, however, since in either scenario the re-action is the same, the robots will turn towards each other. Furthermore we may note that messages received from neighbours that are not directly connected, i.e. neighbours positioned at a diagonal, will always have lower intensity values. However, since the *LibIrcom* library preferentially processes high intensity messages, the proportion of messages received from indirect neighbours, and thus the influence they exert, will be lower than that of direct neighbours. In the worst case scenario robots will over eagerly turn towards each other, and as will become apparent in section 5, this is not always a bad thing.

In an attempt to reduce the constant changes in direction witnessed in the static synchronisation example, and to improve the time taken for the robots to converge upon a common heading, we also implement a new method for translating the relative headings of neighbouring modules into motor commands. Rather than incrementally updating an internal desired heading, at each control cycle we calculate the average direction of all the most recently detected headings. This value, h, which belongs to the range $-\pi < h \leq \pi$ is used to determine the speed of the robot's motors. For values of $h < 0$ the robot will turn left and for values of $h > 0$ will turn right, the speed at which the robot turns is proportional to the magnitude of h. For values of $h = 0$ and for control cycles in which no messages are received, the turning speed of the robot's motors is set to zero.

In communicating the relative angle at which a neighbour was detected, the robots transmit the number of the sensor, rather than the angle itself. Furthermore, if $|h| > \frac{\pi}{2}$, indicating that the robot will make a fast turn, to preempt this movement the number of the sensor that is transmitted is incremented or decremented depending upon whether the robot is turning left or right.

Finally, based upon the knowledge that a high intensity signal is indicative of a close alignment between two sensors, we can define certain sensor pairings which, when the intensity of the signal is high, should not influence the movement of the robots. For example, in figure 4b, if robot 1 receives a high intensity message on sensor 3, that was sent from sensor 7 of robot 2, the relative heading of robot 2 will be set to 0. Note that although the alignment between robots 1 and 2 in this scenario is not perfect, it is considered 'good enough' for the task at hand, and preferential to the robots continuously changing direction.

4.3   Obstacle Avoidance

Every sensor which has not recently received a message from another robot, and does not neighbour with a sensor that has recently received a message from another robot, contributes to obstacle avoidance. At each control cycle, the sensors which have detected the presence of an obstacle each create a new desired heading, based upon the position of the sensor. The distance to the detected object is used to assign a weight in the range $(0, 1)$ to each of these new headings, where the closer the obstacle is, the larger the weight. These weighted headings are added to the relative headings of the robots neighbour's, and as before, the average heading h is used to determine the speed of the robots motors. In effect, this is equivalent to assuming that there is a neighbouring robot directly facing every sensor which perceives an obstacle. As well as attempting to align with their neighbours, robots attempt to 'align' with obstacles, with closer obstacles exerting a greater influence over the alignment.

Finally, to ensure that the robots always continue to move forward, we add a small positive bias to the speed of each of the robot's motors.

5   Results

In this section we present the results of a series of experiments conducted using groups of between two and four e-pucks, each equipped with the modular e-puck extension. In the first set of experiments, using a group of stationary robots, we compare the performance of the static synchronisation strategy with our own approach to alignment. After showing our approach to be amenable to the task of stationary alignment, we demonstrate its ability to control a group of mobile robots. At the same time, we observe the robustness of our approach in terms of its ability to recover from perturbations which cause the group to split apart.

5.1 Stationary Alignment

In this set of experiments we compare our approach with the static synchronisation strategy from the *LibIrcom* library. Experiments were conducted using
groups of two, three and four stationary robots, arranged as shown in figure 5a.

For each controller and each of the three arrangements, 20 individual runs
were conducted. The orientation of the robots was randomised at the start of
each run and the absolute heading of each robot was recorded at one second
intervals over a period of 100 seconds. Throughout all of the experiments, data
was collected using an overhead camera and computer tracking software.

To assess the effectiveness of the approaches in terms of the ability of the
robots to converge towards a common heading, we use the same polarisation
metric as the authors of [7]. The polarisation $P(G)$ of a group of robots G is
defined as the sum of the distance between the heading of every robot and its
angular nearest neighbour θ_{ann}. More formally shown by equation 1.

$$P(G) = \sum_{i \in G} \theta_{ann}(i). \tag{1}$$

Figures 5b-d plot the mean polarisation of the two approaches for each of the
three module configurations. As is evident by the eventual low polarisation values
in all of the figures, in every experimental run the modules were observed to
converge to and maintain a common heading. In comparing the two approaches,
there is no statistically significant difference between the eventual polarisation
of each set of experiments. However, in every configuration, we can observe that
convergence is faster for the experiments utilising the new approach to alignment.
Furthermore, during the convergence phase (between around 0 and 30 seconds)
the variance in the polarisation of the static synchronisation approach greater.

5.2 Collective Locomotion

With the integration of the obstacle avoidance behaviour, we now apply our
approach to the task of controlling the collective locomotion of a group of mobile
units. The approach was tested for the same configurations used in section 5.1
and, in an enclosed arena ($\sim 0.5 \times 0.7m$), was shown to be capable of effectively
coordinating the motion of all three groups. A single run, lasting 30 minutes, was
conducted for each configuration. The average position of the robots over the
full period is plotted in figure 6. Videos of the experiments are provided online[1].

In all three scenarios the robots were able to successfully navigate the arena
without colliding with the arena walls. For the two and four robot configurations
all of the modules remained attached to one another throughout. In the three
module configuration, for a short period of time one module broke away from the
group, only to rejoin soon after. The ability of the module to rejoin the group
highlights an important property of our approach, that it is robust to perturbations in the group structure. To further examine this property we conducted

---

[1] http://www-users.york.ac.uk/~ljm505/modular_epucks.html.

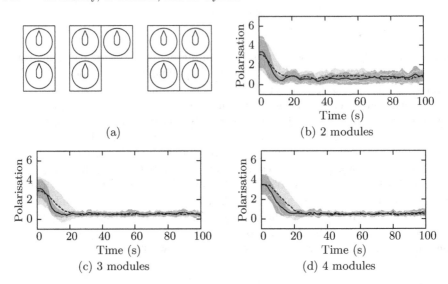

Fig. 5. Figures (b-d) plot the mean polarisation ± one standard deviation, for each of the three configurations in (a). The static synchronisation approach is represented by the dashed line and the lighter grey region, and our new approach is represented by the solid line and the darker region.

another experiment in which three robots were placed in different corners of the arena and left to operate for 10 minutes.

In figure 6d the average pairwise distance between each of the robots is plotted over the 10 minute period. As can be seen in the figure, the robots start far away from one another and gradually converge to a close proximity at around the 5 minute mark. For the remainder of the experiment they remain within close proximity of each other. As shown in figure 6e, what happened in this particular experiment was that at point i two of the modules physically joined together to form a two module structure. Shortly after, at point j the third module joined to complete the three module configuration shown in figure 5a. The robots then remained in this configuration until the end of the run.

It is important to note that this self-assembly behaviour was not pre-programed, it emerges purely due to the interaction of the robots and their environment. Specifically, it can be said to result from a combination of at three factors. Firstly the enclosed arena ensures that robots never stray too far away from one another. Secondly, the alignment behaviour ensures that robots all head in a similar direction. Finally, the design of the e-puck extension ensures that if two robots come into close proximity their magnetic docking interfaces will cause them to 'snap' together. Furthermore, although there is no explicit cohesion behaviour, the implementation of virtual sensors introduced in section 4 may cause robots to move towards each other when they mistakenly believe themselves to be aligned with the blind spot of another robot. These factors combine to produce the semi-stochastic self-assembly behaviour observed in figure 6e.

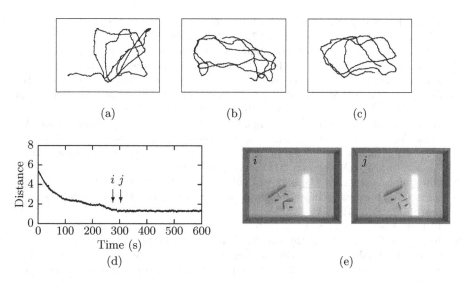

Fig. 6. The average position of groups of two (a), three (b) and four (c) e-pucks equipped with the modular extension, recorded over a 30 minute period, and the pairwise distance between three robots recorded over a 10 minute period (d-e)

6   Conclusions

We have presented the design of a structural extension that may be used to transform the e-puck platform into a *mobile-lattice* modular robotic system. As a proof of concept we described a controller for coordinating the collective locomotion of a group of e-pucks equipped with the extension. The controller was shown to be capable of synchronising the alignment of the group, as well as exhibiting robustness to perturbations which threaten the group's integrity. We conclude that our modular e-puck extension represents a viable low cost platform for research into the control of self-reconfigurable modular robotic systems.

Acknowledgments. The authors would like to thank James Hilder and Martin Trefzer for their invaluable input. The SYMBRION project is funded by the European Commission, within the 7th Framework Programme. FP7-ICT-2007.8.2.

References

1. Cianci, C.M., Raemy, X., Pugh, J., Martinoli, A.: Communication in a Swarm of Miniature Robots: The e-Puck as an Educational Tool for Swarm Robotics. In: Şahin, E., Spears, W.M., Winfield, A.F.T. (eds.) SAB 2006 Ws 2007. LNCS, vol. 4433, pp. 103–115. Springer, Heidelberg (2007)
2. English, S., Gough, J., Johnson, A., Spanton, R., Sun, J.: Formica (2012), http://formica.srobo.org
3. GCtronic: Elisa 3 (2012), http://www.gctronic.com/doc/index.php/Elisa_3

4. Gilpin, K., Kotay, K., Rus, D., Vasilescu, I.: Miche: Modular shape formation by self-disassembly. Int. J. Rob. Res. 27, 345–372 (2008)
5. Gilpin, K., Rus, D.: Self-disassembling robot pebbles: New results and ideas for self-assembly of 3d structures. In: IEEE International Conference on Robotics and Automation Workshop "Modular Robots: The State of the Art", pp. 94–99 (2010)
6. Groß, R., Bonani, M., Mondada, F., Dorigo, M.: Autonomous self-assembly in swarm-bots. IEEE Transactions on Robotics 22(6), 1115–1130 (2006)
7. Gutierrez, A., Campo, A., Dorigo, M., Donate, J., Monasterio-Huelin, F., Magdalena, L.: Open e-puck range & bearing miniaturized board for local communication in swarm robotics. In: IEEE International Conference on Robotics and Automation, ICRA 2009, pp. 3111–3116 (May 2009)
8. Gutiérrez, Á., Tuci, E., Campo, A.: Evolution of neuro-controllers for robots alignment using local communication. International Journal of Advanced Robotic Systems 6(1), 25–34 (2009)
9. K-Team Corporation: K-Team Mobile Robotics (2012), http://www.k-team.com
10. Kernbach, S., Scholz, O., Harada, K., Popesku, S., Liedke, J., Raja, H., Liu, W., Caparrelli, F., Jemai, J., Havlik, J., Meister, E., Levi, P.: Multi-Robot Organisms: State of the Art. In: ICRA10, Workshop on "Modular Robots: State of the Art", Anchorage, pp. 1–10 (2010)
11. Kernbach, S.: Jasmine swarm robot platform (2012), http://www.swarmrobot.org
12. Liu, W., Winfield, A.F.: Open-hardware e-puck linux extension board for experimental swarm robotics research. Microprocessors and Microsystems 35(1), 60–67 (2011)
13. Rubenstein, M., Hoff, N., Nagpal, R.: Kilobot: A low cost scalable robot system for collective behaviors. Tech. Rep. TR-06-11, Harvard University (June 2011), ftp://ftp.deas.harvard.edu/techreports/tr-06-11.pdf
14. Mondada, F., Bonani, M., Raemy, X., Pugh, J., Cianci, C., Klaptocz, A., Magnenat, S., Christophe Zufferey, J., Floreano, D., Martinoli, A.: The e-puck, a robot designed for education in engineering. In: Proceedings of the 9th Conference on Autonomous Robot Systems and Competitions, pp. 59–65 (2009)
15. Mondada, F., Pettinaro, G.C., Guignard, A., Kwee, I.W., Floreano, D., Deneubourg, J.L., Nolfi, S., Gambardella, L.M., Dorigo, M.: Swarm-bot: A new distributed robotic concept. Autonomous Robots 17, 193–221 (2004)
16. O'Grady, R., Pinciroli, C., Groß, R., Christensen, A.L., Mondada, F., Bonani, M., Dorigo, M.: Swarm-Bots to the Rescue. In: Kampis, G. (ed.) ECAL 2009, Part I. LNCS, vol. 5777, pp. 165–172. Springer, Heidelberg (2011)
17. Şahin, E., Spears, W.: Swarm Robotics: SAB 2004 International Workshop, Santa Monica, CA, USA, July 17 (2004); revised selected papers. LNCS. Springer (2005)
18. Wei, H., Cai, Y., Li, H., Li, D., Wang, T.: Sambot: A self-assembly modular robot for swarm robot. In: 2010 IEEE International Conference on Robotics and Automation (ICRA), pp. 66–71 (2010)
19. Yim, M., Shen, W.M., Salemi, B., Rus, D., Moll, M., Lipson, H., Klavins, E., Chirikjian, G.: Modular self-reconfigurable robot systems [grand challenges of robotics]. IEEE, Robotics Automation Magazine 14(1), 43–52 (2007)
20. Yim, M., Shirmohammadi, B., Sastra, J., Park, M., Dugan, M., Taylor, C.: Towards robotic self-reassembly after explosion. In: IEEE/RSJ International Conference on Intelligent Robots and Systems, IROS 2007, pp. 2767–2772 (2007)
21. Zykov, V., Chan, A., Lipson, H.: Molecubes: An open-source modular robotics kit. In: IROS 2007 Self-Reconfigurable Robotics Workshop (2007)

Task Partitioning via Ant Colony Optimization for Distributed Assembly

James Worcester and M. Ani Hsieh

Drexel University, Philadelphia, USA
{jbw68,mhsieh1}@drexel.edu

Abstract. We address the distributed assembly of a structure by a team of homogeneous robots. We present an ant-colony-optimization (ACO) based algorithm to partition general 2- and 3-D assembly tasks into N separate subtasks. The objective is to determine an allocation or partitioning strategy that minimizes the workload imbalance between the robots that allow for maximum assembly parallelization. This objective is achieved by extending ACO to apply to a team of ants dividing a set of tasks, with pheromone marking connections between tasks guiding decisions on task allocation. We present simulation results for various 2-D and 3-D structures and discuss the advantages of the ACO formulation in the context of other existing approaches.

1 Introduction

The challenge in distributed autonomous assembly of general two and three-dimensional structures lies in the complex interplay between the demands on global planning and coordination and local manipulation and perception. Successful autonomous and distributed assembly systems must have the ability to 1) sense and manipulate the various assembly elements; 2) interact with the desired structure at all stages of the assembly process while ensuring correctness of each assembly step; and 3) satisfy global structural properties such as static stability and structural integrity. Existing approaches to the distributed assembly problem generally fall under three categories: self-assembly, assembly task partitioning, and the synthesis of complete assembly strategies that can be executed with limited sensing and actuation capabilities.

In the self-assembly approach, the components mix freely until an appropriate combination occurs, at which point a robot performs the appropriate action to combine them [7,10]. This area is generally analyzed with chemical reaction networks, and deals with concentrations of various parts present in the workspace. As such, it is ideally suited to problems that have large numbers of parts and robots, where many copies of a completed structure are desired. It also has the advantage of dealing with multiple types of materials by considering them to be different chemical species. We are interested in the development of distributed autonomous assembly strategies for application in the areas of macro-scale manufacturing and automation. In this problem space, distributed autonomous assembly is representative of the general class of tightly-coupled tasks that is of much interest in multi-agent robotics research [3].

M. Dorigo et al. (Eds.): ANTS 2012, LNCS 7461, pp. 145–155, 2012.

In recent years, the execution of tightly-coupled tasks by multi-robot teams has mostly focused on cooperative grasping and manipulation of a single object by a team of robots [1, 5, 9, 11, 14]. However, automated assembly involves the coordination of many robots and their interactions with various assembly components whose placements must respect certain precedence constraints to ensure the final integrity of the desired structure. Existing approaches addressing distributed macro-scale assembly include [8, 15, 17, 18]. In [15], the strategy consists of designing local attachment rules for the assembly components and assembly is achieved by robots endowed with the ability to communicate locally with the components in the assembly structure to determine whether a placement is allowed. Mass-based partitioning of a desired structure is achieved through iterative applications of Voronoi decomposition in [17, 18]. Each robot in the team is then tasked to assemble the components located within each Voronoi cell. The advantage of this approach is that workload allocation can be further improved during the assembly process based on the amount of assembled components in each cell and employing the robot's positions as the new Voronoi centers. While this method works well for two dimensional structures, it is not clear how this strategy extends to three dimensions. Lastly, the synthesis of assembly instructions for special cubic structures by a team of quadrotors is discussed in [8]. While the assembly instructions can be executed by quadrotor teams of any size, correctness of the assembly strategy is achieved through serial execution of the assembly instructions. As such, this approach does not take advantage of the potential for parallelization afforded by a multi-robot team.

In this work, we present an ant-colony-optimization (ACO) [4, 13] based solution to the assembly partitioning problem . The primary contribution of this work is the modification of ACO to manage teams of cooperating agents, rather than to determine a policy for a single agent. Where traditional ACO uses groups of ants exploring the search space of solutions for a single ant, we use groups of teams of ants to explore the search space of solutions for a single team. We create N teams of M ants each. Each team acts independently during a generation, but pheromone is shared across teams, allowing them to learn from each others' experience. Each team has a manager which directs the interaction of the team members, orchestrating a sequential node-claiming sequence.

The remainder of the paper is organized as follows: Section 2 describes our methodology. Section 3 outlines our results, and Section 4 provides discussion of the results and directions for future work.

2   Methodology

We determine the set of starting nodes by computing the angular density of the structure about the center of mass, and then spacing the starting nodes such that the wedge mapped out between any two starting nodes has the same portion of the mass of the overall structure, subject to the restriction that starting nodes must be on the exterior of the top surface of the structure. The same set of starting nodes is then provided to all team managers so that pheromone can be meaningfully shared between teams, allowing them to learn from each others' experiences. The algorithm is then run for a prespecified number of generations. In each generation, the ants within a team will collectively divide the task according to the pheromone present, then score their proposed solution according to a metric based on workload variance, deposit their own pheromone in proportion to the quality of their solution, and finally reset their states in preparation for the next generation. This is shown in Alg. 2.1.

Algorithm 2.1. Algorithm Overview

0: choose starting nodes
    for i = 1 to number of generations **do**
        for j = 1 to N **do**
            Team j plans a task allocation (Alg. 2.2)
            Team j scores its solution
        end for
        for j = 1 to N **do**
            Team j deposits pheromone
            Team j resets its plan to hold only starting nodes
        end for
    end for

2.1   Baseline Strategy

We begin by describing our baseline strategy, which we label DAACO (Distributed Assembly by Ant Colony Optimization). In each generation, we use the existing pheromone to plan a decomposition of the structure into individual tasks. This is achieved by each ant sequentially claiming a single node, continuing until no unclaimed nodes remain. An individual ant makes its decision on which node to claim based on summing the total amount of pheromone leading to each potential target node from all nodes currently part of its task. That is, for each target node j, it computes a probability of taking that node according to equation 1:

$$p_j = ((\sum_i x_{ij}) + p_{min})/\sum_k ((\sum_i x_{ik}) + p_{min}) \tag{1}$$

where p_j is the probability of claiming node j, x_{ij} is the pheromone on the edge between i and j, and p_{min} is a constant that provides a small chance of claiming each node, even in the absence of pheromone. The sums only consider nodes for j that are adjacent to the ant's current task, and only consider nodes for i that are within the ant's current task. By considering all edges leading to the target node, we make it more likely that an ant will claim new tasks that share multiple adjacencies with the current task, leading to a more compact overall task for the ant.

The purpose of p_{min} is to introduce a possibility of exploring previously un-tried assignments. Effectively this provides a noise term to the exploration of the search space, giving a possibility of exiting a local minimum. The pheromone is globally initialized to a value of zero, meaning that initial decisions are chosen from a uniform distribution over all adjacent nodes. To increase solution diversity, an ordering of the ants is randomly generated by the team manager for each cycle (each ant claims at most one node during a cycle). The manager also determines when all nodes have been claimed, at which point the solution is scored. This process is summarized in Alg. 2.2.

Algorithm 2.2. Planning for a team

---

while There are unclaimed nodes **do**
   order = randomized permutation of ants within team
   for i = order **do**
     for k = neighbors of current task **do**
       scores(k) = $\sum$ pheromone between k and current task
     end for
     choose a node with probability proportional to scores(k) + p_{min}
     if Ant i found a claimable node **then**
       mark that node as claimed
     end if
   end for
end while

Between the planning and scoring phases, the pheromone graph is subjected to a global decay, removing a set fraction of the old pheromone each generation. This has the effect of attaching more importance to more recent generations. The reason for the timing between planning and scoring is to allow pheromone deposited in generation i to be used in generation $i + 1$ before it is subjected to decay. This means it is possible to increase the decay to a point where all pheromone is erased before new pheromone is deposited, making each generation dependent only on the results of the immediately preceding generation. A decay rate of d means $(d * 100)\%$ of the pheromone is removed at this step.

A metric based on the variance of the workload of each ant is employed by the team manager to score the solution. The metric is given by Eq. 2. This metric will provide a score scaled between 0 and 1, with a higher score indicating a better performance. This score is based on the entire team's performance, and is then passed to each individual ant to be used in depositing pheromone.

$$score = 1/(1 + var(WL)) \tag{2}$$

After the team's manager has computed a team score, each ant deposits an amount of pheromone equal to the score to each edge connecting a pair of nodes within the ant's task. Finally, at the end of each generation every ant is reset to contain only its assigned start node before the next generation begins.

After all generations are concluded, a solution is extracted from the population of ants by having one team run one last generation with a slight difference. Rather than stochastically choosing nodes according to the probabilities described above, each ant selects a node by deterministically selecting the node that would have the maximum probability, described by equation 3, where c is the choice made. This allows us to extract a solution that from the best knowledge the pheromone represents without adding the stochasticity found in a typical generation.

$$c_j = \max_j(\sum_i x_{ij})$$ (3)

2.2 Variant Strategies

We consider two variants on the baseline strategy. The first, which we label DAACO-D, provides an alternative way of depositing pheromone. As the baseline strategy deposits pheromone on all connections within the current task, it does not designate a direction, so the pheromone graph is undirected. This means that an ant claiming a node on either side of an edge with a high value is likely to take the node on the other side. Since this may not be desirable behavior for nodes near one of the starting points, DAACO-D uses a directed pheromone graph. To determine where to deposit pheromone on this directed graph, Dijkstra's algorithm is run on an ant's complete task assignment to determine a distance back to the start for every node. Pheromone is then only deposited on edges leading from a lower distance to a higher distance.

Our second variant, DAACO-S, allows ants to claim nodes that have already been taken by another ant, in order to more quickly reach an equal workload by not forcing an ant to stop taking nodes in a situation where all adjacent nodes have been claimed. In order to avoid ants repeatedly trading nodes back and forth, three restrictions are placed on this behavior. First, an ant will only consider stealing a node if there are no unclaimed nodes adjacent to its current task. Second, an ant will only steal nodes if its current workload is below the target workload (based on an equal distribution of the total). Finally, ant i will only steal a node from ant j if j has at least as much work as i. In order to encourage fewer stolen nodes in successive generations, an ant that loses a node will remove a fraction of the pheromone connecting it to that node.

3   Results

We test the algorithm on types of structures consisting of towers connected by paths, with holes between the paths where nothing is to be built. We vary the number of robots dividing the structure and the decay rate of the pheromone. Each map is also compared against the results of the algorithm described in [16] run on the same map. In this algorithm, the assembly task is initially divided by running Dijkstra's algorithm with multiple starting nodes, one for each robot. This leaves each robot with a tree representation of its task, where the root (the starting node) is guaranteed to be on the external boundary of the structure. By successively building leaves and removing built nodes from its tree, a robot can complete its task without the danger of becoming trapped in a partially built structure. The algorithm then goes through a node-trading phase which attempts to equalize the workload by exchanging leaves or branches while maintaining the tree property of each task. This is a deterministic algorithm, and hence generates only one solution for a given assembly task, in contrast to DAACO and its variants, which explore the solution space by varying pheromone levels.

Results are compared using the variance of the workload between different robots, with the goal being that this variance should be minimized in an effective plan. Our base structure consists of 9 3x3 towers, built out of 351 pieces, shown in Fig. 1(a). Each reported result for DAACO and its variants is the average of five runs, with each run lasting 20 generations. If parameters are not explicitly stated, the experiment is done with 8 robots, using a decay rate of 0.1.

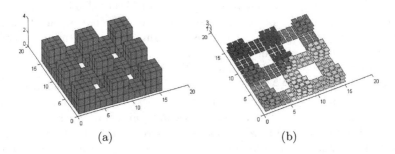

(a)   (b)

Fig. 1. (a) The base structure, consisting of nine towers connected by ground paths. (b) A typical decomposition, in this case by DAACO-S using 8 robots. Different colors represent the tasks of different robots.

First, we analyze the effects of using different numbers of robots to build this structure. For each number, we apply DAACO, DAACO-S, DAACO-D, and the Dijkstra-based algorithm from [16]. Results are shown in Table 1. Each entry is the variance of the workloads of the robots. Generally the deterministic Dijkstra-based algorithm has the best performance, closely followed by DAACO-S, while the basic DAACO has higher workload variance, and DAACO-D is consistently the worst. A typical decomposition is shown in Fig. 1(b), generated by DAACO-S for eight robots. However, the deterministic algorithm, as it only generates one solution per problem, will occasionally encounter a situation that provides a poor result. One instance of this can be seen for 6 robots dividing the base structure. Although the deterministic algorithm generally produces slightly better results than DAACO-S, in this case DAACO-S vastly outperforms the poor solution chosen by the deterministic algorithm. These solutions are shown in Fig. 2.

Table 1. Performance as a Function of Team Size

Algorithm	Number of Robots						
	2	3	4	5	6	7	8
DAACO	0.50	0.8	6.83	2.80	109.5	34.3	9.84
DAACO-S	0.50	0.20	0.78	0.40	3.5	1.01	0.98
DAACO-D	198.9	964.6	379.2	368.4	351.1	223.5	50.9
Dijkstra-based Algorithm	0.50	0	0.25	0.20	81.1	0.48	0.13

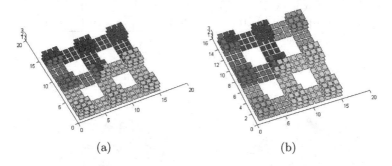

(a)   (b)

Fig. 2. Solutions for six robots, as solved by DAACO-S (a) and the deterministic algorithm (b). Tasks are delineated by different colors.

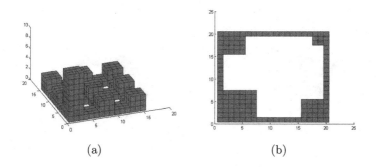

(a)   (b)

Fig. 3. Two asymmetric structures. (a) Tower structure with one tower triple the height of the rest (b) 2-d structure with lopsided areas.

Next, we examine the results of the two structures shown in Fig. 3 to determine the algorithm's robustness to asymmetry. In one structure, one of the towers is much taller than the others, while the second is a 2-D structure with lopsided areas. Table 2 shows a direct comparison between these cases. We note that these asymmetric cases can cause problems for the deterministic algorithm, while DAACO-S still performs well. The plans generated for these structures are shown in Figs. 4 and 5.

Varying the decay rate of the pheromone (what percentage evaporates between each generation) has little effect on the resulting workload variance, as shown in Table 3. These results were generated on the base structure.

Table 2. Results on Asymmetric Structures

Algorithm	One Tall Tower	2-d asymmetric
DAACO	48.3	10.2
DAACO-S	6.73	4.97
DAACO-D	79.8	65.0
Dijkstra-based Algorithm	41.1	29.4

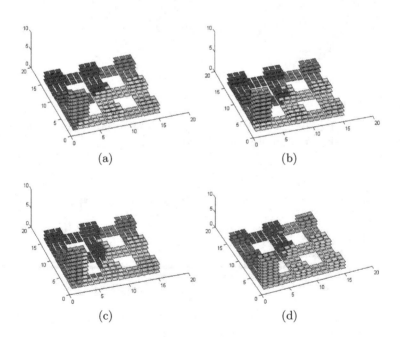

(a)   (b)

(c)   (d)

Fig. 4. Plans created for asymmetric tower structure by (a) DAACO, (b) DAACO-S, (c) DAACO-D, and (d) deterministic algorithm.

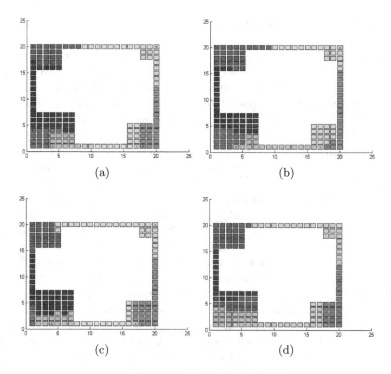

Fig. 5. Plans created for 2-D structure with lopsided areas by (a) DAACO, (b) DAACO-S, (c) DAACO-D, and (d) deterministic algorithm.

Table 3. Performance with Different Decay Rates

Algorithm	Decay Rate				
	0	0.1	0.5	0.75	1
DAACO	5.50	9.84	6.24	5.73	6.75
DAACO-S	0.58	0.98	0.41	0.53	0.47
DAACO-D	46.4	45.5	45.8	44.7	49.7

4   Discussion and Future Work

The results show that allowing ants to steal nodes from each other greatly improves the performance of DAACO-S on this task, giving it comparable performance to the Dijkstra-based algorithm from [16] in most cases, and superior performance in some. This performance appears to be largely independent of how much pheromone decay is present. Breaks in symmetry tend to be problematic for the deterministic approach, but are handled well by DAACO-S. In contrast, DAACO-D displays performance generally worse than DAACO. This may be because not adding pheromone between nodes at the same distance from the starting point weakens the incentive to tightly cluster the tasks chosen, and allows claiming of more distant tasks which can block off other ants, leaving them with smaller workloads.

One aspect of this algorithm worth noting is that it can be used to maintain connectivity back to an external node, similar to the Dijkstra-based algorithm. By requiring the starting points to be on the exterior of the structure and limiting newly claimed nodes to be adjacent to already possessed nodes, DAACO and DAACO-D provide contiguous tasks that contain part of the exterior of the structure. This means each robot can plan a way to build its own part that avoids being trapped in a partially complete structure. As discussed in [6], when using Voronoi methods, robots can have entirely internal tasks, leaving them no way to escape the structure if other robots build a wall around them.

DAACO-S in our implementation is not guaranteed to maintain a contiguous task as another robot could steal a node that disconnects some part of the task. However, this can be fixed by explicitly checking for each stolen node whether contiguouity would be broken. One direction for future work is to add a method to perform this check in constant time regardless of task size. This will be done by having each node maintain a distance from the root, which can be easily calculated when the node is added to the task. One direct method would then be to only allow stealing of nodes that do not have any neighbors with a higher distance. This would prevent tasks from being separated, but would also greatly limit the number of nodes available. A more promising direction is to apply a local Dijkstra starting from each neighbor with a higher distance, which terminates at the first node other than the stolen node which has a distance no higher than the stolen node. Essentially what this is doing is checking for an alternate path back to the root.

Another area for future work is to apply an idea from Simulated Annealing, and allow p_{min} to decay over time, starting with a high value to encourage early exploration of the solution space, with the best solution being further refined as the noise represented by p_{min} decreases.

Finally, we would like to apply these methods to our experimental testbed, described in [16], where it was used with the deterministic approach presented in that paper. Other hardware platforms that could be used with this approach include those used in [8], [12], [2].

References

1. Berman, S., Lindsey, Q., Sakar, M.S., Kumar, V., Pratt, S.: Experimental study and modeling of group retrieval in ants as an approach to collective transport in swarm robotic systems. Proceedings of the IEEE, Special Issue on Swarming in Natural and Engineered Systems (2011)
2. Bolger, A., Faulkner, M., Stein, D., White, L., Yun, S., Rus, D.: Experiments in decentralized robot construction with tool delivery and assembly robots. In: IEEE/RSJ International Conference on Intelligent Robots and Systems (2010)
3. Chaimowicz, L., Sugar, T., Kumar, V., Campos, M.F.M.: An Architecture for Tightly Coupled Multi-Robot Cooperation. In: Proc. IEEE Int. Conf. on Rob. & Autom., Seoul, Korea, pp. 2292–2297 (May 2001)

4. Dorigo, M., Caro, G.D., Gambardella, L.M.: Ant algorithms for discrete optimization. Artificial Life, 137–172 (1999)
5. Fink, J., Hsieh, M.A., Kumar, V.: Multi-robot manipulation via caging in environments with obstacles. In: Proc. IEEE International Conference on Robotics and Automation (ICRA 2008), Pasadena, CA, pp. 1471–1476 (May 2008)
6. Hsieh, M., Rogoff, J.: Complexity measures for distributed assembly tasks. In: Proc. of the 2010 Performance Metrics for Intelligent Systems Workshop (PerMIS 2009), Baltimore, Maryland (September 2010)
7. Klavins, E., Burden, S., Napp, N.: Optimal rules for programmed stochastic self-assembly. In: Proc. Robotics: Science and Systems II, Atlanta, GA, pp. 9–16 (2007)
8. Lindsey, Q.J., Mellinger, D., Kumar, V.: Construction of cubic structures with quadrotor teams. Robotics: Science and Systems (June 2011)
9. Mataric, M.J., Nilsson, M., Simsarian, K.: Cooperative Multi-Robot Box-Pushing. In: Proc. IEEE/RSJ International Conference on Intelligent Robots and Systems (IROS 1995), Pittsburgh, Pennsylvania, pp. 556–561 (August 1995)
10. Matthey, L., Berman, S., Kumar, V.: Stochastic Strategies for a Swarm Robotic Assembly System. In: Proc. 2009 IEEE International Conference on Robotics and Automation (ICRA 2009), Kobe, Japan, pp. 1953–1958 (2009)
11. Pereira, G.A.S., Kumar, V., Campos, M.F.M.: Decentralized Algorithms for Multirobot Manipulation via Caging. International Journal of Robotics Research 23, 783–795 (2004)
12. Peterson, K., Nagpal, R., Werfel, J.: Termes: an autonomous robotic system for three-dimensional collective construction. In: Robotics: Science and Systems (2011)
13. Sauter, J.A., Matthews, R., Parunak, H.V.D., Brueckner, S.: Evolving adaptive pheromone path planning mechanisms. In: Autonomous Agents and Multi-Agent Systems (AAMAS 2002), Bologna, Italy, pp. 434–440 (2002)
14. Sugar, T., Kumar, V.: Multiple Cooperating Mobile Manipulators. In: Proc. 1999 IEEE International Conference on Robotics and Automation (ICRA 1999), Detroit, Michigan, pp. 1538–1543 (May 1999)
15. Werfel, J., Bar-Yam, Y., Nagpal, R.: Building patterned structures with robot swarms. In: Proc. of the 19th Int. Joint Conf. on Artificial Intelligence (IJCAI 2005), Pasadena, CA USA, pp. 1495–1502 (July 2009)
16. Worcester, J., Rogoff, J., Hsieh, M.: Constrained Task Partitioning for Distributed Assembly. In: Proc. IEEE/RSJ International Conference on Intelligent Robots and Systems (IROS 2011), San Francisco, California (September 2011)
17. Yun, S.K., Rus, D.: Adaptation to robot failures and shape change in decentralized construction. In: Proc. of the Int. Conf. on Robotics & Automation (ICRA 2010), Anchorage, AK, USA, pp. 2451–2458 (May 2010)
18. Yun, S.-k., Schwager, M., Rus, D.: Coordinating Construction of Truss Structures Using Distributed Equal-Mass Partitioning. In: Pradalier, C., Siegwart, R., Hirzinger, G. (eds.) Robotics Research. STAR, vol. 70, pp. 607–623. Springer, Heidelberg (2011)

The Self-adaptive Comprehensive Learning Particle Swarm Optimizer

Adiel Ismail[1,2] and Andries P. Engelbrecht[2]

[1] Department of Computer Science, University of the Western Cape, South Africa
aismail@uwc.ac.za
[2] Department of Computer Science, University of Pretoria, South Africa
engel@cs.up.ac.za

Abstract. Particle swarm optimization (PSO) has been applied successfully to a wide range of optimization problems. Appropriate values for control parameters of the particle swarm optimization (PSO) algorithm are critical to its success. This paper proposes that the control parameters of PSO be embedded in the position vector of particles and dynamically adapted while the search is in progress, relieving the user from specifying appropriate values before the search commences. Application of the Self-Adaptive Comprehensive Learning Particle Swarm Optimizer (SACLPSO) to 9 well known test functions show an improvement in performance on most of the functions compared to CLPSO and a tuned PSO.

1 Introduction

Particle swarm optimization (PSO) is a nature inspired population based stochastic optimization approach which was originally developed by Eberhart and Kennedy [3]. PSO is appealing to optimization because it is easy to implement, no gradient information is required, and it is computationally inexpensive due to low memory and CPU requirements [3].

Despite its simplicity, the success of PSO largely depends on selecting appropriate values for its control parameters, i.e. the inertia weight, w, and acceleration coefficients c_1 and c_2. Incorrectly chosen parameter values may lead to suboptimal solutions, premature convergence, stagnation of the algorithm, slower convergence, or even to divergent or cyclic behaviour [13],[14]. Optimal control parameter values are also problem dependent and may be different for different particles in the swarm. Determining optimal static control parameters manually for the PSO is time consuming.

Numerous PSO variants dynamically adapt the control parameters to improve the performance of the PSO. These include the time-varying parameter control strategies such as the linearly decreasing inertia weight [10] and maximum velocity [12], the non-linearly adjusted inertia weight [1], and the time-varying acceleration coefficients [7]. A fuzzy system adapts the inertia weight in [11]. Two swarms alternate in optimizing the objective function and the PSO control parameters separately in [5]. Control parameters are self-adapted by growing

M. Dorigo et al. (Eds.): ANTS 2012, LNCS 7461, pp. 156–167, 2012.
© Springer-Verlag Berlin Heidelberg 2012

and shrinking the swarm respectively based on under or improved performance of individual particles in 'Tribes' of Clerc [2].

Despite exhibiting good performance on well-known test functions, the basic PSO tends to converge prematurely in strongly multi-modal test functions. Poor swarm diversity has been identified as one of the causes of premature convergence of the basic PSO [8]. Correctly chosen parameter values ensure swarm diversity and thus exploration which is vital for the PSO in reaching an optimal solution. Preferably, the PSO search should start with a high diversity and maintain it for a longer period while a lower diversity is desirable when approaching convergence. Results reported for the Comprehensive Learning PSO (CLPSO) of Liang *et al* [4] on multi-modal functions indicate that the CLPSO generally strikes a good balance between high and low diversity when fine-tuning a solution.

This paper proposes the Self-Adaptive Comprehensive Learning PSO (SACLPSO) which is a modification to the CLPSO by dynamically determining appropriate values for the CLPSO control parameters. The position vectors are augmented to also contain the inertia weight and the acceleration coefficient which are adjusted together with the decision variables using the PSO update equations. Velocity, personal best position and global best position are also augmented to $(D+2)$-dimensional vectors. This approach of including the control parameters in an augmented position vector can easily be applied to other PSO variants.

The rest of the paper is organized as follows: Section 2 provides an overview of PSO. An overview of the CLPSO is presented in section 3. The SACLPSO is presented in section 4. The experiments and their results are presented and discussed in section 5. The paper is concluded in section 6.

2   Overview of PSO

A swarm of particles in PSO fly through the search space to find an optimal solution to an optimization problem. Each particle represents a potential solution to the optimization problem and is equipped with a position and a velocity. When PSO starts, the particles are randomly distributed throughout the search space. Each particle subsequently adjusts its velocity in relation to the best position found so far and in relation to the best position of all particles in a defined neighborhood. The position of a particle is updated using the particle's velocity. The best position of particle i is denoted by $\mathbf{x}_i$ and the velocity by $\mathbf{v}_i$. The personal best position of particle i is represented as $\mathbf{xpbest}_i$. The best position in the entire swarm is referred to as $\mathbf{xGbest}$. The global best and personal best positions are also updated over time. The position and velocity update equations are:

$$v_i^d(t+1) = w \cdot v_i^d(t) + c_1 \cdot r_1^d(t) \cdot (xpbest_i^d(t) - x_i^d(t)) \tag{1}$$
$$+ c_2 \cdot r_2^d(t) \cdot (xGbest^d(t) - x_i^d(t))$$
$$x_i^d(t+1) = x_i^d(t) + v_i^d(t+1) \tag{2}$$

where $d = 1, 2, ..., D$, $i = 1, 2, ..., S$, and S is the size of the swarm; w is the inertia weight with $0 \leq w < 1$; c_1 and c_2 are two positive constants, called the *acceleration constants*; $\mathbf{r}_1$ and $\mathbf{r}_2$ are two vectors containing random numbers, with each random number uniformly distributed in $(0, 1)$; and t indicates the iteration number. The second and third terms in equation (1) are respectively referred to as the cognitive and the social components.

3   Comprehensive Learning Particle Swarm Optimizer

The Comprehensive Learning Particle Swarm Optimizer (CLPSO) of Liang *et al* [4] addresses the problem associated with premature convergence in the basic PSO by removing the social component from velocity update equation (1), and by allowing each position vector component of a particle to be attracted stochastically to the corresponding personal best position vector component of any other particle in the swarm. Velocity is updated using

$$v_i^d(t+1) = w \ v_i^d(t) + c \ r_1^d(t)(xpbest_{f_i(d)}^d(t) - x_i^d(t)) \tag{3}$$

where $\mathbf{f}_i = [f_i(1), f_i(2), f_i(3), ..., f_i(D)]$ and $f_i(d) = i_1$, with $d \in \{1, 2, 3, ..., D\}$ and $i_1 \in \{1, 2, 3, ..., S\}$; S denotes the size of the swarm and $\mathbf{f}_i$ defines which particles' personal best positions to use when updating each dimension of the velocity of particle i.

The basic PSO updates a particle's velocity using the particle's personal best and the swarm's global best positions, while in the extreme case equation (3) may result in a particle's velocity to be updated by using information from as many as D distinct particles when each vector component refers to a different particle, i.e. $\{f_i(d) \mid d = 1, 2, 3, ..., D\} = \{i_1 \mid i_1 = 1, 2, 3, ..., S\}$, where i_1 refers to the index of the particle. The decision whether to use a particle's own personal best position or that of another particle depends on a learning probability, LP_i. The learning probabilities which range from 0.05 to 0.5 were empirically developed by Liang *et al* and were computed using,

$$LP_i = 0.05 + 0.45 \cdot \frac{(\exp(\frac{10 \cdot (i-1)}{S-1}) - 1)}{(\exp(10) - 1)} \tag{4}$$

Experiments conducted by Liang *et al* indicated that different learning probabilities equip particles with different exploration/exploitation abilities. Liang *et al* subsequently proposed a different learning probability for each particle in the swarm. The learning probability assigned to a particle is fixed to the particle for the entire execution of the CLPSO algorithm.

CLPSO updates the velocity of each particle using a set of particles referred to as *exemplars* [4]. Exemplars are selected as follows: A random number uniformly distributed in $(0, 1)$ is generated for each dimension of particle i. If this random number exceeds the corresponding learning probability, LP_i, then the corresponding dimension will be updated using the particle's own personal best, otherwise the dimension will be updated using the personal best of another particle as determined by a tournament selection procedure. In the latter approach two particles are randomly chosen from the swarm, excluding the particle being updated. The particle with a better personal best value is subsequently selected to update the corresponding dimension of the velocity of particle i. This procedure is repeated for all dimensions of particle i.

If all dimensions of the position of particle i refer to its own personal best positions, then one dimension of particle i is randomly chosen and updated by the corresponding dimension of another randomly selected particle's personal best position.

If a particle's personal best does not improve for a predetermined period (also referred to as the refreshing gap, m), a new set of exemplars is selected for the particle. Liang et al empirically determined 7 as a good value for m on their set of test functions. To keep track of the number of consecutive iterations that showed no improvement in a particle's personal best, each particle i is assigned a counter, $flag_i$. For a detailed description of CLPSO refer to [4].

Liang et al reported that the CLPSO performed better than a number of modified PSO algorithms in 10 of their 16 test functions. This makes the CLPSO algorithm a good candidate for self-adapting the control parameters of PSO.

4   Self-adaptive Comprehensive Learning PSO

The Self-Adaptive Comprehensive Learning PSO (SACLPSO) is an adaptation of the CLPSO where the inertia weight and acceleration coefficient are self-adapted during the search process. The position vector of each particle in SACLPSO is augmented to contain both the inertia weight, w, and the acceleration coefficient, c. The first D dimensions of the position vector represent a potential solution to the optimization problem, while the particle's inertia weight and acceleration coefficient are stored in dimensions $D{+}1$ and $D{+}2$ of the position vector, respectively. Thus, each particle in SACLPSO has its own inertia weight and acceleration coefficient. Note that only the first D dimensions of the position vector are used when evaluating a particle's fitness. Velocity, personal best position and global best position vectors are also augmented to $(D{+}2)$-dimensional vectors. When a swarm is created the vector components corresponding to the decision variables are initialized to random values in a defined domain, while the vector components for the inertia weight and the acceleration coefficient values of each particle are initialized to random values in the acceptable ranges [0.1, 1.0] and [0.1, 3.0], respectively. The learning probabilities which are fixed during the entire execution of SACLPSO are initialized using equation (4).

The following operations apply to each particle in the swarm: A new set of exemplars for a particle is selected as outlined in CLPSO when the SACLPSO commences or as soon as $flag_i$ is equal to or greater than the refreshing gap m. When a new set of exemplars is selected for particle i, the counter $flag_i$ is reset to zero. The control parameters, w and c, are extracted from the position vector and used to update the velocity of a particle using equation (3) and clamped if required. The position of a particle is subsequently updated using equation (2). The personal best and global best positions are only updated if the position of the particle lies within the search domain. An update of the personal best signals an improvement, and hence $flag_i$ is reset. If the personal best of particle i is not updated, $flag_i$ is incremented. To prevent the SACLPSO algorithm from searching for potential solutions outside the search space, a value for any dimension of an updated position that exceeds the boundary of the search space is immediately reassigned to a random value in the domain. The SACLPSO algorithm appears in Algorithm 1 where max_{iter} refers to the maximum number of iterations.

The SACLPSO requires additional storage space for the weight and acceleration coefficients of each particle. Additional processing is also required to access, extract and update these additional two vector components compared to the CLPSO.

Algorithm 1. SACLPSO algorithm

```
Create a swarm of D+2-dimensional particles with
position vector augmented to contain w and c
Initialize learning probabilities, LP_i, using equation (4)
Repeat max_iter times (k = 1 to max_iter)
    Repeat S times (i = 1 to S)
        if( flag_i ≥ m) or (k = 1) then
            select a set of exemplars for particle i
            reset counter, flag_i ← 0
        Endif
        Extract w from position vector of particle i
        Extract c from position vector of particle i
        Repeat D times (d = 1 to D + 2)
            Update v_i^d using equation (3)
            Clamp velocity if necessary
            Update x_i^d using equation (1)
        Next D
        if x_i ∈ [x_min, x_max] then
            if fitness(x_i) < fitness(xpbest_i) then
                xpbest_i = x_i
                flag_i = 0
                if fitness(x_i) < fitness(gBest) then
                    gBest = x_i
                Endif
            Else
                flag_i = flag_i + 1
            Endif
        else
            Reassign vector position components
            that exit search space randomly
            to search domain
        Endif
    Next i
Next k
```

---

5   Experiments and Results

The aim of this section is to describe and report on the experiments performed in this paper. For this purpose, section 5.1 describes the experiments and defines the test functions and its parameters, while section 5.2 reports the results of the experiments.

5.1   Experimental Procedure

The principle goal of this paper is to investigate the performance of the proposed SACLPSO which self-adapts the control parameters of CLPSO, bearing in mind that the SACLPSO searches a larger dimensional space of $D + 2$ compared to the D dimensional space searched by the CLPSO. Performance was based on the fitness of particles. To compare the performance of the SACLPSO with the CLPSO and a tuned PSO, 9 test functions listed in table 1 were used. The test set consisted of the unimodal Sphere function and 8 multi-modal functions including the Rotated Ackley, which has been rotated using Salomon's method [9]. The domain refers to the space in which the optimum was searched for.

Table 1. Definitions and parameters of test functions

Function (where $D = 30$)	Domain	Name
$f_1(\mathbf{x}) = \sum_{i=1}^{D} x_i^2$	$[-100, 100]^D$	Sphere
$f_2(\mathbf{x}) = \sum_{i=1}^{\frac{D}{2}} 100(x_{2i} - x_{2i-1}^2)^2 + (1 - x_{2i-1})^2$	$[-10, 10]^D$	Rosenbrock
$f_3(\mathbf{x}) = -20 \cdot \exp\left(-0.2 \cdot \sqrt{\frac{1}{D}\sum_{i=1}^{n} x_i^2}\right)$ $- \exp\left(\frac{1}{n}\sum_{i=1}^{D}\cos(2\pi x_i)\right) + 20 + e$	$[-32, 32]^D$	Ackley
$f_4(\mathbf{x}) = \frac{1}{4000}\sum_{i=1}^{D} x_i^2 - \prod_{i=1}^{D}\cos(\frac{x_i}{\sqrt{i}}) + 1$	$[-600, 600]^D$	Griewank
$f_5(\mathbf{x}) = \sum_{i=1}^{D}\left(\sum_{k=0}^{kmax}[a^k\cos(2\pi b^k(x_i + 0.5))]\right)$ $- D\sum_{k=0}^{kmax}[a^k\cos(2\pi b^k \cdot 0.5)$ $a = 0.5, b = 3, kmax = 20$	$[-0.5, 0.5]^D$	Weierstrass
$f_6(\mathbf{x}) = \sum_{i=1}^{D}(x_i^2 - 10\cos(2\pi x_i) + 10)$	$[-5.12, 5.12]^D$	Rastrigin
$f_7(\mathbf{x}) = \sum_{i=1}^{D}(y_i^2 - 10\cos(2\pi y_i) + 10)$ where $y_i = \begin{cases} x_i & \text{if } |x_i| < \frac{1}{2} \\ \frac{round(2x_i)}{2} & \text{if } |x_i| \ge \frac{1}{2} \end{cases}$	$[-5.12, 5.12]^D$	Non-continuous Rastrigin
$f_8(\mathbf{x}) = 418.98 \times D - \sum_{i=1}^{D} x_i \sin\left(\sqrt{|x_i|}\right)$	$[-500, 500]^D$	Schwefel
$f_9(\mathbf{x}) = -20 \cdot \exp\left(-0.2 \cdot \sqrt{\frac{1}{D}\sum_{i=1}^{n} x_i^2}\right)$ $- \exp\left(\frac{1}{n}\sum_{i=1}^{D}\cos(2\pi x_i)\right) + 20 + e$ $y = M * x$	$[-32, 32]^D$	Rotated Ackley

The optimal set of parameters for the tuned PSO was determined by comparing the average global best values yielded by a limited number of combinations of w, c_1 and c_2 on the test functions after 1000 iterations. The inertia weight ranged from 0.4 to 1.0 in increments of 0.025, while both acceleration coefficients ranged from 0.6 to 2.4 in increments of 0.075. The average of the global best values over 50 independent simulations was used to evaluate the performance for each set of PSO control parameters. The best yielding set of parameters for each test function was chosen as parameters for the PSO. The parameters for the tuned PSO for each function are listed in table 2.

The performance of the SACLPSO, as measured by the average global best value over 30 simulations, was compared to that of the CLPSO and a tuned PSO using the parameters listed in Table 2. For all experiments, each swarm consisted of 40 particles. All experiments were run for 2×10^5 function evaluations, noting that 40 function evaluations are required per iteration by all PSO approaches. The swarm size and maximum number of function evaluations are similar to that chosen by Liang *et al* for their experiments in [4].

Table 2. Parameter settings of tuned PSO for each test function

Function	PSO		
	w	c_1	c_2
f_1	0.525	2.025	1.80
f_2	0.625	1.20	2.025
f_3	0.60	1.875	2.025
f_4	0.60	2.10	1.65
f_5	0.725	1.475	1.85
f_6	0.775	2.10	1.05
f_7	0.75	2.025	1.20
f_8	0.45	2.40	1.875
f_9	0.70	2.175	1.275

Table 3. Average values for control parameters for SACLSPO and p-values

Function	SACLPSO average w	SACLPSO average c	SACLPSO vs CLPSO p-value	SACLPSO vs PSO p-value
f_1	0.482	1.103	0.032	2.87E-11
f_2	0.490	1.325	0.013	2.87E-11
f_3	0.428	1.140	**5.43E-05**	2.87E-11
f_4	0.445	1.147	**1.05E-05**	0.917
f_5	0.399	1.207	**2.87E-11**	**2.87E-11**
f_6	0.283	1.268	**4.29E-11**	**2.87E-11**
f_7	0.264	1.254	**6.17E-10**	**2.87E-11**
f_8	0.385	1.275	**1.12E-09**	**2.87E-11**
f_9	0.409	0.964	**2.28-07**	**1.14E-7**

The effect of SACLPSO on diversity was also investigated in this paper. Olorunda and Engelbrecht investigated a number of diversity measures in [6] and concluded that the average distance around the swarm center is a more robust measure than swarm diameter or radius in the presence of outliers. Hence, the diversity measure used in this paper is the 'average distance around the swarm center' as defined in [6].

5.2 Experimental Results

The average values for the inertia weight, w, and the acceleration coefficient, c, for the SACLPSO were calculated at each iteration over the 30 simulations; results are given in table 3. In order to establish whether the results produced by the SACLPSO algorithm are statistically different from the results produced by CLPSO and the PSO, the non-parametric Mann-Whitney U-test was conducted. The p-values from the test are included in table 3. A p-value less than 0.05 indicates that the performance of the two algorithms are statistically different with 95% confidence. Entries in bold in table 3 indicate that the SACLPSO has outperformed the other algorithm. The SACLPSO has outperformed the CLPSO and the PSO in 7 and 5 of the 9 test functions, respectively.

The average global best values over 30 simulations are tabulated in table 4 for the tuned PSO, CLPSO and SACLPSO for each of the 9 test functions.

Subfigures (a) to (j) in figure 1 plot the logarithm of the average global best values over 30 simulations for the various test functions for each of the three PSO approaches. The logarithm of the average diversity over 30 simulations for the various test functions are plotted for the tuned PSO, CLPSO and SACLPSO in subfigures (a) to (i) in figure 2.

The basic PSO with optimized parameters performed much better than CLPSO and SACLPSO on function f_1, the unimodal Sphere function. The tuned PSO also converged much faster than both the CLPSO and SACLPSO. Both the CLPSO and SACLPSO improved their minimum, although extremely slowly. The CLPSO and SACLPSO achieved fairly similar results on the Sphere function. Figure 2(a) indicates that the SACLPSO maintained a slightly higher diversity than CLPSO, with a corresponding slightly lower performance as reflected in figure 1(a). The continued high diversity maintained by both CLPSO and SACLPSO towards the end of the search could have resulted in their poor performance. The CLPSO and SACLPSO could not successfully move from exploration to exploitation when convergence is reached on the simple unimodal functions. The omission of the global best term from the velocity update equation in CLPSO and SACLPSO resulted in particles not being attracted explicitly to the single global minimum when applied to the simple unimodal Sphere function. Particles were instead attracted to positions which were constructed from personal best positions. Omission of the global best term from the velocity update equation caused delayed attraction and subsequent slowed convergence to the local minimum in the case of unimodal functions.

Table 4. Average global best over 30 simulations for tuned PSO, CLPSO and SACLPSO

Function	PSO Mean	CLPSO Mean	SACLPSO Mean
f_1	$7.73E - 95 \pm 2.93E - 94$	$6.44E - 13 \pm 2.92E - 13$	$7.45E - 12 \pm 2.63E - 11$
f_2	$6.05E + 00 \pm 2.23E + 00$	$2.12E + 01 \pm 2.54E + 00$	$2.62E + 01 \pm 1.27E + 01$
f_3	$9.80E - 15 \pm 3.30E - 15$	$2.88E - 07 \pm 6.76E - 08$	$1.87E - 07 \pm 1.60E - 07$
f_4	$2.11E - 02 \pm 4.56E - 02$	$7.79E - 09 \pm 1.08E - 08$	$1.45E - 08 \pm 4.98E - 08$
f_5	$2.90E + 00 \pm 1.84E + 00$	$4.74E - 06 \pm 2.26E - 06$	$1.04E - 08 \pm 1.10E - 08$
f_6	$2.27E + 01 \pm 6.41E + 00$	$8.94E - 05 \pm 1.00E - 04$	$2.38E - 13 \pm 2.67E - 13$
f_7	$1.33E + 01 \pm 8.01E + 00$	$1.06E - 03 \pm 6.86E - 04$	$6.21E - 10 \pm 3.06E - 09$
f_8	$2.57E + 03 \pm 5.96E + 02$	$1.69E - 09 \pm 1.49E - 09$	$7.84E - 11 \pm 1.50E - 10$
f_9	$2.08E + 00 \pm 8.61E - 01$	$1.54E - 02 \pm 4.29E - 02$	$1.46E - 02 \pm 7.50E - 02$

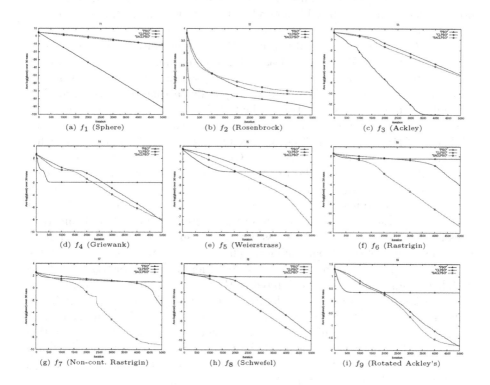

(a) f_1 (Sphere)   (b) f_2 (Rosenbrock)   (c) f_3 (Ackley)

(d) f_4 (Griewank)   (e) f_5 (Weierstrass)   (f) f_6 (Rastrigin)

(g) f_7 (Non-cont. Rastrigin)   (h) f_8 (Schwefel)   (i) f_9 (Rotated Ackley's)

Fig. 1. Plots of average gbest for functions f_1 to f_9

The tuned PSO also performed much better than both the CLPSO and the SACLPSO on function f_2, the Rosenbrock function as reflected in figure 1(b). The tuned PSO improved its minimum fitness value quickly over the first 300 iterations, with a corresponding reduction in diversity, whereafter the minimum fitness continued to decrease at a much slower rate. As illustrated in figure 2(b), the diversity of the tuned PSO on Rosenbrock also increased from iteration 350 as some particles were drawn away from the global minimum towards local minima. An inspection also revealed that more particles were exiting the search domain after 2000 iterations, which also lead to an increase in the diversity, since particles were not re-initialized to the domain. The CLPSO reached a slightly lower fitness than the SACLPSO.

For function f_3, the Ackley function, a tuned PSO converged initially much faster than the CLPSO and SACLPSO, but was eventually exceeded by CLPSO and SACLPSO (i.e. around 10000 iterations or 40000 evaluations, not shown in graph). The small spikes in the graph depicting the diversity for PSO on the Ackley function in figure 2(c) showed that particles wandered off or explored the search areas around the minimum but were subsequently drawn back to the minimum. The tuned PSO performed the best for the Ackley function.

The tuned PSO converged much faster than both CLPSO and SACLPSO on functions f_1, f_2 and f_3 (i.e. the Sphere, Rosenbrock and the Ackley functions, respectively) as reflected in figures 1(a) to 1(c) and managed to reach much lower fitness values compared to CLPSO and SACLPSO within the 2×10^5 function evaluations.

The SACLPSO outperformed the tuned PSO on the multi-modal functions, f_4 to f_9 (i.e. Griewank, Weierstrass, Rastrigin, Non-continuous Rastrigin, Schwefel and Rotated Ackley functions, respectively) based on the Mann-Whitney U-Test (refer to table 3). Figures 1(d) to 1(i) indicate that the tuned PSO had difficulty optimizing these functions. The tuned PSO converged prematurely on the Weierstrass and Rastrigin functions as reflected in figures 1(e) and 1(f), while the CLPSO and SACLPSO continued to improve their solutions. A higher diversity is maintained for longer by SACLPSO and CLPSO compared to the tuned PSO on the multi-modal functions as reflected in figures 2(d) and 2(e). Oscillation or wandering of particles are indicated by the spikes in figure 2(d) in the case of the tuned PSO applied to the Griewank function, which however lead to no corresponding improvement of the solution as reflected in figure 1(d). This implies that the tuned PSO was not able to successfully escape from local minima in search of the global minimum. The tuned PSO was also unsuccessful in escaping from local minima in the case of the Weierstrass and Rastrigin functions with behaviour similar to that exhibited by the Griewank function. The graphs of multi-modal functions f_5 and f_6 in figures 1(e) and 1(f) also show that SACLPSO converged much quicker than the CLPSO with the additional advantage that no parameter tuning was required for both the inertia weight and the acceleration coefficient. The poor performance of the tuned PSO is accompanied by much lower diversity compared to SACLPSO and CLPSO on functions f_4, f_5 and f_8 (i.e. Griewank, Weierstrass, Schwefel functions, respectively).

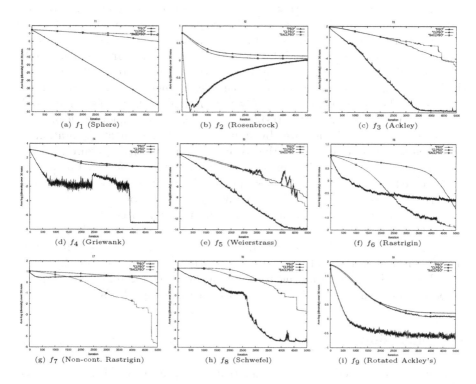

Fig. 2. Plots of average diversity for functions f_1 to f_9

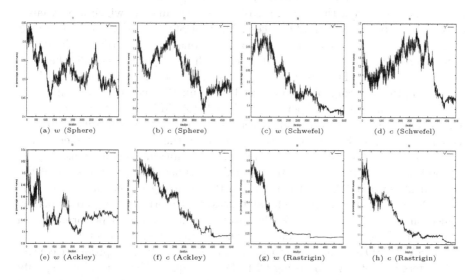

Fig. 3. Plots for average of parameters w and c of all particles for functions f_1, f_3, f_6 and f_8

Figures 1(g) and 1(h) show that the SACLPSO outperformed the CLPSO on functions f_7 and f_8. In these cases the PSO converged prematurely.

Figure 3 visualizes the average values of the inertia weight, w, and the acceleration coefficient, c, of the SACLPSO for functions f_1, f_3, f_6 and f_8. The graph in figure 3(a) indicates a decrease in the inertia weight up to 1300 iterations, whereafter it increased, indicating that particles changed from exploitation to exploration after the 1300 iterations, however without much success as indicated in figure 1(a). Figures 3(c) and 3(d) show that w decreased to a low value of 0.37, while c decreased initially followed by an increase and subsequent exploration of the search space as confirmed by the corresponding diversity in figure 2(h). In figure 3(e), w decreased until approximately 3000 iterations, followed by a sudden increase to enable SACLPSO to escape from local minima in search of better optima as reflected in figure 1(c). Figure 3(g) and 3(h) show that both w and c decreased rapidly. The small value of w indicates that successful exploration and exploitation of the search space was achieved by the larger c value.

The results showed that the SACLPSO performed at least as well as the CLPSO on most of the multi-modal functions and in seven cases much better than the CLPSO, despite having to search a larger $D + 2$ dimensional space compared to the smaller D dimensional space searched by CLPSO.

6   Conclusion

This paper presented the Self-Adaptive Comprehensive Learning PSO (SACLPSO) where the control parameters (i.e. inertia weight, w, and acceleration coefficient, c) are self-adapted by extending particles of the CLPSO. Each particle is equipped with its own set of control parameters which are dynamically adapted by the SACLPSO process. The CLPSO's strategy does not restrict updating of a particle's velocity to its own personal best and that of the global best particle, but extends updating to include the best positions of all other particles in the swarm. This approach contributed to the success of the SACLPSO in self-adapting the control parameters. The Mann-Whitney U-Test results indicate that the SACLPSO outperformed the CLPSO in 7 of the 9 test functions. The SACLPSO algorithm produced sensible values for the control parameters as reflected in table 3 and the plots of averages of the control parameter values.

The SACLPSO succeeded in optimizing the multi-modal functions at least as good as the CLPSO and outperformed the tuned PSO. The results of the experiments have indicated that the SACLPSO converged much faster than the CLPSO on most of the multi-modal functions. Unfortunately, poorer performance on unimodal functions is the price paid for improved performance on multi-modal functions in accordance to the 'no free lunch theorem' [15].

The SACLPSO algorithm relieves the user from specifying appropriate control parameters for optimization using CLPSO and requires the user to only specify (a) the function to optimize, (b) the domain to search, and (c) the terminating condition(s) presented. This effectively reduces the optimization involving a PSO to optimization using a black box.

References

1. Chatterjee, A., Siarry, P.: Nonlinear inertia weight variation for dynamic adaptation in particle swarm optimization. Comput. Oper. Res. 33(3), 859–871 (2004)
2. Clerc, M.: TRIBES, A parameter free particle swarm optimizer, Math stuff for PSO (2002), http://www.mauriceclerc.net
3. Eberhart, R.C., Kennedy, J.: A New Optimizer Using Particle Swarm Theory. In: 6th International Symposium on Micromachine and Human Science, pp. 39–43. IEEE Service Center, Piscataway (1995)
4. Liang, J.J., Qin, A.K., Suganthan, P.N., Baskar, S.: Comprehensive Learning Particle Swarm Optimizer for Global Optimization of Multimodal Functions. Transactions on Evolutionary Computation 10(3) (June 2006)
5. Meissner, M., Schmuker, M., Schneider, G.: Optimized Particle Swarm Optimization (OPSO) and its application to artificial neural network training. BMC Bioinformatics 2006 7, 125 (2006)
6. Olorunda, O., Engelbrecht, A.P.: Measuring Exploration/Exploitation in Particle Swarms using Swarm Diversity. In: IEEE World Congress on Computational Intelligence (CEC 2008), pp. 1128–1134 (2008)
7. Ratnaweera, A., Halgamuge, S.M., Watson, H.: Self-Organizing hierarchical particle swarm optimiser with time-varying acceleration coefficients. IEEE Transactions on Evolutionary Computation 8(3), 240–255 (2004)
8. Riget, J., Vesterstrøm, J.S.: A Diversity-Guided Particle Swarm Optimizer - the ARPSO. Technical report, EVALife, Denmark (2002)
9. Salomon, R.: Reevaluating genetic algorithm performance under coordinate rotation of benchmark functions. BioSystems 39, 263–278 (1996)
10. Shi, Y., Eberhart, R.C.: Parameter selection in particle swarm optimization. In: 7th Annual Conference on Evolutionary Programming, New York, pp. 591–600 (1998)
11. Shi, Y., Eberhart, R.C.: Fuzzy adaptive particle swarm optimization. In: IEEE Congress on Evolutionary Computation (CEC 2001), vol. 1, pp. 101–106. IEEE Press (2001)
12. Schutte, F., Groenwold, A.A.: A study of Global Optimization using Particle Swarms. Journal of Global Optimization 31, 93–108 (2005)
13. Trelea, I.C.: The Particle Swarm Optimization Algorithm: Convergence Analysis and Parameter Selection. Information Processing Letters 85(6), 317–325 (2003)
14. Van den Bergh, F., Engelbrecht, A.P.: A Study of Particle Swarm Optimization Particle Trajectories. Information Sciences 176(8), 937–971 (2006)
15. Wolpert, D.H., Macready, W.G.: No free lunch theorems for optimization. IEEE Transactions on Evolutionary Computation 4, 67–82 (1997)

Towards Swarm Calculus: Universal Properties of Swarm Performance and Collective Decisions

Heiko Hamann

Artificial Life Laboratory of the Department of Zoology
Karl-Franzens University Graz, Austria
heiko.hamann@uni-graz.at

Abstract. The search for generally applicable methods in swarm intelligence aims to gain new insights about natural swarms and to develop design methodologies for artificial swarms. The ideal would be a 'swarm calculus' that allows to calculate key features such as expected swarm performance and robustness on the basis of a few parameters. A path towards this ideal is to find methods and models that have maximal generality. We report two models that might be examples of exceptional generality. First, we present an abstract model that describes the performance of a swarm depending on the swarm density based on the dichotomy between cooperation and interference. Second, we give an abstract model for decision making that is inspired by urn models. A parameter, that controls the feedback based on the current consensus, allows to understand the effects of an increasing probability for positive feedback over time in a decision making system.

1 Introduction

Research in the context of swarm intelligence is important in biology to gain new insights about natural swarms and also in fields aiming for artificial swarms, such as swarm robotics, to obtain sophisticated design methodologies. The ideal tools would allow to calculate swarm behavior, performance, stability, and robustness based on few observed parameters in case of a natural swarm system or based on few designed parameters in case of an artificial swarm. We call this highly desired set of tools 'swarm calculus' (calculus in its general sense).

Models will surely be an important part of swarm calculus. In order to define a general methodology of understanding and designing swarm systems, general properties and generally applicable models need to be found. Today only few models exist that have the potential to become general swarm models. Biological swarm models are particularly distinguished by their variety [23,22,27,6,5]. Typically each biological challenge is answered by a specialized model. The desire for a model with applicability to all natural swarms seems to be small in that community. In the field of artificial swarms, such as robot swarms, the desire for generality seems to be bigger which is, for example, expressed by several models of swarm robotics [10,1,24,18]. The idea of these models is to support the design of swarm robotic systems within a maximal range of applications. They focus

M. Dorigo et al. (Eds.): ANTS 2012, LNCS 7461, pp. 168–179, 2012.

on features that describe quantities of the swarm behavior, such as robot distributions or required times for certain tasks and typically struggle between the intended generality and having direct connections between the model and the robot behavior. If we abandon, however, the demand for a detailed description of behavioral features and focus only on high-level features such as overall performance or the macroscopic process of a collective decision then a higher degree of generality is achievable. In this paper, we identify two models of universal properties of swarm systems concerning the dependence of swarm performance on swarm density and the dependence of collective decisions on positive feedback.

2   Universal Properties of Swarm Performance

It is quite clear that a function of swarm performance depending on swarm density cannot be a simple linear function. For a true swarm scenario a very low density (e.g., corresponding to one agent in the whole area) has to result in low performance because there is no cooperation. With increasing density the performance increases because more and more cooperation is possible (assuming that cooperation is an essential beneficial part of swarms). Even a superlinear performance increase is possible in this interval [20]. At some critical/optimal density the improvement in cooperation possibilities will be lower than the drawback of high densities, namely interference [15]. With further increase of the density the performance is decreasing. Hence, swarms generally face a tradeoff between beneficial cooperation and obstructive interference.

It turns out that not only these qualitative properties are similar in many swarm systems but also the actual shapes of swarm performance over swarm size plots (see Fig. 1(a)). Examples are the performance of foraging in a group of robots (Fig. 1(b) and Fig. 10a in [15]), the activation dynamics and information capacity in an abstract cellular automaton model of ants (Figs. 1b and 1c in [19]), and even in the sizes of social networks (Fig. 8b in [26]). Furthermore, notice that these shapes are typical in probability distributions such as Weibull, Wigner, and log-normal. A related set of models are traffic models of flow over density. The 'fundamental diagram' of traffic flow [16] is symmetric, more realistic models propose at least two asymmetric phases of free and synchronized flow. Actual measurements on highways show curves with shapes similar to Fig. 1(a) (e.g., see Fig. 6-4 in [17]). In these models, there exist two densities for a given flow (except for the maximum flow) similar to the situation here where we have two swarm densities for a given swarm performance.

Having identified the two main components (cooperation and interference) and the typical shape of these plots we can define a simple model. The idea is to fit this model to empirical data for verification and predictions.

2.1   Simple Model of Swarm Performance

For a given bounded, constant area A the swarm density ρ is defined by the swarm size N according to $\rho = N/A$. We define the swarm performance P depending on swarm size N by

$$P(N) = C(N)(I(N) - d) = a_1 N^b a_2 \exp(cN), \tag{1}$$

for parameters $c < 0$, $a_1, a_2, b > 0$, and $d \geq 0$ (see Fig. 1(a)). Parameter d is subtracted to force a decrease to zero ($\lim_{N \to \infty} I(N) - d = 0$). The swarm performance depends on two components C and I. First, the swarm effort without negative feedback is defined by the cooperation function (see also Fig. 1(a))

$$C(N) = a_1 N^b. \tag{2}$$

This function can be interpreted as the potential for cooperation in a swarm that would exist without certain constraints, such as physical collisions. The same formula was used by Breder [4] to model the cohesiveness of a fish school and by Bjerknes and Winfield [2] to model swarm velocity in emergent taxis. However, they used parameters of $b < 1$ while we are using mostly values of $b > 1$. Second, the interference function (see also Fig. 1(a)) is defined by

$$I(N) = a_2 \exp(cN) + d, \tag{3}$$

with d used for scaling (e.g., $\lim_{N \to \infty} I(N) = d$). The exponential decrease seems to be a reasonable choice, for example, compare Fig. 10b in [15] which shows an exponentially decreasing efficiency per robot in a foraging task.

2.2 Examples

To prove the wide applicability of this simple model we fit it to some swarm performance plots that were available. We briefly investigate four scenarios: foraging in a group of robots [15], collective decision making [12] based on BEECLUST [25], aggregations in tree-like structures and reduction to shortest paths [9] similar to [14], and the emergent taxis scenario (also sometimes called 'alpha algorithm') [21,3].

Given the data of the the overall performance, the four parameters of eq. 1 can be directly fitted to it. That is what we do for the first three of our four examples in Fig. 1. The equation can be well fitted to the empirical data. In case of the foraging scenario (Fig. 1(b)) we also have data about the efficiency per robot. We can use the model parameters, that were obtained by fitting the model to the overall performance, to predict the efficiency per robot. This is done by scaling the interference function linearly and plotting it against the efficiency per robot. The satisfying result is shown in Fig. 1(b).

We analyze the forth example, emergent taxis, in more detail. The following empirical data is based on a simple simulation. This simulation is noise-free and therefore robots move in straight lines except for u-turns according to the emergent taxis algorithm. First, we measure the performance that is achieved without cooperation. This is done by defining a random behavior that ignores any characteristic feature of the actual emergent taxis algorithm. For example, in the emergent taxis algorithm, robots count the number of neighbors and do u-turns if this number drops below a threshold α. To obtain the cooperation-free behavior we have set this parameter to $\alpha = 0$ in the simulation. Hence, no robot will

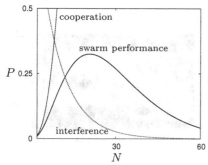

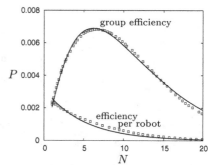

(a) Model of cooperation and interference, examples of swarm performance (eq. 1), cooperation (eq. 2), and interference (eq. 3) depending on swarm size.

(b) Foraging in a group of robots, eq. 1 fitted to group efficiency (upper solid line), prediction of interference (lower solid line, efficiency per robot, linearly rescaled), data points extracted from Fig. 10 in Lerman et al. [15]; P gives group/robot efficiency

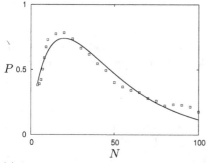

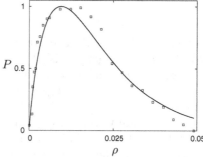

(c) Collective decision making [12] based on BEECLUST [25]; values of $P = 1$ would indicate that 100% of the swarm have found a decision; $P = 0$ indicates symmetry between options

(d) Aggregation in tree-like structures and reduction to shortest path [9]; P gives the ratio of successful runs

Fig. 1. Model of cooperation and interference and three scenarios with fitted performance P according to eq. 1

ever u-turn and they basically disperse in the arena. A simulation run is stopped once a robot touches a wall. The performance of the swarm P is measured by the total distance covered by the swarm's barycenter multiplied by the swarm size (i.e., an estimate of how much distance was effectively covered summed over all robots). The performance obtained by this random behavior can be fitted using the interference function of eq. 3. The well fitted interference function and the empirically obtained data is shown in Fig. 2(a) labeled 'random'. In a second step, we keep the interference function fixed and fit the full model of swarm performance P (eq. 1) to the data from the actual emergent taxis scenario by only varying the cooperation function (i.e., fitting a_1 and b while

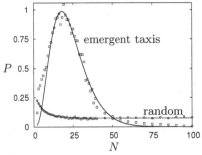
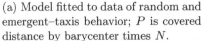
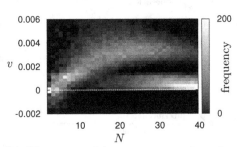

(a) Model fitted to data of random and emergent–taxis behavior; P is covered distance by barycenter times N.

(b) Histogram of barycenter speeds v for different swarm sizes. Note the bimodality about in the interval $N \in [16, 40]$.

Fig. 2. Performance of a random behavior and the actual self-organized emergent taxis behavior (also sometimes called 'alpha algorithm') [21,3] with fitted model (eq. 1); histogram showing two phases

keeping a_2, c and d fixed). The fitted swarm performance model[1] is shown in Fig. 2(a) labeled 'emergent taxis'. This simple model is capable of predictions, if the interference function has been fitted and we fit the cooperation function only to a small interval of, for example, $N \in [15, 25]$ (i.e., including the maximum performance).

Note that we are working with a single value (average) to describe the performance which does not fully catch the system's behavior. At least in some scenarios, as here in the emergent taxis scenario, the performance does not just decrease due to increasing interference. Instead, two coexisting phases of behaviors emerge: functioning swarms moving forward and pinned swarms with extreme numbers of u-turns. In emergent taxis this is shown, for example, by a histogram of barycenter speeds in Fig. 2(b). For $N < 15$ the mean of a unimodal distribution increases with increasing N. Starting at about $N = 15$ a second phase of slowly moving swarms emerges generating a bimodal distribution. Hence, given the fully deterministic implementation of our simulation, there are two classes of initial states (robot positions and orientations) that determine the two extremes of success or total failure. In other scenarios the interference might be increased in a different process continuously, for example, by saturation of target areas with robots.

3   Universal Properties of Collective Decisions

In the following we investigate macro models of collective decisions. One of the most general and at the same time simplest model of collective decisions is a model of only one state variable $s(t)$ which gives the temporal evolution of a

---

[1] Fitted parameters: $a_1 = 0.01061$, $b = 3.237$, $a_2 = 0.2138$, $c = -0.1823$, $d = 0.075$.

swarm fraction that is in favor of one of the options in a binary decision process. If we assume that there is no initial bias to either option (i.e., full symmetry), then we need a tie breaker for $s = 0.5$. A good choice for the tie breaker is noise because any real swarm will be noisy. The average change of s depending on itself per time $(\overline{\Delta s(s)/\Delta t})$ is of interest. Given that the system should be able to converge to one of two options plus the symmetric case of $s = 0.5$ we end up with at least three zeros for $\overline{\Delta s(s)/\Delta t}$ and consequently at least a cubic function. Instead of developing a model, that predefines such a function, we prefer a model that allows this function to emerge from a simple process. In swarms the tendency to a certain option once symmetry is overcome (say, for $s = 0.5 + \epsilon$ towards $s = 1$) is typically a result of positive feedback. Hence, we define such a process depending on probabilities of positive feedback next.

3.1   Simple Model of Collective Decisions

We use simple models inspired by the urn model of the Ehrenfests [7] which they introduced in the context of statistical mechanics and entropy. Eigen and Winkler reported similar models to show the effect of positive feedback [8]. Here we use an urn model that has optionally positive or negative feedback depending on the system's current state and depending on a stochastic process. The urn is filled with N marbles which are either red or blue. The game's dynamics is turn-based. First a marble is drawn with replacement followed by replacing a second one influenced by the color of the first marble. The probability of drawing a blue marble is implicitly determined by the current number of blue marbles $B(t)$ in the urn. The subsequent replacement of a second marble effects either a positive or a negative feedback. The feedback is determined explicitly by a probability

$$P(s, \varphi) = \varphi \sin(\pi s) \tag{4}$$

that is based on the current ratio s of either the blue marbles in the urn $s = b(t)$ or the ratio of red marbles $s = r(t)$. The constant $\varphi \in [0, 1]$ defines the 'sign' and the intensity of the feedback. For $\varphi < 0.5$ negative feedback is predominant and for $\varphi > 0.5$ an interval around $s = 0$ emerges for which positive feedback is predominant. Say we draw a blue marble, we notice the color, and put it back into the urn. Then our model defines that with probability $P(b(t), \varphi)$ a red marble will be replaced by a blue one (i.e., a positive feedback event because drawing a blue one increased the number of blue marbles) and with probability $1 - P(b(t, \varphi))$ a blue one will be replaced by a red one (i.e., a negative feedback event because now drawing a blue one decreased the number of blue marbles). Hence, the probability $P(s, \varphi)$ gives the probability of positive feedback. $P(s, \varphi)$ is plotted for different settings of φ in Fig. 3(a). There is maximum probability for positive feedback for the fully symmetric case of $s = 0.5$ as clearly seen in Fig. 3(a). For $s = 0$ and $s = 1$ we have $P(s, \varphi) = 0$ because no positive feedback is possible (either all marbles are already blue or all marbles are red and therefore no blue one can be drawn). For $\varphi \leq 0.5$ the probability of positive feedback is small $(\varphi \leq 0.5, \forall s : P(s, \varphi) \leq 0.5)$, consequently the system is stable and kept around

$s = 0.5$. The analogy of this model to a collective decision making scenario is the following. The initial drawing resembles the frequency of individual decisions in the swarm proportional to s within the turn-based model. The replacement of the second marble resembles the effect of a swarm member convincing another one about its decision or of being convinced of the opposite. Based on the above definitions the average expected change $\overline{\Delta B}$ of blue marbles B can be calculated by summing over the four cases: drawing a blue or red marble, followed by positive or negative feedback, multiplied by the 'payoff' in terms of blue marbles respectively. Using the symmetry $P(b, \varphi) = P(1 - b, \varphi)$ we get

$$
\begin{aligned}
\Delta B(b) = \quad & bP(b, \varphi)(+1) + b(1 - P(b, \varphi))(-1) \\
& + (1 - b)P(1 - b, \varphi)(-1) + (1 - b)(1 - P(1 - b, \varphi))(+1) \\
= \quad & 4(P(b, \varphi) - 0.5)(b - 0.5).
\end{aligned} \tag{5}
$$

In Fig. 3(b) we compare the theoretical average change per round $\overline{\Delta B / \Delta t}$ according to eq. 5 to the empirically obtained average change of $B(t)$ in terms of number of marbles for the different settings of φ. The agreement between theory and empiric data is close to perfect as expected. Two zeros s_1 and s_2 emerge additionally to $s_0 = 0.5$ for $\varphi > 0.5$: $s_1 = \frac{1}{\pi} \arcsin(\frac{1}{2\varphi})$ and $s_2 = 1 - \frac{1}{\pi} \arcsin(\frac{1}{2\varphi})$. Positive values of $\overline{\Delta B(s) / \Delta t}$ for $s < 0.5$ represent dynamics that has a bias towards $s = 0.5$ and negative values represent dynamics with a bias towards $s = 0$ and vice versa for the other half ($s > 0.5$).

Fig. 3(c) gives an estimate of the asymptotic behavior of this urn model for varied feedback intensity φ. It shows a pitchfork bifurcation at $\varphi = 0.5$ which is to be expected based on Fig. 3(b). Between $\varphi = 0.5$ and $\varphi = 0.75$ the curve defined by $\overline{\Delta B(s) / \Delta t}$ becomes cubic and generates two new stable fixed points while the former at $s = 0.5$ becomes unstable.

3.2   Examples

Next we want to compare the data from our urn model (Fig. 3(b)) to data from more complex models, such as the density classification scenario [13]. First we need a more general equation than eq. 5. We obtain it by introducing a scaling constant c that scales the average change for payoffs different from 1.

$$
\Delta s(s) = 4c(P(s, \varphi) - 0.5)(s - 0.5) \tag{6}
$$

The density classification scenario [13] is about a swarm of red and green agents moving around randomly. Their only interaction is constantly keeping track of those agents' colors they bump into. Once an agent has seen five agents of either color it changes its own color to that it has encountered most. Here, s gives the ratio of red agents. The name of this scenario is due to the idea that the swarm should converge to that color that was initially superior in numbers. It turns out that the averaged change $\overline{\Delta s(s) / \Delta t}$ (see Fig. 3(d)) starts with a curve similar to that of $\varphi = 0$ in Fig. 3(b) and then converges slowly to a curve that is similar to that of $\varphi = 0.75$. Early in the simulation there is mostly negative feedback forcing values close to $s = 0.5$. With increasing time the negative feedback decreases which results finally in positive feedback for $s \in [0.23, 0.77]$. Comparing Fig. 3(b) to Fig. 3(d) indicates a good qualitative agreement between our urn model and the density classification scenario. Given that the curves in Fig. 3(d) converge over time to the final shape which is resembled by our model for increasing φ in Fig. 3(b), one can say that positive feedback builds up slowly over time in the density classification scenario. By fitting eq. 6 to the data shown in Fig. 3(d) we get estimates for the feedback intensity φ. From the earliest and steepest line to the latest and only curve with positive slope in $s = 0.5$ we get values of $\varphi \in [0, 0, 0, 0.007, 0.304, 0.603]$ for times $t \in [100, 200, 400, 800, 1600, 3200]$. By continuing this fitting for additional data not shown in Fig. 3(d), we are able to investigate the temporal evolution of feedback intensity φ according to our model. In Fig. 3(e), the data points of feedback intensity φ obtained by fitting are shown and also a negative exponential function that was fitted to the data. This result supports the assumption of a negative exponential increase of positive feedback in this system as already stated in [11].

Other examples showing similarities to the $\varphi = 0.75$-graph in Fig. 3(b) are Figs. 2B and 3B in Yates et al. [28] which show the drift coefficient dependent on the current alignment of a swarm (average velocity). While the data obtained from experiments with locusts (Fig. 2B in [28]) is too noisy, we use the data from their model (Fig. 3B in [28]) to fit our model. The result is shown in Fig. 3(f). We obtain a maximal positive feedback of $\varphi = 1$.

4   Discussion and Conclusion

We have reported two abstract swarm models with high generality because we would like to get towards a swarm calculus. The first model describes the dependency of swarm performance on swarm density by separation into two parts: cooperation and interference. It explains the existence of an optimal or critical swarm density at which the peak performance is reached. The second model describes the dynamics of collective decision processes based on the existence and intensity of feedback. It explains how the cubic functions of decision revision emerge by an increase of positive feedback over time.

The first model is simple and somewhat obvious because the existence of optimal swarm densities is well known. However, the authors are not aware of any explicit introduction of a similar model combined with a validation by fitting the model to data from diverse swarm applications. Despite its simplicity the model has the capability to give predictions of swarm performance, especially, if the available data, to which it is fitted, includes an interval around the optimal density. That way this model might serve as a swarm calculus of swarm performance. In addition, we want to draw attention to the problem of masking special density-dependent properties by only investigating the mean performance. The example shown in Fig. 2(b) documents the existence of phases in swarm systems.

The second model is also abstract but has a higher complexity and is more conclusive because it allows for mathematical derivations. Based on our urn

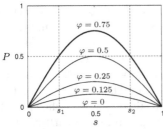

(a) Examples of setting the probability of positive feedback for intensities of feedback $\varphi \in \{0, 0.125, 0.25, 0.5, 0.75\}$.

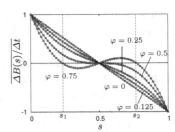

(b) Average change of $B(t)$ in terms of marbles, lines according to eq. 5, squares give empirical data, number of samples is 8×10^5 for each possible s, 64 marbles.

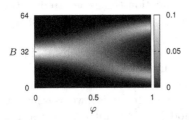

(c) Normalized histogram of blue marbles B over intensity of feedback φ after $t = 200$ steps, initialized to $B(0) \in \{32, 33\}$, indicating a pitchfork bifurcation at $\varphi = 0.5$.

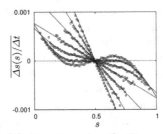

(d) Density classification scenario [13], change of the ratio of red robots for different times during simulation, squares give empirical data (from [11]), lines are fitted according to eq. 6.

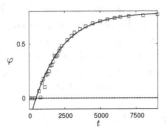

(e) Negative exponential function $\varphi(t) = 0.786 - \exp(-5 \times 10^{-4}t)$ fitted to feedback intensities obtained from the density classification scenario.

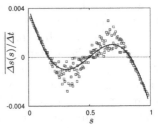

(f) Model fitted to data from Fig. 3B of Yates et al. [28] (local model of swarm alignment in locusts) by $\varphi = 1$ (and $c = 4.134 \times 10^{-3}$); data scaled to $s \in [0, 1]$.

Fig. 3. Settings of the positive feedback probabilities, resulting average change in $B(t)$ in the urn model over the ratio of marbles s, histogram of blue marbles for varied intensity of feedback φ, comparison of model and results from the density classification scenario [13], increase of positive feedback over time, and comparison of model and results from Yates et al. [28]

model for positive feedback decision processes the emerging cubic function of decision revision can be derived (see eq. 5). Here this 'cubic function' is actually trigonometric but alternatively one can choose $P(s,\varphi) = \varphi(1 - 4(s - 0.5)^2)$ yielding $\Delta s(s) = 2(s - 0.5) - 16(s - 0.5)^3$. Hence, we generate the function of decision revision based on our urn model which allows for an interpretation of how the function emerges while, for example, in [28] this function is measured in a local model. Our model of collective decisions might qualify as a part of swarm calculus because those decision revision functions seem to be a general phenomenon in swarms.An interesting result is also the negatively exponential increase of the positive feedback over time in the density classification task (see Fig. 3(e)). Note that this increase seems to be independent from respective values of s. Furthermore, values close to the bounds ($s \approx 1$ or $s \approx 0$) are not observed. An investigation of the underlying processes is beyond this paper but we want to state two ideas. First, the final saturation phase ($\lim_{t\to\infty} \varphi = 0.8$) is most likely caused by explicit noise in the simulation. The agent–agent recognition rate was set to 0.8 which keeps $P(s = 0.5, \varphi) < 1$. Second, the initial fast increase of φ (after a transient which might also be caused by the simulation because agents revise their color only after a minimum of five agent–agent encounters) might be caused by locally emerging sub-groups of homogeneous color within small areas that generate 'islands' of early positive feedback. Time-variant positive feedback was also observed in BEECLUST-controlled swarms as reported before [12]. Hence, a feedback system as given in Fig. 4 seems to be a rather common situation in swarm systems. In terms of the above urn model we can mimic this situation, say A is the number of blue marbles (w.l.o.g.), B is the probability of drawing a blue marble, P is the probability of positive feedback (i.e., this edge can also negatively influence A), and C is an unspecified state variable that increases feedback (φ) over time and is influenced by an additional, unknown process. This triggers the question of what C can be and how it influences the feedback process independent of the current swarm consensus s.

We get maximally positive feedback $\varphi = 1$ for the data of [28] (see Fig. 3(f)) with the effect that situations of low alignment ($s \approx 0.5$) are left as fast as possible. This reinforces the findings of Yates et al. [28] about the diffusion coefficient. A major feature of the self-organizing processes in the swarm seems

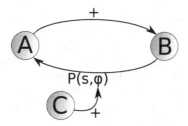

Fig. 4. Time-variant feedback system; here for increasing probability of pos. feedback

to be that times in states of low aligned are minimized by the system (Yates et al.: "A higher diffusion coefficient at lower alignments suggests that the locusts 'prefer' to be in a highly aligned state").

The result of this paper is that generally applicable swarm models, that have simple preconditions, exist. To apply the model of swarm performance, only a concept of swarm density is necessary and to apply the model of collective decisions only a consensus variable of a binary decision is necessary. Despite their simplicity, both models have enough explanatory power to give insights about swarm processes such as the interplay of cooperation and interference and the installation of positive feedback. Hence, we contend that it is possible to generate a set of models and methods of general applicability for swarm science, that is, to create a swarm calculus.

Acknowledgments. The author thanks Payam Zahadat, Jürgen Stradner and the anonymous reviewers for very helpful comments that improved the manuscript.

References

1. Berman, S., Kumar, V., Nagpal, R.: Design of control policies for spatially inhomogeneous robot swarms with application to commercial pollination. In: IEEE Intern. Conf. on Robotics and Automation (ICRA 2011), pp. 378–385 (2011)
2. Bjerknes, J.D., Winfield, A.: On fault-tolerance and scalability of swarm robotic systems. In: Proc. Distributed Auton. Robotic Syst, DARS 2010 (2010)
3. Bjerknes, J.D., Winfield, A., Melhuish, C.: An analysis of emergent taxis in a wireless connected swarm of mobile robots. In: IEEE Swarm Intelligence Symposium, pp. 45–52. IEEE Press, Los Alamitos (2007)
4. Breder, C.M.: Equations descriptive of fish schools and other animal aggregations. Ecology 35(3), 361–370 (1954)
5. Camazine, S., Deneubourg, J.L., Franks, N.R., Sneyd, J., Theraulaz, G., Bonabeau, E.: Self-Organizing Biological Systems. Princeton Univ. Press (2001)
6. Edelstein-Keshet, L.: Mathematical models of swarming and social aggregation. Robotica 24(3), 315–324 (2006)
7. Ehrenfest, P., Ehrenfest, T.: Über zwei bekannte Einwände gegen das Boltzmannsche H-Theorem. Physikalische Zeitschrift 8, 311–314 (1907)
8. Eigen, M., Winkler, R.: Laws of the game: how the principles of nature govern chance. Princeton University Press (1993)
9. Hamann, H.: Modeling and Investigation of Robot Swarms. Master's thesis, University of Stuttgart, Germany (2006)
10. Hamann, H.: Space-Time Continuous Models of Swarm Robotics Systems: Supporting Global-to-Local Programming. Springer (2010)
11. Hamann, H., Meyer, B., Schmickl, T., Crailsheim, K.: A Model of Symmetry Breaking in Collective Decision-Making. In: Doncieux, S., Girard, B., Guillot, A., Hallam, J., Meyer, J.-A., Mouret, J.-B. (eds.) SAB 2010. LNCS (LNAI), vol. 6226, pp. 639–648. Springer, Heidelberg (2010)
12. Hamann, H., Schmickl, T., Wörn, H., Crailsheim, K.: Analysis of emergent symmetry breaking in collective decision making. Neural Computing & Applications 21(2), 207–218 (2012)

13. Hamann, H., Wörn, H.: Embodied computation. Parallel Processing Letters 17(3), 287–298 (2007)
14. Hamann, H., Wörn, H.: Aggregating Robots Compute: An Adaptive Heuristic for the Euclidean Steiner Tree Problem. In: Asada, M., Hallam, J.C.T., Meyer, J.-A., Tani, J. (eds.) SAB 2008. LNCS (LNAI), vol. 5040, pp. 447–456. Springer, Heidelberg (2008)
15. Lerman, K., Galstyan, A.: Mathematical model of foraging in a group of robots: Effect of interference. Autonomous Robots 13, 127–141 (2002)
16. Lighthill, M.J., Whitham, G.B.: On kinematic waves. II. A theory of traffic flow on long crowded roads. Proceedings of the Royal Society of London A 229(1178), 317–345 (1955)
17. Mahmassani, H.S., Dong, J., Kim, J., Chen, R.B., Park, B.: Incorporating weather impacts in traffic estimation and prediction systems. Tech. Rep. FHWA-JPO-09-065, U.S. Department of Transportation (September 2009)
18. Milutinovic, D., Lima, P.: Cells and Robots: Modeling and Control of Large-Size Agent Populations. Springer (2007)
19. Miramontes, O.: Order-disorder transitions in the behavior of ant societies. Complexity 1(1), 56–60 (1995)
20. Mondada, F., Bonani, M., Guignard, A., Magnenat, S., Studer, C., Floreano, D.: Superlinear Physical Performances in a SWARM-BOT. In: Capcarrère, M.S., Freitas, A.A., Bentley, P.J., Johnson, C.G., Timmis, J. (eds.) ECAL 2005. LNCS (LNAI), vol. 3630, pp. 282–291. Springer, Heidelberg (2005)
21. Nembrini, J., Winfield, A.F.T., Melhuish, C.: Minimalist coherent swarming of wireless networked autonomous mobile robots. In: Hallam, B., et al. (eds.) Proc. of the 7th Intern. Conf. on Simulation of Adaptive Behavior (SAB), pp. 373–382. MIT Press, Cambridge (2002)
22. Okubo, A.: Dynamical aspects of animal grouping: Swarms, schools, flocks, and herds. Advances in Biophysics 22, 1–94 (1986)
23. Okubo, A., Levin, S.A.: Diffusion and Ecological Problems: Modern Perspectives. Springer, Berlin (2001)
24. Prorok, A., Correll, N., Martinoli, A.: Multi-level spatial models for swarm-robotic systems. The International Journal of Robotics Research 30(5), 574–589 (2011)
25. Schmickl, T., Hamann, H.: BEECLUST: A swarm algorithm derived from honeybees. In: Xiao, Y. (ed.) Bio-inspired Computing and Communication Networks. CRC Press (March 2011)
26. Strogatz, S.H.: Exploring complex networks. Nature 410(6825), 268–276 (2001)
27. Vicsek, T., Zafiris, A.: Collective motion. arXiv:1010.5017v1 (2010)
28. Yates, C.A., Erban, R., Escudero, C., Couzin, I.D., Buhl, J., Kevrekidis, I.G., Maini, P.K., Sumpter, D.J.T.: Inherent noise can facilitate coherence in collective swarm motion. PNAS 106(14), 5464–5469 (2009)

A Hybrid Particle Swarm Optimization Algorithm for the Open Vehicle Routing Problem

Yannis Marinakis[1] and Magdalene Marinaki[2]

[1] Decision Support Systems Laboratory,
Department of Production Engineering and Management,
Technical University of Crete, Chania, Greece
marinakis@ergasya.tuc.gr
[2] Industrial Systems Control Laboratory,
Department of Production Engineering and Management,
Technical University of Crete, Chania, Greece
magda@dssl.tuc.gr

Abstract. This paper introduces a new hybrid algorithmic nature inspired approach based on Particle Swarm Optimization, for successfully solving one of the most popular supply chain management problems, the Open Vehicle Routing Problem. The Open Vehicle Routing Problem (OVRP) is a variant of the classic vehicle routing problem in which the vehicles do not return in the depot after the service of the customers. The proposed algorithm for the solution of the Open Vehicle Routing Problem, the Hybrid Particle Swarm Optimization (HybPSO), combines a Particle Swarm Optimization (PSO) Algorithm, the Variable Neighborhood Search (VNS) Strategy and a Path Relinking (PR) Strategy. The algorithm is suitable for solving large-scale open vehicle routing problems within short computational time. Two sets of benchmark instances are used in order to test the proposed algorithm.

1 Introduction

Particle Swarm Optimization (PSO) is a population-based swarm intelligence algorithm that was originally proposed by Kennedy and Eberhart [9]. PSO simulates the social behavior of social organisms by using the physical movements of the individuals in the swarm. Its mechanism enhances and adapts to the global and local exploration. Most applications of PSO have concentrated on the optimization in continuous space but in the last years the PSO algorithm is used also in discrete optimization problems.

The **Open Vehicle Routing Problem (OVRP)** is the variant of the classic vehicle routing problem where the vehicles do not return in the depot after the service of the customers [14]. The real life application of the Open Vehicle Routing Problem concerns the case where either the company does not have vehicles at all or the vehicles owned by the company are not enough in order to use them for the distribution of the products to the customers. In both cases

M. Dorigo et al. (Eds.): ANTS 2012, LNCS 7461, pp. 180–187, 2012.
© Springer-Verlag Berlin Heidelberg 2012

the company has to hire a number of vehicles in order to realize the distribution of the products. When the vehicles finish their jobs they do not return to the company. This problem also belongs in the category of the third party logistics (3PL) problems. From the combinatorial optimization point of view, the main difference between the Vehicle Routing Problem and the Open Vehicle Routing Problem is that in the first case the route is a hamiltonian cycle while in the second case the route is a hamiltonian path [1]. Usually two different objectives are used in OVRP, the first one is the minimization of the required number of vehicles and, then, for this number of vehicles the total travel distance is, also, minimized and the second one is the minimization of the corresponding total traveled distance. The Open Vehicle Routing Problem was first published in [15] but since then for the following twenty years it received little study. In the last ten years, a number of publications using different heuristic and metaheuristic algorithms for the OVRP have been published. It should be noted that the Open Vehicle Routing Problem is an NP-hard problem, and, thus, the instances with a large number of customers can not be solved in optimality within reasonable time. For this reason, a large number of approximation techniques has been proposed for its solution. These techniques are classified into three main categories: the classical heuristics, the single solution based metaheuristics and the population based metaheuristics. For analytical descriptions of the solution algorithms for the Open VRP please see [10,13,18].

In this paper, we would like to develop a competitive Nature Inspired method based on Particle Swarm Optimization for the solution of the Open Vehicle Routing Problem and to test its efficiency compared to other Nature Inspired and Classic Metaheuristic algorithms. Thus, in this paper, we demonstrate how a nature inspired intelligent technique, the Particle Swarm Optimization (PSO) [9] and two metaheuristic techniques, the Variable Neighborhood Search (VNS) [8] and the Path Relinking (PR) [7] can be incorporated in a hybrid scheme in order to give very good results for the Open Vehicle Routing Problem (OVRP). The rest of the paper is organized as follows: In the next section the proposed algorithm, the Hybrid Particle Swarm Optimization (HybPSO) is presented and analyzed in detail. Computational results are presented and analyzed in the third section while in the last section conclusions and future research are given.

2   Hybrid Particle Swarm Optimization Algorithm

In this paper, a hybrid PSO (HybPSO) algorithm is used for the solution of the OVRP. In PSO algorithm, initially a set of particles is created randomly where each particle corresponds to a possible solution. Each particle has a position in the space of solutions and moves with a given velocity. One of the key issues in designing a successful PSO for the Open Vehicle Routing Problem is to find a suitable mapping between Open Vehicle Routing Problem solutions and particles in PSO. Each particle is recorded via the path representation of the tour, that is, via the specific sequence of the nodes.

For example, if we have a particle (solution) with ten nodes, a possible path representation is the following:

1 3 8 5 4 10 1 6 9 7 2

with node number 1 is denoted the depot and nodes 2 through 10 denote the customers. The difference between the Open Vehicle Routing Problem and the Capacitated Vehicle Routing Problem is that in the first the vehicles do not return to the depot. Thus, the difference in the calculation of a cost function for each particle is that we do not add the cost between the last customer and the depot, i.e. in the previous example the cost (distances) between customer 10 and the depot and customer 2 and the depot are omitted.

As the calculation of the velocity of each particle is performed by Equation (1) (see below), the above mentioned representation should be transformed appropriately. We transform each element of the solution into a floating point in the interval (0,1], calculate the velocities and the positions of all particles and, then, convert back the particles' positions into the integer domain using relative position indexing [11].

The position of each individual (called particle) is represented by a d-dimensional vector in problem space $x_i = (x_{i1}, x_{i2}, ..., x_{id})$, $i = 1, 2, ..., N$ (N is the population size and n is the number of the vector's dimension), and its performance is evaluated on the predefined fitness function. The velocity v_{ij} represents the changes that will be made to move the particle from one position to another. Where the particle will move depends on the dynamic interaction of its own experience and the experience of the whole swarm. There are three possible directions that a particle can follow: to follow its own path, to move towards the best position it had during the iterations ($pbest_{ij}$) or to move to the best particle's position ($gbest_j$). The velocity and position equations are updated as follows (constriction PSO) [3]:

$$v_{ij}(t + 1) = \chi(v_{ij}(t) + c_1 rand_1(pbest_{ij} - x_{ij}(t)) + c_2 rand_2(gbest_j - x_{ij}(t))) \quad (1)$$

and

$$x_{ij}(t + 1) = x_{ij}(t) + v_{ij}(t + 1) \quad (2)$$

where

$$\chi = \frac{2}{|2 - c - \sqrt{c^2 - 4c}|} \quad \text{and} \quad c = c_1 + c_2, c > 4 \quad (3)$$

t is the iterations counter, c_1 and c_2 are the acceleration coefficients, $rand_1$ and $rand_2$ are two random variables in the interval $(0, 1)$. A local search strategy based on the Variable Neighborhood Search (VNS) algorithm [8] is applied in each particle in the swarm in order to improve the solutions produced from the particle swarm optimization algorithm. In this paper, the VNS algorithm is used with the following way. Initially, the number of local search algorithms is selected. The local search strategies for the Open Vehicle Routing Problem are distinguished between local search strategies for a single route and local search strategies for multiple routes. The local search strategies that are chosen and belong to the category of the single route interchange are the well known methods for the TSP, the 2-opt and the 3-opt. In the single route interchange all the routes have been created in the initial phase of the algorithm. The Local Search Strategies for Single Route Interchange try to improve the routing decisions. The Local Search Strategies for Multiple Route Interchange try to improve the assignment decisions. This, of course, increases the complexity of the algorithms but gives the possibility to improve even more the solution. The multiple route interchange local search strategies that are used are the 1-0 relocate, 2-0 relocate, 1-1 exchange and 2-2 exchange [6].

As we do not want to increase the complexity of the algorithm, it is decided to apply in each particle one local search combination of algorithms per iteration. For this reason, a VNS operator C_{VNS} is selected that controls which local search algorithm is applied. The C_{VNS} value is compared with the output of a random number generator, $rand_i(0, 1)$. If the random number is less or equal to the C_{VNS}, then, the first local search algorithm is used. Then, if the random number is less or equal to the $2 * C_{VNS}$, then, the second local search algorithm is used, and so on. As we would like to have not only simple local search algorithms but also their combinations we select ten local search algorithms, the six previously mentioned methods (2-opt, 3-opt, 1-0 relocate, 2-0 relocate, 1-1 exchange and 2-2 exchange) and four combinations (2-opt with 1-0 relocate, 2-opt with 1-1 exchange, 2-opt with 3-opt and 1-1 exchange and 2-opt with 3-opt, 1-0 relocate and 1-1 exchange). Thus, the C_{VNS} operator is set equal to 0.1 and only for 10% of the cases a time consuming local search procedure is applied in the problem.

Finally, after the completion of an iteration, a path relinking strategy [7] for exploring trajectories between the best particle and a number of other particles of the swarm is applied. During the path relinking procedure, if a better solution than the current best solution is found, then, the current best solution is replaced by this solution. In this algorithm the best particle plays the role of the starting solution and in each iteration the other random particles play the role of target solutions. We are using random particles for the target solutions in order to give to the best particle more exploration abilities by combining not only the best particle with its neighbor particles but also with equal probabilities with all the particles in the swarm. If a better solution than the current best solution is found, then, the current best solution is replaced by this solution. In each iteration of the algorithm the optimal solution of the whole swarm and the optimal solution of each particle are kept. The algorithm stops when a maximum number of iterations has been reached.

3   Results and Discussion

The algorithm was implemented in Fortran 90 and was compiled using the Lahey f95 compiler on a Intel Core 2 DUO CPU T9550 at 2.66 GHz, running Suse Linux 9.1. The algorithm was tested on two sets of benchmark problems, the 14 benchmark problems proposed by Christofides [2] and the 8 large scale open vehicle routing problems proposed by Li et al. [10]. Each instance of the first set contains between 51 and 200 nodes including the depot. The location of the nodes is defined by their Cartesian co-ordinates and the travel cost from node i to j is assumed to be the respective Euclidean distance. Each problem includes capacity constraints while the problems 6-10, 13 and 14 have, also, maximum route length restrictions (mtl) and non zero service times (st). For the first ten problems, nodes are randomly located over a square, while for the remaining ones, nodes are distributed in clusters and the depot is not centred. The maximum allowed route length has been multiplied by 0.9 compared to the one considered for the VRP [13]. The second set of instances contains between 200 and 480 nodes including the depot. Each problem instance includes capacity constraints. In Table 1 in columns 2-5 the most important characteristics (number of nodes (n), Capacity of Vehicles (Q), maximum route length restrictions (mtl) and service times (st)) of each of the data sets are presented. The parameters of the proposed algorithm are selected after thorough testing. A number of different alternative values were tested and the ones selected are those that gave the best computational results concerning both the quality of the solution and the computational time needed to achieve this solution. The selected parameters are: number of particles equal to 50, number of generations equal to 1000 and $c_1 = c_2 = 2.05$. The efficiency of the HybPSO algorithm is measured by the quality of the produced solutions. The quality is given in terms of the relative deviation from the best known solution, that is $\omega = \frac{(c_{HybPSO} - c_{BKS})}{c_{BKS}}\%$, where c_{HybPSO} denotes the cost of the solution found by HybPSO and c_{BKS} is the cost of the best known solution.

To test the performance of the proposed algorithm we applied HybPSO 10 times to each test problem. In Table 1, two different best solutions are presented. The first best known solution (BKS1) is obtained using first the minimization of the number of vehicles and, then, the minimization of the total distance traveled. The other best solution (BKS2) is obtained by minimizing only the total distance traveled. As it has, already, been mentioned in the description of the problem it is very important to use the smallest number of vehicles as in the real life application of the Open Vehicle Routing Problem the finding of the best routes by hiring as less as possible number of vehicles is the main concern. Thus, initially the Open Vehicle Routing Problem is solved with the proposed algorithm using the hierarchical objective function, where initially the number of vehicles is minimized and, then, for this number of vehicles the total travel distance is, also, minimized. The number of vehicles (NV), the best results (BR), the quality of the best solution (ω), the average results (AR), the median, the standard deviation (stdev), the variance (var) and the CPU time in minutes are presented in the first part of Table 1 in columns 7 to 14 for Christofides benchmark instances. Afterwards, the Open Vehicle Routing Problem is solved for Christofides benchmark instances with the single objective function (the total distance traveled) and the results are presented in the second part of Table 1. It should be noted that in the second part of Table 1, there are only the instances in which the algorithm with the use of the single objective function produced different results from the ones produced from the algorithm when the hierarchical objective function was used. In the last part of Table 1, the results for Li et al. benchmark instances with hierarchical objective function are given.

Table 1. Results of HybPSO

	n	Q	mtl	st	BKS1	NV	BR	ω	AR	median	stdev	var	CPU
Results with hierarchical objective function in Christofides benchmark instances													
C1	51	160	∞	0	416.06 [1]	5	416.06	0.00	416.37	416.23	0.39	0.15	0.10
C2	76	140	∞	0	567.14 [5]	10	567.14	0.00	567.28	567.31	0.12	0.01	0.35
C3	101	200	∞	0	639.74 [10]	8	639.74	0.00	639.83	639.86	0.09	0.01	1.10
C4	151	200	∞	0	733.13 [12]	12	735.29	0.29	735.77	735.91	0.32	0.10	2.17
C5	200	200	∞	0	893.39 [18]	16	895.79	0.27	895.95	895.92	0.14	0.01	3.28
C6	51	160	180	10	412.96 [1]	6	412.96	0.00	413.26	413.28	0.27	0.07	0.21
C7	76	140	144	10	583.19 [12]	10	583.19	0.00	583.56	583.53	0.32	0.10	0.37
C8	101	200	207	10	644.63 [1]	9	644.79	0.02	645.02	645.03	0.15	0.02	0.58
C9	151	200	180	10	757.84 [12]	13	759.81	0.26	759.91	759.87	0.10	0.01	1.42
C10	200	200	180	10	875.67 [12]	17	878.49	0.32	879.02	878.94	0.41	0.17	3.25
C11	121	200	∞	0	682.12 [12]	7	682.12	0.00	682.36	682.43	0.15	0.02	1.19
C12	101	200	∞	0	534.24[12]	10	535.49	0.23	535.65	535.61	0.15	0.02	1.35
C13	121	200	648	50	904.04 [4]	11	904.04	0.00	904.39	904.43	0.20	0.04	1.28
C14	101	200	936	90	591.87 [12]	11	592.58	0.12	592.70	592.67	0.12	0,01	1.52
Results with minimization of the total distance in Christofides benchmark instances													
	n	Q	mtl	st	BKS2	NV	BR	ω	AR	median	stdev	var	CPU
C1	51	160	∞	0	412.96 [16]	6	412.96	0.00	413.13	413.09	0.18	0.03	0.17
C2	76	140	∞	0	564.06 [16]	11	564.06	0.00	564.27	564.28	0.18	0.03	0.37
C3	101	200	∞	0	639.26 [18]	9	639.26	0.00	639.83	639.86	0.09	0.02	0.47
C5	200	200	∞	0	869 [18]	17	872.28	0.38	872.55	872.51	0.18	0.03	2.59
C7	76	140	144	10	568.49 [10]	11	569.12	0.11	569.48	569.51	0.24	0.05	0.47
C9	151	200	180	10	756.38 [10]	14	758.15	0.23	758.42	758.45	0.17	0.03	1.23
C11	121	200	∞	0	678.54 [17]	10	678.54	0.00	678.89	678.90	0.26	0.06	1.39
C13	121	200	648	50	896.5 [10]	12	897.25	0.08	897.52	897.51	0.23	0.05	1.52
Results with hierarchical objective function in Li et al. benchmark instances													
	n	Q	mtl	st	BKS1	NV	BR	ω	AR	median	stdev	var	CPU
O1	200	900	∞	0	6018.52 [10]	5	6023.25	0.08	6023.53	6023.53	0.14	0.02	2.37
O2	240	550	∞	0	4557.38 [18]	9	4557.89	0.01	4558.14	4558.13	0.24	0.06	3.12
O3	280	900	∞	0	7731 [18]	7	7734.28	0.04	7735.01	7735.11	0.42	0.18	3.35
O4	320	700	∞	0	7253.2 [18]	10	7268.23	0.21	7268.45	7268.4	0.20	0.04	3.45
O5	360	900	∞	0	9193.15 [18]	8	9201.28	0.09	9201.68	9201.48	0.60	0.36	3.57
O6	400	900	∞	0	9793.72 [18]	9	9797.28	0.04	9798.03	9798	0.47	0.22	4.14
O7	440	900	∞	0	10347.7 [18]	10	10352.29	0.04	10352.58	10352.53	0.18	0.03	4.32
O8	480	1000	∞	0	12415.36 [18]	10	12419.25	0.03	12419.62	12419.65	0.15	0.02	4.51

It can be seen from Table 1, that the HybPSO algorithm for Christofides benchmark instances, in seven out of fourteen instances in the first case and in five out of fourteen instances in the second case has reached the best known solution. For the rest instances, in the first case (when a hierarchical objective function is used) the quality of the solutions is between 0.02% and 0.32% and the average quality for the fourteen instances is 0.11%. For the second case (when only the travel distance is minimized) the quality of the solutions is between 0.02% and 0.38% and the average quality for the fourteen instances is 0.13%. The standard deviation in both cases is between 0.09 and 0.41. The variance in both cases is between 0.01 and 0.17. Also, in this Table the computational time needed (in minutes) for finding the best solution by HybPSO is presented. The CPU time needed is significantly low and only for the instances with number of nodes equal to 200 is larger than 3 minutes. The algorithm is also tested for the large scale benchmark instances proposed by Li et al [10]. The results of the second data set are presented in the last part of Table 1. In this data set, we present only results for the hierarchical objective function where first the number of vehicles is minimized and, afterwards, the total distance traveled is minimized. The quality of the solutions for the 8 instances is between 0.01% and 0.21% and the average quality is 0.07%. The standard deviation is between 0.14 and 0.60 and the variance is between 0.02 and 0.36. Also, in this Table the computational time needed (in minutes) for finding the best solution by HybPSO is presented. The CPU time needed is significantly low and is never larger than 5 minutes.

4   Conclusions

In this paper, a new algorithm based on the Particle Swarm Optimization for the solution of the Open Vehicle Routing Problem is presented. This algorithm is a hybridization of the Particle Swarm Optimization algorithm with the Variable Neighborhood Search algorithm and with the Path Relinking Strategy. As a number of different variants of the Particle Swarm Optimization algorithm have been published, mainly using a different equation for the calculation of the velocities, we used the constriction Particle Swarm Optimization. Another issue that we have to deal with was the fact that the PSO algorithm is suitable for continuous optimization problems. Thus, it was a challenge to find an effective transformation of the solutions of PSO in discrete values without loosing information from this procedure. The algorithm was tested in the two benchmark instances that are usually used in the literature. As some publications use a hierarchical objective function and others only the minimization of the total distance traveled we test our algorithm in both cases taking efficient results for both of them. Our future research will be focused in two different directions, the solution of the OVRP using other nature inspired techniques like Clonal Selection Algorithm, Artificial Bee Colony etc. and the use of the proposed algorithm for solving even more complicated problems like the Open Vehicle Routing Problem with Stochastic Demands or the Open Vehicle Routing with Time Windows.

References

1. Brandao, J.: A tabu search algorithm for the open vehicle routing problem. European Journal of Operational Research 157(3), 552–564 (2004)
2. Christofides, N., Mingozzi, A., Toth, P.: The vehicle routing problem. In: Christofides, N., Mingozzi, A., Toth, P., Sandi, C. (eds.) Combinatorial Optimization. Wiley, Chichester (1979)
3. Clerc, M., Kennedy, J.: The particle swarm: explosion, stability and convergence in a multi-dimensional complex space. IEEE Transactions on Evolutionary Computation 6, 58–73 (2002)

4. Fleszar, K., Osman, I.H., Hindi, K.S.: A variable neighbourhood search algorithm for the open vehicle routing problem. European Journal of Operational Research 195, 803–809 (2009)
5. Fu, Z., Eglese, R., Li, L.: A new tabu search heuristic for the open vehicle routing problem. Journal of the Operational Research Society 56(2), 267–274 (2005)
6. Gendreau, M., Laporte, G., Potvin, J.-Y.: Vehicle routing: modern heuristics. In: Aarts, E.H.L., Lenstra, J.K. (eds.) Local Search in Combinatorial Optimization, pp. 311–336. Wiley, Chichester (1997)
7. Glover, F., Laguna, M., Marti, R.: Scatter search and path relinking: Advances and applications. In: Glover, F., Kochenberger, G.A. (eds.) Handbook of Metaheuristics, pp. 1–36. Kluwer Academic Publishers, Boston (2003)
8. Hansen, P., Mladenovic, N.: Variable neighborhood search: Principles and applications. European Journal of Operational Research 130, 449–467 (2001)
9. Kennedy, J., Eberhart, R.: Particle swarm optimization. In: Proceedings of 1995 IEEE International Conference on Neural Networks, vol. 4, pp. 1942–1948 (1995)
10. Li, F., Golden, B., Wasil, E.: The open vehicle routing problem: Algorithms, large-scale test problems, and computational results. Computers and Operations Research 34, 2918–2930 (2007)
11. Lichtblau, D.: Discrete optimization using Mathematica. In: Callaos, N., Ebisuzaki, T., Starr, B., Abe, J.M., Lichtblau, D. (eds.) World Multi-Conference on Systemics, Cybernetics and Informatics (SCI 2002). International Institute of Informatics and Systemics, vol. 16, pp. 169–174 (2002)
12. Pisinger, D., Ropke, S.: A general heuristic for vehicle routing problems. Computers and Operations Research 34, 2403–2435 (2006)
13. Repoussis, P.P., Tarantilis, C.D., Braysy, O., Ioannou, G.: A hybrid evolution strategy for the open vehicle routing problem. Computers and Operations Research 37, 443–455 (2010)
14. Sariklis, D., Powell, S.: A heuristic method for the open vehicle routing problem. The Journal of the Operational Research Society 51(5), 564–573 (2000)
15. Schrage, L.: Formulation and structure of more complex realistic routing and scheduling problem. Networks 11, 229–232 (1981)
16. Tarantilis, C., Diakoulaki, D., Kiranoudis, C.: Combination of geographical information system and efficient routing algorithms for real life distribution operations. European Journal of Operational Research 152(2), 437–453 (2004)
17. Tarantilis, C., Ioannou, G., Kiranoudis, C., Prastacos, G.: Solving the open vehicle routing problem via a single parameter metaheuristic algorithm. Journal of the Operational Research Society 56, 588–596 (2005)
18. Zachariadis, E.E., Kiranoudis, C.T.: An open vehicle routing problem metaheuristic for examining wide solution neighborhoods. Computers and Operations Research 37, 712–723 (2010)

A Self-adaptive Heterogeneous PSO
Inspired by Ants

Filipe V. Nepomuceno and Andries P. Engelbrecht

Department of Computer Science, University of Pretoria, Pretoria, South Africa
filinep@gmail.com, engel@cs.up.ac.za

Abstract. Heterogeneous particle swarm optimizers have been proposed where particles are allowed to implement different behaviors. A selected behavior may not be optimal for the duration of the search process. Since the optimality of a behavior depends on the fitness landscape it is necessary that particles be able to dynamically adapt their behaviors. This paper introduces two new self-adaptive heterogeneous particle swarm optimizers which are influenced by the ant colony optimization meta-heuristic. These self-adaptive strategies are compared with three other heterogeneous particle swarm optimizers. The results show that the proposed models outrank the existing models overall.

1 Introduction

Particle swarm optimization (PSO) is a stochastic optimization technique introduced by Kennedy and Eberhart [6,11]. PSOs contain a swarm of particles that move around in an n-dimensional search space trying to find an optimal solution to an optimization problem. Each particle's position represents a candidate solution and each particle has a velocity which determines the particle's next position. Homogeneous PSOs use the same position update and the same velocity update for all particles. This means that all the particles exhibit the same search patterns.

One of the problems that PSOs face is the exploration versus exploitation problem [8]. By making the PSO heterogeneous, the swarm can have multiple search patterns. This allows a better balance between exploration and exploitation. Previous work done on heterogeneous PSO (HPSO) includes experiments by Montes de Oca et al [15], the TRIBES PSO [3], the static HPSO (sHPSO) and dynamic HPSO (dHPSO) models [8], the adaptive learning PSO-II (ALPSO-II) [13], and the difference proportional probability PSO (DPP-PSO) [18]. Some of these approaches have shortcomings, e.g. the ALPSO-II is computationally expensive, and the DPP-PSO, sHPSO and dHPSO cannot adapt to the changing search landscape characteristics as the particles move through the search space.

This paper aims to overcome these shortcomings by proposing two self-adaptive heterogeneous models inspired by the foraging behavior of ants modeled with the ant colony optimization meta-heuristic (ACO-MH) [5]. The swarm contains a behavior pool which contains different behaviors (update equations).

M. Dorigo et al. (Eds.): ANTS 2012, LNCS 7461, pp. 188–195, 2012.

The behaviors have an associated pheromone concentration which determines the probability of a particle choosing that behavior.

The proposed strategies are evaluated on a subset of the CEC 2005 benchmark functions and compared to the dHPSO, ALPSO-II and DPP-PSO. The results show that the proposed self-adaptive HPSO strategies perform well on unimodal and multimodal functions.

The rest of this paper is organized as follows: Section 2 provides background on PSOs and existing HPSO algorithms used for comparison in this paper. Section 3 introduces the proposed self-adaptive strategies. Section 4 details the experimental procedure followed and the results are presented and analyzed in Section 5. The paper is concluded in Section 6.

2 Background

This section provides details on the original PSO and heterogeneous PSO.

2.1 Particle Swarm Optimization

The original PSO is based on the papers by Kennedy and Eberhart [6,11]. Each particle keeps track of the best position it has found called the particle's personal best or *pbest*. Particles are grouped together into neighborhoods and the best position of all the particles' *pbests*, called the neighbourhood best or *nbest*, is recorded. Particles initially start in random positions in the search space and iteratively update their velocity and position. The following equations, with the addition of the inertia weight introduced by Shi and Eberhart [17], are used:

$$v_{ij}(t+1) = wv_{ij}(t) + c_1r_{1j}(t)(y_{ij}(t) - x_{ij}(t)) + c_2r_{2j}(t)(\hat{y}_j(t) - x_{ij}(t)) \quad (1)$$

$$x_{ij}(t+1) = x_{ij}(t) + v_{ij}(t+1) \quad (2)$$

where $v_{ij}(t)$ represents the ith particle's velocity in the jth dimension at iteration t, $x_{ij}(t)$ is the particle's position, $y_{ij}(t)$ is the particle's *pbest*, $\hat{y}(t)$ is the neighborhood's *nbest*, w is the inertia weight to avoid sudden changes in direction, $r_{1j}, r_{2j} \sim U(0,1)$ and c_1 and c_2 are constant acceleration coefficients. The velocity and position updates define a particle's search behavior.

2.2 Heterogeneous Particle Swarm Optimization

HPSO algorithms have a behavior pool and a behavior selection strategy. Behaviors which have been used in behavior pools are

- Original PSO with inertia weight (PSO) [6,11,17]
- Cognitive-only model (Cog-PSO) [9]
- Social-only model (Soc-PSO) [9]
- Bare-bones (BB-PSO) and modified bare-bones (BBMod-PSO) [10]

- Quantum PSO (QSO) [1]
- Time-varying inertia weight PSO (TVIW-PSO) [17]
- Time-varying acceleration coefficients (TVAC-PSO) [16]
- Fully informed particle swarm (FIPS) [14]

The dynamic HPSO (dHPSO), proposed by Engelbrecht [8], selects behaviors randomly from the behavior pool if the particle's *pbest* has not improved for ten iterations. A critique against the dHPSO is that the behavior selection is random and no information about the search process is used to guide the selection towards the most promising behaviors.

Spanvello and Montes de Oca's [18] difference proportional probability PSO (DPP-PSO) allows particles to change their behaviors to the *nbest*'s behavior based on a probability calculated by how much better the *nbest*'s fitness is compared to their own. Additionally, the DPP-PSO has a number of rigid particles for each behavior which do not change their behavior at all. This is to ensure that all behaviors occur in the swarm. One of the issues with the DPP-PSO is that it only contains two behaviors (FIPS and the original PSO with inertia weight) so there is not an adequate range of behavioral diversity to help in the swarm's search.

Li and Yang's [13] adaptive learning particle swarm optimizer-II (ALPSO-II) works as follows: progress values are kept for each particle and rewards are calculated based on the progress. A new behavior is then chosen probabilistically based on a selection ratio calculated using the rewards. The ALPSO-II also contains an archive position, *abest*, which stores the best solution found throughout the whole search. Every iteration each particle has a chance to update the *abest* position by replacing each element of the *abest* individually. If the replacement results in a better fitness, then the *abest* keeps that element. The main issue with ALPSO-II is that it is overly complex and computationally expensive. The *abest* update procedure can increase the number of function evaluations per iteration drastically for higher dimensional problems.

3   Pheromone Based Particle Swarm Optimizer

This section introduces the two proposed self-adaptive HPSO strategies.

Both the strategies' behavior pools consist of the original PSO with inertia weight, Cog-PSO, Soc-PSO, BB-PSO, BBMod-PSO, QSO, TVIW-PSO and TVAC-PSO.

The self-adaptive strategies are inspired by the foraging behavior of ants as modeled in the ant colony optimization meta-heuristic (ACO-MH) [5]. Ants are able to find the shortest route to a food source by secreting pheromone on the trails to the food source. Ants probabilistically follow the routes with the higher concentrations of pheromone. Over time, the pheromone evaporates making the routes less likely to be chosen if the ants do not continue using the route.

The pheromone heterogeneous particle swarm optimizer (pHPSO) uses these concepts to select a behavior for a particle. Each behavior, b, in the behavior pool represents a candidate route, the particles represent ants and the pheromone concentration, p_b, represents the fitness of a behavior. Fitter behaviors have higher pheromone concentrations.

Each particle is initially assigned a random behavior from the behavior pool with the probability $\frac{1}{B}$ where B is the total number of behaviors in the behavior pool. The initial pheromone concentration of each behavior is also $\frac{1}{B}$. Each iteration consists of four phases: behavior selection, particle update, pheromone update and pheromone evaporation.

During behavior selection, a new behavior is probabilistically chosen using probabilities computed using the pheromone concentrations when a particle stagnates. A particle is considered stagnant if its *pbest* does not improve for ten iterations as per [12]. The probability for choosing behavior b is

$$prob_b(t) = \frac{p_b}{\sum_{i=1}^{B} p_i} \tag{3}$$

The particles then update their positions and velocities using their assigned behaviors during the particle update phase.

The next phase is updating the pheromone concentrations. Assuming minimization, the pheromone concentration is updated using one of the following strategies:

- Constant strategy (pHPSO-const)

$$p_b(t) = p_b(t) + \sum_{i=1}^{S_b} \begin{cases} 1.0 & \text{if } f(x_i(t)) < f(x_i(t-1)) \\ 0.5 & \text{if } f(x_i(t)) = f(x_i(t-1)) \\ 0.0 & \text{if } f(x_i(t)) > f(x_i(t-1)) \end{cases} \tag{4}$$

where S_b is the number of particles using behavior b. This strategy rewards behaviors if they improve or maintain a particle's fitness regardless of the magnitude of the improvement. The update values were chosen as a starting point and other values will be investigated in the future.
- Performance based (linear) strategy (pHPSO-lin)

$$p_b(t) = p_b(t) + \sum_{i=1}^{S_b} (f(x_i(t-1)) - f(x_i(t))) \tag{5}$$

Using this strategy behaviors are rewarded in proportion to the improvement of a particle's fitness over two iterations. A minimum concentration of 0.01 is used to prevent zero and negative concentrations.

Roulette wheel selection is biased to the more successful behaviors. To maintain diversity in behavior space and enhance its exploration, pheromone concentrations of all behaviors evaporate using

$$p_b(t+1) = \frac{\left(\sum_{i=1,i\neq b}^{B} p_i \right)}{\sum_{i=1}^{B} p_i} \times p_b \tag{6}$$

The amount of evaporation is proportional to a behavior's pheromone concentration, e.g. if $p_b(t)$ is 90% of the total pheromone concentrations then evaporation will decrease it by 90%.

In comparison to the heterogeneous strategies discussed in Section 3, the pheromone-based self-adaptive HPSO strategies have the following advantages:

- computationally less expensive than the ALPSO-II with less control parameters,
- behaviors are self-adapted based on the success of individual behaviors, and
- better exploration of the behavior space by using pheromone evaporation

4   Experimental Setup

This section provides information on the functions used to compare the different heterogeneous PSO strategies as well as the control parameters used for the algorithms. All functions and algorithms were implemented in CIlib (http://www.cilib.net). The test functions used to compare the different algorithms are functions $f_1 - f_{14}$ of the CEC 2005 benchmark functions [19]. The experiments were run 50 times on each function for 1000 iterations in dimensions 10 to 100 in increments of ten. Each swarm contained 30 particles.

The behaviors used an inertia weight, w, of 0.729844 and acceleration coefficients, c_1 and c_2, of 1.496180 [2]. The QSO used a cloud radius of 5, a value in between the values used in [12] and [1]. The TVIW-PSO decreased its inertia weight from 0.9 to 0.4 [7] and the TVAC-PSO increased its social acceleration coefficient from 0 to 2.5 and decreased its cognitive acceleration coefficient from 2.5 to 0 [16]. The value of 0 for the minimums was used for the behavior to mimic the Cog-PSO and Soc-PSO. The DPP-PSO used five rigid particles per behavior and $\beta = 5$ [18].

5   Results and Analysis

This section analyzes the results obtained for the experiments.

Table 1 summarizes the average rank of each algorithm over all the functions for each dimension. The numbers in bold indicate the highest rankings. In terms of scalability, the pHPSOs obtained the highest ranks for each dimension with the pHPSO-const obtaining the best overall rank. The linear pHPSO achieved better ranks in the lower dimensions and the constant pHPSO in the higher dimensions. The other algorithms ranked very similarly to each other overall with the DPP-PSO ranking the best of the three followed by the dHPSO then the ALPSO-II.

Figure 1 visualizes the scalability results for certain functions. The pHPSO strategies appeared to be unaffected by the increase in dimensionality for functions f_1, f_2, f_4, f_6, f_7 and f_{11}. For functions f_3, f_5, f_{10}, f_{13} and f_{14} the pHPSO strategies scaled linearly, and exponentially for functions f_9 and f_{12}. The f_8 function was the only one with a logistic trend. Compared to the ALPSO-II, the

Table 1. Average Ranks Over All Functions per Dimension

Dimensions	ALPSO-II	DPP-PSO	dHPSO	pHPSO-const	pHPSO-lin
10	4.15±1.64	3.07±0.88	3.14±1.55	2.43±0.72	**2.21±1.15**
20	3.86±1.68	3.36±1.11	3.07±1.33	2.75±1.24	**1.96±0.77**
30	3.57±1.68	3.5±1.05	3.43±1.45	2.36±0.97	**2.14±1.06**
40	3.57±1.68	3.64±0.97	3.29±1.39	**2.07±0.88**	2.43±1.24
50	3.43±1.63	3.43±0.98	3.64±1.44	2.36±1.29	**2.14±0.83**
60	3.43±1.64	3.71±0.88	3.43±1.45	**2.0±0.93**	2.43±1.18
70	3.36±1.67	3.29±1.03	3.64±1.34	**2.21±1.32**	2.5±1.05
80	3.5±1.68	3.29±0.88	3.71±1.39	**2.0±0.85**	2.5±1.3
90	3.36±1.67	3.5±0.91	3.79±1.42	**2.0±1.07**	2.35±0.89
100	3.5±1.68	3.43±0.82	3.57±1.45	2.29±1.28	**2.21±0.94**
Mean	3.57±0.23	3.42±0.18	3.47±0.23	**2.24±0.23**	2.3±0.17

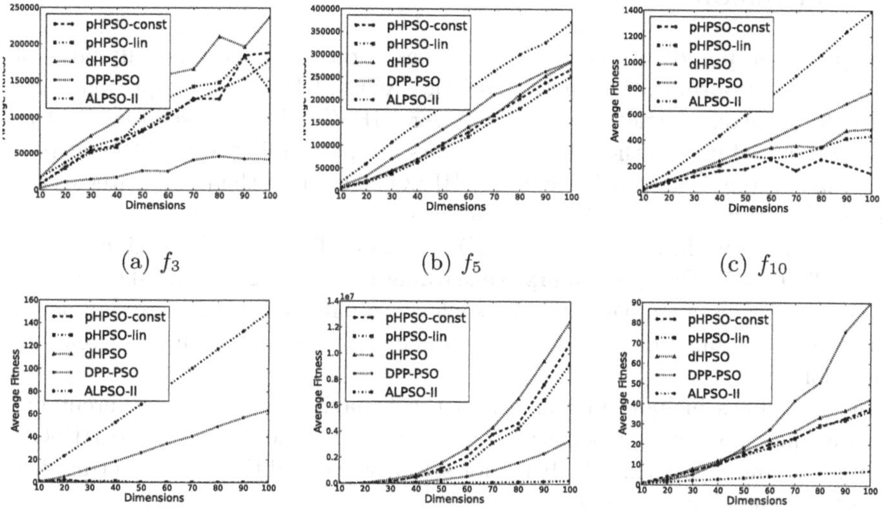

(a) f_3 (b) f_5 (c) f_{10}

(d) f_{11} (e) f_{12} (f) f_{13}

Fig. 1. Scalability for Functions f_3, f_5 and f_{10} to f_{13}

pHPSO strategies scaled better on five of the functions, worse on three functions and the same on six of the functions. The DPP-PSO algorithm scaled better on nine of the functions, worse on two of the functions and the same on two of the functions. Compared to the dHPSO the pHPSO strategies scaled better on five of the functions and the same on the rest of the functions. The scalability patterns of the dHPSO were similar to the pheromone HPSO strategies.

The Friedman test with the Bonferroni-Dunn post-hoc test [4] was used to show that, with 95% confidence, the pHPSO strategies perform significantly better than the other strategies over all dimensions and functions. Figure 2 visualizes the comparison of the algorithms with the Bonferroni-Dunn test. Algorithms

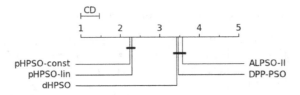

Fig. 2. Critical difference (CD) diagram comparing the algorithms with the Bonferroni-Dunn post-hoc test

grouped with a bold line indicate that there is no significant difference between them.

6   Conclusion

This paper proposed two new strategies based on the pheromone updates of the ant colony optimization meta-heuristic (ACO-MH) to self-adapt behaviors in a heterogeneous particle swarm optimizer (HPSO). The two strategies select behaviors based on whether those behaviors are performing well in the current search landscape. Compared to existing HPSO algorithms the new strategies are computationally simpler and are self-adaptive.

Comparisons with the dynamic HPSO (dHPSO), difference proportional probability PSO (DPP-PSO) and adaptive learning PSO-II (ALPSO-II) showed that the new strategies outranked the others when evaluated on a number of unimodal and multimodal functions and that they scale relatively well with an increase in dimensionality.

Future studies include an analysis of the behavior pool, using different behavioral change triggers, a sensitivity analysis of the pheromone-based HPSO's parameters and comparing the behavior selection capabilities with other models using the same behavior pool.

References

1. Blackwell, T., Branke, J.: Multi-swarm Optimization in Dynamic Environments. In: Raidl, G.R., Cagnoni, S., Branke, J., Corne, D.W., Drechsler, R., Jin, Y., Johnson, C.G., Machado, P., Marchiori, E., Rothlauf, F., Smith, G.D., Squillero, G. (eds.) EvoWorkshops 2004. LNCS, vol. 3005, pp. 489–500. Springer, Heidelberg (2004)
2. Clerc, M., Kennedy, J.: The Particle Swarm - Explosion, Stability, and Convergence in a Multidimensional Complex Space. IEEE Transactions on Evolutionary Computation, 58–73 (2002)
3. Cooren, Y., Clerc, M., Siarry, P.: Performance Evaluation of TRIBES, an Adaptive Particle Swarm Optimization Algorithm. Swarm Intelligence 3, 149–178 (2009)
4. Demšar, J.: Statistical Comparisons of Classifiers Over Multiple Data Sets. The Journal of Machine Learning Research, 1–30 (2006)
5. Dorigo, M.: Optimization, Learning and Natural Algorithms (in Italian). Ph.D. thesis, Dipartimento di Elettronica, Politecnico di Milano, Milan, Italy (1992)

6. Eberhart, R., Kennedy, J.: A New Optimizer using Particle Swarm Theory. In: Proceedings of the Sixth International Symposium on Micro Machine and Human Science, pp. 39–43 (1995)
7. Eberhart, R., Shi, Y.: Comparing Inertia Weights and Constriction Factors in Particle Swarm Optimization. In: Proceedings of the IEEE Congress on Evolutionary Computation, pp. 84–88 (2000)
8. Engelbrecht, A.P.: Heterogeneous Particle Swarm Optimization. In: Dorigo, M., Birattari, M., Di Caro, G.A., Doursat, R., Engelbrecht, A.P., Floreano, D., Gambardella, L.M., Groß, R., Şahin, E., Sayama, H., Stützle, T. (eds.) ANTS 2010. LNCS, vol. 6234, pp. 191–202. Springer, Heidelberg (2010)
9. Kennedy, J.: The Particle Swarm: Social Adaptation of Knowledge. In: Proceedings of the IEEE International Congress on Evolutionary Computation, pp. 303–308 (1997)
10. Kennedy, J.: Bare Bones Particle Swarms. In: Proceedings of the IEEE Swarm Intelligence Symposium, pp. 80–87 (2003)
11. Kennedy, J., Eberhart, R.: Particle Swarm Optimization. In: Proceedings of the IEEE International Joint Conference on Neural Networks, pp. 1942–1948 (1995)
12. Leonard, B., Engelbrecht, A., van Wyk, A.: Heterogeneous Particle Swarms in Dynamic Environments. In: Proceedings of the IEEE Swarm Intelligence Symposium, pp. 1–8 (2011)
13. Li, C., Yang, S.: Adaptive Learning Particle Swarm Optimizer-II for Global Optimization. In: Proceedings of the Congress on Evolutionary Computation, pp. 1–8 (2010)
14. Mendes, R., Kennedy, J., Neves, J.: The Fully Informed Particle Swarm: Simpler, Maybe Better. IEEE Transactions on Evolutionary Computation, 204–210 (2004)
15. Montes de Oca, M., Peña, J., Stützle, T., Pinciroli, C., Dorigo, M.: Heterogeneous Particle Swarm Optimizers. In: Proceedings of the IEEE Congress on Evolutionary Computation, pp. 698–705 (2009)
16. Ratnaweera, A., Halgamuge, S., Watson, H.: Self-Organizing Hierarchical Particle Swarm Optimizer with Time-Varying Acceleration Coefficients. IEEE Transactions on Evolutionary Computation, 240–255 (2004)
17. Shi, Y., Eberhart, R.: A Modified Particle Swarm Optimizer. In: Proceedings of the IEEE Congress on Evolutionary Computation, pp. 69–73 (1998)
18. Spanevello, P., Montes de Oca, M.: Experiments on Adaptive Heterogeneous PSO Algorithms. In: Proceedings of the Doctoral Symposium on Engineering Stochastic Local Search Algorithms, pp. 36–40 (2009)
19. Suganthan, P.N., Hansen, N., Liang, J.J., Deb, K., Chen, Y.P., Auger, A., Tiwari, S.: Problem Definitions and Evaluation Criteria for the CEC 2005 Special Session on Real Parameter Optimization. Tech. rep., Nanyang Technological University (2005)

A "Thermodynamic" Approach to Multi-robot Cooperative Localization with Noisy Sensors

Yotam Elor and Alfred M. Bruckstein

Department of Computer Science and the Goldstein UAV and Satellite Center,
Technion, Haifa, Israel
{yotame,freddy}@cs.technion.ac.il

Abstract. In a previous paper [1], we proposed a new approach to the simultaneous cooperative localization of a very large group of simple robots capable of performing dead-reckoning and sensing the relative position of nearby robots. The idea behind the proposed averaging process is the following: every time two robots meet, they simply average their location estimates. This paper extends the results of [1] by considering noisy relative location measurements and by presenting a novel analysis based on the *Well Mixing Movement Pattern* assumption. The results of this paper are more precise than what was previously reported. Nevertheless, when considering the limit of a large group of robots, and after a long "stabilization" time, the final results turn out to be identical.

1 Introduction

Localization is the task of estimating a robot's self location in space and has been identified as one of the key problems in robotics. In the variant of the localization problem that we shall consider, it is assumed that, initially, every robot knows its precise location in a commonly agreed upon coordinate system. Every robot then uses only odometry in order to track its location, by a process which is sometimes called "dead-reckoning". However, due to noisy sensor readings, in time, the self location estimate diverges from the robot's real location. When a group of robots perform localization, the localization error can be reduced by sharing information between them. In order to do so, some simple *exteroceptive* capabilities are needed. We shall assume that a robot is able to sense the relative location of nearby robots and to communicate with them.

The proposed cooperative localization algorithm is denoted by "Encounter Averaging" (EA). In EA, every robot moves in the area while maintaining an estimate of its location using odometry and whenever two robots are within sensing and communication range they "meet", i.e. average their location estimates. In this work, we consider movement patterns which are "well mixing" in the sense defined below.

Definition 1 (Well Mixing Movement Pattern, WMMP). *If the probability of a meeting between any two robots at any given time is constant then the robots follow a well mixing movement pattern.*

M. Dorigo et al. (Eds.): ANTS 2012, LNCS 7461, pp. 196–203, 2012.

Let $p(r_i, r_j; t)$ be the probability that robots r_i and r_j meet at time t. The movement pattern is WMMP, by definition, if for any two robots $r_i \neq r_j$ and any time t, we have $p(r_i, r_j; t) = p$ where p is a constant. As an example of a movement pattern which is well mixing, we proposed in [1] the "random billiard walk" (RBW). Due to space limitations the analysis of RBW is omitted from this paper and can be found in the TR [2]. A simple "independent error" model (IEM) is considered. In IEM, the odometry errors incurred at each step are independent from the state of the robot. The localization errors accumulate as two-dimensional Gaussian variables with linearly increasing variance.

Due to space limitations the proofs of the theorems and many other details are omitted from this paper, they can be found in our readily available technical report [2].

2   The Encounter Averaging Process

In our work time is discrete i.e. $t = 0, 1, 2...$ A group of M identical independent robots is considered. The robots are modeled as points on the plane. Let J be the matrix of all ones of size $M \times M$ and I - the identity matrix of size $M \times M$. The location of robot r_i at time t in respect to a fixed reference frame is denoted by the vector $X_i(t) = [x_i(t), y_i(t)]^T$ where $x_i(t)$, $y_i(t)$ are the robot's coordinates. Let $v(t)$ be the robot speed and $\phi_i(t)$ its direction at time t. The robot coordinates are readily updated as follows: $X_i(t+1) = X_i(t) + [\cos(\phi_i(t)), \sin(\phi_i(t))]^T v(t)$. The location estimate of robot r_i at time t is denoted by $\hat{X}_i(t) = [\hat{x}_i(t), \hat{y}_i(t)]^T$. Initially $\hat{X}(0) = X(0)$. The estimate error is given by the vector $\tilde{X} = \hat{X} - X = [\tilde{x}_i(t), \tilde{y}_i(t)]^T$. According to IEM, the localization errors added at each time step are distributed normally, i.e. $\hat{X}_i(t+1) = \hat{X}_i(t) + X_i(t+1) - X_i(t) + [n_{i,x}(t), n_{i,y}(t)]^T$ where $n_{i,x}(t)$ ($n_{i,y}(t)$) is the normal noise with variance σ_0^2 added to $\hat{x}_i$ ($\hat{y}_i$) at time t.

Average Upon Meeting

Let Z_{ij} be the relative location of robot r_i in respect to r_j, i.e. $Z_{ij} = X_i - X_j$. In our previous work [1] it was assumed that upon meeting the robots sense the relative location of each other (Z_{ij} and Z_{ji}) accurately. In this work, we consider the case where the measurements of Z_{ij} and Z_{ji} are noisy. Let $\hat{Z}_{ij}$ be Z_{ij} as measured by robot r_j. The measurement errors are modeled as independent normal noise i.e. $\hat{Z}_{ij}(t) = Z_{ij}(t) + n_{ij}(t)$ where $n_{ij}(t) = [n_{ij,x}(t), n_{ij,y}(t)]^T$, $n_{ij,x}(t)$ ($n_{ij,y}(t)$) is the normal noise with variance σ_Z^2 added to the x-component (y-component) of $\hat{Z}_{ij}$ at time t. Let $C_Z = E[n_{ij}(t)n_{ji}(t)]/\sigma_Z^2$. Two cases are considered:

1. $\hat{Z}_{ij}$ and $\hat{Z}_{ji}$ are independent i.e. robots r_i and r_j estimate the relative position independently. In this case we have $C_Z = 0$.
2. $\hat{Z}_{ij} = -\hat{Z}_{ji}$ i.e. the relative location estimates of robots r_i and r_j agree. In this case we have $C_Z = -1$. Agreement can be achieved by the following

process: Each of the robots measure the relative position of the other robot. Denote the results of this measurement by $\hat{Z}_{ij}^0$ and $\hat{Z}_{ji}^0$. The robots transmit their estimations to each other and each of the robots average it's estimation with the additive inverse of the value just received. The resulting estimations are $\hat{Z}_{ji} = \frac{1}{2}\left(\hat{Z}_{ij}^0 - \hat{Z}_{ji}^0\right)$ and $\hat{Z}_{ji} = \frac{1}{2}\left(\hat{Z}_{ji}^0 - \hat{Z}_{ij}^0\right)$ i.e. the estimates agree.

In our proposed cooperative self-localization scheme, whenever two robots meet, they apply the following meeting protocol. Let r_i, r_j be the two robots that meet at time t. The meeting protocol is described for robot r_i; r_j simultaneously follows the same procedure. Upon meeting, r_i asks r_j "what is your estimate of my location?". r_j replies with $\hat{X}_j\left(t^-\right) + \hat{Z}_{ij}\left(t\right)$ i.e.

$$\underbrace{\begin{bmatrix} \hat{x}_j\left(t^-\right) \\ \hat{y}_j\left(t^-\right) \end{bmatrix}}_{\hat{X}_j(t^-)} + \underbrace{\begin{bmatrix} x_i\left(t\right) \\ y_i\left(t\right) \end{bmatrix} - \begin{bmatrix} x_j\left(t\right) \\ y_j\left(t\right) \end{bmatrix} + \begin{bmatrix} n_{ij,x}\left(t\right) \\ n_{ij,y}\left(t\right) \end{bmatrix}}_{\hat{Z}_{ij}(t)} \tag{1}$$

where the values of t^- are the values before the meeting. Then, r_i sets his location estimate to be the average of his previous estimate and the coordinates received from r_j, i.e.

$$\hat{x}_i\left(t\right) = \frac{\hat{x}_i\left(t^-\right) + \left(\hat{x}_j\left(t^-\right) + x_i\left(t\right) - x_j\left(t\right) + n_{ij,x}\left(t\right)\right)}{2} \tag{2}$$

$$\tilde{x}_i\left(t\right) = \hat{x}_i\left(t\right) - x_i\left(t\right) = \frac{\tilde{x}_i\left(t^-\right) + \tilde{x}_j\left(t^-\right)}{2} + \frac{1}{2}n_{ij,x}\left(t\right) \tag{3}$$

and the same for $\hat{y}$. Therefore the new error of each of the robots is the average of their old errors plus half of the error in estimating the relative location.

3   Analysis: The Covariance Evaluation Process

The IEM assumption is that $\tilde{x}_i$ and $\tilde{y}_i$ are independent therefore they can be analyzed separately. Hence only one coordinate, the x-error will be analyzed here. The same results apply to y as well.

Let P_t be the covariance matrix of the localization errors in x at time t. Where the components of P_t are denoted by $\sigma_{ij}\left(t\right)$ and given by $\sigma_{ij}\left(t\right) = \text{Cov}\left[\tilde{x}_i\left(t\right), \tilde{x}_j\left(t\right)\right]$. Let $\bar{P}_t = E\left[P_t\right]$ where the expectation is over all robot meetings prior to time t. The time course of $\bar{P}_t$ under EA is described in the following theorem.

Theorem 1. *Under the WMMP assumption, $\bar{P}_t$ is given by*

$$\bar{P}_t \simeq \left[\frac{\sigma_0^2}{M} + \frac{p}{4}\left(1 + C_Z\right)\sigma_Z^2\right] \cdot J \cdot t + \left[\frac{2\sigma_0^2}{Mp} + \frac{\sigma_Z^2}{2}\right] \cdot I \tag{4}$$

To examine the optimality of EA, a lower bound on any cooperative localization algorithm is presented. The bound is obtained by applying the optimal Kalman Filter.

Theorem 2. *Considering IEM and any cooperative localization algorithm, the expected variance of the localization error of any robot is bounded by*

$$E\left[\tilde{x}_i\left(t\right)^2\right] \geq \frac{\sigma_0^2}{M}t \tag{5}$$

where M is the number of robots and $\tilde{x}_i\left(0\right) = 0$.

The Effect of a Landmark

Consider a landmark placed in a fixed point in the environment. The robots know the exact coordinates of the landmark. Every robot that is within the landmark sensing range senses the relative location of the landmark accurately and updates his localization accordingly. Similarly to the WMMP assumption, it is assumed that the probability that any robot will sense the landmark at any time t is constant. That probability is denoted by p_l and derived in [2]. In case the system comprise a landmark, $\bar{P}_t$ converges to the steady state provided in the following theorem.

Theorem 3. *Under the WMMP assumption, when the system comprises a landmark, the steady state of $\bar{P}_t$ is given by*

$$\bar{P}_\infty \simeq \left[\frac{1}{2Mp_l}\sigma_0^2 + \frac{Mp\left(1 + C_Z\right) + 2C_Zp_l}{8Mp_l}\sigma_Z^2\right] \cdot J \tag{6}$$
$$+ \left[\frac{2}{Mp}\sigma_0^2 + \frac{1}{2}\sigma_Z^2\right] \cdot I$$

4 Discussion and Simulations

The time course of $\bar{P}_t$ can be roughly described by the following: While moving, the robots accumulate localization error. Since errors accumulated by different robots are statistically independent, only the values of the main diagonal of $\bar{P}_t$ increase. Upon meeting, and applying EA, the robots spread the error from the main diagonal to the rest of the matrix. Actually, EA does not decrease, and might even increase the sum of all elements of $\bar{P}_t$. Nevertheless, the EA process "spreads the error" from the main diagonal to the rest of the matrix. Since the robots' localization errors are determined solely by the values of the main diagonal, spreading some of the error from the main diagonal is desired.

When there is no landmark, according to Theorem 1, $\bar{P}_t$ is given by Equation 4 i.e. all elements of $\bar{P}_t$ grow linearly in time with the same pace while the elements of the main diagonal are slightly larger. The constant gap between the values of the main diagonal and the rest of $\bar{P}_t$ is due to the time required for the errors to average over the robots.

Denote by $\sigma_{diag}^2\left(t\right)$ the value of the main diagonal of $\bar{P}_t$ and recall that the expected localization error of a robot is normal with zero mean and variance of $\sigma_{diag}^2\left(t\right)$. Since we are mainly interested in the expected localization error, the discussion will focus on the value of $\sigma_{diag}^2\left(t\right)$. For brevity, consider four cases:

Case 1. (no landmark, $\sigma_Z^2 = 0$). Considering the case with no landmark and no relative location measurement error, by Theorem 1, $\sigma_{diag}^2(t)$ is given by $\sigma_{diag}^2(t) \simeq \frac{\sigma_0^2}{M} \cdot t + \frac{2\sigma_0^2}{Mp}$ i.e. $\sigma_{diag}^2(t)$ comprises a time dependent component and a constant component. Recall that when no error correction mechanisms are applied, $\sigma_{diag}^2(t) = \sigma_0^2 \cdot t$. Hence by applying EA, the error growth rate is reduced by a factor of M. However, a constant component is added. This constant component is a result of the time the odometry errors require to average over the robots and is inversely proportional to the frequency of meetings (Mp). By Theorem 2, the optimal cooperative localization algorithm employing a Kalman filter based on all possible relative location observations yields $\sigma_{diag}^2(t) = \frac{\sigma_0^2}{M} \cdot t$. Hence, rather surprisingly, the localization estimates provided by EA are optimal up to a constant i.e. asymptotically optimal.

Case 2. (no landmark, $\sigma_Z^2 > 0$, $C_Z = 0$). When the relative location measurements are independent ($C_Z = 0$), by Theorem 1, $\sigma_{diag}^2(t)$ is given by $\sigma_{diag}^2(t) \simeq \left[\frac{\sigma_0^2}{M} + \frac{p}{4}\sigma_Z^2 \right] \cdot t + \frac{2\sigma_0^2}{Mp} + \frac{\sigma_Z^2}{2}$. Due to the noisy relative location measurements, both the slope and the constant component of σ_{diag}^2 are larger in comparison to Case 1. The slope is larger since, in this case, the relative location measurement errors incurring at every meeting increase the total amount of noise in the system. The addition to the time dependent component is given by $\frac{p}{4}\sigma_Z^2 \cdot t$ i.e. proportional to the amount of error added in each meeting (σ_Z^2) and to the frequency of meetings (p). Hence, in the long term, frequent meeting will increase the localization error rather than decrease it.

Case 3. (no landmark, $\sigma_Z^2 > 0$, $C_Z = -1$). When the relative location measurements agree ($C_Z = -1$), by Theorem 1, $\sigma_{diag}^2(t)$ is given by $\sigma_{diag}^2(t) \simeq \frac{\sigma_0^2}{M} \cdot t + \frac{2\sigma_0^2}{Mp} + \frac{\sigma_Z^2}{2}$ i.e. the slope of $\sigma_{diag}^2(t)$ equals to the slope of Case 1. Recall that the slope of $\sigma_{diag}^2(t)$ equals to the rate of noise accumulation in the system. When the relative location measurements agree, a meeting does not add noise to the system. Hence these errors do not affect the slope of $\sigma_{diag}^2(t)$. Comparing to the optimal cooperative localization algorithm employing a Kalman filter based on all possible relative location observations (Theorem 2) we have asymptotically optimal expected error.

A comparison between cases 2 and 3 reveals relative location measurements which agree ($C_Z = -1$) yields a significantly better localization error than uncorrelated errors ($C_Z = 0$). Furthermore, $C_Z = -1$ can be easily achieved by the simple relative measurement averaging process described in the beginning of Section 3. Hence it is recommended to apply the process in every meeting prior to applying EA.

Case 4. (with landmark, $\sigma_Z^2 > 0$, $C_Z = -1$). In all three cases above, σ_{diag}^2 increases linearly in time. The error can be made bounded by introducing a landmark. By Theorem 3, with a landmark, the stable state localization error is given by $\sigma_{diag}^2(\infty) \simeq \frac{\sigma_0^2}{2Mp_l} + \frac{2\sigma_0^2}{p} + \frac{1}{2}\sigma_Z^2$. Whenever a robot sense the landmark, some localization error is removed from $\bar{P}_t$. The amount of error removed is

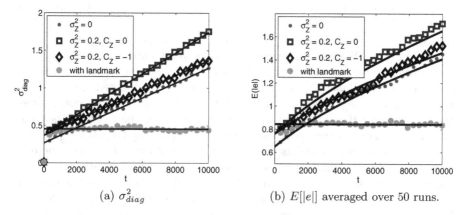

(a) σ^2_{diag}

(b) $E[|e|]$ averaged over 50 runs.

Fig. 1. Comparison of the four cases on a torus. The solid lines are the theoretical predictions and the markers are the simulation results.

proportional to the localization error of the robot. Therefore, as $\bar{P}_t$ contains more error, more error will be removed each time a robot sense the landmark. Since error is accumulated at a constant rate, the process converges to a steady state in which the error accumulation rate equals the error removal rate.

Extensive simulations were performed in order to validate the above presented analytical results. The following parameters were computed from experimental data: $\sigma^2_{diag}(t) = \frac{1}{M} \sum_{i=1}^{M} [P_t]_{ii}$ and $E[e(t)] = \frac{1}{M} \sum_{i=1}^{M} \sqrt{\tilde{x}_i^2(t) + \tilde{y}_i^2(t)}$ i.e. σ^2_{diag} is the variance of the localization error averaged over the robots and $E[e]$ is the localization error averaged over the robots. Observe Figure 1 for a comparison between the four cases discussed above. The values of σ^2_{diag}, measured in a single run for each of the cases are presented in Figure 1a. The experiments show that the predictions of σ^2_{diag} are accurate for all cases. This is expected since RBW is indeed WMMP on the torus, as shown in [2]. The average error was found to be very noisy for a single run. Hence the mean of the average error over 50

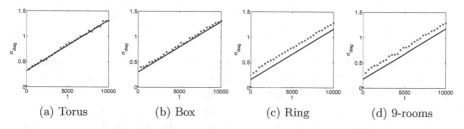

(a) Torus   (b) Box   (c) Ring   (d) 9-rooms

Fig. 2. σ^2_{diag} for a single run in every environment. The solid lines are the theoretical predictions and the markers are the simulation results.

runs is presented in Figure 1b. It can be observed that the expected error is also predicted well.

The simulations have shown that the predictions are accurate when the environment is a torus. We have experimented with several additional environments. Sketches of the environments can be found in [2]. Experiment results for a single run in every environment are presented in Figure 2. For all tested environment, the growth rate of σ^2_{diag} was predicted well but the constant component was found to be higher then expected. Recall that this gap is the result of the time required to average the error over the robots and is given by $2\sigma^2_0/Mp + \frac{1}{2}\sigma^2_Z$ (for case 3). On the torus, the robots travel freely hence at every time step there is a probability of Mp to meet a "fresh" robot i.e. a robot with relatively low covariance. In other words, on the torus, RBW is WMMP. On the contrary, when the environment is fragmented, there is a higher probability to meet a "dirty" robot i.e. a robot with high shared covariance due to a recent meeting. Putting it another way, RBW is less WMMP. Meeting a "fresh" robot reduces the localization error much more efficiently that meeting a "dirty" one. Hence the error spreads less efficiently and the gap between σ^2_{diag} and the optimal Kalman filter is larger than predicted.

5   Relation to Previous Work

Due to space limitations, only the most relevant work is presented here, for a wider survey, see [1] and the TR [2]. About ten years ago, Sanderson[7] proposed a cooperative localization mechanism based on a central (non-distributed) Kalman Filter. Roumeliotis and colleagues[5,4] presented a distributed version of KF in which the computation required to maintain the covariance matrix is distributed between the robots. However, every meeting between two robots implies an update of at least $2M$ components of the covariance matrix. Furthermore, all robots must be aware of every update of the covariance matrix thus every meeting implies a computation complexity of $\Theta\left(M^2\right)$ and communication between all robots.

In distinction from the previous work, in EA, the computation complexity implied by a meeting is $\Theta\left(1\right)$ and the only communication required is between the two meeting robots. Furthermore, since EA is asymptotically optimal, the benefits of using variants of KF are limited to reducing the constant gap between EA and the optimum achievable. These benefits diminish when considering long time scales.

Roumeliotis and Rekleitis were the first to analyze the performance of KF[6]. Later, Mourikis and Roumeliotis [3,4] analyzed KF assuming a fixed RPMG i.e. every robot averages its location with a fixed set of other robots. By fixing the RPMG, they have been able to obtain an exact analysis of the localization process. They also considered changes of the RPMG, but discuss the system state after stabilization. The model used by Mourikis and Roumeliotis is more conventional than IEM. Nevertheless, the analysis of both models produces similar results, see the discussion in [1].

6   Conclusion

We presented the error averaging (EA) localization scheme inspired by the optimal Kalman filter (KF) proposed by Sanderson[7] and Roumeliotis et al.[5]. The idea behind EA is simple: Whenever two robots meet, they average their location estimates. While being asymptotically optimal, EA requires considerably less communication and computation then KF.

While performing EA, during every meeting, the two meeting robots are required to know their relative location. Noisy relative location measurements were considered. Generally, these errors increase the localization error. However, we have shown that in case the relative location measurements of the two robots agree, the localization error is (almost) unaffected by these errors. A simple averaging process which makes the relative location estimates agree was proposed. Applying this process prior to EA is highly recommended.

We analyzed the expected localization quality of EA assuming the movement pattern of the robots is random and well mixing (WMMP) i.e. the probability of a meeting between any two robots at any time is constant. As an example of such a movement pattern, we presented the random billiard walk (RBW). Simulations have shown that the analysis is accurate when the environment is a torus. Hence, RBW is indeed well mixing on the torus. When the environment includes obstacles, RBW is less WMMP. In that case, the time dependent component of the error propagation is predicted well however the constant is somewhat higher than expected.

Acknowledgements. This research was supported by the Technion Goldstein UAV and Satellite Center.

References

1. Elor, Y., Bruckstein, A.M.: A Thermodynamic Approach to the Analysis of Multirobot Cooperative Localization under Independent Errors. In: Dorigo, M., Birattari, M., Di Caro, G.A., Doursat, R., Engelbrecht, A.P., Floreano, D., Gambardella, L.M., Groß, R., Şahin, E., Sayama, H., Stützle, T. (eds.) ANTS 2010. LNCS, vol. 6234, pp. 36–47. Springer, Heidelberg (2010)
2. Elor, Y., Bruckstein, A.M.: A thermodynamic approach to multi-robot cooperative localization with noisy sensors. Tech. rep., Computer Science Department, Technion Haifa, Israel (2012)
3. Mourikis, A., Roumeliotis, S.: Performance analysis of multirobot cooperative localization. IEEE Trans. on Robotics 22(4), 666–681 (2006)
4. Mourikis, A.I., Roumeliotis, S.I.: Predicting the performance of cooperative simultaneous localization and mapping. The Int. J. of Robotics Research 25(12) (2006)
5. Roumeliotis, S., Bekey, G.: Distributed multirobot localization. IEEE Trans. on Robotics and Automation 18(5), 781–795 (2002)
6. Roumeliotis, S.I., Rekleitis, I.M.: Propagation of uncertainty in cooperative multirobot localization: Analysis and experimental results. Auton. Robots 17(1) (2004)
7. Sanderson., A.C.: A distributed algorithm for cooperative navigation among multiple mobile robots. Advanced Robotics 12(15), 335–349 (1997)

AcoSeeD: An Ant Colony Optimization for Finding Optimal Spaced Seeds in Biological Sequence Search

Dong Do Duc[1], Huy Q. Dinh[2], Thanh Hai Dang[3],
Kris Laukens[3,4], and Xuan Huan Hoang[5]

[1] Institute of Information Technology, Vietnam National University, Hanoi, Vietnam
[2] Center for Integrative Bioinformatics, Max F Perutz Laboratories,
University of Vienna and Medical University, Vienna, Austria
[3] Biomina - Biomedical Informatics Research Center Antwerp, Antwerp University
Hospital / University of Antwerp, Edegem, Belgium
[4] Advanced Database Research and Modelling (ADReM),
University of Antwerp, Belgium
[5] University of Technology (UET), Vietnam National University, Hanoi, Vietnam
dongdoduc@vnu.edu.vn, huy.dinh@univie.ac.at

Abstract. Similarity search in biological sequence database is one of the most popular and important bioinformatics tasks. Spaced seeds have been increasingly used to improve the quality and sensitivity of searching, for example, in seeded alignment methods. Finding optimal spaced seeds is a NP-hard problem. In this study we introduce an application of an Ant Colony Optimization (ACO) algorithm to address this problem in a metaheuristics framework. This method, called AcoSeeD, builds optimal spaced seeds in an elegant construction graph that uses the ACO standard framework with a modified pheromone update. Experimental results demonstrate that AcoSeeD brings a significant improvement of sensitivity while demanding the same computational time as other state-of-the-art methods. We also introduces an alternative way of using local search that exerts a fast approximation of the objective function in ACO.

1 Introduction

The revolution of sequencing technologies is increasingly yielding a tremendous number of biological sequences, which are stored in numerous databases (e.g NCBI gene bank). As a consequence, searching for similarity or local alignments between biological sequences from large databases is among the most popular bioinformatics tasks. It is therefore crucial to develop search algorithms that are highly sensitive and time-efficient. The pioneer work for sequence similarity search, which has been proposed by Smith and Waterman [10], uses dynamic programming to generate the exact solution but demands a quadratic running time. Nevertheless, the current growth of data sets does not allow this class of methods to work sufficiently efficient in terms of computional time. Heuristic alternatives, such as BLAST [1], have been used instead. Those methods are based

M. Dorigo et al. (Eds.): ANTS 2012, LNCS 7461, pp. 204–211, 2012.
© Springer-Verlag Berlin Heidelberg 2012

on an approximate match between two biological sequences (namely genes, proteins or even the whole genome) that is called a seed. A seed is a string denoting the similarity between biological sequences. Seeded-alignment is widely-used in biological sequence searching applications, recently for example in short-read mapping and genome assembly algorithms for next-generation sequencing data. To obtain search results with high sensitivity, the spaced seed finding method proposed by ([9], [12]) allows for relax matching, thus allows for much more flexibility in alignments. Related methods such as Mandala [12] and Iedera [8] were developed and successfully implemented in a number of alignment methods (e.g BFAST[5], PatternHunter II [9], SHRiMP[2]). To evaluate the quality of a spaced seed, Li et al. [9] introduced dynamic programming for computing its sensitivity (i.e the probability of that a seed set matches an alignment) of a given multiple spaced seeds. Furthermore, Ilie et al. [6] proposed a heuristic approach called Overlap Complexity (OC) that approximates this sensitivity in polynominal computational time. More recently, the state-of-the-art method for finding the optimal spaced seed, called SpEED [7], has been introduced. SpEED uses a popular meta-heuristic method, i.e. hill climbing, together with OC heuristics. It was demonstrated to improve the sensitivity and running time in comparison to previous existing methods. In this regard, we propose an application of ACO for finding multiple spaced seeds. Ant Colony Optimization [4] is a meta-heuristic technique based on simulating the behaviors of a real ant colony. Our method is called AcoSeeD and uses an adaption of the MAX-MIN Ant system that allows an ant colony to travel in a useful construction graph to build spaced seeds. The experimental results demonstrate that the method outperforms the existing state-of-the-art method for finding space seeds, namely SpEED, in all configuration settings of test cases given the same number of intermediate solutions.

2   Spaced Seed Optimization Problem

Under the assumption of the Bernoulli model, a random sequence R of length N consisting of either 0(mismatch) or 1(match) is used to represent a sequence alignment with a matching probability [1]. A spaced seed s of 1(match) and $*$(match/mismatch) is said to hit R if s can be aligned with R at the 1 position. A set S of k spaced seeds is said to hit R if at least one of these hits R. For example, a set of seeds $\{11*1, 1*11\}$ can hit the following sequences $\{100110100001,$ $1000010110001, 1000011110001, 1101001011001\}$. A spaced seed s is associated with a weight w, indicating the number of 1 in the string. The problem of finding multiple spaced seeds is described as follows: Given a matching sequence R of length N and p being the matching probability between two biological sequences, find a set of k spaced seeds of weight w that maximize the hit to R. This problem is NP-hard [9]. It remains valid either in the case of given or unknown seed length. In this paper, we also present an ACO application to find the corresponding seed length with respect to the sensitivity.

3   AcoSeeD: Ant Colony Optimization for Spaced Seeds

3.1   Construction Graph

A construction graph (Fig. 1A)) is defined to have k rectangles of size $w \times (l_{max} - w)$. Each ant builds k seeds by traveling on each rectangle either up or right (Fig. 1B) from the start node at the coordinate $(i, 0, 0)$ for rectangle $i, i = 1 \ldots k$. Such a travel corresponds to adding '1'(right) or '*'(up) to the current seed. The process stops when ant i travels to the node $(i, w, length_i - w)$ where $length_i \leq l_{max}$ is the respective length of seed i. We note that $length_i$ can be given or found by another ACO procedure that will be presented later in this paper. Thanks to its special orientation, it is always guaranteed that the ant colony builds the seed of weight w (an example in Fig. 1C). The pheromone concentration τ denotes how likely the ant colony building seed i at coordinate (x, y) by choosing

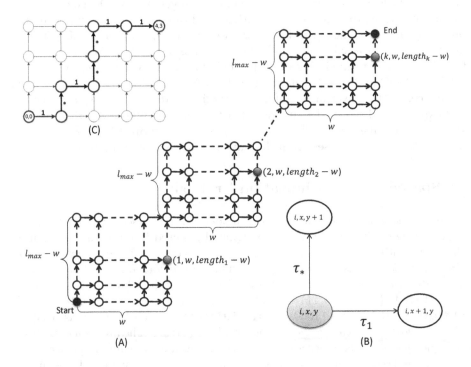

Fig. 1. Construction graph and seed building procedure. (A) Construction graph for building a set of k spaced seeds of length w. **(B)** The direction of an ant's travel path. **(C)** An example of building spaced seeds of weight 4 and length 7. The path $(RU RUU RR)$ of an ant as depicted represents the seeds $1 * 1 * *11$.

either orientation Up(τ_*, coordinate $(x, y+1)$) or Right(τ_1, coordinate $(x+1, y)$) (Fig. 1B) probabilistically according to the following probability

$$P^i_{(x,y)}(v) = \frac{\tau^i_{x,y,v}}{\tau^i_{x,y,*} + \tau^i_{x,y,1}}, v \in \{*, 1\} \tag{1}$$

The pheromone is updated following the adapted MAX-MIN Ant System rule [11], [3]. In more detail, the path s_{i-best} of the i-best ant at which the highest sensitivity is obtained at current iteration is used for updating the pheromone in the construction graph as follows

$$\tau^i_{x,y,v} \leftarrow (1 - \rho)\tau^i_{x,y,v} + \Delta\tau, v \in \{*, 1\}, \Delta\tau = \begin{cases} \rho\tau_{max} & (x, y, v) \in s_{i-best} \\ \rho\tau_{min} & otherwise \end{cases} \tag{2}$$

3.2   ACO-Based Seed Length Identification

We also apply ACO to identify the optimal length for each seed separately based on the construction graph described in Fig. 2. Ants choose the next nodes according to

$$P_i(l) = \frac{\tau_{i,l}\eta_{i,l}}{\sum_{h=v}^{l_{max}} \tau_{i,h}\eta_{i,h}}, v = \begin{cases} l_{min} & i = 1 \\ length_{i-1} & i > 1 \end{cases} \tag{3}$$

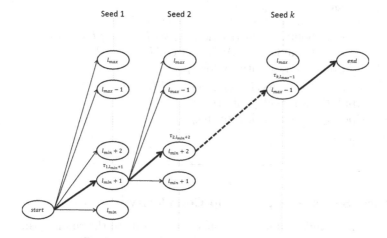

Fig. 2. ACO construction graph for the identification of seed lengths. From the starting node in the construction graph, each ant chooses one of the following nodes $(1, l_{min}), (1, l_{min} + 1), \ldots, (1, l_{max})$ as such that the seed 1 has the respective length $l_{min}, l_{min} + 1, \ldots, l_{max}$. Because the seed length is increased, the ant chooses the node $(i, length_{i-1}), (i, l_{min} + 1), \ldots, (i, l_{max})$ where $i = 2, .., k$.

where $\tau_{i,l}$ indicates how likely these ants choose as such that the seed i has a length l. Heuristic information is computed as follows

$$
\begin{cases}
0.5 & (i > 1)\&(l = length_{i-1}) \\
1.0 & (i = 1)\|((l > length_{i-1})\&(l \leq l_{max} - (k - i))) \\
0.1 & otherwise
\end{cases}
\tag{4}
$$

Here the seed i with a length equal to the length of seed $(i - 1)$ will be chosen with the priority of 0.5. The seed with a length larger than the length of its preceding seed (i.e, $(i-1)$) and smaller than $l_{max} - (k - i)$ (for $k - i$ succeeding seeds still have chance to be chosen) will be chosen with the priority of 1.0. Otherwise the priority is 0.1. The pheromone update rule is similarly applied using the rule described above (see formula 2).

3.3   AcoSeeD Algorithm

Overall, AcoSeeD works as outlined in the following scheme:

Algorithm 1. Pseudo code of the AcoSeeD algorithm

Data: w, k, p, N
Output: The optimal spaced seed s_{best} set w.r.t the sensitivity

begin
    $s_{g-best} \leftarrow null$; Estimating l_{min}, l_{max};
    while *stop conditions not satisfied* **do**
        foreach $i = 1..N_{ant}$ **do**
            Determine the seed length; {*section 3.2*}
            $s_i \leftarrow$ SolutionConstruction(); {*seed built by the ant i^{th}*}
            $s_i \leftarrow$ LocalSearch(s_i); {*using OC heuristics*}
            Computing sensitivity for s_i: $F(s_i)$;
        $s_{i-best} \leftarrow$ **argmax**$(F(s_1), F(s_2), .., F(s_{n_a}))$;
        ApplyPheromoneUpdate (s_{i-best});
        Update the global best seed s_{g-best};
    Output s_{g-best};
end

3.4   Local Search Using Overlap Complexity

After each ant completes building a spaced seed, due to the running time of the original sensitivity computation, the local search exerted in [7] is performed using an objective function based on the OC heuristic. The OC is an approximation function for the sensitivity that can speed up the computational time, compared to the exponential computational time of the dynamic programming algorithm [9]. Starting from the spaced seed built by the current ant, the local search tries to swap between 1 and * for each seed without changing its weight to obtain a new spaced seed with a better approximated sensitivity.

4 Experimental Results

4.1 Datasets

To compare with existing methods including the state-of-the-art method SpEED, we experimentally evaluated the spaced seed identification based on the parameter settings that were practically used in a number of popular biological sequence alignment/search programs such as SHRiMP[2], PatternHunter II [9], BFAST[5]. SHRiMP consists of 15 datasets with a small number of seeds (i.e. $k = 4$) whereas each of the two others uses 3 datasets with a large set of seeds ($k = 10, 16$). PatternHunter II is the largest dataset with a matching pattern of length $N = 64$ whereas for the two others $N = 50$. These datasets have a seed weight w ranging from 10 to 20 and a matching probability p from 0.70 to 0.95.

4.2 Comparison Results

To obtain a fair comparison with the state-of-the-art work [7], we performed AcoSeeD search for $N_{solutions} = 5000$ solutions as done in [7], each was generated once and was then used in the OC-based local search to improve sensitivity.

Specifically, in total $N_{ants} = 50$ ants were used for each of $N_{loops} = 100$ loops to determine $N_{solutions} = N_{ants} * N_{loops}$ sets of spaced seeds. Hence, the computational complexity of both two methods are $\mathcal{O}(N_{solutions} * (ls + o))$, where

Table 1. Experimental comparison using the SHRiMP dataset: Results between AcoSeeD and the existing methods (Mandala [12], Iedera [8], SpEED [7] (*in italic*) for a small number of seeds. The column "ACO-best" and "ACO-worst" represents the AcoSeeD sensitivity for the best and the worst seed, respectively. In addition, the average AcoSeeD sensitivity value over 10 runs is given in the last column. The sensitivity of other methods are retrieved from the SpEED paper [7].

w	p	Mandala	Iedera	SpEED-best	ACO-best	ACO-worst	ACO-average
			SHRiMP: 4 seeds ($N = 50$)				
	0.75	90.6608	90.6802	*90.9098*	**90.9757**	90.9104	90.9513
10	0.8	97.7316	97.7586	*97.8337*	**97.8584**	97.8467	97.8521
	0.85	99.7283	99.7437	*99.7569*	**99.7624**	99.7599	99.7614
	0.75	83.0512	83.2413	*83.3793*	**83.5349**	83.4207	83.4728
11	0.8	94.7845	94.935	*94.9861*	**95.0636**	95.0144	95.037
	0.85	99.1929	99.2189	*99.2431*	**99.2498**	99.2451	99.2478
	0.8	90.258	90.3934	*90.575*	**90.6576**	90.6147	90.6328
12	0.85	98.0786	98.0781	*98.1589*	**98.1786**	98.1682	98.1766
	0.9	99.8633	99.8773	*99.8821*	**99.8866**	99.8845	99.8853
	0.85	84.3838	84.5795	*84.8212*	**85.0328**	84.915	84.9829
16	0.9	97.3023	97.2806	*97.4321*	**97.483**	97.464	97.4712
	0.95	99.9287	99.9331	*99.9388*	**99.9429**	99.9414	99.9419
	0.85	72.1954	72.1695	*73.1664*	**73.3357**	73.2432	73.27
18	0.9	93.0855	93.0442	*93.712*	**93.7912**	93.7597	93.7778
	0.95	99.6603	99.669	*99.75*	**99.7617**	99.7575	99.7599

ls and o are the complexity of the local search and sensitivity computating procedure as the objective function, respectively. We further set other ACO parameters for AcoSeeD, being: (1) the pheromone evaporation factor $\rho = 0.3$, (2) the upper bound of pheromone trail $\tau_{max} = 1.0$, (3) the lower bound of pheromone trail $\tau_{min} = \tau_{max}/W$ where $W = 2*w*k$ for the seed length finding and $W = 2*w*w*k$ for the seed building process. The difference between pheromone bounds is thus set proportionally to the number of graph nodes.

Table 1 demonstrates that the performance in terms of sensitivity increases from 0.007% to 0.134% in all test cases of the SHRiMP dataset. As noted by Illie et al. (2011) in the SpEED paper [7], a 1% sensitivity improvement is significant. This indicates that using a better seed can help bringing in additional 3 billion nucleotides to be mapped for the 100× coverage of the human genome. The difference between AcoSeeD and SpEED indicates that a significant number of nucleotides can be additionally added to the information extracted from the sequencing data. Futhermore, AcoSeeD gained a higher sensitivity for all 10 runs compared to the best result obtained with SpEED. Interestingly, for all datasets the worst solution (i.e spaced seed) among 10 runs has a higher sensitivity compared to the best result obtained from SpEED. Fig. 3 shows a performance comparison in terms of sensitivity between AcoSeeD and SpEED (both the first and the last run) after running on the PatternHunter II and BFAST dataset. Even though the SpEED shows good performances from the first to the last result based on the OC heuristics, AcoSeeD still yields improved performances compared to SpEED. Our method yielded an improvement of up to 0.89% for the PatternHunter II dataset and 2.33% for the BFAST. This allows us to conclude that the AcoSeeD approach can significantly boost sequence alignment mapping for high coverage sequencing of large genomes.

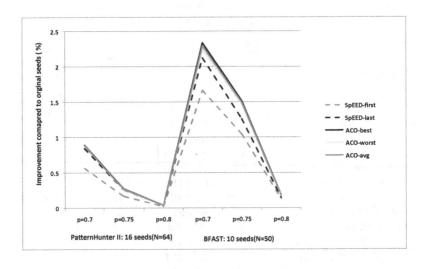

Fig. 3. Experimental performance comparison for large size datasets

5   Conclusions

In this paper, we proposed an ACO-based approach for tackling the problem of finding spaced seeds for biological sequence searching. Our method, AcoSeeD, used a construction graph in which each spaced seed is built as a forward-only path in a separate rectangle graph and integrated the refined MAX-MIN pheromone update procedure [3]. A flexible and quick local search procedure based on the Overlap Complexity heuristic is also applied to boost the quality of the seed. The experimental results and comparisons based on several benchmark datasets demonstrate that AcoSeeD outperforms existing methods in terms of sensitivity without consuming extra computing time.

Acknowledgments. We would like to thank Prof. von Haeseler for the introduction of the spaced seed problem. This work is partially supported by Vietnam National Foundation for Science & Technology Development (NAFOSTED) and the TRIG project at University of Engineering and Technology, VNU Hanoi.

References

1. Altschul, S.F., Gish, W., Miller, W., Myers, E.W., Lipman, D.J.: Basic local alignment search tool. J. Mol. Biol. 215(3), 403–410 (1990)
2. David, M., Dzamba, M., Lister, D., Ilie, L., Brudno, M.: SHRiMP2: sensitive yet practical SHort Read Mapping. Bioinformatics 27(7), 1011–1012 (2011)
3. Do Duc, D., Dinh, H.Q., Hoang Xuan, H.: On the Pheromone Update Rules of Ant Colony Optimization Approaches for the Job Shop Scheduling Problem. In: Bui, T.D., Ho, T.V., Ha, Q.T. (eds.) PRIMA 2008. LNCS (LNAI), vol. 5357, pp. 153–160. Springer, Heidelberg (2008)
4. Dorigo, M., Stutzle, T.: Ant Colony Optimization. The MIT Press, Cambridge (2004)
5. Homer, N., Merriman, B., Nelson, S.F.: BFAST: an alignment tool for large scale genome resequencing. PLoS ONE 4(11), e7767 (2009)
6. Ilie, L., Ilie, S.: Multiple spaced seeds for homology search. Bioinformatics 23(22), 2969–2977 (2007)
7. Ilie, L., Ilie, S., Bigvand, A.M.: SpEED: fast computation of sensitive spaced seeds. Bioinformatics 27(17), 2433–2434 (2011)
8. Kucherov, G., Noe, L., Roytberg, M.: A unifying framework for seed sensitivity and its application to subset seeds. J. Bioinform. Comput. Biol. 4(2), 553–569 (2006)
9. Li, M., Ma, B., Kisman, D., Tromp, J.: PatternHunter II: highly sensitive and fast homology search. Genome Inform. 14, 164–175 (2003)
10. Smith, T.F., Waterman, M.S.: Identification of common molecular subsequences. J. Mol. Biol. 147(1), 195–197 (1981)
11. Stuetzle, T., Hoos, H.: Max-min ant system. Future Gener. Comp. Sy. 16, 889–914 (2000)
12. Sun, Y., Buhler, J.: Designing multiple simultaneous seeds for DNA similarity search. J. Comput. Biol. 12(6), 847–861 (2005)

Analysis of Ant-Based Routing
with Wireless Medium Access Control

Rui Fang[1], Zequn Huang[2], Louis Rossi[1], and Chien-Chung Shen[2]

[1] Mathematical Sciences
[2] Computer & Information Sciences
University of Delaware, Newark, DE, USA
{ruifang,rossi}@math.udel.edu, {zehuang,cshen}@cis.udel.edu

Abstract. Although ant-based routing protocols have been shown empirically to perform well in multi-hop wireless networks, there lack mathematical frameworks to rigorously characterize their behaviors. The paper takes the first and a modest step by modeling the cross-layer interaction between a basic ant-based routing protocol and a realistic medium access control protocol on a simple topology. The merit of the model is validated via comparison between the Matlab numerical analysis of equilibrium behavior and the QualNet simulation with realistic wireless communications.

1 Introduction

Ant-based routing protocols have been successfully applied to exploit routes in multi-hop networks [2,3,6,4]. In these protocols, there are a number of protocol parameters that control the deposition and evaporation of pheromone as well as the exploratory routing of the ants. However, the mathematical modeling and analysis of ant-based protocols was limited to wired networks because the models did not include particular pathological features of wireless networks such as the *hidden terminal problem*. In this paper, we present a study using a rigorous model of the ant-based routing protocol BARP (Basic Ant-based Routing Protocol) on top of a mathematical model of the wireless medium access control (MAC) protocol MACA (Multiple Access with Collision Avoidance). Given the intrinsic complexity of wireless medium access control and its cross-layer interaction with ant-based routing, we take the first and a modest step by modeling and analyzing the integrated behavior on a simple six-node topology shown in Figure 3.

2 Related Work and Background

Previous Work. There have been a variety of contributions in the study of biologically inspired networking algorithms. Yoo, La and Makowski rigorously studied a simple two router ant-based system with multiple parallel routes [9]. The study rigorously determined the long-time asymptotics for the system. This work was augmented by Punyaslok and Baras [5] who modeled the arrival times of data and control packets along parallel routes between two routers. Similar to

M. Dorigo et al. (Eds.): ANTS 2012, LNCS 7461, pp. 212–219, 2012.
© Springer-Verlag Berlin Heidelberg 2012

our work, the stochastic problem is mapped to a system of ordinary differential equations (ODEs). The authors identify stationary states and analyze their stability. For larger networks, Bean and Costa developed a framework for studying ant-based systems, connecting equilibrium solutions with Wardrop equilibrium, a special case of Nash equilibrium, from traffic flow theory [1]. Saleem et al. have developed mathematical frameworks for the analysis and measurement of collision probabilities to routing overhead, route optimality and energy consumption [7]. Along similar lines, Zhahid et al. have developed a mathematical framework for analyzing beehive based protocols. [10].

MACA MAC Protocol. To address the hidden terminal problem, MACA adopts *virtual* carrier sensing to replace *physical* carrier sensing, where a sender and a receiver handshake via RTS (Request To Send) and CTS (Clear To Send) control packets before sending data. After the handshake, the sender can send its data packet without incurring collisions with neighboring nodes. Although collisions may occur between RTS packets, MACA can reduce the chance of collisions between data packets as long as RTS packets are significantly shorter than data packets. However, data packets can still collide with RTS packets.

BARP Ant-Based Routing Protocol. BARP models a network as a directed graph. Each link is weighted by pheromone values, which determine how ants will travel in the network along multi-hop routes. BARP uses two different types of ants. Ants traveling from source s, seeking route to destination d. are called "forward ants." Once a forward ant reaches the destination, it becomes a "backward ant," and will trace back to the source from the destination, depositing pheromone along the route it takes. Using pheromone tables on each node, ant-based routing protocols deploy forward ants to discover possible routes between pairs of nodes, and optimize routing tables to enhance shorter, desirable routes via pheromone deposition by backward ants and discard longer, less efficient routes via evaporation of pheromone.

Analytical Framework for BARP. In our modeling framework, the behaviors of ant-based routing are characterized by three general rules: route discovery, route reinforcement (deposition) and route decay (evaporation). By considering ant-based routing as a dynamic process, we further identify three critical time increments. The increment h_1 is the amount of time between evaporation events on each node. The increment h_2 is the amount of time between deployment of ants from a source node s. The increment h_3 is the time required for an ant control packet to move from one node to the next. We assume that $h_1 < h_3 < h_2$. An ant at node i will move to node j with probability p_{ij}

$$p_{ij} = (\tau_{ij})^\beta / \sum_{h \in N_i} (\tau_{ih})^\beta \qquad (1)$$

where τ_{ij} represents the pheromone values on the link from node i to node j, N_i is the set of all connected neighbors of nodes i and β is the routing exponent, which controls whether single-path routes or multi-path routes are selected. The forward ants then traverse the network following the Markov process according to a transition matrix $P^{(n)}(\beta) = [p_{ij}]$ at the $n^{th}h_3$ time step,

$$\mathbf{y}^{(n+1)} = \mathbf{y}^{(n)} P^{(n)}(\beta). \tag{2}$$

Here the kth component of the density vector $\mathbf{y}^{(n)}$ is the probability of finding an ant on the kth node of the network. The routing protocol defines how the matrix $P^{(n)}(\beta)$ evolves from one iteration to the next through pheromone deposition and evaporation.

The behavior of this ant-based routing protocol are elaborated in [8], and in particular, an analytic model is derived:

$$\tau_{ij}^{(n+1)} = \underbrace{(1 - h_1\kappa_1)^{(h_2/h_1)} \tau_{ij}^{(n)}}_{\text{evaporation}} + \underbrace{h_2\kappa_2 \sum_{k=1}^{\infty} \frac{1}{k^p} \tilde{p}_{ij}^{sd}(k)}_{\text{deposition}}, \tag{3}$$

where κ_1 is an evaporation rate, κ_2 is a deposition rate and $\tilde{p}_{ij}^{sd}(k)$ is the probability of an ant following a k-hop route from source node s to destination node d passing through link ij without any cycles. The link undergoes h_2/h_1 evaporation events between step 1 and step 5, and it is understood that many transitions of (2) occur for every one transition of (3). Also, the summation is the expected inverse hop count, $\left\langle \frac{1}{H_{sd}} \right\rangle$ for a single ant. A stationary state occurs when (2) and (3) are independent of the time step n and satisfy the system,

$$\Lambda\tau_{ij} = \sum_{k=1}^{\infty} \frac{1}{k} \tilde{p}_{ij}^{sd}(k) \tag{4}$$

where τ_{ij} is an equilibrium pheromone distribution and $\Lambda = \frac{\kappa_1}{\kappa_2}$ is called pheromone deposition number. Note that $\tilde{p}_{ij}^{sd}(k)$ depends upon τ_{ij}.

3   Stochastic Modeling of BARP with MACA

In Sections 3.1 and 3.2, we first explore the operational details of MACA with RTS/CTS handshakes and data transmissions. The objective is to understand how MACA manages packet collision. In particular, we model the behavior of MACA in both two-sender and three-sender scenarios. In Section 3.3, we integrate the MACA model with the analytical model of BARP.

3.1   Two-Sender Scenario with MACA

We start from a two-sender scenario with following assumptions: (i) senders are hidden from each other; (ii) senders are synchronized at the beginning; (iii) RTS and CTS packets have the same size; (iv) no path loss and packet loss during the propagation. Figure 1 illustrates the topology for the scenario and the associating MACA timeline: sender 1 randomly chooses a time t_1 (e.g. $t_1=\lambda_1$ in the timeline) between 0 and CW to send a RTS packet RTS_1 by broadcasting; after a delay of $\sigma+T_D$, receiver obtains RTS_1, then sends a CTS packet CTS_1 by broadcasting immediately; when the sender receives CTS_1 after another delay of $\sigma + T_D$, it begins to transmit data packet by broadcasting immediately.

Based on the results of QualNet simulation using realistic communication models, we make three key observations:

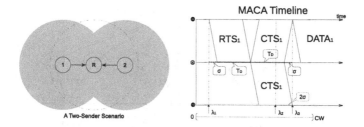

Fig. 1. σ denotes the propagation delay; T_D denotes the transmission delay; $\lambda_{1,2,3}$ are three critical moments; CW denotes the back-off window size

#1. If one terminal is receiving a packet while another packet arrives, then both packets will be corrupted.

#2. If one terminal is sending a packet while another packet arrives, then both packets will be dropped (inward packet is ignored, the signal of outward packet is weakened).

#3. In the PHY layer, sending has a higher priority than receiving.

Thus, given the second sender also randomly choosing a time t_2 (assume $t_2 > t_1$ here) between 0 and CW to send a RTS packet RTS_2, there are three possibilities:

1) If $t_2 < \lambda_2 = \lambda_1 + 2T_D$, RTS_2 either collides with RTS_1, according to observation #1, or interrupts the sending of CTS_1, based on the observation #2. No data packet will be sent and both senders will resend RTS packet following the rules of exponential back-off mechanism (back-off window size doubles) after a period of RTS timeout.

2) If $\lambda_2 < t_2 < \lambda_2 + 2\sigma = \lambda_3$, CTS_1 will successfully arrive at sender 1 but not at sender 2 according to the observation #3. Sender 1 then sends the data packet which will collide with RTS_2 provided the size of the data packet $\gg$ the size of RTS packet.

3) If $t_2 > \lambda_3$, both senders will successfully receive CTS_1. Then sender 2 will become silence so that sender 1 successfully sends the data packet.

For the case of $t_2 < t_1$, by symmetry the analysis is the same. We define the time that j-th sender sends RTS packets with back-off window size $2^{n-1}CW$ as

$$T_j^{(n)} = (n-1)\tilde{T} + \sum_{k=1}^{n} t_j^{(k)}, \qquad t_j^{(n)} \sim U(0, 2^{n-1}CW) \;\; i.i.d, t_j^{(0)} = 0 \qquad (5)$$

where $\tilde{T}$ is the length of RTS timeout.

From the analysis above, we develop a stochastic model for the two-senders case. Figure 2 shows the directed diagram of states. In particular, the transition possibilities are given by the aggregating behaviors of the RTS-competing process. By symmetry we only give the probabilities for node 1. All the other transition probabilities unlabeled in the figure are equal to 1 because there are only two senders in this scenario.

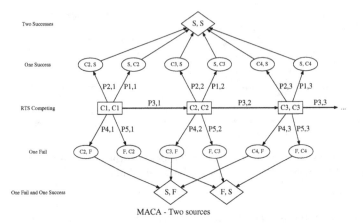

Fig. 2. Directed diagram for the Markov chain: S represents the data packet is successfully sent. F corresponds to data packet being corrupted, and C_i's, $i = 1, 2, 3, \cdots$ mean sender is competing with others (if any) by randomly sending RTS packet within period of back-off window size $2^{i-1}CW$. The states, $(s_1(t), s_2(t))$, where $s_1, s_2 \in \{S, F, C_1, C_2, C_3, \cdots\}$, show the status of (sender1, sender2) at time t.

$$P1, n = P\left(T_2^{(n)} - T_1^{(n)} > 2(T_D + \sigma)\Big||T_2^{(m)} - T_1^{(m)}| < 2T_D, m = 0, 1, 2, \cdots, n-1\right)$$

$$P3, n = P\left(|T_2^{(n)} - T_1^{(n)}| < 2T_D\Big||T_2^{(m)} - T_1^{(m)}| < 2T_D, m = 0, 1, 2, \cdots, n-1\right)$$

$$P5, n = P\left(2T_D < T_2^{(n)} - T_1^{(n)} < 2(T_D + \sigma)\Big||T_2^{(m)} - T_1^{(m)}| < 2T_D, m = 0, 1, 2, \cdots, n-1\right)$$

3.2   Three-Sender Scenario with MACA

We also generalize the mathematical model for MACA to a scenario with three senders and one receiver. Following the notation in Figure 2, a form of 3-tuple

$$\left(s_1(t), s_2(t), s_3(t)\right), \qquad s_1, s_2, s_3 \in \{S, F, N, C_1, C_2, C_3, \cdots\}$$

is used to represent the states of (sender1, sender2, sender3) at time t. Here a new status 'N' is added, which represents that a sender receives other CTS packet so that it freezes for a specific amount of time. By symmetry, we only consider sender 1. Theoretically, starting from any state, $(C_{i_1}, C_{i_2}, C_{i_3})$ in one transition we have six new possible states:

$(C_{i_1+1}, C_{i_2+1}, C_{i_3+1})$: No data packets will be sent due to the collision of RTS packets, or failing to receive a CTS.

$(C_{i_1}, C_{i_2+1}, C_{i_3+1})$: Senders 2 and 3 send RTS packets and fail while sender 1 is still waiting to send.

(S, N, N) : Sender 1 delivers the packet successfully while the other two freeze.

(F, N, C_{i_3+1}) : The RTS packet from sender 3 collides with the data packet from sender 1 and sender 2 freezes.

(F, C_{i_2+1}, N) : The RTS packet from sender 2 collides with the data packet from sender 1 and sender 3 freezes.

$(F, C_{i_2+1}, C_{i_3+1})$: Both RTS packets from sender 2 and 3 collide with the data packet from sender 1.

Once sender 1 gets to the states 'S' or 'F', we go back to the two-sender case. We point out that the Markov process of the system with three senders is much more complicated, and it is unlikely that we will find a regular repeating structure as in the two-sender case.

3.3 Analysis of BARP with MACA

Given the simple topology in Figure 3, we now integrate MACA protocol into BARP. Since the maximum neighbors for each node is two, we only consider the MACA model for the two-sender scenario. Also, we assume that the probability of a sender successfully sending packet only relates to whether other nodes, in the communicating range of the receiver, have packets to send. Thus, we define a new component, $y_D^{(n)}$ which represents the probability of finding an ant dropped at the n-th time step in the network, to the original density vector of ants $\mathbf{y}^{(n)}$.

Based on the MACA modeling in Section 3.1, if we set the RTS retransmission limit as L times and let δ be the probability of sender 1 fails to deliver data packet, then $\delta \approx \sum_{n=1}^{L} \prod_{i<n}(P3, i)(P5, n) + \prod_{i=1}^{L}(P3, i)$, $P3, 0 := 0$. This approximation is accurate in general when $L > 5$. The corresponding transition matrix for the forward ants now becomes

$$\bar{P}^{(n)}(\beta, \mathbf{y}^{(n)}) = \left((p_{ij}^{(n)} * S_j(y_l^{(n)})) \right), \qquad S_j(y_l^n) = \begin{cases} 1 - \delta y_l^{(n)}, & l \in N_j, l \neq d \\ 1, & \text{otherwise.} \end{cases}$$

By the definition of $y_D^{(n)}$, we get:

$$y_D^{(n)} = \sum_{i,j} y_i^{(n)} (1 - p_{ij}^{(n)} S_j(y_l^{(n)})) \tag{6}$$

For modeling the backward ants and the existence of equilibrium solution, we add one link from d back to s and one link from D back to s both with transition probability of 1, that is,

$$y_s^{(n+1)} = y_d^{(n)} + y_D^{(n)} \quad \text{and} \quad \mathbf{y}^{(n)} \cdot \mathbf{1} + y_D^{(n)} = 1 \quad \text{(normalization)} \tag{7}$$

Finally, our stationary solutions for both pheromone and density of ants satisfy $\mathbf{y} = \mathbf{y} * \bar{P}(\beta, \mathbf{y})$ as well as (4), (6), and (7).

4   Evaluation and Validation

We validate the developed model by comparing the Matlab numerical results of solving its steady state solution with the QualNet simulation results of executing

path β	1→2→3→4→5	1→6→5
0	0.178177 / 0.137059	0.356880 / 0.297402
0.5	0.118665 / 0.117521	0.476191 / 0.470853
2	0 / 0	0.714286 / 0.713762

β	0	0.5	2
Matlab	3.68	2.92	0.00
Qualnet	5.12	3.01	0.00

Fig. 3. At left, a simple network topology. At center and right, pheromone distribution and drop rate ($\times 10^4$) comparisons.

MACA and BARP protocols with realistic wireless communications, using the six-node topology of Figure 3.

By using Matlab's **fsolve** subroutine, we compute the steady state solution for both the pheromone distribution and the ant drop rate. The initial value of pheromone on each link is 1, and the starting probability density vector of ants is $(1, 0, 0, 0, 0, 0)$.

The QualNet simulation uses the parameters summarized in Table 1. Along the two paths (1→2→3→4→5 and 1→6→5) from the source to the destination, forward ants sent from nodes 4 and 6 will collide at node 5. The source originates one forward ant every two seconds. In the simulation, after receiving an ant, a node does not forward the ant until the next integer second. In this way, we ensure that node 4 and node 6 will compete sending packet to the destination at exactly the same time, which corresponds to the modeled two-sender scenario. The proposed analysis only models the behavior of forward ants. Backward ants trace their steps back to the source through a 'wired' interface at each hop to avoid colliding with forward ants sent wirelessly. We perform Matlab numerical computation and QualNet simulation with different β values, as they affect pheromone distribution and ant drop rate.

Both Matlab numerical results and QualNet simulation results of pheromone distribution (τ_{ij} on the link from node i to node j) are presented together in Figure 3 (center). Each entry has the format $\frac{x}{y}$ where x denotes the Matlab result and y denotes the QualNet result. Figure 3 (right) compares the Matlab and the QualNet results of ant drop rate with different β values. When $\beta = 0$, ants choose the two paths with equal probability, which then results in more collisions at the destination. As β increases, ants favor the shorter path 1→6→5 with higher pheromone concentration, which leads to less collisions at the destination. When β is 2, all the ants choose the path 1→6→5 with no collisions at the destination.

Table 1. Qualnet (left) and BARP parameters (right) used for simulations

Terrain size	1500×1500 m^2
Number of nodes	6
Mobility	none
Radio range	up to 500 m
PHY protocol	802.11b
Bandwidth	2 Mbps
MAC protocol	MACA

Ant interval	2 second
Decay interval	2 second
β	0, 0.5, 2
h_1	0.3
k_1	1
h_2	1
k_2	1

5   Conclusion

Modeling of ant-based routing in the context of multi-hop wireless networks is challenged by the intrinsic complexity of wireless medium access control (such as the hidden terminal problem) and its cross-layer interaction. Leveraging our previous work of modeling and analyzing ant-based routing protocols on wired networks, this paper investigates the integration of such model with a mathematical model of a practical wireless medium access control protocol. Comparable results from the numerical analysis of the equilibrium solution to the integration model and the QualNet simulation with realistic protocol models and wireless communications validate the efforts.

Acknowledgments. The work is supported by Army SBIR Contract #W911QX-09-C-0076.

References

1. Bean, N., Costa, A.: An analytic modelling approach for network routing algorithms that use "ant-like" mobile agents. Comp. Networks 49(2), 243–268 (2005)
2. Di Caro, G., Dorigo, M.: AntNet: Distributed Stigmergetic Control for Communications Networks. Journal of Artificial Intelligence Research 9, 317–365 (1998)
3. Di Caro, G., Ducatelle, F., Gambardella, L.: AntHocNet: An Adaptive Nature-Inspired Algorithm for Routing in Mobile Ad Hoc Networks. European Transactions on Telecommunications, Special Issue on Self-organization in Mobile Networking 16(5), 443–455 (2005)
4. Ducatelle, F., Di Caro, G., Gambardella, L.: Principles and applications of swarm intelligence for adaptive routing in telecommunications networks. Swarm Intelligence 4(3), 173–198 (2010)
5. Purkayastha, P., Baras, J.S.: Convergence results for ant routing algorithms via stochastic approximation and optimization. In: Proceedings of the 46th IEEE Conference on Decision and Control, pp. 340–345. IEEE, Piscataway (2007)
6. Rajagopalan, S., Shen, C.C.: ANSI: A Swarm Intelligence-based Unicast Routing Protocol for Hybrid Ad hoc Networks. Journal of System Architecture, Special issue on Nature Inspired Applied Systems 52(8-9), 485–504 (2006)
7. Saleem, M., Khayam, S., Farooq, M.: A formal performance modeling framework for bio-inspired ad hoc routing protocols. In: ACM Genetic and Evolutionary Computation Conference (GECCO), pp. 103–110. ACM, New York (2008)
8. Torres, C.E., Rossi, L.F., Keffer, J., Li, K., Shen, C.C.: Modeling, analysis and simulation of ant-based network routing protocols. Swarm Intelligence 4(3), 221–244 (2010), http://www.springerlink.com/index/10.1007/s11721-010-0043-7
9. Yoo, J.H., La, R.J., Makowski, A.M.: Convergence results for ant routing. In: Conf. Info. Sci. and Systems. IEEE, Piscataway (2004)
10. Zahid, S., Shahzad, M., Ali, S., Farooq, M.: A comprehensive formal framework for analyzing the behavior of nature-inspired routing protocols. In: IEEE Congress on Evolutionary Computation, CEC 2007, pp. 180–187. IEEE, Piscataway (2007)

Ant-Based Approaches
for Solving Autocorrelation Problems

Ilias S. Kotsireas[1], Konstantinos E. Parsopoulos[2],
Grigoris S. Piperagkas[2], and Michael N. Vrahatis[3]

[1] Department of Physics and Computer Science, Wilfrid Laurier University,
Waterloo, Canada
ikotsire@wlu.ca
[2] Department of Computer Science, University of Ioannina, Greece
{kostasp,gpiperag}@cs.uoi.gr
[3] Department of Mathematics, University of Patras, Greece
vrahatis@math.upatras.gr

Abstract. We propose two ant–based formulations for solving autocorrelation problems. The formulations are combined with different ACO
variants. Preliminary experiments of the derived approaches are conducted on two hard instances of the problem. Their performance is compared to an efficient Tabu Search algorithm, offering useful conclusions
and motivation for further investigation.

1 Introduction

Several difficult combinatorial problems can be defined in a succinct way via
the concepts of *periodic* and *non–periodic autocorrelation functions* (PAF and
NPAF, respectively) associated with a finite binary or ternary sequence. Various metaheuristics have been previously employed in the search for solutions of
similar combinatorial problems, with varying degrees of success.

The present paper aims at triggering the interest of the Ant Colony Optimization (ACO) research community in solving such combinatorial problems
through ant–based approaches. For this purpose, we propose two ant–based formulations. To the best of our knowledge, this is the first attempt of formulating
such problems in the specific algorithmic framework. As case study, we use our
formulations to find *Hadamard matrices with two circulant cores*, a problem that
can be defined via the PAF associated to two binary sequences. Nevertheless,
the proposed ant–based formulations can be applied with minor modifications
to any combinatorial problem defined via PAF and NPAF.

The sequences that arise as solutions to these problems are useful in a wide variety of applications, ranging from code–division multiple–access (CDMA) communication systems to pulse compression of radar signals. The reader is referred
to [6] and [8] for further details and application areas. Additional applications in
Coding Theory can be found in [3]. The rest of the paper is organized as follows:
Section 2 offers brief descriptions of the problems while Section 3 introduces our
ant–based formulations. Experimental results are presented in Section 4. The
paper concludes with Section 5.

M. Dorigo et al. (Eds.): ANTS 2012, LNCS 7461, pp. 220–227, 2012.

2   Autocorrelation Problems

Let n be an odd positive integer. A finite sequence of length n with elements from the alphabet $\{-1, +1\}$ is called a *binary sequence*. Similarly, a finite sequence of length n with elements from the alphabet $\{-1, 0, +1\}$ is called a *ternary sequence*. The PAF associated to a finite sequence $\mathbf{a} = (a_1, \ldots, a_n)$ of length n, is a sequence $(PAF(\mathbf{a}, 0), PAF(\mathbf{a}, 1), \ldots, PAF(\mathbf{a}, n-1))$, also of length n where,

$$PAF(\mathbf{a}, s) = \sum_{i=1}^{n} a_i a_{i+s}, \qquad s = 0, 1, \ldots, n-1. \tag{1}$$

The quantity $i+s$ is taken modulo n whenever $i+s > n$. On the other hand, the NPAF associated to the finite sequence $\mathbf{a}$ is defined as $(NPAF(\mathbf{a}, 0), NPAF(\mathbf{a}, 1), \ldots, NPAF(\mathbf{a}, n-1))$ where,

$$NPAF(\mathbf{a}, s) = \sum_{i=1}^{n-s} a_i a_{i+s}, \qquad s = 0, 1, \ldots, n-1. \tag{2}$$

Chapter 7 of [3] contains a comprehensive description of the properties of the two autocorrelation functions defined above.

Given two finite (binary or ternary) sequences $\mathbf{a}$ and $\mathbf{b}$ of length n, we can request that their respective *PAF* or *NPAF* values (with the exception of the value at $s = 0$) add up to a constant, i.e.:

$$PAF(\mathbf{a}, s) + PAF(\mathbf{b}, s) = c_{PAF}, \qquad NPAF(\mathbf{a}, s) + NPAF(\mathbf{b}, s) = c_{NPAF}, \tag{3}$$

where $s = 1, 2, \ldots, n-1$. In general, sequences that satisfy these requirements are called *complementary*. When the values of the constants c_{PAF} and c_{NPAF} are small, i.e., less than 2 in absolute value, such sequences are said to exhibit *low (auto)correlation* and they have important engineering applications [6].

There are some particularly important cases of combinatorial problems that can be defined via the aforementioned setup. In our work, we focused on the case of binary sequences with $c_{PAF} = -2$, which are related to *Hadamard matrices with two circulant cores* or equivalently to *Generalized Legendre pairs* [5]. The solution sequences of the aforementioned problems are also subject to *Diophantine Equations* (DEs) that shall be satisfied by the solutions. For instance, in our case study the corresponding DE is:

$$sa^2 + sb^2 = 1, \tag{4}$$

where $sa = a_1 + \cdots + a_n$ and $sb = b_1 + \cdots + b_n$. Equation (4) has four solutions, up to sign. In our study we focus on the case where $sa = 1$ and $sb = 1$.

3   Proposed Ant–Based Approaches

In the following paragraphs, we introduce two different formulations of autocorrelation problems within the framework of ant–based algorithms.

3.1   Approach Based on Binary Ants

Let n be the length (positive odd integer) of each one of the two sequences and let $N = 2n$. Then, a candidate solution has the following form:

$$\mathbf{x} = \left(\underbrace{x_1, x_2, \ldots, x_n,}_{\text{sequence a}} \quad \underbrace{x_{n+1}, x_{n+2}, \ldots, x_N}_{\text{sequence b}} \right)^{\top}. \tag{5}$$

The corresponding optimization problem is N–dimensional and it is defined as the *minimization* of the objective function:

$$F(\mathbf{x}) = \left| \sum_{i=1}^{n} a_i - 1 \right| + \left| \sum_{i=1}^{n} b_i - 1 \right| + \sum_{s=1}^{(n-1)/2} \left| PAF(\mathbf{a}, s) + PAF(\mathbf{b}, s) + 2 \right|, \tag{6}$$

where $PAF(\mathbf{a}, s)$ and $PAF(\mathbf{b}, s)$ are defined according to Eq. (1). In order to put the problem in the ACO framework we shall define a table of pheromones, i.e., weights for the possible component values of a candidate solution. The probabilities of selecting -1 or $+1$ for the component x_i of a new candidate solution $\mathbf{x}$, are defined as follows:

$$p_{i,(-)} = \frac{w_{i,(-)}^{\alpha} \eta_{i,(-)}^{\beta}}{w_{i,(-)}^{\alpha} \eta_{i,(-)}^{\beta} + w_{i,(+)}^{\alpha} \eta_{i,(+)}^{\beta}}, \qquad p_{i,(+)} = \frac{w_{i,(+)}^{\alpha} \eta_{i,(+)}^{\beta}}{w_{i,(-)}^{\alpha} \eta_{i,(-)}^{\beta} + w_{i,(+)}^{\alpha} \eta_{i,(+)}^{\beta}}, \tag{7}$$

where $w_{i,(-)}$, $w_{i,(+)}$, are the corresponding pheromone levels (weights) for the values -1 and $+1$; α and β are user–defined parameters controlling the strength of each term; and η is a function of desirability of the corresponding component, i.e., it defines its significance in the solution vector.

The value of the component x_i is determined by drawing a uniformly distributed random number, i.e., $x_i = -1$, if $\mathbf{rand}() < p_{i,(-)}$, otherwise $x_i = +1$. The same selection procedure is independently applied for all components. Instead of one, K ants can be used to construct K candidate solutions at each iteration. We will call this set the *colony* in our approach. Nevertheless, the construction procedure is identical for all ants.

If t denotes the iteration number, the colony can be denoted as $\mathbf{S}^{(t)} = \left\{ \mathbf{x}_1^{(t)}, \mathbf{x}_2^{(t)}, \ldots, \mathbf{x}_K^{(t)} \right\}$ with $\mathbf{x}_i^{(t)} = \left(x_{1,i}^{(t)}, x_{2,i}^{(t)}, \ldots, x_{N,i}^{(t)} \right)^{\top}$, $i = 1, 2, \ldots, K$. After generating the K candidate solutions of the t–th iteration, their evaluation with the objective function $F(\mathbf{x})$ of Eq. (6) takes place and the pheromones are updated as follows:

$$w_{i,j}^{(t+1)} = (1 - \rho) w_{i,j}^{(t)} + \Delta w_{i,j,k}^{(t)}, \qquad j \in \{-1, +1\}, \ i = 1, 2, \ldots, K, \tag{8}$$

where $\Delta w_{i,j,k}^{(t)} = V_k^{(t)}$, if $x_{k,i}^{(t)} = j$; otherwise $\Delta w_{i,j,k}^{(t)} = 0$, $k = 1, 2, \ldots, N$. The increment $V_k^{(t)}$ can be either fixed for all ants or inversely proportional to the objective value of each contributing ant, i.e., $V_k^{(t)} = 1/F(\mathbf{x}_i^{(t)})$ or $V_k^{(t)} = Q$.

Different ant–based algorithms are distinguished by considering different groups of contributing ants. In *Ant Colony Optimization* [1] (ACO) only new ants produced at each iteration contribute to the pheromone update. In *Elitist Ant System* [4] (EAS), in addition to the currently constructed ants, also the overall best ant contributes to the pheromones. In the *Max–Min Ant System* [7] (MMAS) scheme the pheromones are bounded within a range $[w_{min}, w_{max}]$ and initialized to their maximum values. Also, they are re–initialized to their maximum value whenever stagnation is detected. In contrast to the previous variants, only the best ant of the current iteration or the overall best ant deposits pheromones (we considered only the latter case).

These three popular variants were also considered in our experiments with two minor modifications. Specifically, we adopted a fixed lower bound for the pheromones in all variants (not only for MMAS). This decision aimed at avoiding the actual elimination of component values with very small pheromones in the selection procedure. Also, the algorithm was restarted whenever there was no improvement of the overall best solution for a predefined number of function evaluations. This number was defined as a fraction of the maximum available computational budget. Apart from these modifications, some additional alterations proved to enhance the algorithm's performance and they are described in the following section.

3.2   Performance Enhancing

The construction of candidate solutions can be modified to ensure that the produced solutions will be feasible with respect to the DEs, i.e., the sums of their components will be equal to 1 for both their sequences. Specifically, each sequence has length n and constitutes of values in $\{-1, +1\}$. Hence, we can build a candidate solution by determining its components in pairs of complementary values, i.e., if one component receives -1 then another randomly selected component automatically receives $+1$. At the end, there will be one remaining component that is set directly to $+1$. Thus, -1 appears in $(n-1)/2$ components while $+1$ appears in $(n+1)/2$ components.

This procedure produces candidate solutions that, by construction, satisfy the DEs. Therefore, the first two terms terms in the objective function can be dropped, resulting in the following form:

$$F(\mathbf{x}) = \sum_{s=1}^{(n-1)/2} \left| PAF(\mathbf{a}, s) + PAF(\mathbf{b}, s) + 2 \right|, \qquad (9)$$

that replaces the one defined in Eq. (6). The performance of the algorithm can be further enhanced by incorporating local search. We adopted the procedure used in [2] within the framework of a very efficient Tabu Search approach.

3.3   Approach Based on Components Permutation

An alternative ant–based approach, yet closer to the general principles of the original ACO algorithms, is based on the formulation of the problem as a search procedure for the best permutation of components. More specifically, we can define a candidate solution as a permutation of solution components indices:

$$\mathbf{x} = \left(\underbrace{c_1^{\mathsf{a}}, c_2^{\mathsf{a}}, \ \dots \ , c_n^{\mathsf{a}}}_{\text{permutation for seq. a}}, \quad \underbrace{c_1^{\mathsf{b}}, c_2^{\mathsf{b}}, \ \dots \ , c_n^{\mathsf{b}}}_{\text{permutation for seq. b}} \right)^{\mathsf{T}}, \tag{10}$$

where $c_j^{\mathsf{a}} = i$, $i \in \{1, \dots, n\}$, denotes that the i-th component of the actual (binary) sequence $\mathbf{a}$ possesses the j-th position in the specific permutation defined by $\mathbf{x}$. Then, we build a binary vector by translating $\mathbf{x}$, assuming that components that appear in the first $(n+1)/2$ positions of the permutation are assigned the value $+1$, while the rest are assigned the value -1, i.e.:

$$\mathbf{y_x} = \left(\underbrace{a_1, a_2, \dots, a_n,}_{\text{sequence a}} \quad \underbrace{b_1, b_2, \dots, b_n}_{\text{sequence b}} \right)^{\mathsf{T}}, \quad a_i, b_i \in \{-1, +1\}, \ i = 1, 2, \dots, n.$$

$$\tag{11}$$

where a_i (resp. b_i) $= +1$, if c_j^{a} (resp. c_j^{b}) $= i$ for j such that $1 \leqslant j \leqslant (n+1)/2$; otherwise a_i (resp. b_i) $= -1$. Apparently, this permutation–based representation of the ants requires also different pheromone table representation than that of Section 3.1. Indeed, a pheromone entry $w_{i,j}^{\mathsf{a}}$ for sequence $\mathbf{a}$ defines the weight (pheromone level) for the case where component index j appears immediately after index i in the permutation of sequence $\mathbf{a}$ of a candidate solution. The corresponding quantities are defined by weights $w_{i,j}^{\mathsf{b}}$ for sequence $\mathbf{b}$.

The objective value of the ant $\mathbf{x}$ is defined through its corresponding binary translation $\mathbf{y_x}$, i.e., $F(\mathbf{x}) = F(\mathbf{y_x})$. Since, by definition, the DEs hold for the produced translated vectors $\mathbf{y_x}$, we can use the objective function defined in Eq. (9) instead of Eq. (6). The same ant–based variants along with all modifications and performance enhancing techniques mentioned in the previous section, were also used with this formulation.

4   Experimental Results

We report indicative experimental results for the ant–based approaches defined in the previous sections for PAF problems of length $n = 29$ and 39. We shall mention that $n = 77$ is the smallest value for which this is an open problem. Henceforth, we will denote as "Bin" the approach based on binary ants and "Per" the one based on permutations. The basic ACO algorithm will be denoted as "A", the EAS as "B" and the MMAS as "C". Finally, the fixed pheromone increment approach will be denoted as "a", while the proportional one as "b".

Regarding the parameter setting, the maximum function evaluations was $\text{fev}_{\max} = 200 \times 10^6$, while the maximum evaluations for restart (if no improvement) was $R = \text{fev}_{\max}/5$. The pheromone scaling factor of Eq. (8) was $\rho = 0.1$ and the fixed pheromone increment was set to $Q = 0.001$. The pheromones were bounded in the range $[0.01, 1.0]$, while the parameters η, α and β in Eq. (7) were

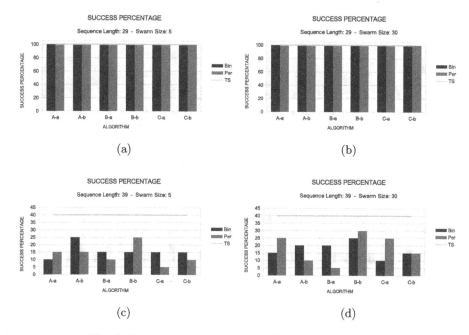

Fig. 1. Success percentages per problem and swarm size

all set to 1. Finally, two numbers of ants were considered, namely 5 and 30. The number of experiments conducted per approach was 20. Each experiment was terminated as soon as a global minimizer was found or the available computational budget was exceeded. An experiment was considered as successful only if an optimal solution was detected.

In order to provide a measure of performance for the proposed ant–based approaches, we performed the same number of independent experiments also for the TS approach proposed in [2] for the same computational budget. For comparison purposes, we also conducted Wilcoxon rank–sum tests for each pair of algorithms per problem and swarm size, and we recorded the number of favorable (denoted with "+"), unfavorable (denoted with "-") and neutral (denoted with "=") comparisons for 95% significance level. However, we shall underline that no effort was paid in fine–tuning the ant–based approaches in the comparisons, because a thorough comparison among the different methodologies was out of the scope of the present paper. Thus, we used the TS performance mostly as a reference point for a preliminary assessment of the proposed methods.

The results are graphically illustrated in Figs. 1 and 2. Specifically, Fig. 1 illustrates the success percentage of each algorithm per problem and swarm size, i.e., the percentage of experiments where it managed to detect a global optimizer within the available computational budget. The bars refer to the Bin and Per ant–based approaches, while the corresponding TS performance for the same experimental setting is depicted as a horizontal line. On the other hand, each bar

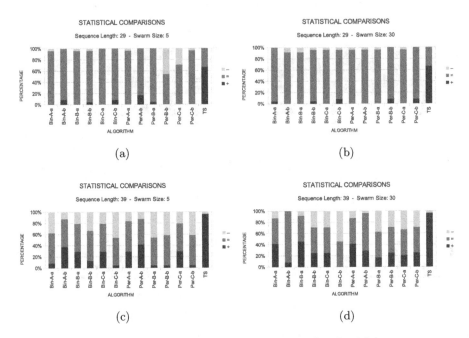

Fig. 2. Statistical comparison tests among the algorithms

in Fig. 2 illustrates the percentage of positive, negative and equal comparisons of the corresponding approach with the rest of the algorithms.

A close inspection of the results offers intuition on the algorithms' performance. Regarding the success percentages of the algorithms, as we see in Fig. 1, all approaches were completely successful for the case of sequence length $n = 29$. However, the picture radically changes for the (much harder) problem of $n = 39$. The performance of all algorithms, including TS, plunges by at least 40%. Moreover, the ant–based approaches exhibit also different behavior with respect to the swarm size. For the case of $K = 5$ ants, the Bin approaches have superior performance than Per for the 4 out of 6 variants, as depicted in Fig. 1(c). Yet, the Per approaches outperformed Bin for the A–a (ACO with fixed pheromone increments) and B–b (EAS with proportional increments) cases. Increasing the swarm size to $K = 30$, significantly improves the performance of Per approaches, especially for the C variant (MMAS). Also, Per remains better than Bin for A–a and B–b. However, even the Bin approaches achieve better performance in 3 out of 6 variants, compared to the 5 ants case. Thus, the first impression is that higher swarm size can rise the probability of successful experiments.

Inspecting Fig. 2, we can verify that the case $n = 29$ can be efficiently solved by all algorithms. In most cases, the algorithms exhibit statistically insignificant differences in performance but outperformed by TS in almost 60% of the cases. Again, increasing swarm size seems to produce essentially identical performance among ant–based approaches. However, the picture becomes more complicated in the $n = 39$ case. In this cases, the approaches with fixed pheromone increments have a clear increasing trend of positive comparisons for ACO and EAS. On the other hand, some of the approaches with proportional increments seem to loose part of their efficiency, especially for Bin. This behavior can be ascribed to the faster biasing towards the best performing ants offered due to the proportional increments, in combination with the higher dimensionality and degree of difficulty.

5 Conclusions

We presented two different ant–based formulations for tackling autocorrelation problems. Various combinations with different ACO–based approaches were considered and tested on two problems of different dimensionality and degree of difficulty. The proposed approaches were compared against a specialized TS approach with verified efficiency. The results are promising, offering space for further improvement by proper fine–tuning of the ant–based approaches. Also, they reveal that swarm size can play a role in the algorithms' performance profiles. However, the exact tendency of each approach remains to be investigated in depth. This will be the main subject of our future work.

References

1. Bonabeau, E., Dorigo, M., Théraulaz, G.: Swarm Intelligence: From Natural to Artificial Systems. Oxford University Press, New York (1999)
2. Chiarandini, M., Kotsireas, I.S., Koukouvinos, C., Paquete, L.: Heuristic algorithms for Hadamard matrices with two circulant cores. Th. Com. Sc. 407, 274–277 (2008)
3. Colbourn, C.J., Dinitz, J.H. (eds.): Handbook of combinatorial designs. Discrete Mathematics and its Applications. Chapman & Hall/CRC, Boca Raton (2007)
4. Dorigo, M., Maniezzo, V., Colorni, A.: Ant system: Optimization by a colony of cooperating agents. IEEE Trans. SMC – Part B 26(1), 29–41 (1996)
5. Fletcher, R.J., Gysin, M., Seberry, J.: Application of the discrete Fourier transform to the search for generalised Legendre pairs and Hadamard matrices. Australas. J. Combin. 23, 75–86 (2001)
6. Golomb, S.W., Gong, G.: Signal design for good correlation. Cambridge University Press, Cambridge (2005)
7. Stützle, T., Hoos, H.H.: Max–min ant system. Future Generation Computer Systems 16, 889–914 (2000)
8. Tran, L.C., Wysocki, T.A., Mertins, A., Seberry, J.: Complex Orthogonal Space-Time Processing in Wireless Communications. Springer (2006)

Collision-Induced "Priority Rule" Governs Efficiency of Pheromone-Communicating Swarm Robots

Ryusuke Fujisawa[1], Shigeto Dobata[2], Yuuta Sasaki[1],
Riku Takisawa[1], and Fumitoshi Matsuno[3]

[1] Hachinohe Institute of Technology, Aomori, Japan
swarm.ant@gmail.com
[2] University of the Ryukyus, Okinawa, Japan
dobatan@gmail.com
[3] Kyoto University, Kyoto, Japan
matsuno@me.kyoto-u.ac.jp

Abstract. The recruiting system in foraging ant colonies is a typical example of swarm intelligence. The system is underpinned by the use of volatile pheromones which form a trail connecting from nest to food. We have incorporated this property into the behavior of the swarm of real robots. Because the trail is narrow, avoiding overcrowding on the trail, as well as in the environment, is a critical issue in maintaining efficiency of the swarm behavior. In this paper, we studied how "priority rule,h a behavioral rule under which a robot is given priority over the other robot in collision, affect the group-foraging performance of pheromone-mediated swarm robots. Using real robot experiments, we found that the alteration in the priority rules can have substantial effects on the group-foraging performance. Our results highlight the importance of implementing "fine-tuningh algorithms to improve the performance of complex swarm systems.

1 Introduction

1.1 Swarm and Pheromone Communication in Ants

We define the term "swarmh as a distributed autonomous system, in which each individual acts autonomously only according to local information in the given environment without any global information [1]. A global-level behaviour of the swarm emerges through frequent local interactions among individuals. This emergence has two remarkable properties: robustness through which a swarm can adapt to changes in its internal states, and flexibility through which it can adapt to changes in its external states (e.g., the environment) [2].

Individuals of social insects communicate with one another to form a swarm, known as a colony. Among others, ants and termites are known to form especially complex societies, and their formation is often facilitated by using pheromones [3].

M. Dorigo et al. (Eds.): ANTS 2012, LNCS 7461, pp. 228–235, 2012.

A pheromone is a chemical or set of chemicals produced by a living organism that transmits information to other members of the same species [3]. In this paper, we focus on foraging behaviour of ants using a pheromone. When an ant finds food and brings it back to the nest, it secretes a pheromone that forms a trail. Other ants trace the pheromone trail and can reach the food. An ant stops to lay down the pheromone trail when it cannot find the food. Consequently, the pheromone trail volatilizes (or diffuses) into the environment, making the previous information meaningless to the ants. The algorithm of this indirect recruiting system is a simple but advanced communication method. Indeed, "Ant Colony Optimization" [4] was inspired by the above-explained mechanism.

1.2   Related Studies

In swarm robotics, several studies using real or virtual pheromones have been reported previously. Sugawara *et al.* [5] and Garnier *et al.* [6] achieved the foraging behaviour of ants using a swarm of robots and a virtual pheromone (with a projector and screen). These studies represented a well-conceived measurement system. Pheromone diffusion is an important factor in real pheromone studies, and implementing it is a very difficult problem. To adjust the duration of the pheromone signal, the pheromone should be, for example, mixed with other substance(s) to change concentration of the pheromone. In addition, there are few high-performance chemical sensors available; these difficulties have led the researchers to use a virtual pheromone. Shimoyama *et al.* [7] achieved pheromone tracking behaviour using a "chimeric" system implementing real insect antennae and pheromone, but they did not consider swarm behaviour, and the use of biomaterials is usually difficult for swarm robotics. Purnamadjaja *et al.* [8] studied swarm robots that communicate using two real chemical substances. The latter regulates a gas sensor in a refined way. However, only one robot secretes the pheromone, so this system allows for only one-sided communication. In the previous study, we focused on the effect of concentration of the pheromone on the performance of group-foraging [9].

1.3   Priority on the Pheromone Trail

A critical issue in managing the swarm system is how to control for overcrowding. The negative impact of overcrowding on swarm performance becomes crucial especially in a larger swarm size (Kriger *et. al* [10]), even though direct and thus potentially damaging collision itself could be avoided in some way (e.g. [11]). In real ant colonies, the existence of priority rules like the one in the present study has been demonstrated ([12, 13, 14]). Also in ants, the priority rules are induced when two ants collide; such a situation most likely occurs on the pheromone trail. Moreover, some studies showed experimentally that the rule contributes to efficient transportation ([13, 14]). These findings suggest that a "fine-tuning" of the trail-foraging system have played a crucial role in the adaptive evolution of the ant colony systems. Implementing similar condition-dependent fine-tuning may sometimes improve the performance of robot swarm, as well as the swarm algorithm itself. Although collision-avoiding algorithms are routinely implemented in swarm robotics, to our knowledge, previous studies have not assessed directly how they could contribute to the group performance. In this experimental study, we implemented collision-induced "priority rules" in our trail pheromone-based robot swarm and assessed the effects of the alteration in the rules on the group-foraging performance.

2   Swarm Behaviour Algorithm

2.1   Basic Algorithm

We assumed a finite experimental field with only agents, a food and a nest. The task of the swarm is to find a food in the field, just like foraging ant colonies. To accomplish this task, an agent can attract other agents indirectly using a pheromone secretion. We used the swarm behaviour algorithm for group foraging using pheromone communication [9], which is described as a deterministic finite automaton. The algorithm shown in Fig. 1 can read as follows: We defined the following three states $S_i (i = 1, 2, 3)$, six perceptual cues (stimuli) $P_j (j = 1, \cdots, 6)$ and three effector cues

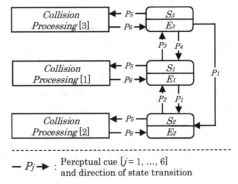

Fig. 1. State transition rule for swarm behaviour

(actions) $E_k (k = 1, 2, 3)$. The agent whose state is S_i selects the action E_k $(i = k)$. If the agent in state S_i detects the perceptual cue P_j, the state of the agent transits to S_k (Fig. 1). The details of S_i, P_j, and E_k are as follows. S_i: S_1, Search (Agent does not have any information of the food); S_2, Attraction (Agent has the location information of the food); S_3, Tracking (Agent has only the direction information of the location of the food). P_j: P_1, Contact with food; P_2, Arrival at nest; P_3, Presence of pheromone; P_4, Timeout; P_5, Collision with object; P_6, Completion of collision processing. E_k: E_1, Random walk; E_2, Secrete pheromone along the nest direction; E_3, Follow the pheromone path toward the food. We assumed that all agents can detect the direction of the nest, which we feel is a reasonable assumption.

2.2   Collision Processing and "Priority Rules"

We propose the following interaction rules. When colliding, an robot is designed to take one of the following two reactions, "Stay" and "Back", according to its current internal states(S_i) that are perceived by the robot itself. During the reaction "Stay", the robot stops moving for a given time (1[sec]) and then regains

Table 1. Description of the "priority rules"

Patterns	BSB	BBS	BBB	SBB	SBS	SSB	BSS	SSS
S_1	Back	Back	Back	Stop	Stop	Stop	Back	Stop
S_2	Stop	Back	Back	Back	Back	Stop	Stop	Stop
S_3	Back	Stop	Back	Back	Stop	Back	Stop	Stop

Actions after collision are described. "Backh means disengagement from collision point, keeping the head in the same direction as before. "Stayh means temporary stop. See the main text for details.

the same internal state as it took when colliding. During the reaction "Back", the robot moves directly backward (10[cm]) from its position, and then regains the same internal state. This behavior was originally implemented to avoid potential collision-induced congestion [1]. The robot can take different reactions depending on each of the three internal states (S_1-S_3), so that there arise eight possible combinations of reaction rules (Table 1). The term "priority rules" is most suitable when the combinations are NBS and NSB (N = S,B hereafter), i.e., when the reaction rules are invoked on the pheromone trail. Nevertheless, we hereafter use this term to indicate the total set of these combinations.

3   Hardware and Experimental Design

We have developed robots which can tune the duration of pheromone activity [15]. The robot is shown in Fig. 2. The robot is cylinder shape, diameter 150 [mm], height 225 [mm], weight 1.45 [kg] and speed 0.1 [m/s]. Power source is six series-connected Ni-MH batteries (1.2 [V] 4500 [mAh]). The robot is constructed by four layers, and each layer is supported by spacers. At first (bottom) layer, there are two DC motors, two alcohol sensors, two micro pump and discharge spout for alcohol. There are color

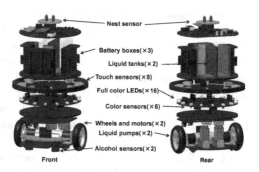

Fig. 2. Overview of a developed robot (AR-GOS02)

sensors, full-color LEDs and push switches for detecting collision at second layer. There are tank for alcohol and six batteries at third layer. At fourth layer, there are system circuit board, LED, and LCD indicator, Wireless USB, power circuit and nest sensor. Batteries are connected on power circuit at fourth layer. The system has eight micro-computers(CY8C29466), two masters and six slaves.

Figure 3 shows the experimental field. A nest and a food are set on the opposite side. The field size is 3600 [mm] × 3600 [mm], and is surrounded by walls. Nest size is $\phi600$ [mm], food size is $\phi300$ [mm], and food detection area is $\phi600$ [mm]. Initial positions of the robots were set randomly on the field. The duration of experiment was 20 [min]. We ran experiments ten times for each of the eight priority rules (Table 1), and the number of foraging was recorded as a measure of swarm performance. The effects of swarm size and reaction rules on the swarm performance were analyzed statistically using multiple Poisson regression.

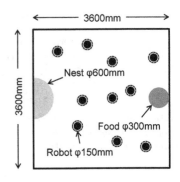

Fig. 3. Experimental field for pheromone comm. robots

In order to assess the effects of alteration of reaction rules at each state, we compared 12 pairs of priority rules which differ only at one of the three states. The effects of swarm size - 2 (denoted as x_1), change of reaction rules from S to B (denoted as x_2; S=0, B=1), and the interaction of x_1 and x_2, on the swarm performance (denoted as y) were analyzed statistically using multiple regression with the model: $y = \beta_0 + \beta_1 x_1 + \beta_2 x_2 + \beta_{1\times2}(x_1 \times x_2) + \epsilon$. The intercept β_0 and the slopes (β_1, β_2, $\beta_{1\times2}$) of the variables were tested against $\beta = 0$ using t-tests.

4   Results

Figure 4, 5 shows some typical results of the experiments with ten robots. Under the priority rule BSB (Fig. 4), the robots communicate with one another, indicating that the priority rule is effective for foraging behavior. In stark contrast, under the priority rule SSB (Fig. 5), we observed many clusters of colliding robots on the experimental field (indicated by black circles in Fig. 5), which developed during the run (ca. 5 [min] after the onset). In the cluster, the robots were stuck at each other and could not disengage from it. This comparison highlights the fact that an alteration of the reaction rule at only one state can drastically affect the swarm performance.

Figure 6 shows the performance of the swarm (number of times of foraging per 20 min trial, $n = 10$ each) for each priority rule and the swarm size (i.e., number of robots). For statistical analyses, we paired these priority rules based on the presence/absence of rule B at each of the three states, so as to assess how rule B affects the swarm performance at each of these states. Table 2 shows the results of multiple regression analyses with the model described in Section 3.2. (Note that x_2 and thus β_2 correspond to different states for different pairs.). Briefly, for each comparison, β_0 corresponds to the extrapolated intercept at swarm size = 2 under the reaction rule N = S, β_1 corresponds to the slope of swarm performance against swarm size under the reaction rule N = S, β_2 measures how the alteration of the reaction rule N from S to B affects the swarm performance

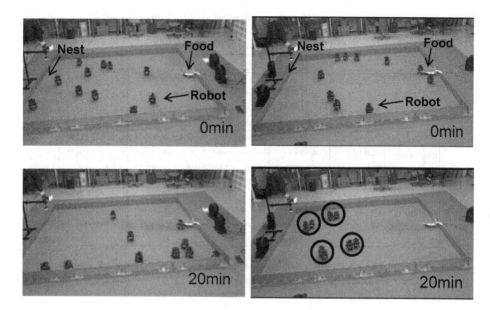

Fig. 4. Snapshots of swarm behavior under the priority rules BSB

Fig. 5. Snapshots of swarm behavior under the priority rules SSB

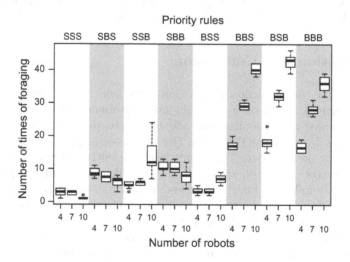

Fig. 6. Experimental result (Horizontal axis is number of robots, vertical axis is number of foraging)

(measured at the extrapolated intercept at swarm size = 2), and $\beta_{1\times2}$ measures how the alteration of the reaction rule N from S to B affects the slope against swarm size. Our aim is to assess the effects of the change of a reaction rule at each state, so hereafter we consider only β_2 and $\beta_{1\times2}$. In the comparisons of reaction

Table 2. Statistical analyses of the effects of reaction rule change at each stage assessed by multiple regressions

Test	Comparison	β_0	t	β_1	t	β_2	t	$\beta_{1\times2}$	t
Rule change at S_1	SSS to BSS	3.57	7.224***	-0.267	-3.007**	-2.07	-2.960**	0.867	6.911***
	SBS to BBS	9.65	17.612***	-0.450	-4.573***	0.117	0.151	4.283	30.778***
	SSB to BSB	0.85	0.663	1.483	6.440***	10.12	5.578***	2.517	7.726***
	SBB to BBB	11.75	13.826***	-0.417	-2.730**	-0.900	-0.749	3.633	16.832***
Rule change at S_2	SSS to SBS	3.57	7.616***	-0.267	-3.170**	6.083	9.185***	-0.183	-1.541
	BSS to BBS	1.50	2.633*	0.600	5.863***	8.267	10.259***	3.233	22.341***
	SSB to SBB	0.85	0.673	1.483	6.536***	10.90	6.099***	-1.900	-5.920***
	BSB to BBB	10.96	12.497***	4.000	25.38***	-0.117	-0.094	-0.783	-3.514***
Rule change at S_3	SSS to SSB	3.57	3.122**	-0.267	-1.300	-2.716	-1.681	1.750	6.031***
	BSS to BSB	1.50	1.964	0.600	4.374***	9.467	8.765***	3.400	17.527***
	SBS to SBB	9.65	13.50***	-0.450	-3.505***	2.100	2.077*	0.033	0.184
	BBS to BBB	9.77	13.65***	3.833	29.846***	1.083	1.071	-0.617	-3.395**

The coefficients of the regression model βs are shown, which were tested against $\beta = 0$ using t-tests. *: $p < 0.05$, **: $p < 0.01$, ***: $p < 0.001$.

rules at S_1, the signs of β_2 varied among comparisons, whereas $\beta_{1\times2}$ was always positive (and significantly different from 0). In contrast, in the comparisons of reaction rules at S_2 and S_3, the signs of β_2 were mostly significantly positive (at least not different from 0), whereas $\beta_{1\times2}$ varied among comparisons.

5   Discussion and Conclusion

We found that the alteration of reaction rules from S to B had substantial (mostly positive) effects on group-foraging performance. Moreover, statistical analyses revealed that the alteration affects the group-foraging performance in different ways depending on the states. The alterations at S_2 and S_3 improved the group-foraging performance. This result has an intuitive interpretation: robots take these states on the pheromone trail, and efficient use of the pheromone trail is directly linked to foraging success. Meanwhile, these alterations showed no constant effect on an increasing group size. This result might be attributed to the fact that the trail length on which robots can exist increases only as the square-root of the field size. The alteration at S_1 improved the group-foraging performance under increased group size (i.e., altered the slope of group-foraging performance against group size from negative to positive), but not the performance itself. In our observation, local clustering of the searching robots (Fig. 5) was observed mainly under the priority rules SNN. Therefore, this result suggests that the collision-induced priority rule has an important role in avoiding the negative impact of overcrowding on the field.

In this paper, we studied how "priority rules" affect the group-foraging performance of pheromone-mediated swarm robots. The priority rules are induced when two robots collide on the pheromone trail and/or on the field. Using real robot experiments, we found that the alteration in the reaction rules, components of a priority rule, can have substantial effects on the performance. Our results highlight the importance of implementing "fine-tuning" algorithms to improve the performance of complex swarm systems. In future study, the scalability of the improving effects of priority rules on group performance should be investigated by numerical simulations.

References

1. Fujisawa, R., Imamura, H., Hashimoto, T., Matsuno, F.: Communication using pheromone field for multiple robots. In: Proc. IEEE/RSJ 2008 International Conference on Intelligent Robots and Systems (2008)
2. Bonabeau, E., Dorigo, M., Theraulaz, G.: Swarm Intelligence. Oxford University Press (1999)
3. Hölldobler, B., Wilson, E.: The superorganism: the beauty, elegance, and strangeness of insect societies. WW Norton & Company (2009)
4. Dorigo, M., Stützle, T.: Ant Colony Optimization. Bradford Books (2004)
5. Sugawara, K., Kazama, T., Watanabe, T.: Foraging behavior of interacting robots with virtual pheromone. In: Proc. IEEE/RSJ Int. Conf. on Intelligent Robots and Systems (IROS 2004), vol. 3, pp. 3074–3079 (2004)
6. Garnier, S., Tache, F., Combe, M., Grimal, A., Theraulaz, G.: Alice in pheromone land: An experimental setup for the study of ant-like robots. In: Proc. IEEE Swarm Intelligence Symposium (SIS 2007), April 1-5, pp. 37–44 (2007)
7. Shimoyama, I., Kanzaki, R.: Biological type micromachine. Journal of Society of Biomechanisms 22, 152–157 (1998) (in Japanese)
8. Purnamadjaja, A.H., Russell, R.A.: Guiding robots behaviors using pheromone communication. Autonomous Robots 23, 113–130 (2007)
9. Fujisawa, R., Dobata, S., Kubota, D., Imamura, H., Matsuno, F.: Dependency by Concentration of Pheromone Trail for Multiple Robots. In: Dorigo, M., Birattari, M., Blum, C., Clerc, M., Stützle, T., Winfield, A.F.T. (eds.) ANTS 2008. LNCS, vol. 5217, pp. 283–290. Springer, Heidelberg (2008)
10. Krieger, M., Billeter, J., Keller, L.: Ant-like task allocation and recruitment in cooperative robots. Nature 406, 992–995 (2000)
11. Chang, D., Shadden, S., Marsden, J., Olfati-Saber, R.: Collision avoidance for multiple agent systems. In: Proceedings of 42nd IEEE Conference on Decision and Control, 2003, vol. 1, pp. 539–543. IEEE (2003)
12. Burd, M., Archer, D., Aranwela, N., Stradling, D.: Traffic dynamics of the leaf-cutting ant, atta cephalotes. The American Naturalist 159, 283–293 (2002)
13. Dussutour, A., Fourcassié, V., Helbing, D., Deneubourg, J.: Optimal traffic organization in ants under crowded conditions. Nature 428, 70–73 (2004)
14. Dussutour, A., Beshers, S., Deneubourg, J., Fourcassié, V.: Priority rules govern the organization of traffic on foraging trails under crowding conditions in the leaf-cutting ant atta colombica. Journal of Experimental Biology 212, 499–505 (2009)
15. Fujisawa, R., Shimizu, Y., Matsuno, F.: Effectiveness of tuning of pheromone trail lifetime in attraction of robot swarm. In: Proc. on International Symposium on System Integration, SII 2011, D2-2 (2011)

Dynamic Load Balancing Inspired by Cemetery Formation in Ant Colonies

Ronald Klazar and Andries P. Engelbrecht

Department of Computer Science, Faculty of Engineering, Built Environment and Information Technology, University of Pretoria, Pretoria, South Africa
{rklazar,engel}@cs.up.ac.za

Abstract. Loosely connected distributed computing systems present a changing environment to the programs that they execute. Dynamic load balancing (DLB) algorithms are employed to address the problem of re-locating tasks when parts of a distributed computing system become unavailable while other parts become idle. This paper presents a novel DLB algorithm based on cemetery formation in ant colonies. The algorithm builds on previous work to formulate ant-inspired DLB algorithms that aim to reduce the time needed to complete the parallel execution of multiple, independent tasks, where resources as well as tasks are diverse with respect to their performances and durations, respectively. The new algorithm is compared with its predecessors, based on division of labour in ant colonies, and pure, opportunistic load balancing, established as the baseline.

1 Introduction

Dynamic task allocation (DTA) is a continuous process that aims to reduce the time required to complete a set of tasks by a set of workers operating in a changing environment. Reduction in completion time is achieved at the cost incurred by the switching of workers' tasks.

Within a distributed computing system, the environment is transformed by the availability of individual computing resources and the process of reallocating tasks manifests as dynamic load balancing (DLB). *Load balancing* is here synonymous with *load sharing*, as described by Wang and Morris [10], and DLB is categorised, according to Casavant and Kuhl's taxonomy [4], as a global scheduling algorithm that operates within a changing (dynamic) environment, consisting of physically distributed, cooperative resources.

Earlier work [7] showed that a distributed computing system that employed only opportunistic load balancing (OLB) [6], or *cycle soaking*, would exhibit deteriorating performance as the resources diverged increasingly with respect to individual performance. The authors introduced a DLB algorithm (DLB_{DL}), based on division of labour in ant colonies, that aims to effect a better (though not necessarily optimal) distribution of tasks by making use of a load characterisation heuristic. DLB_{DL} improved overall task completion time, relative to the

M. Dorigo et al. (Eds.): ANTS 2012, LNCS 7461, pp. 236–243, 2012.

established baseline and, as expected, utilized more network bandwidth than the OLB algorithm.

Returning to existing work on modelling the behaviours of real ants, another method presents itself as a possible inspiration for a DLB strategy. To wit, certain species of ant group the dead members of their colonies in cemeteries, which the living members of the colony organize without centralized coordination or direct communication between participating workers. Experiments conducted by Deneubourg et al. [5] have led to a simple model of this behaviour that is described in detail in [2] and is commonly referred to as *cemetery formation*. A subsequent, rigorous analysis of the cemetery formation model was conducted by Theraulaz et al. in [9].

This paper presents an alternative to the approach by division of labour and introduces a variation of the DLB_{DL} algorithm, referred to as DLB_{CF} herein, that is inspired by the formation of cemeteries in ant colonies. The viability of DLB_{CF} is herein discussed and the algorithm is compared with its predecessor.

Related work by Montresor et al. [8] describes a DLB algorithm that is based on a variation of cemetery formation. The algorithm is used by Messor, which is an application that supports the parallel execution of independent subtasks on a computational grid. Ants in the Messor application wander the network and distribute tasks instead of clustering them. This is achieved by altering the normal behaviour of a cemetery formation algorithm such that an ant drops a task only once it has observed a low frequency of similar tasks over a period of time.

Cao [3] describes a DLB algorithm that draws inspiration from the random walk performed by ants that form cemeteries. In this case, an ant visits resources at random and for a certain number of steps. In so doing, the ant records the location of a single resource with the highest load amongst those resources that were visited. The ant then performs another walk of equal length to locate a node with a low load, after which it brokers a transfer of tasks between the two nodes it has recorded.

Bertelle et al. [1] present a DLB algorithm for distributed computing systems that is based on the same principles as Ant Colony Optimization. The targeted application takes into account tasks that exhibit dependencies amongst each other and must communicate during their execution.

The DLB algorithm presented in this paper is aimed at a distributed computing system that executes independent tasks in parallel. The algorithm does not employ agents and, instead, the idle, potentially faster resources themselves perform the task of wandering the network by sending queries to other, potentially slower resources to acquire the tasks that the slower resources host.

The remainder of the paper is structured as follows. Section 2 rationalizes the task allocation mechanism, Section 3 describes the method used to analyse the new algorithm and discusses the results of the analysis, and Section 4 ends the paper with some concluding remarks.

2   Task Allocation Inspired by Cemetery Formation

The multiple, independent tasks that constitute a single, larger problem, here termed the *project*, may either outnumber the independent resources in a distributed computing system or they may not. In the former case, an OLB strategy is sufficient to distribute tasks to all resources (one task per resource), as this approach will maximise the utilization of the computing system. However, once fewer tasks than resources remain, some resources will be idle while others will continue to finish the remaining tasks. In this case, the idle resources may either be faster processors than the busy resources or the busy resources may become unavailable due to being engaged by their actual owners or users.

A DLB strategy is employed to determine when an idle resource would be able to perform a task in a shorter period of time than a busy resource and then to broker a migration of the task, hosted by the slower resource, to the faster resource.

The approach taken in this study is inspired by cemetery formation. While busy resources continue to execute tasks, idle resources wander the network in search of resources with sufficiently lower processing capabilities to warrant the reallocation of a task. However, unlike the model described in [2], idle resources are not represented by an actual agent that wanders from one host to another. Instead, an idle resource searches the network by sending queries to other resources in the computing system.

The determination of the difference in processing performance between two resources is expressed by a normalized scalar value, referred to as the *shortfall*. The shortfall calculation was introduced in [7] and is briefly repeated here. The shortfall, s, is

$$s = \exp\left(-a\frac{W_S(T)}{Wmax_D}\right) \tag{1}$$

where S and D are the potential source and destination of a task, respectively, $Wmax$ is the maximum work that can be done by a resource per unit of time, $W(T)$ is the amount of work being done at time T, and a determines the steepness. The specific values of $W_S(T)$ and $Wmax_D$ may vary arbitrarily.

When a resource becomes idle and the only remaining tasks to process are already allocated to other resources, the idle resource begins to search the network for a task that it will be able to execute faster than the resource currently hosting the task.

The idle resource chooses another, remote resource in the network at random and sends a query to the chosen resource. The query message includes $Wmax_D$, the maximum processing capability of the idle resource. If the remote resource hosts a task, then the resource will compute a shortfall value based on the value of $Wmax_D$, obtained from the query message, and its own, current performance value, $W_S(T)$.

The remote resource uses the shortfall value in place of the item frequency to compute P_d, as in [2]. If the remote resource drops its task, then the task is transmitted to the idle resource that issued the causal query.

The probability to pick up a task is not calculated by DLB_{CF} because the *pick-up* action is implicit in the exchange of a task between two resources.

DLB_{CF} is not a direct mapping of the original cemetery formation model described in [2] to a distributed computing system. Nevertheless, the effect of DLB_{CF} on task allocation is to gather tasks dispersed over all resources and cluster those tasks at only the fastest resources in the system.

3   Analysis

Testing of the new DLB algorithm was conducted using the simulation system described in [7]. No specific network topology was tested and the overheads of a particular network stack, including application protocols, were not taken into account. Instead, only the time taken to complete a project and the bandwidth usage characteristics of the DLB algorithm were recorded and analyzed. This section describes the DLB_{CF} algorithm, the parameters that control the performance of the new algorithm, details the design of the empirical study, and presents the results of the experimental tests.

3.1   The Experimental Model

The experimental test bed used to simulate the load balancing strategies is identical to that described in [7]. A resource operating according to DLB_{CF} operates as follows. The resource first queries the project server for a task. The resource executes its task to completion and submits the result to the project server, after which the resource requests another task. If no task is available from the project server, then the resource begins to prospect for tasks amongst other resources in the distributed computing system. The resource will continue to prospect until either it finds and acquires a task from another resource or the time limit for prospecting has been reached. When prospecting times out, the resource once again queries the project server for a task.

3.2   Simulation Control Parameters

The parameters that control the composition and performance of the simulated distributed computing system are as described in [7]. The parameters that affect the DLB algorithm are described next.

Performance Data Size: The performance data is the value of $Wmax_D$, as transmitted by an idle resource. The bandwidth usage of these messages is recorded by the simulator and the performance data size stipulates the size of the performance data message.

Maximum Prospecting Range: An idle resource is not guaranteed to find a busy resource, that happens to be slower, due to the fact that it chooses resources randomly when looking for a task. Consequently, the idle resource must repeat its query to other resources as long as it has not acquired a task. The maximum prospecting range determines the upper bound for the number of resources to query per time step. Increasing this parameter increases the amount of bandwidth required to effect the search for suboptimal task distributions.

Maximum Prospecting Duration: At some point in time, an idle resource must check for the possibility of a new project having been deployed on the project server. Were idle resources not to perform this check, they would not become aware of the case that a project was completed and a new project should be processed next. The maximum prospecting duration determines the upper bound for the number of time steps that an idle resource searches for tasks amongst other resources in the system before it queries the project server for a new task.

3.3 Design of the Empirical Test

The aim of the empirical analysis is: 1) to show that the employment of DLB_{CF} in a distributed computing system reduces the time taken to complete a project, as compared with the baseline result, which is derived by the employment of an OLB strategy only; 2) to compare the performance of DLB_{CF} with that of DLB_{DL}; and 3) to determine the bandwidth usage characteristics of both DLB algorithms.

The tests are performed to produce a trend in completion time with respect to an increasing diversity of resource performances. Likewise, as it is unrealistic to assume that all tasks will require exactly the same amount of computation to produce a result, each test considers an increasing diversity of task durations as well.

Each degree of resource diversity is obtained by randomly selecting an incremental number of resources that deviate from the mean performance of resources in the range of possible performance values. The average absolute deviation is computed over 30 such samples to produce the resource performance dispersion value. The task duration diversities are computed similarly.

To simulate the effects of users engaging the resources they control, thus preempting the execution of tasks hosted by those resources, a processor variance is introduced to the tests. At each time step, and for each resource, a new processor performance is computed by multiplying a resource's maximum processing performance by a randomly chosen factor, v, for $v \in [0, 1]$.

Each simulation is run 30 times to produce a mean turnaround time (project completion time) and mean bandwidth usage.

The parameter values used to specify the distributed computing system as well as the DLB_{DL} algorithm were taken from [7], with the following exceptions. The maximum prospecting range and stimulus period of DLB_{DL} were changed to

99 and 1, respectively. The former is a correction of the previous value and the latter is used to set resources to broadcast a stimulus as often as possible. A detailed description of these parameters can be found in [7].

The parameter values used to specify the $DLBCF$ algorithm were set as follows. Performance data size, maximum prospecting range and maximum prospecting duration were set to 64.0×10^{-6}, 99, and 1, respectively. a, θ_2, and n were set to 9, 0.0001, and 9, respectively.

The algorithms were were tested for viability. Consequently, the stimulus period of DLB_{DL} and the maximum prospecting range of DLB_{CF} were set to their respective logical limits, such that the lowest possible turnaround time and the highest possible bandwidth usage could be measured.

3.4   Results of the Viability Test

The results are presented here as surface plots, depicting, for each algorithm, including the baseline, the turnaround time and bandwidth usages against increasing resource performance dispersion and increasing task duration dispersion. Significance testing was conducted to determine whether or not the algorithms could be reliably distinguished by their performance. A discussion of the results follows.

Turnaround Time: Figure 1a shows the turnaround time when DLB_{DL} was employed. The DLB_{DL} distribution differs significantly from the baseline distribution by Mann-Whitney with $U = 1299.0, n_1 = n_2 = 100$ at a significance level of 0.05 (two-tailed). The mean turnaround time of DLB_{DL} is 231.246, with a standard deviation of 7.332. However, the shape of the DLB_{DL} surface suggests that DLB_{DL} is susceptible to the same flaw as an OLB algorithm, with respect to scalability.

Figure 1b shows the turnaround time when DLB_{CF} was employed. The DLB_{CF} distribution differs significantly from the baseline distribution with $U = 55.0, n_1 = n_2 = 100$, and differs from the DLB_{DL} distribution with $U = 57.0, n_1 = n_2 = 100$ at a significance level of 0.05 (two-tailed). DLB_{CF} was superior to DLB_{DL} in terms of mean performance, with a mean turnaround time of 211.224 and standard deviation of 1.844. Additionally, DLB_{CF} exhibited a more consistent turnaround time as resource performance and task duration dispersions increased, suggesting that DLB_{CF} is more scalable than DLB_{DL}.

The mean turnaround time of the baseline is 253.761, with a standard deviation of 17.341, showing that both DLB_{DL}

Bandwidth Usage: Figure 2a shows the bandwidth usage for DLB_{DL}. The mean bandwidth usage is 0.00220, with a standard deviation of 0.00013. The DLB_{DL} distribution differs from that of the baseline with $U = 1011.0, n_1 = n_2 = 100$ at a significance level of 0.05 (two-tailed). As expected, turnaround time decreased at the cost of an increase in bandwidth usage.

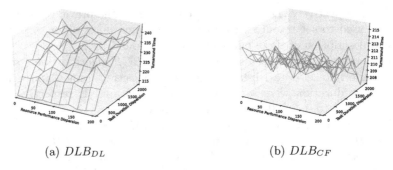

(a) DLB_{DL} (b) DLB_{CF}

Fig. 1. Turnaround Time vs. Resource Performance Dispersion, Task Duration Dispersion

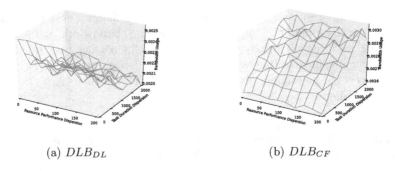

(a) DLB_{DL} (b) DLB_{CF}

Fig. 2. Bandwidth Usage vs. Resource Performance Dispersion, Task Duration Dispersion

Figure 2b shows the bandwidth usage for DLB_{CF}. The mean bandwidth usage is 0.00283, with a standard deviation of 0.00011. The DLB_{CF} distribution differs from the baseline distribution with $U = 0.0, n_1 = n_2 = 100$ and from the DLB_{DL} distribution with $U = 0.0, n_1 = n_2 = 100$ at a significance level of 0.05 (two-tailed). Once again, bandwidth usage costs were higher with a correspondingly lower turnaround time.

The mean bandwidth usage of the baseline is 0.00177 with a standard deviation of 0.00026.

Of note is that DLB_{CF} exhibited the lowest bandwidth usage deviation amongst the baseline and DLB_{DL}, supporting the observation that the bandwidth usage of DLB_{CF} remained consistent even as resource performances and task durations became more diverse.

4 Conclusion

The results of the viability test showed that both ant-inspired DLB algorithms improved upon turnaround time in the parallel execution of multiple, independent tasks. However, while the algorithm inspired by division of labour effected an improvement in performance, the DLB algorithm inspired by cemetery formation showed the most promise. The deciding factor was the consistency of performance in turnaround time as the differences amongst resources and tasks increased.

Even so, a real application will have to consider the performance capabilities of its particular network topology. While both of the DLB algorithms presented in this paper have the potential to lower turnaround time, the crucial difference between the two algorithms lies in the means that each employs to search for tasks. To wit, DLB_{DL} broadcasts queries, while DLB_{CF} queries the members of the network iteratively.

References

1. Bertelle, C., Dutot, A., Guinand, F., Olivier, D.: Organization detection for dynamic load balancing in individual-based simulations. Multiagent and Grid Systems 3(1), 141–163 (2007)
2. Bonabeau, E., Dorigo, M., Theraulaz, G.: Swarm Intelligence: From Natural to Artificial Systems, 1st edn. Oxford University Press (1999)
3. Cao, J.: Self-organizing agents for grid load balancing. In: Proceedings of the 5th IEEE/ACM International Workshop on Grid Computing, pp. 388–395. IEEE Computer Society (2004)
4. Casavant, T., Kuhl, J.: A taxonomy of scheduling in general-purpose distributed computing systems. IEEE Transactions on Software Engineering 14(2), 141–154 (1988)
5. Deneubourg, J.L., Goss, S., Franks, N., Sendova-hanks, A., Detrain, C., Chrtien, L.: The dynamics of collective sorting: robot-like ants and ant-like robots. In: Meyer, J.A., Wilson, S. (eds.) Proceedings of the First International Conference on Simulation of Adaptive Behavior: From Animals to Animats, pp. 356–363 (1991)
6. Freund, R.F., Siegel, H.J.: Guest editor's introduction: Heterogeneous processing. Computer 26, 13–17 (1993)
7. Klazar, R., Engelbrecht, A.P.: Dynamic load balancing inspired by division of labour in ant colonies. In: IEEE Symposium on Swarm Intelligence (SIS), pp. 1–8 (April 2011)
8. Montresor, A., Meling, H., Babaoğlu, Ö.: Messor: Load-Balancing through a Swarm of Autonomous Agents. In: Moro, G., Koubarakis, M. (eds.) AP2PC 2002. LNCS (LNAI), vol. 2530, pp. 125–137. Springer, Heidelberg (2003)
9. Theraulaz, G., Bonabeau, E., Nicolis, S.C., Sol, R.V., Fourcassi, V., Blanco, S., Fournier, R., Joly, J.L., Fernndez, P., Grimal, A., Dalle, P., Deneubourg, J.L.: Spatial patterns in ant colonies. Proceedings of the National Academy of Sciences 99(15), 9645–9649 (2002)
10. Wang, Y.T., Morris, R.J.: Load sharing in distributed systems. IEEE Transactions on Computers C-34(3), 204–217 (1985)

Feasibility of an Ant Colony Optimization Algorithm for Multi-leaf Collimator (MLC) Aperture Definition and Beam Weighting in Volumetric Modulated Arc Therapy (VMAT) Radiotherapy Treatment Planning

Owen Clancey and Matthew Witten

Witten Clancey Partners, LLC, Great Neck, New York, USA
owen.clancey@gmail.com, witten@earthlink.net

Abstract. Volumetric Modulated Arc Therapy (VMAT) is a sophisticated radiotherapy treatment delivery modality in which a medical linear accelerator arcs around a patient, with concurrent dynamic variation of multi-leaf collimator aperture, dose rate, and gantry speed, to produce a radiation dose distribution which delivers a highly conformal dose to the target while minimizing the incidental irradiation of normal tissue. Treatment planning for VMAT is an inverse problem, requiring optimization of the linear accelerator parameters to produce the desired radiation dose distribution, which is specified by dose-volume objectives. In this study, the feasibility of an ant colony algorithm for VMAT treatment planning is demonstrated by the ability of the algorithm to produce a treatment plan, which satisfies given dose-volume objectives, for a phantom target/critical structure geometry. Three experiments were conducted: one in which the optimization included only heuristic information, one in which there was exclusively a pheromone trail update, and one where there was both a pheromone trail update and an applied heuristic. The results indicate that the use of both a pheromone trail update and heuristic information during the optimization yields solutions of the highest quality.

1 Introduction

1.1 Radiation Therapy Treatment Delivery

Modern external beam radiation therapy, for treatment of malignant cancers, benign lesions, and functional conditions, is delivered via a medical linear accelerator (linac). The linac is a gantry-mounted system, with the gantry rotating about a single point in space, called the isocenter. Linacs are capable of producing megavoltage photon beams, which are collimated using a tertiary (i.e. after both the primary collimator and secondary jaws) beam aperture-defining device, the multi-leaf collimator (MLC). The MLC consists of many pairs of tungsten leaves, which can be accurately and precisely driven to prescribed positions by

M. Dorigo et al. (Eds.): ANTS 2012, LNCS 7461, pp. 244–251, 2012.

the treatment delivery software. The MLC allows for the conformal shaping of the radiation beam, such that the shape of the beam can be made to match the contours of an irregularly-shaped tumor, while shielding adjacent critical organs-at-risk (OARs), thereby minimizing the probability of sequelae induced by the incidental irradiation of these structures.

1.2 Volumetric Modulated Arc Therapy(VMAT)

VMAT is an extension of so-called intensity modulated radiation therapy (IMRT) [6]. In IMRT, the MLC leaves are adjusted dynamically to produce a modulation in photon fluence, allowing steep dose gradients to be produced throughout the treatment field. VMAT is also a dynamic treatment; the gantry continuously moves in an arc about the patient, and the MLC leaves, gantry speed, and dose rate are varied simultaneously to produce a highly conformal radiation dose distribution. The treatment is quite rapid, with a duration of delivery of approximately 70-160 sec [1].

1.3 Ant Colony Optimization for VMAT Treatment Planning

Treatment planning for VMAT is an inverse problem, wherein the desired dose distribution is specified, and the machine parameters necessary to produce the dose distribution are determined via optimization. There are currently several different approaches to VMAT treatment planning [2] - [8]. It is the observation of the authors of the present work that such methods tend to be slow, when patient throughput is considered in the clinical setting. The user interfaces may be somewhat awkward. Finally, direct inspection of the solutions reveals that the MLC leaf trajectories tend to include many noisy jumps throughout the gantry rotation. Clearly, a new approach might offer some improvement. The analogy between the path an MLC leaf may take as the gantry rotates around the patient, and the path of an ant on its search for a food source, motivates the application of an ant colony approach to the VMAT treatment planning problem.

In the present work, an ACO algorithm for the optimization of MLC leaf trajectories and dose rates is proposed, and its feasibility is demonstrated. The algorithm was used to produce an optimized treatment plan for a phantom containing volumes representing a target and a critical OAR. The algorithm was able to produce optimized MLC leaf trajectories and dose rates, and consequently a treatment plan satisfying the specified dose objectives, in a clinically relevant optimization time.

2 Materials and Methods

2.1 Objective Function

A dosimetric objective function was used to score the treatment plans derived from the ant paths. The objective function was of a quadratic form, including terms expressing the deviation in the doses at optimization points from the desired doses, summed in quadrature, with the contribution from each volume of interest multiplied by a user-selectable weight. The DVH constraints were implemented in the manner of Spirou and Chui [7]. The objective function included terms representing the target, as well as terms representing the OARs, as shown in Eq. 1:

$$
f(\boldsymbol{x}, \boldsymbol{w}, \boldsymbol{d}, \boldsymbol{v}) = \mathcal{H}(v_{p,min} - v_{t,min})w_{t,min} \sum_{i=1}^{n_t} \mathcal{H}(\delta_{thres,min} - \sum_{j=1}^{b} DDC_{ij}x_j)
$$

$$
\times (\sum_{j=1}^{b} DDC_{ij}x_j - d_{p,min})^2 + \mathcal{H}(v_{t,max} - v_{p,max})
$$

$$
\times w_{t,max} \sum_{i=1}^{n_t} \mathcal{H}(\sum_{j=1}^{b} DDC_{ij}x_j - \delta_{thres,max})
$$

$$
\times (\sum_{j=1}^{b} DDC_{ij}x_j - d_{p,max})^2 + \sum_{l=1}^{org} [\sum_{m=1}^{c_{lm}} \mathcal{H}(v_{lm} - v_{p,lm})w_{lm}
$$

$$
\times \sum_{k=1}^{n_l} \mathcal{H}(\sum_{j=1}^{b} DDC_{kj}x_j - \delta_{thres,lm})
$$

$$
\times (\sum_{j=1}^{b} DDC_{kj}x_j - \delta_{thres,lm})^2] \ , \quad (1)
$$

where $\boldsymbol{x}$ is a vector of beam weights, $\boldsymbol{d}$ is a vector of doses associated with the dose-volume objectives, $\boldsymbol{v}$ is a vector of volumes associated with the dose-volume objectives (paired with the vector of doses), $\mathcal{H}$ is the Heaviside function, subscript t refers to the target, subscript p refers to the prescription dose, n_t is the number of points within the target, b is the number of beam weights, org is the number of critical organs, c_{lm} is the mth DVH objective for the lth critical organ, and n_l is the number of points in the lth critical organ.

In addition, $\delta_{thres,min}$ is the dose to that point in the target such that when all points in the target are sorted, points for which the dose is less than or equal to $\delta_{thres,min}$ cause the minimum dose-volume objective for the target to be violated, $\delta_{thres,max}$ is the dose to that point in the target such that when all points in the target are sorted, points for which the dose is greater than or equal to $\delta_{thres,max}$ cause the maximum dose-volume constraint for the target to be violated, and $\delta_{thres,lm}$ is the dose to that point in the lth critical organ such that when all points in the organ are sorted, points for which the dose is greater than or equal to $\delta_{thres,lm}$ cause the mth dose-volume objective for the organ to be violated.

2.2 Algorithmic Structure

The Ant System algorithm [3] was used for the optimization. The pseudocode for the algorithm appears below:

```
Procedure VMAT
     Set parameters
     Calculate heuristic and pheromone values
     While (Termination condition not met) do
          Construct apertures using random proportional rule
          Weight apertures using SQP
          Fitness evaluation of weighted apertures
          Update pheromones
     End
End
```

Each ant traced out a tour which was mapped, via a linear mapping, to a possible leaf path trajectory. A treatment plan was constructed by using all the leaf paths of all the leaves of the MLC to create the apertures for dose delivery. The beam weights (or dose rates) were then optimized with sequential quadratic programming, before being scored using the dosimetric fitness function of Eq. 1. A fitness-based pheromone update was then applied before the next iteration. In all cases, the algorithm was terminated when the fitness value was < 1 or a run-time of 600 sec was reached.

The gantry rotation of a full 360 degrees was subdivided into 5 separate arcs of 72 degrees each, for which distinct MLC apertures were optimized. As discussed previously, there were 24 leaf pairs, i.e. there were 2 banks, right and left, of 12 leaves each. For each leaf, the range of possible MLC leaf positions was discretized into 10 equally-spaced intervals. The number of ants per leaf was $m = 100$, and the evaporation constant was $\rho_0 = 0.5$. Each treatment plan was a set $\{A^i\}_{i=1}^5$ of MLC apertures constructed from the leaf trajectories, which were derived from the ant paths. There were thus 100 treatment plans generated per iteration.

In order to set initial pheromone values, it was noted that open apertures have an objective function value of on the order of $f_0 = 10^3$, which was used to set the initial pheromone values to

$$\tau_0 = m/f_0 \ . \tag{2}$$

Some problem-specific knowledge was applied to determined the starting MLC leaf positions, namely: as a first approximation to the solution, it was possible to construct open apertures which simply ensure target coverage. To convert this knowledge into a heuristic, η was represented by a monotonically nondecreasing function of leaf position, with η increasing as the leaf was positioned further from the isocenter. Each leaf was constrained such that it could not allow irradiation beyond 3 mm further from the isocenter than the target, which accounted for the penumbra of the beam produced by the leaf edge. Tour construction used the Random Proportional Rule [4]:

$$p_{ijkl} = [\tau_{ijkl}]^{\alpha}[\eta_{ijkl}]^{\beta}/(\sum_{n \in N_{ijk}} [\tau_{ijkn}]^{\alpha}[\eta_{ijkn}]^{\beta}) \text{ if } n \in N_{ijk} \ , \qquad (3)$$

where i is the index of the aperture number of the plan, j indicates the jth MLC leaf, k is an index denoting the position, in the $(i$th $- 1)$, aperture of the jth MLC leaf, and l is an index denoting the position, in the ith aperture, of the jth MLC leaf.

The pheromone update was fitness-based [4], where,

$$\tau_{ijkl} \leftarrow (1 - \rho)\tau_{ijkl} + \sum_{n=1}^{b} \Delta\tau_{ijkl}^{n},$$

$$\text{where } \Delta\tau_{ijkl}^{n} = 1/f,$$

$$\text{if arc } (i, j, k, l) \text{ belongs to } A^{n},$$

$$\text{otherwise } \Delta\tau_{ijkl}^{n} = 0 \ . \quad (4)$$

Note that in Eq. 4, A^{n} is the nth aperture of treatment plan A, b is the total number of apertures, and f is the objective function value of treatment plan A. In this manner, the pheromone update reinforced those tours which produced dosimetrically favorable treatment plans.

2.3   Phantom Geometry

The phantom was an infinite cylinder of 300 mm diameter. The target was cylinder concentric with the phantom, of 100 mm diameter and 100 mm height. The critical structure was a cylinder abutting the target, of diameter 60 mm.

2.4   DVH Constraints

All treatment plans were optimized to meet the following DVH objectives, listed in Tab. 1. Note that "Ring 10 mm" and "Ring 50 mm" are annular structures, at distances of 10 mm and 50 mm from the target respectively, that were introduced to control the lower isodoses of the radiation dose distribution, restricting the "bleeding out" of dose.

Table 1. DVH Objectives

Structure	Volume (%)	Dose (cGy)	Weight
Target	95	100	1
Target	0	105	1
Critical Organ	10	100	0.5
Critical Organ	50	50	0.5
Ring 10 mm	0	100	0.5
Ring 50 mm	0	65	0.5

3   Results and Discussion

Cumulative DVH graphs are shown for each case in subsequent subsections. The cumulative DVH is a clinical tool that plots the volume of a structure that receives at least a certain dose against the radiation dose received.

3.1   Heurstic Information Only

This was the case where $\alpha = 0$ and $\beta = 1$. The cumulative DVH for this case is shown in Fig. 1.

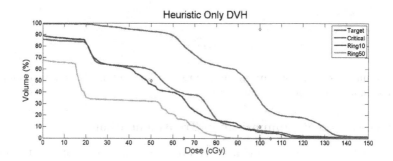

Fig. 1. Cumulative DVH for heuristic-only optimization. Note that the target (in red) is not well-covered at all.

3.2   Learning Only

This was the case where $\alpha = 1$ and $\beta = 0$. The cumulative DVH for this case is shown in Fig. 2.

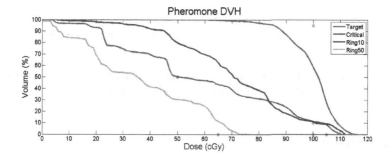

Fig. 2. Cumulative DVH for learning-only optimization. The stigmergy has helped to improve target coverage.

3.3 Learning and Heuristic Information

This was the case where $\alpha = 1$ and $\beta = 1$. The cumulative DVH for this case is shown in Fig. 3.

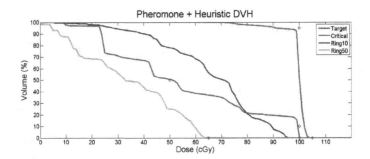

Fig. 3. Cumulative DVH for learning and heuristic information. The combination prodces a plan that covers the target quite well.

3.4 Fitness-Based Comparison of Treatment Plans

The plot in Fig. 4 compares the average objective function values of the treatment plans as a function of time. Clearly, the convergence of the case where both heurstic information and learning are used in the optimization is superior.

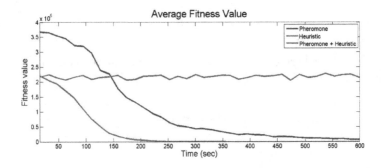

Fig. 4. Plot of average objective function values as a function of time. The convergence properties of the heuristic + learning case are clearly superior.

4 Conclusion

As has been demonstrated, ACO shows much promise for application to the problem of MLC leaf trajectory sequencing and dose rate optimization in VMAT.

Clearly, heuristic information acts in a synergistic fashion with the natural stigmergy of the algorithm to produce dosimetrically superior plans.

The authors intend to develop the ACO for VMAT treatment planning optimization more thoroughly in future work. It needs to be applicable to problems of a wide variety of geometries, not the simple one of the phantom in this study. It must admit the use of a much finer subdivision of the whole 360 degree arc of gantry rotation. There must also be further development of the heuristic information applied to the problem, to aid in the creation of initial MLC apertures.

References

1. Bzdusek, K., Friberger, H., Eriksson, K., Hardemark, B., Robinson, D., Kaus, M.: Development and Evaluation of an Efficient Approach to Volumetric Arc Therapy Planning. Med. Phys. 36, 2328 (2009)
2. Craft, D., McQuaid, D., Wala, J., Chen, W., Salari, B.T.: Multicriteria VMAT Optimization. Med. Phys. 39, 686 (2012)
3. Dorigo, M.: Optimization, Learning and Natural Algorithms. PhD Thesis. Dipartimento di Ellettronica, Politecnico di Milano, Milan (1992)
4. Dorigo, M., Stuetzle, T.: Ant Colony Optimization. MIT, Cambridge (2004)
5. Hoegele, W., Loeschel, R., Merkle, N., Zygmanski, P.: An Efficient Inverse Radiotherapy Planning Method for VMAT Using Quadratic Programming Optimization. Med. Phys. 39, 444 (2012)
6. Otto, K.: Volumetric Modulated Arc Therapy: IMRT in a Single Gantry Arc. Med. Phys. 35, 310 (2008)
7. Spirou, S., Chui, C.: A Gradient Inverse Planning Algorithm with Dose-Volume Constraints. Med. Phys. 25, 321 (1998)
8. Vanetti, E., Nicolini, G., Nord, J., Peltola, J., Clivio, A., Fogliata, A., Cozzi, L.: On the Role of the Optimization Algorithm of RapidArc Volumetric Modulated Arc Therapy on Plan Quality and Efficiency. Med. Phys. 38, 5844 (2011)
9. Yang, Y., Xing, L.: Optimization of Radiotherapy Dose-Time Fractionation with Consideration of Tumor Specific Biology. Med. Phys. 32, 3666 (2005)

Formica ex Machina: Ant Swarm Foraging from Physical to Virtual and Back Again

Joshua P. Hecker[1], Kenneth Letendre[1,2], Karl Stolleis[1],
Daniel Washington[1], and Melanie E. Moses[1,2]

[1] Department of Computer Science, University of New Mexico, Albuquerque, USA
[2] Department of Biology, University of New Mexico, Albuquerque, USA
{jhecker,melaniem}@cs.unm.edu, {kletendr,stolleis}@unm.edu

Abstract. Ants use individual memory and pheromone communication to forage efficiently. We implement these strategies as distributed search algorithms in robotic swarms. Swarms of simple robots are robust, scalable and capable of exploring for resources in unmapped environments. We test the ability of individual robots and teams of three robots to collect tags distributed in random and clustered distributions in simulated and real environments. Teams of three real robots that forage based on individual memory without communication collect RFID tags approximately twice as fast as a single robot using the same strategy. Our simulation system mimics the foraging behaviors of the robots and replicates our results. Simulated swarms of 30 and 100 robots collect tags 8 and 22 times faster than teams of three robots. This work demonstrates the feasibility of programming large robot teams for collective tasks such as retrieval of dispersed resources, mapping, and environmental monitoring. It also lays a foundation for evolving collective search algorithms *in silico* and then implementing those algorithms *in machina* in robust and scalable robotic swarms.

1 Introduction

One goal of swarm robotics is to engineer groups of simple, low-cost robots that can cooperate as a cohesive unit to accomplish collection and exploration tasks such as mapping, monitoring, search and rescue, and foraging for resources in unmapped environments [4,5,8]. Ideally, robotic swarms are capable of exploring unknown environments without the benefit of prior knowledge to guide them. Individuals must adapt to sensor error and motor drift, and the swarm must function given variation, errors, and failures in individual robots.

Biology often provides inspiration for approaches to achieve these design goals [4,6,8,18]. Biologically-inspired decentralized approaches have enhanced scalability and robustness by removing single points of failure from communication bottlenecks and rigid control structures. Such approaches have not yet reached the level of emergent coordination observed in natural systems [24].

Our robots are designed to mimic colonies of seed harvester ants who forage using a combination of individual memory and pheromone trails. Robots are

M. Dorigo et al. (Eds.): ANTS 2012, LNCS 7461, pp. 252–259, 2012.

equipped with a sensor suite which mimics the real ants: time-based odometry approximates physical location analogous to the ants' stride integration [26], and ultrasound ranging measures distance to objects and corrects for drift similar to an ant's landmark-based navigation [13]. Pheromone-like communication of previously successful search locations is used to improve search performance. Robots search for radio-frequency identification (RFID) tags, and upon finding them, return to a central 'nest.' Robot locations are transmitted over one-way wireless communication to a server for data logging; occasional two-way communication allows virtual pheromones to direct robots to previously found tag locations.

We program our robots with search algorithms derived from our previous work that used an agent-based model (ABM) guided by genetic algorithms (GA) to replicate foraging behaviors of seed harvester ants [11,15]. We duplicate parameters from the ant model in the robots. We modified the ABM to replicate the constraints of the robot hardware, and to model the behavior and environment of the robots in their search for RFID tags. This parallel physical and simulated implementation allows us to compare results from analogous experiments *in machina* as implemented in physical robots and *in silico* in the ABM (as in [7,16]). In additional ABM experiments we scale up the size of the swarm, the number of tags, and the size of the area in which the simulated robots search.

2   Background

Swarm Robotics: Like ant colonies and other complex biological systems, robotic swarms have potential to utilize efficient, robust, distributed approaches to physical tasks. Effective algorithms for swarm robotics must extend beyond simulation to intelligently deal with the complexities of navigating in real environments [7,16,17]. Our approach balances the benefit of centralized information exchange with the scalability of decentralized autonomous search [2,19,23]. We use evolutionary algorithms to determine the parameters of individual behavior that result in effective collective action, as in [9,11,22,25].

Biological Ants: Our algorithms are largely inspired by foraging in *Pogonomyrmex* desert seed-harvester ants [10]. These foragers typically leave their colony's single nest, travel in a relatively straight line to some location on their territory, and then switch to a correlated random walk to search for seeds.

When a forager finds a seed, it brings it directly back to the nest. Foragers often return to the location where they previously found a seed in a process called site fidelity [3,10,20], which reduces future search times. It is unclear exactly how often these ants lay and follow pheromone trails [12,13,21], but our recent work indicates occasional laying of pheromone trails to dense piles of food may be an effective component of these ants' foraging strategies [11,15].

Models: We used GAs to find the optimal balance of site fidelity and pheromone communication in simulated ant colonies [15]. We simulated ant foraging using a set of ABMs of foragers on a grid, with parameters that specify how ants travel from the nest, search, and use site fidelity and pheromone communication. These parameters are optimized by a GA to maximize seed intake rate.

Previous simulations show that ants increase foraging rates with rare pheromone use ($< 10\%$ of foraging trips), particularly in the clustered distribution where the intake rate doubles with the addition of pheromone [15].

The ant foraging ABM was modified to model our swarm robots and our experimental setup. The simulation provides both a theoretical benchmark and a basic architecture for using GAs to optimize simulated robots within the constraints imposed by the physical hardware. All *in machina* experiments have been duplicated *in silico*.

3   Methods

3.1   Hardware

Our robots use an Arduino microcontroller with a compass, ultrasound, wireless card, and RFID reader. These allow the robots to localize at a central 'nest,' measure distance (object 100 cm away: mean error = 2.7 cm, $\sigma = 2.24$), and calculate odometry (round trip of 10 m: mean error = 21 cm, $\sigma = 6.6$). Robots avoid collisions by rotating clockwise until the object has been cleared.

3.2   Search Algorithm

The search behavior used by the robots to locate RFID tags is shown in Fig. 1.

1. Set Search Location: Robots begin at the nest in the center and randomly select an initial search site location, encoded as a distance d and heading h.
2. Travel to Search Site (yellow path) Traveling robots go straight to the search location while avoiding collisions with other robots, correcting for motor drift, and communicating events to the server for later analysis.
3. Search for Tag (blue path): The robot moves in a correlated random walk with direction θ at time t drawn from a normal distribution centered around direction θ_{t-1} and standard deviation $SD = \omega + \gamma/t_s^\delta$. ω determines the degree of turning during an uninformed search. In a search informed by memory or communication, γ/t_s^δ determines an initial additional degree of turning which decreases over time spent searching. This mimics ants' tight turns in an initially small area that expand to explore a larger area over time [11].
4. Travel to Nest (pink path): The robot returns to the known nest location. In pheromone experiments, the tag location (d, h) is reported to the server if $C > 1$, where C is the count of other tags detected in the 8-cell neighborhood of the collected tag in the simulation or discovered in one 360° rotation of the real robot.
5. Set Next Search Location: On subsequent trips, d and h are determined by either returning to the previously found tag location if $C > 0$, otherwise d and h are communicated from the pheromone list on the server.

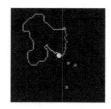

Fig. 1. A robot begins its search at a globally shared central nest site (center circle) and **sets a search location**. The robot then **travels to the search site** (yellow line). Upon reaching the search location, the robot **searches for tags** (blue line) until tags (red squares) are found. After searching, the robot **travels to the nest** (purple line).

3.3 Experimental Design

Each experimental trial on a concrete surface runs for a maximum of one hour. A cylinder marks the center 'nest' to which the robots return once they have located a tag. This center point is used for localization and error correction by the robots' ultrasonic sensors. All robots involved in a trial are initially placed near the cylinder. We program each robot to stay within a 3 m radius 'virtual fence'. In every experiment, 32 RFID tags are arranged in one of three different patterns: random, clustered, or power law (Fig. 2). Experiments are replicated under identical conditions for individual robots and for groups of three bots.

Robot locations are continually transmitted over one-way WiFi communication to a central server and logged for analysis. When a tag is found, its unique identification number is transmitted back to the server, providing us with a detailed record of tag discovery. Tags can only be read once, simulating seed retrieval. The central server also acts as a coordinator for virtual pheromone trails using two-way communication. Locations deemed important enough to require a pheromone value (i.e. those with two or more tags discovered by the robot) are added to a list data structure with a pheromone value of 1. Each location's associated pheromone value p_i is decayed exponentially over time by the server: $p_{t+1} = p_t * .995^\eta$, where η is the number of seconds between time t and $t + 1$. When a location's pheromone value has dropped below a threshold of 0.001, it is removed from the list. As each robot returns to the nest, the server selects a location from the list (if available) and transmits it to the robot.

Our simulations replicate the physical dimensions of the robots, their speed while traveling and searching, and the area over which they can detect an RFID tag, with spatial dimensions that reflect the distribution of tags in the 3 m area. Like the real robots, simulated robots avoid collisions by turning to the right to move past other robots, and search for a simulated hour.

We also simulated the behavior of the robots in a much larger area in which tags are distributed in the same density but in such large numbers that even large swarms of robots collect only a fraction of the available tags. We simulated 1, 3, 30, and 100 robots to observe the scaling properties of the system.

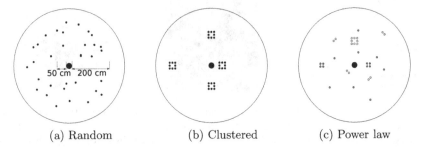

(a) Random   (b) Clustered   (c) Power law

Fig. 2. 32 RFID tags scattered in a ring between 50 cm and 200 cm in (a) the uniform random distribution. The clustered distribution (b) has four piles of eight tags placed at 90° intervals at 50, 100, 150, and 200 cm in relation to the central nest. The power law distribution (c) uses piles of varying size and number: one large pile of eight tags at 125 cm, two medium piles of four tags at 75 and 175 cm, four small piles of two tags at 50, 100, 150, and 200 cm, and eight randomly placed tags.

4   Results

We analyze the rates at which robots retrieve tags from each distribution, individually or in teams of three, in real robots and in simulation. Unless otherwise noted, results for each experimental treatment are averaged over five robot experiments and twenty simulations. Error bars indicate one standard deviation.

Time to collect 32 tags is shown in Fig. 3. In robots and in simulation, three robots collect tags faster than one robot, however, the speedup varies over the course of the experiments (i.e., the red and blue lines are not parallel). When we average time to collect n tags, where n varies between 1 and the maximum number of tags collected, we find that 3 robots collect tags approximately twice as fast as 1 robot.

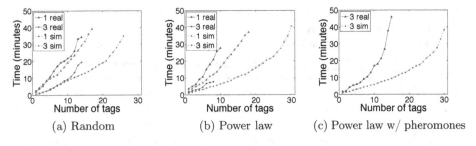

(a) Random   (b) Power law   (c) Power law w/ pheromones

Fig. 3. Time for 1 and 3 robots, real and simulated, to collect tags arranged in (a) random and (b) power law distributions using only site fidelity, and (c) for 3 robots on a power law distribution using pheromones and site fidelity.

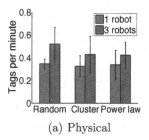
(a) Physical

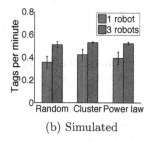
(b) Simulated

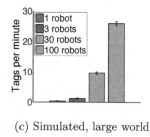
(c) Simulated, large world

Fig. 4. Rate of tag discovery per minute of experiment time for 1 and 3 (a) physical and (b) simulated robots in the 3 m area using only site fidelity, as well as (c) 1, 3, 30, and 100 simulated robots collecting tags in a large world with site fidelity and pheromones.

Figure 4 shows the the rate of tag collection per minute of experiment time for physical and simulated robots. Each bar denotes the collection rate over a particular tag distribution. We were not able to distinguish a significant effect of tag distribution on tag collection rate by the robots (General Linear Model [GLM]: $p > 0.1$; $n = 18$); but we did find a significant effect of distribution on tag collection rate using the larger sample size in simulation (GLM: $p < 0.001$; $n = 120$). In the simulations, the fastest tag collection was in the clustered distribution, followed by power law and then random distributions.

5   Discussion

We used ABMs and GAs to translate foraging behaviors of seed harvesting ants into algorithms for teams of RFID tag–seeking robots. We tested two algorithms: one in which robots rely on individual memory of locations of previously found tags (mimicking site fidelity), and one in which robots share tag locations as waypoints (mimicking pheromones) via a server that acts as the robots' nest.

Three robots find tags approximately twice as fast as 1 robot when using site fidelity. Site fidelity is an effective foraging strategy in ants and robots. It is extremely simple and easily encoded into very simple devices, including devices much simpler than the robots we used here. The approach is also highly parallelizable because it requires no communication among robots or the server.

Our approach, similar to [7], lays a foundation to explore the interplay between simulation and experiments with real robots. Simulated and real experiments with 1 and 3 robots using site fidelity show similar foraging rates (Fig. 3(a),(b) and Fig. 4(a),(b)), although simulated robots are slightly faster. This results from real robots having more difficulty with avoiding each other, physical hardware limitations, imperfect localization, and the possibility that real robots confuse each other with the nest.

Simulated foraging is highly scalable whether using site fidelity alone, or site fidelity augmented with pheromones when multiple tags are found in the same location. When we scale up to 100 robots in unbounded environments with many tags, teams of 100 robots collect resources 66 times faster than a single robot (Fig. 4(c)). This 34% decline in per-robot efficiency results from increased travel distance–an unavoidable consequence of central place foraging [14].

We implemented pheromone communication in real robots by having robots report found tag locations to a central server. Mimicking a strategy that was effective in our ant simulations, robots communicated a location as a waypoint to the server if the robot saw at least 2 additional tags in the vicinity. The server implements a simple pheromone algorithm and reports those locations to other robots. When we add this pheromone-like behavior to our robots, we observe robots clearing large clusters of tags faster; however, pheromones decreased the average tag collection rate in real robots relative to tag collection using only site fidelity. We attribute the lack of success primarily to error propagation: pheromones decrease performance when robots get lost and communicate incorrect locations to other robots, similar to [1].

Our results suggest that the approach of combining individual memory with communication at a central nest can transform simple robots into effective swarms that are scalable and robust to the loss or malfunction of a few individuals. Results of our 3 robot experiments include several instances in which one robot became lost or malfunctioned, but the other two robots continued their task. Such systems could be used for search and rescue, searching for resources or obstacles, and even biomedical applications using nano-robots.

Our next steps are to use a GA to optimize parameters that maximize efficiency and/or robustness in the robot ABM, and then import those parameters into the robots. For example, currently the robots report a pheromone to the server if there are 2 or more additional tags in the local neighborhood of the last tag found. We will use the GA to optimize the decision to lay pheromone and follow pheromone trails vs. returning to the last site food was found, optimizing the balance between shared and private information. Preliminary analysis suggests that the GA can evolve a pheromone-laying rule that significantly improves foraging over our current implementation. We will also extend analysis to different distributions, and will increase scalability by mimicking features of large ant colonies such as the use of mobile nests and of multiple nests.

Acknowledgments. This work was funded by NSF EF #1038682 and DARPA CRASH #P-1070-113237.

References

1. Bailis, P., Nagpal, R., Werfel, J.: Positional communication and private information in honeybee foraging models. Swarm Intelligence, 263–274 (2010)
2. Banerjee, S., Moses, M.: Scale invariance of immune system response rates and times: perspectives on immune system architecture and implications for artificial immune systems. Swarm Intelligence 4(4), 301–318 (2010)
3. Beverly, B., McLendon, H., et al.: How site fidelity leads to individual differences in the foraging activity of harvester ants. Behavioral Ecology 20(3), 633–638 (2009)

4. Bonabeau, E., Dorigo, M., Theraulaz, G.: Swarm intelligence: from natural to artificial systems. Oxford University Press, USA (1999)
5. Cao, Y., Fukunaga, A., Kahng, A.: Cooperative mobile robotics: Antecedents and directions. Autonomous Robots 4(1), 7–27 (1997)
6. Deneubourg, J., Goss, S., Franks, N., Sendova-Franks, A., et al.: The dynamics of collective sorting robot-like ants and ant-like robots. In: From Animals to Animats: Proc. of the 1st Int'l Conf. on Simulation of Adaptive Behavior, pp. 356–363 (1991)
7. Dorigo, M., Floreano, D., et al.: Swarmanoid: a novel concept for the study of heterogeneous robotic swarms. Tech. rep., Technical Report TR/IRIDIA/2011-014, IRIDIA, Université Libre de Bruxelles, Brussels, Belgium (2011)
8. Dorigo, M., Sahin, E.: Swarm robotics–special issue editorial. Autonomous Robots 17(2-3), 111–113 (2004)
9. Dorigo, M., Trianni, V., Şahin, E., Groß, R., Labella, T., et al.: Evolving self-organizing behaviors for a swarm-bot. Autonomous Robots 17(2), 223–245 (2004)
10. Flanagan, T., Letendre, K., Moses, M.E.: Quantifying the Effect of Colony Size and Food Distribution on Harvester Ant Foraging. PLoS ONE (in review)
11. Flanagan, T., Letendre, K., et al.: How Ants Turn Information into Food. In: Proceedings of the 2011 IEEE Conference on Artificial Life, pp. 178–185 (2011)
12. Gordon, D.: The spatial scale of seed collection by harvester ants. Oecologia 95(4), 479–487 (1993)
13. Hölldobler, B.: Recruitment behavior, home range orientation and territoriality in harvester ants, Pogonomyrmex. Behav. Ecol. and Sociobio. 1(1), 3–44 (1976)
14. Krieger, M., Billeter, J., Keller, L.: Ant-like task allocation and recruitment in cooperative robots. Nature 406, 992–995 (2000)
15. Letendre, K., Moses, M.E.: Ant foraging strategies: Site fidelity and recruitment alone and in combination (in review)
16. Mayet, R., Roberz, J., Schmickl, T., Crailsheim, K.: Antbots: A feasible visual emulation of pheromone trails for swarm robots. Swarm Intell., 84–94 (2011)
17. Moeslinger, C., Schmickl, T., Crailsheim, K.: Emergent flocking with low-end swarm robots. Swarm Intelligence, 424–431 (2011)
18. Mondada, F., Pettinaro, G., Kwee, I., Guignard, A., Gambardella, L., Floreano, D., Nolfi, S., Deneubourg, J., Dorigo, M.: SWARM-BOT: A swarm of autonomous mobile robots with self-assembling capabilities. In: Proc. of the Intl. Workshop on Self-organisation and Evolution of Social Behaviour, pp. 307–312 (2002)
19. Moses, M., Banerjee, S.: Biologically Inspired Design Principles for Scalable, Robust, Adaptive, Decentralized Search and Automated Response (RADAR). In: Proceedings of the 2011 IEEE Conference on Artificial Life, pp. 30–37 (2011)
20. Moses, M.: Metabolic scaling from individuals to societies. Ph.D. thesis, University of New Mexico (2005)
21. Mull, J., MacMahon, J.: Spatial variation in rates of seed removal by harvester ants (Pogonomyrmex occidentalis) in a shrub-steppe ecosystem. Am. Nat. (1997)
22. Nolfi, S., Florin, D.: Evolutionary robotics: The biology, intelligence, and technology of self-organizing machines. MIT Press (2000)
23. Parker, L.: Designing control laws for cooperative agent teams. In: IEEE International Conference on Robotics and Automation, pp. 582–587. IEEE (1993)
24. Sharkey, A.: Robots, insects and swarm intelligence. Artificial Intelligence Review 26(4), 255–268 (2006)
25. Trianni, V., Nolfi, S.: Engineering the Evolution of Self-Organizing Behaviors in Swarm Robotics: A Case Study. Artificial Life 17(3), 183–202 (2011)
26. Wittlinger, M., Wehner, R., Wolf, H.: The ant odometer: stepping on stilts and stumps. Science 312(5782), 1965 (2006)

Improving Peer Review with ACORN: ACO Algorithm for Reviewer's Network

Mark Flynn and Melanie Moses

Computer Science Department
University of New Mexico, Albuquerque, NM, USA
mflynn@unm.edu, melaniem@cs.unm.edu

Abstract. Peer review, our current system for determining which papers to accept for journals and conferences, has limitations that impair the quality of scientific communication. Under the current system, each paper receives an equal amount of attention regardless of how good the paper is. We propose to implement a new system for conference peer review based on ant colony optimization (ACO) algorithms. In our model, each reviewer has a set of ants that goes out and finds articles. The reviewer assesses the paper that the ant brings and the reviewer's ants deposit pheromone that is proportional to the quality of the review. Subsequent ants select the next article based on pheromone strength. We used an agent-based model to determine that an ACO-based paper selection system will direct reviewers' attention to the best articles and correctly rank them based on the papers' quality.

1 Introduction

The peer review system is the cornerstone of the vast majority of modern scientific communication. It is the method for determining which research is suitable for dissemination and where it should appear. Despite the success of the current system, there are some disadvantages of peer review. There are questions of fairness and bias towards established authors, and how big a role chance plays in determining whether a paper is accepted[15]. Computer science publishing is based on conference proceedings. A small group of reviewers is tasked with determining which papers are suitable for presentation at the conference and later inclusion in the proceedings and also assigning them to groups based on the paper's topic. The restricted pool of reviewers means that each reviewer must assess many papers and each paper can only be seen by a few reviewers. Furthermore, each paper receives the same amount of attention from the reviewers regardless of how good the paper is. Peer review purports to objectively determine which papers are suitable for publication. However, when this has been tested experimentally, the probability that reviewers agree with each other is no better than chance[17] and that the process is very poor at identifying flaws[8].

ACO algorithms have been used to efficiently allocate limited resources, such as for the traveling salesperson problem (TSP)[19], engineering applications such as the design of VLSI chips[1] network routing[12] and data mining[16]. The

M. Dorigo et al. (Eds.): ANTS 2012, LNCS 7461, pp. 260–267, 2012.

ACO algorithm is a metaheuristic that has been used to solve combinatorial optimization problems.

We propose to implement a new system for computer science peer review based on ant colony optimization (ACO) algorithms. In our model, each reviewer has a set of ants that goes out and finds articles. The reviewer assesses the paper that the ant brings according to the criteria specified by the conference organizers and the ant deposits pheromone that is proportional to the quality of the review. Each subsequent ant then samples the pheromones and probabilistically selects the next article based on the strength of the pheromones. We used an agent-based model (ABM) to determine if an ACO-based paper selection system will direct reviewers' attention to the best articles and if the average quality of papers increases with each round of reviews. Additionally, if the goal is to determine which papers will be accepted, the model can also be used to determine which papers exceed a given cutoff. For example, if the conference can only accept the top 40% of the papers they receive; those papers that are closest to the cutoff would receive the most scrutiny. We also looked at the sensitivity of the model to amount of agreement on paper quality and the degree of trust among the reviewers on convergence of the model on the target paper quality. To assess the utility of our approach, we compared our algorithm to a recommender system based on latent factor analysis.

2   Methods

To test whether our ACO network would be useful for evaluating and sorting papers for a CS conference, we simulated the peer review process using an agent-based model. The agents in this model are ants that search through the papers and bring them to the reviewers. Paper quality was modeled as a normal distribution. The mean of the distribution was a quality score which could be considered the ground truth. This would be the paper's score if it was reviewed by a large number of reviewers such that further reviews would be unlikely to change the score. Each of these means was drawn from an overall normal distribution in order to reflect the diversity of papers a conference is likely to receive, and the amount of diversity was determined by the distributions standard deviation. This overall standard deviation controlled how dissimilar the paper qualities were. Each paper had its own standard deviation, for its own distribution which determines how widely the reviews for the paper can vary. The higher the paper's standard deviation, the less likely different reviewers will agree with each other. This was a parameter of the model that we varied to examine the effect of reviewer agreement on the ability of the network to converge on the target paper score.

Another factor we considered was reviewer bias; each reviewer may have a tendency to rate papers either higher or lower than the mean. We modeled this by skewing the normal distribution from which the paper scores were drawn by a factor that was unique for each reviewer. This skew factor was chosen by randomly selecting a factor from a normal distribution with a 0 mean and a standard deviation which was varied from 0 to 4 to determine the effect of the amount of bias on the algorithm's ability to pick the best papers. Each review consisted of selecting a score from this skewed normal distribution.

To ensure that each paper was reviewed at least once, each ant randomly selected a paper until all papers had received one review. The reviewers selected the score (on a scale of 1 to 10) from the skewed normal distribution and placed a pheromone trail to the paper that is equal to the reviewers score. For subsequent rounds of reviews, the ants sample the pheromone trails and select the next paper for review probabilistically based on the average quality of the reviews for each paper up to that point. Since paper quality is static, we did not include evaporation as has been done for other implementations of the ACO algorithm [18]. The probability of a $paper_i$ being selected by $reviewer_j$ was determined using an exponential equation:

$$
p_{ij} = \begin{cases} \dfrac{b^{(\bar{\tau}_i - \tau_\mu)}}{\sum_{i \in N_j} b^{(\bar{\tau}_i - \tau_\mu)}} & \text{if } i \in N_j, \\ 0 & \text{otherwise.} \end{cases}
\tag{1}
$$

Where N_j is the list of unread papers for $reviewer_j$, $\bar{\tau}_i$ is the mean pheromone value for the ith paper, τ_μ is the average pheromone value for all papers. The base factor, b, reflects how much the reviewers trust the opinions of the other reviewers. The effect of this equation is that the higher the base factor, the more likely that the papers other reviewers rated highly are selected. The exponential form was chosen for (1) to implicitly model the positive feedback effect of ants reinforcing pheromone trails. The base factor was the same for each paper. We varied b between 1 and 2 to investigate the role of trust in directing reviewers attention to the best papers.

To assess how our algorithm matches up to other methods for selecting papers, we compared our algorithm with other methods for selecting papers to be reviewed. First we used a greedy algorithm that always selected the best paper that the reviewer has not reviewed yet. Unlike our ant-based algorithm, papers were selected deterministically based on the quality of the previous reviews, instead of probabilistically. Next, we tried recommender system algorithms, which are used extensively by online retailers to direct customers to products they might like[14]. We used a type of recommender system called collaborative filtering where the previous history of reviews is used to predict whether a user will like other items. We used a type of collaborative filtering called latent factor analysis[3] to detect underlying patterns in the user-response matrix (URM) to predict ratings for un-reviewed papers. Reviewers were directed to the papers that the algorithm predicted would get the highest score for that reviewer. One problem inherent to collaborative filtering is making recommendations when there is no history. We used the greedy algorithm when the recommender algorithm was unable to select a new paper. This is not a problem for the ACO algorithm since it assumes that all users will have similar opinions about all of the items.

We compared the ability of each algorithm (ACO, greedy and SVD) to pick the best paper given the variability of the papers and the biases of the reviewers. We determined the correlations between the *a priori* paper quality (the ground truth that was determined before the simulation was run) and the number of reviews the paper received. We also determined the correlation between paper quality and the average quality of the papers reviewed for each round of reviews. Each round was considered one time step and the pheromone trails were updated after each review. Each simulation was run 20 times to average the variability due to the stochastic elements of the simulations. We analyzed the response of the three algorithms to varying levels of reviewer bias by varying the standard deviation of the zero-mean normal distribution from which the skew factors were drawn and the effects of paper quality variability by varying the standard deviation of the distribution from which the paper means are drawn. The skew factor for each reviewer determines the amount the paper score distribution deviates from the normal distribution, while the standard deviation determines the width of the normal distribution. Each paper would then consist of a unique distribution for each reviewer determined by the mean and standard deviation for that paper and the skew factor for the reviewer.

3 Results

Our goal was to determine whether an ACO algorithm could direct reviewers' attention to the simulated papers that were deemed most important. First, we tested the ability of our algorithm to determine which papers were the best (based on the quality assigned at the beginning of the simulation) and how sensitive this determination was to variation in the parameters. The base factor (b) was set to 2 and the standard deviation of the paper reviews was set to 2. We found that there was a positive correlation between the quality of a paper and the number of reviews it receives (Fig. 1).

To determine the interaction between base factor and the standard deviation of the paper scores, the Pearson product-moment correlation coefficient was computed for each combination of base factor and standard deviation. Figure 2 shows the effects of these interactions on the correlation of the number of papers a reviewer has evaluated up to that point and the quality of the papers reviewed. There was a large increase in this correlation between 1 and 1.25 and then the correlation plateaued above 1.5. This correlation was less sensitive to decreasing the amount of agreement among reviewers.

The number of reviews a paper received was also very dependent on the b for values between 1 and 1.25 and plateaued above 1.5. However, the effect of increasing the variability of the reviews was much less; there were only significant decreases for values of b equal to 1.5 or below (Table 1).

We compared the performance of the ACO, greedy and recommender algorithms in their ability to find the best paper. Figure 3 shows that all three were able to direct the ants to the best papers, with the ACO and greedy algorithms outperforming the recommender system.

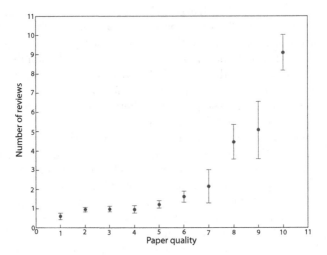

Fig. 1. Plot of number of reviews (±SEM) for each paper of a given quality. Higher quality papers receive more reviews.

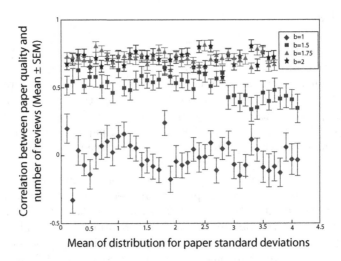

Fig. 2. Decreasing the influence of other reviewers opinions on paper selection decreases correlation between paper quality and the number of reviews a paper receives

Table 1. correlations (r) and significance values (p) for paper quality vs. number of reviews

	$b = 1$	$b = 1.25$	$b = 1.5$	$b = 1.75$	$b = 2$
r	-0.1313	-0.6248	-0.4827	-0.1910	0.0431
p	0.4131	0.0000	0.0014	0.2316	0.7891

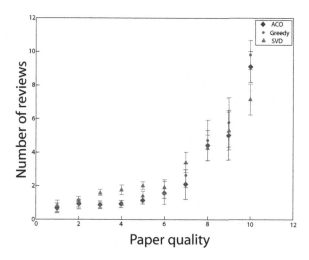

Fig. 3. Comparison of ACO, greedy and recommender algorithms

None of the algorithms were affected by the amount of skew in the range that was tested (p= 0.6344, 0.1632, 0.3079, respectively). Both the ACO and greedy algorithms were significantly different from the recommender algorithm ($p <$ 0.0001 for both) while the ACO algorithm was better than the greedy algorithm ($p < 0.001$). When we tested the ability of all three algorithms to correctly rank papers, however, we found that the ACO algorithm was better at determining where the papers should be ranked (Fig. 4).

4   Conclusion

We found that our system for changing the peer review process can successfully direct reviewers attention to the best papers. The best papers received the most reviews and the algorithm could rank the papers correctly. We found that the ACO algorithm was robust to decreasing reviewer agreement while remaining sensitive to changes in the base factor necessary for emphasizing the best papers. Changing the goal to selecting papers nearest to a cutoff for acceptance is equivalent to selecting the best paper, since it is only a matter of rescaling the paper scores by distance from the cutoff. This would favor the papers nearest the cutoff instead of the papers that received the best reviews.

While all three algorithms were able to find the best papers, the ACO-based algorithm was more robust to inaccurate reviews. The probablistic nature of the ACO algorithm was less sensitive to errors. While both algorithms use positive feedback to increase the likelihood that the best papers are selected for reviews[7], the greedy algorithm is more susceptible to errors since it always takes the best paper available and if a low quality paper is given an overly generous first review the network is less able to recover. The probabilistic ACO

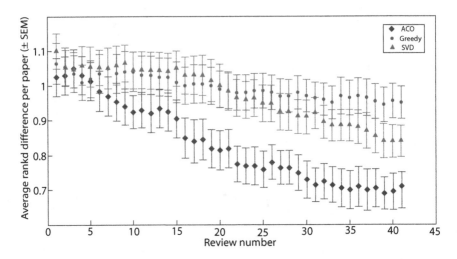

Fig. 4. Comparison of paper ranking by ACO, greedy and recommender algorithms

algorithm exhibits better fault-tolerance because in a sense it is exploring multiple solutions in parallel[7], while the greedy algorithm converges on the best solution at the time, even if it is not close to the optimal. While the reason for the poor performance by the recommender system has not been determined, one possibility could be a problem inherent to this type of algorithm. Collaboration-based recommender systems rely on patterns in the user-item matrix. Especially in the beginning, the user-response matrix is very sparse and so it is unlikely that the performance of the recommender system could be improved.

Acknowledgments. This work was funded by NSF EF #1038682 and DARPA CRASH #P-1070-113237.

References

1. Arora, T., Moses, M.: Using ant colony optimization for routing in VLSI. In: 1st International Conference on Bio-Inspired Computational Methods Used for Difficult Problem Solving: Development of Intelligent and Complex Systems. AIP Conference Proceedings, pp. 145–156 (2009)
2. Beckers, R., Deneubourg, J.L., Goss, S.: Trails and U-turns in the Selection of a Path by the Ant Lasius niger. J. Theor. Biol. 159, 397–415 (1992)
3. Bell, R., Koren, Y., Volinsky, C.: Matrix Factorization Techniques for Recommender Systems. IEEE Computer Society 42, 30–37 (2009)
4. Chubin, D.E., Hackett, E.J.: Peer review and the printed word. In: Peerless Science: Peer Review and U.S. Science Policy. SUNY Press, Albany (1990)
5. Deneubourg, J.L., Lioni, A., Detrain, C.: Dynamics of aggregation and emergence of cooperation. Biol. Bull. 202, 262–267 (2002)
6. Deneubourg, J.L., Pasteels, J.M., Verhaeghe, J.C.: Probablistic Behaviour in Ants: A Strategy of Errors? J. Theor. Biol. 105, 259–271 (1983)

7. Dorigo, M., Maniezzo, V., Colorni, A.: The Ant System: Optimization by a colony of cooperating agents. IEEE Transactions on Systems, Man, and Cybernetics Part B: Cybernetics 26, 29–41 (1996)
8. Godlee, F., Gale, C.R., Martyn, C.N.: Effect on the quality of peer review of blinding reviewers and asking them to sign their reports: a randomized controlled trial. JAMA 280, 237–240 (1998)
9. Goss, S., Aron, S., Deneubourg, J.L., Pasteels, J.M.: Self-organized shortcuts in the Argentine ant. Naturwissenschaften 76, 579–581 (1989)
10. SVD Recommendation System in Ruby, http://www.igvita.com/2007/01/15/svd-recommendation-system-in-ruby
11. Grimm, V.B., et al.: Ecological Modelling 198, 115-126 (2006)
12. Kwang, M.S., Weng, H.S.: Ant colony optimization for routing and load-balancing: survey and new directions. IEEE Transactions on Systems, Man and Cybernetics, Part A: Systems and Humans 33, 560–572 (2003)
13. Melville, P., Mooney, R.J., Nagarajan, R.: Content-Boosted Collaborative Filtering for Improved Recommendations. In: Proceedings of the Eighteenth National Conference on Artificial Intelligence, AAAI 2002, pp. 187–192 (2002)
14. Melville, P., Sindhwani, V.: Recommender Systems. In: Sammut, G., Webb, G. (eds.) Encyclopedia of Machine Learning. Springer, Berlin (2010)
15. Neff, B.D., Olden, J.D.: Is Peer Review a Game of Chance? Bioscience 56, 333–340 (2006)
16. Parpinelli, R.S., Lopes, H.S., Freitas, A.A.: Data mining with an ant colony optimization algorithm. IEEE Transactions on Evolutionary Computation 6, 321–332 (2002)
17. Rothwell, P.M., Martyn, C.N.: Reproducibility of peer review in clinical neuroscience. Is agreement between reviewers any greater than would be expected by chance alone? Brain 123(pt 9), 1964–1969 (2000)
18. Dorigo, M., Birattari, M., Stützle, T.: Ant Colony Optimization: Artificial Ants as a Computational Intelligence Technique. IEEE Computational Intelligence Magazine 1, 39 (2006)
19. Dorigo, M., Gambardella, L.M.: Ant colony system: a cooperative learning approach to the traveling salesman problem. IEEE Transactions on Evolutionary Computation 1, 53–66 (1997)

Learning Finite-State Machines
with Ant Colony Optimization

Daniil Chivilikhin and Vladimir Ulyantsev

Saint-Petersburg National Research University of Information Technologies,
Mechanics and Optics, Saint-Petersburg, Russia
chivilikhin.daniil@gmail.com

Abstract. In this paper we present a new method of learning Finite-State Machines (FSM) with the specified value of a given fitness function, which is based on an Ant Colony Optimization algorithm (ACO) and a graph representation of the search space. The input data is a set of events, a set of actions and the number of states in the target FSM and the goal is to maximize the given fitness function, which is defined on the set of all FSMs with given parameters. Comparison of the new algorithm and a genetic algorithm (GA) on benchmark problems shows that the new algorithm either outperforms GA or works just as well.

1 Introduction

Finite-state machines can be applied to various problems. FSMs have proven to be a good representation of agent strategies [1]. They are also used as efficient representations of large dictionaries [2]. In a programming paradigm called automata-based programming [3] FSMs are used as key components of software systems.

The problem of inducting finite-state machines for a given fitness function has drawn the attention of many researchers. The common approach to this problem is the use of various evolutionary algorithms (EA). In [1] Spears and Gordon used evolutionary strategies (ES) to learn FSMs for the Competition for Resources problem. In [4] and [5] a GA was used for inducting a FSM from test examples with a special crossover operator based on tests. In [2] Lucas and Reynolds used an EA to learn deterministic finite automata from labeled data samples. Another GA was used in [6] to build an optimal solution of the John Muir food trail problem. EA have proven to be efficient in cases when FSMs cannot be built heuristically.

The optimization problem we are solving is formulated in the following way: given the number of states N, a set of events Σ and a set of actions Δ build a FSM with the specified target value of the fitness function f.

We propose a new local-search heuristic method of learning FSMs based on ACO and compare it with GA in terms of performance.

M. Dorigo et al. (Eds.): ANTS 2012, LNCS 7461, pp. 268–275, 2012.

2   ACO Overview

In ACO, the solutions are built by a set of artificial ants which use a stochastic strategy. The solutions can be represented either as paths in the graph, or simply by graph vertices. Each edge (u, v) of the graph (u and v are vertices of the graph) has an assigned pheromone value τ_{uv} and can also have an associated heuristic distance η_{uv}. The pheromone values are modified by the ants in the process of solution construction, while the heuristic distances are assigned initially and are not changed. An ACO algorithm consists of three major steps which are repeated until a viable solution is found or a stop criterion is met. In the first step — ConstructSolutions — each ant explores the graph following a certain path. The ant chooses the next edge to visit according to the pheromone value and heuristic distance of this edge. When an edge has been selected, the ant appends it to its path and moves to the next node. In the next stage — UpdatePheromones — the pheromone values of all graph edges are modified. A particular pheromone value can increase if the edge it is associated with has been traveled by an ant or it can decrease due to evaporation. The amount of pheromone that each ant deposits on a graph edge depends on the quality of the solution built by this ant, which is measured by the fitness function value of this solution. On the last (optional) stage — DaemonActions — some procedure is executed performing actions that cannot be performed by individual ants.

When we apply ACO to FSM generation we have to deal with huge graphs, sometimes consisting of several millions vertices. In our work we apply a variation of the *expansion technique* introduced in [7] – we limit the ant path lengths to reduce the size of the graph we store in memory.

3   Finite-State Machines and Search Space Representation

We formally define a finite-state machine as a sextuple $(S, \Sigma, \Delta, \delta, \lambda, s_0)$. Here, S is a set of states, Σ is a set of input events, Δ is a set of output actions. δ is a transition function mapping a state and an event to another state, i.e. $\delta(s, e) = t$, where $s, t \in S$, $e \in \Sigma$. λ is a transition function mapping a state and an event to an output action, i.e. $\lambda(s, e) = a$, where $s \in S$, $e \in \Sigma$, $a \in \Delta$ and s_0 is the initial state.

Informally speaking, a mutation of a FSM is a small change in its structure. In this work we consider two FSM mutation types:

- **Change transition end state.** For a random transition in the FSM, the transition's end state is set to another state selected uniformly randomly from the set of all states S.
- **Change transition action.** For a random transition in the FSM, the transition's output action is set to another action selected uniformly randomly from the set of actions Δ.

The search space, which is a set of all FSMs with the specified parameters, is represented in the form of a directed graph G with the following properties:

- the vertices of G are associated with FSMs;
- let u be a vertex associated with FSM A_1 and v be a vertex associated with FSM A_2. If machine A_2 lays within one mutation from A_1 then G contains edges $u \to v$ and $v \to u$. Otherwise, nodes u and v are not connected with an edge.

For each pair of FSMs A_1 and A_2 and the corresponding pair of vertices u and v, there exists a path in G from u to v and also from v to u.

4   The Proposed Algorithm

The overall scheme of our algorithm complies with the classical ant colony optimization algorithm with a few modifications. First we generate an initial random solution. While stagnation is not reached, the artificial ants select paths in the graph, building it in process and deposit pheromone on the graph edges.

4.1   Path Construction

First we need to select a node for each ant to start from. If the graph is empty, we generate a random initial solution (a FSM) and place all the ants into the node associated with that solution. This random initial solution is generated by randomly defining the transition functions of a FSM with a fixed number of states. If the number of nodes in the graph is greater than zero, then the start nodes for the ants are selected randomly from the list of nodes in the best path — a path traveled by a certain ant leading to the solution with the highest fitness function value.

Let the artificial ant be located in a node u associated with FSM A. If this node has successors, then the ant selects the next node v to visit according to the rules discussed below — search space expansion and stochastic path selection.

Search Space Expansion. With a probability of p_{new} the ant attempts to construct new edges of the graph by making N_{mut} mutations of A. The procedure of processing a single mutation of machine A is as follows:

- construct a mutated FSM A_{mutated};
- find a node t in graph G associated with A_{mutated}. If G does not contain such a node, construct a new node and associate it with A_{mutated};
- add an edge (u, t) to G.

After all N_{mut} mutations have been made, the ant selects the best newly constructed node v and moves to that node.

Stochastic Path Selection. With a probability of $(1 - p_{\text{new}})$ the ant stochastically selects the next node from the existing successors set N_u of node u. Node v is selected with a probability defined by the classical ACO formula:

$$p_{uv} = \frac{\tau_{uv}^{\alpha} \cdot \eta_{uv}^{\beta}}{\sum_{w \in N_u} \tau_{uw}^{\alpha} \cdot \eta_{uw}^{\beta}}, \tag{1}$$

where $v \in N_u$ and $\alpha, \beta \in [0, 1]$. In our algorithm all the heuristic distances η_{uv} are considered to be equal and do not influence path selection, β does not influence path selection and α equals one at all times.

If u does not have any successors, then the next node is selected according to the search space expansion rule with a probability of 1.0.

4.2   Controlling Graph Growth

We use the following mechanisms for controlling the graph growth rate:

- each ant is given at most n_{stag} steps to make without an increase in its best fitness value. When the ant exceeds this number, it is stopped;
- the whole colony of artificial ants is given at most N_{stag} iterations to run without an increase in the best fitness value. After this number of iterations is exceeded, the algorithm is restarted.

4.3   Pheromone Update

For each graph edge (u, v) we store $\Delta \tau_{uv}^{best}$ – the best pheromone value that any ant has ever deposited on edge (u, v). For each ant path, a sub-path is selected that spans from the start of the path to the best node in the path. The values of $\Delta \tau_{uv}^{best}$ are updated for all edges along this sub-path. Next, for each graph edge (u, v), the pheromone value is updated according to the classical formula:

$$\tau_{uv} = \rho \tau_{uv} + \Delta \tau_{uv}^{best}, \tag{2}$$

where $\rho \in [0, 1]$ is the evaporation rate.

5   Experimental Evaluation

To evaluate the efficiency of our algorithm, we applied it to the following problems:

- inducting finite-state transducers based on test examples [4] [5];
- inducting a finite-state machine for the John Muir food trail problem [6].

5.1   Inducting FSMs from Test Examples

Fitness Evaluation Method. The input data for this problem is the set of possible events, the set of possible actions, the number of states in the target FSM and a set of test examples. Each of the test examples consists of an events sequence Inputs[i] and a corresponding actions sequence Actions[i]. For fitness function evaluation, each events sequence Inputs[i] is given as input to the FSM, and the resulting output sequence Outputs[i] is recorded. After running the FSM on all test examples, the following value is calculated:

$$FF_1 = \frac{1}{n} \sum_{i=1}^{n} \left(1 - \frac{ED\left(Outputs[i], Actions[i]\right)}{max\left(|Outputs[i]|, |Actions[i]|\right)} \right) \tag{3}$$

Here, n is the number of test examples and $ED\,(s_1, s_2)$ denotes the edit distance between strings s_1 and s_2. The final expression for the fitness function has the form:

$$FF_2 = 100 \cdot FF_1 + \frac{1}{100}\left(100 - n_{\text{transitions}}\right) \tag{4}$$

Here, $n_{\text{transitions}}$ is the number of transitions in the FSM. Note that we do not evolve the output sequences on the FSM transitions — we use a technique introduced in [5] and used in [4] called smart transition labeling. The idea is to evolve the numbers of output actions for each transition instead of the output sequences themselves. The output sequences for each transition are selected optimally using a simple algorithm based on test examples.

Alarm Clock Problem Description. An alarm clock has three buttons for setting the current time, setting the alarm to a specific time and turning it on or off. The alarm clock has two operation modes – one mode for setting the current time and another one for setting the alarm time. When the alarm is off, the user can push the buttons H and M to increment the hours and minutes of the current time respectively. If the user presses the A button, the clock is switched to the alarm setting mode. In this mode the same buttons H and M are used to adjust the time when the alarm should sound. When the user presses the A button in this mode, the alarm is set to go off when the current time will be equal to the alarm time. When the alarm is ringing, the user can press the A button to switch it off, however it will automatically turn off after one minute. The alarm clock also contains a timer that increments the current time each minute. This system has four input events and seven output actions.

We compare the efficiency of our algorithm with the results obtained in [6] using a GA. The goal of the experiment was to generate a heuristically built FSM that satisfies all the test examples, has three states and 14 transitions.

Experiment. In the experiment we searched for the solution among FSMs with four nominal states following the experimental setup in [5]. Our algorithn had the following values of parameters: $N - 5$, $\rho - 0.5$, $n_{\text{stag}} - 20$, $N_{\text{stag}} - 4$, $N_{\text{mut}} -20$, $p_{\text{new}} - 0.6$.

We have performed 1000 runs of our algorithm and also 1000 runs of the GA and measured the average number of fitness evaluations used to generate the target FSM. Results show that the ACO algorithm required an average of 53944 fitness evaluations, while GA required more than twice as much — an average of 117977 fitness evaluations. The transition diagram of one of the constructed FSMs is shown on Figure 1. The start state on this diagram and all the other diagrams in this paper is always state 1.

5.2   The Food Trail Problem

Problem Description. The food trail problem, described in [8], is considered to be a benchmark problem for testing the performance of evolutionary algorithms. The objective is to find a program controlling an agent (called an ant) in

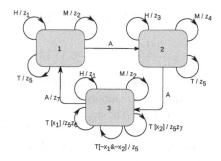

Fig. 1. Finite-state machine for the alarm clock problem

a game performed on a square toroidal field 32 by 32 cells. There are 89 pieces of food (apples) distributed along a certain trail in this field. In the beginning of the game, the ant is located in the leftmost upper cell and is looking east. The field, food trail and the ant's position at the beginning of the game are shown on Figure 2. The black squares indicate the food, the white squares are empty and the gray squares show the trail.

The ant can determine whether the next cell contains a piece of food or not. On each step it can turn left, turn right or move forward, eating a piece of food if the next cell contains one. The target controlling program must allow the ant to eat all 89 apples in no more than 200 steps.

In this problem there are two input events – N (the next cell does not contain an apple) and F (the next cell contains an apple) and three output actions: L (turn left), R (turn right) and M (move forward).

The solution proposed in [3] is to build a finite-state machine controlling the ant. The authors of [6] achieved the best-known solution of this problem using GA. The generated FSMs contained seven states and allowed the ant to eat all 89 apples in less than 200 steps. The construction of such a FSM in two different experiments took the GA 160 and 250 million fitness evaluations respectively.

Experiments. We have performed two different experiments on this problem. In the first experiment we tried to search for the solution among FSMs with seven states, copying the experimental setup of [6]. Our algorithm produced two valid solutions after 143 and 221 million fitness evaluations correspondingly. For the second experiment, we chose to expand the search space and search for the target FSM among FSMs with 12 states. We still wanted the solution FSM to contain only seven states, therefore we modified the classical fitness function:

$$f(A) = n + \frac{200 - n_{\text{steps}}}{200} \tag{5}$$

Here, A is the FSM, n is the number of eaten apples and n_{steps} is the number of the step on which the ant ate the last apple. Our modified fitness function takes into account the number of states visited by the FSM in the process of fitness evaluation:

$$f(A) = n + \frac{200 - n_{\text{steps}}}{200} + 0.1 \cdot (M - N) \tag{6}$$

Here, M is the number of states in the initial FSM and N is the number of visited states. We have performed 30 runs of our algorithm with the following values of parameters: $N - 10$, $\rho - 0.5$, $n_{\text{stag}} - 40$, $N_{\text{stag}} - 200$, $N_{\text{mut}} - 40$, $p_{\text{new}} - 0.5$. This experiment was performed for the ACO algorithm only, because an experiment with the GA algorithm would require certain changes in its code, which we did not have access to.

Results show that in this case our algorithm only requires an average of 37.29 million fitness evaluations to reach the desired solution. The transition diagram of one of the generated FSMs is shown on Figure 3. This machine allows an ant to eat all food in 189 steps.

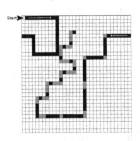

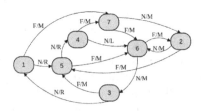

Fig. 2. The field in the food trail problem (John Muir trail)

Fig. 3. Finite-state machine for the food trail problem

6   Conclusion

We have developed an ACO-based local-search heuristic method of learning finite-state machines for a given fitness function. ACO is used to find an optimal vertex in a graph, where vertices are associated with FSMs and edges are associated with mutations of FSMs. The efficiency of the proposed algorithm has been compared to GA on the problem of inducting FST from test examples and on the John Muir food trail problem. On both problems our method has either outperformed GA or worked just as well.

References

1. Spears, W.M., Gordon, D.E.: Evolving finite-state machine strategies for protecting resources. In: Proceedings of the International Symposium on Methodologies for Intelligeng Systems, pp. 166–175 (2000)

2. Lucas, S., Reynolds, J.: Learning dfa: Evolution versus evidence driven state merging. In: The 2003 Congress on Evolutionary Computation (CEC 2003), vol. 1, pp. 351–348 (2003)
3. Polykarpova, N., Shalyto, A.: Automata-based programming. Piter (2009) (in Russian)
4. Tsarev, F., Egorov, K.: Finite-state machine induction using genetic algorithm based on testing and model checking. In: Proceedings of the 2011 GECCO Conference Companion on Genetic and Evolutionary Computation (GECCO 2011), pp. 759–762 (2011), http://doi.acm.org/10.1145/2001858.2002085, doi:10.1145/2001858.2002085
5. Tsarev, F.: Method of finite-state machine induction from tests with genetic programming. Information and Control Systems (Informatsionno-upravljayushiye sistemy, in Russian) (5), 31–36 (2010)
6. Tsarev, F., Shalyto, A.: Use of genetic programming for finite-state machine generation in the smart ant problem. In: Proceedings of the IV International Scientific-Practical Conference "Integrated Models and Soft Calculations in Artificial Intelligence", vol. (2), pp. 590–597 (2007)
7. Alba, E., Chicano, F.: Acohg: dealing with huge graphs. In: Proceedings of the 9th Annual Conference on Genetic and Evolutionary Computing (GECCO 2007), pp. 10–17 (2007), http://doi.acm.org/10.1145/1276958.1276961, doi:10.1145/1276958.1276961
8. Koza, J.: Genetic Programming: On the Programming of Computers by Natural Selection. MIT Press, Cambridge (1992)

Mobbing Behavior and Deceit and Its Role in Bio-inspired Autonomous Robotic Agents

Justin Davis and Ronald Arkin

Mobile Robotics Lab, Georgia Institute of Technology, Atlanta, GA, USA
{justindavis,arkin}@cc.gatech.edu

Abstract. Arabian babblers are highly preyed upon avians living in the Israeli desert. The survival of this species is contingent upon successful predator deterrence known as mobbing. Their ability to successfully defend against larger predators is the inspiration for this research with the goal of employing new models of robotic deception. Using Grafen's Dishonesty Model [8], simulation results are presented, which portend the value of this behavior in military situations.

1 Introduction

Mobbing is an anti-predator behavior mainly displayed in cooperative birds but can also be found in animals such as meerkats [7] and squirrels [10]. This behavior is a prime example of the handicap principle which claims that signals with a high cost must be honest [13]. One such model that incorporates deceit into the handicap principle is Grafen's Dishonesty Model [8]. Our research has created a model based on Grafen's approach. In our researchwe replicate situations encountered during the mobbing process and determine when it is advantageous to deceive. This research extends and expands our previous research in deceptive behavior that focused on human models of cognition [11]. In that earlier work, deception was defined simply as a false communication that benefits the communicator (from [4]), and we continue to use that definition in this paper. One species often associated with the handicap principle that exhibits this mobbing behavior is the Arabian Babbler. The observed behavior of this bird will serve as the inspiration for the robotic simulation that follows.

In this research we model the mobbing process, most importantly group formation during mobbing, integrate Grafen's dishonesty model, and examine its utility in the context of multiagent robotics. Our preliminary results are provided via simulation studiesThe motivation behind this research is for determining when to invoke robotic deception based on principles that transcend individual biological species, specifically in situations when the reward for deceit outweighs the cost of being caught. This can pertain to military operation. For example, a robot that is threatened might feign the ability to combat adversaries: being honest about the robot's abilities risks capture or destruction while deception could possibly drive away the threat. Feigning strength is a tactic used regularly in military combat [2].

M. Dorigo et al. (Eds.): ANTS 2012, LNCS 7461, pp. 276–283, 2012.

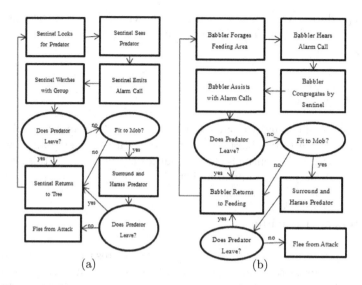

Fig. 1. Mobbing Process for the Sentinel and the Individual Babbler

2 Mobbing Behavior

In this section, we develop the underlying behavior for the deception scenario within which our model is tested. Mobbing is defined as the gathering of members of a group around a potentially dangerous individual. The purpose of this behavior is to deter and drive away potential predators [9]. While it is exhibited by many different species, it is most commonly associated in avians. The mobbing birds react to a perceived threat by surrounding it and cooperatively harassing it, usually by making noises and flapping their wings.

A popular example of mobbing is displayed in the Arabian Babbler (Turdoides squamiceps). In babblers, the behavior is determined by group makeup and individual fitness. A group of babblers can consist of anywhere from 2 to 14 birds [13]. When a group begins to forage in a feeding area, a single babbler assumes the role of sentinel [13]. The sentinel perches in the tree that gives it the best view of its group and approaching predators [12].

The mobbing processes for the sentinel and individual babbler are shown in figures 1a and 1b respectively. It begins when the sentinel spies a potential danger. It responds by emitting an alarm. Upon hearing this alarm call, individual babblers congregate in the sentinel's tree and assist in issuing these alarm calls. If the predator still approaches the group and perches nearby, the babblers approach and mob the predator. The predator responds by either leaving or attacking one of the mobbing birds [13].

While there are several factors in determining the flock's decision to mob, the work described here focuses on an individual babbler's perceived ability to escape. This is the aspect of the mobbing process where deception will be injected into the system. Here, a babbler may deceive regarding its fitness in order to deter the predator. While there is no direct evidence to suggest this occurs in nature, it presents an interesting variation for robotic decisions regarding feigning behavior.

2.1 Sentinel

The role of sentinel is usually assumed by the alpha male or another high-ranking male [13]. For each group of babblers, there is only one sentinel at any given time. In a natural setting, the sentinels change, but for the purposes of this simulation, the sentinel will be predetermined and static.

2.2 Handicap Principle

The Handicap Principle, developed by Zahavi [13], states that if an animal wastes its personal resources to produce a signal, then that signal must be honest. Its application to mobbing is that babblers will not approach a predator if they do not believe they can escape it. If the babbler does approach, it is wasting the resources of cover from the trees and a head start to escape from the predator. By wasting these resources, it is demonstrating that it can survive without them. If it could not tolerate losing these resources and attempts to mob the predator anyway, that babbler becomes vulnerable to an attack. In that case, the babbler would not be able to survive should the predator decide to attack it, and thus deceiving with respect to its low fitness was not the appropriate choice according to the handicap principle.

2.3 Deception

The purpose of this research is to model the mobbing behavior and determine what value it affords robots and what value is added by injecting deception into the process. While Zahavi maintains that signals produced through wasted resources must be honest, Grafen claims there can exist an acceptable level of cheating that will keep the system stable [8]. Grafen details inequalities in which cheating would be the best strategy for the signaler. The derived model is based upon the Philip Sydney game [8].

2.4 Group Control

Mob formation does not have an exact spatial layout and positioning as was the case in our earlier work on formations [3], but some spatial constraints define the mob structure. In earlier work [6], bird lekking behavior was used for group formation in a different context. Utilizing this pre-existing group formation behavior is an easy solution for implementation.

3 Computational Model

3.1 Sentinel and Individual Behavior

The computational model for the sentinel behavior is shown in figures 2a and 2b, and is derived from the behavioral processes shown in figures 1a and 1b. Each component behavioral assemblage (an aggregation of primitive behaviors [1]) and their associated transitions (behavioral triggers) are described extensively in the computational model section of [5](including for the predator).

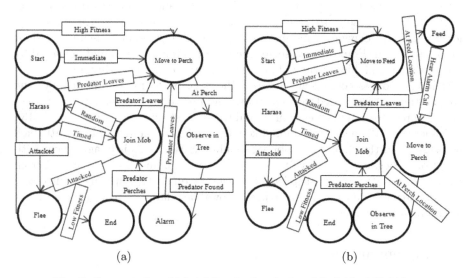

Fig. 2. Computational Model for the Sentinel and Indvidual Babbler

3.2 Grafen's Dishonesty Model

Equation 1 is derived from Grafen's dishonesty model [8].

$$X = 1 + t + 2r(Sd - 1)$$
$$Mob \begin{cases} \text{Yes } Sb > X \\ \text{No } Sb \leq X \end{cases}$$

(1)

where S_b is the individual babbler's fitness, S_d is the predator's fitness as perceived by the individual babbler, r is the relatedness coefficient, and t is the cost of signaling. X represents the risk associated with mobbing this predator. The bounds of all parameters presented, with the exception of X, are 0 and 1. It is important to note that the parameter S_d represents perceived fitness rather than the actual fitness, which will be represented differently in the data analysis. If the inequality is not satisfied, the individual remains in the tree until the predator leaves.

3.3   Deception in Mobbing

Dishonesty is incorporated into the computational model (after [8]) and is used when the individual makes the choice whether to participate in mobbing or not. If the system was entirely honest then the only factors involved in mobbing would be the fitness of the predator and prey and the cost of the signaling. In the honest situation, if the individual has fitness greater than the predator after factoring in signaling cost, then it would always mob. Similarly, if the individual was fitness deficient after subtracting the signal cost, then it would never participate in the completely honest situation. However, when incorporating deception, a relatedness coefficient is included, which allows and influences deceptive behavior. The purpose is to determine when it is the most appropriate strategy for an agent to engage in mobbing independent of whether it is an honest or dishonest signal. Equation 1 assesses the risk of being attacked and devoured by the predator. The higher the risk, the less likely the babbler will mob.

The relatedness coefficient, r, drives the decision to mob and expresses the cooperation between predator and prey. The prey does not want to be chased, and the predator wants an easy meal and to not waste energy during a chase [13]. As r increases, the agents are more likely to cooperate, the risk of being attacked decreases, and the chance of mobbing should increase. This is in agreement with equation 1, because predator fitness, S_d, is between 0 and 1. Subtracting 1 from S_d means that r will be multiplied by a negative quantity, implying an inversely proportional relationship. Figure 6 in [5] shows the relationship of each parameter assuming a linear model.

4   Implementation

The computational model has been implemented in MissionLab[1]. This specific research has only utilized the simulation aspect of MissionLab thus far but we expect to port this model to Pioneer robots in the near future.

The implementation of mob behavior is constructed from multiple previously developed behaviors (Appendices A-C in [5]). Mob formation around the predator is emulated using a sub-FSA containing the lek behavior [6]. For the harassment aspect of mobbing, the change-color behavior is utilized rather than implementing any extravagant motor display. The transition between the mob and harass state is probabilistic. This value is empirically assigned, as we have not found supporting biological data regarding the frequency of harassment during mobbing. After harassing is complete, its color returns to the original state, and the agent is considered back in the mob state.

When being harassed, the predator detects green harassers. During each time cycle, the predator's current frustration value is incremented by 1 for each harassing agent:

$$f_{\text{current}} = f_{\text{previous}} + n \qquad (2)$$

---

[1] MissionLab is freely available for research and educational purposes at: http://www.cc.gatech.edu/ai/robot-lab/research/MissionLab/.

where $f_{current}$ is the current frustration value, $f_{previous}$ is the previous frustration value, and n is the number of harassing agents in a fixed time cycle. If the frustration value exceeds a specified frustration threshold (f_t =100, 125, or 150), the predator leaves and the simulation terminates. If, however, s seconds elapse (in this case arbitrarily 10) and the frustration threshold has not been exceeded, the predator selects a random mobbing prey individual to attack. If the predator has a higher perceived fitness value than the prey individual it selects, then that agent is considered to be bluffing, and the probability of that agent being killed, D_l, is 95%. Conversely if the predator selects an honest mobbing agent, the probability of this agent being killed, D_h, is set to either 5%, 10%, or 15%. The chance of the predator killing an honest mobber is increased across different analyses to represent the effect of a fitter predator.

Each non-sentinel prey evaluates equation 1 whenever in the presence of a predator. Every agent that satisfies this inequality participates in mobbing upon receiving the alarm call from the sentinel. In the results that follow, parameters t, r, and S_d are held constant (t=0.1, r=0.75, S_d=0.5) while the parameters S_b (fitness), f_t (frustration threshold), and D_h (death probability for honest agents) vary. The assigned value for S_b was either 0 (no participation), 0.4 (deceitful participation), or 0.6 (honest participation). All combinations of honest and dishonest mob groups were analyzed for group sizes of 2 through 7 babblers. f_t was assigned a value of 100, 125, or 150 with greater values representing a more patient predator. Finally, the probability of an honest mobber being killed was varied from 0.05, 0.10, and 0.15. As previously mentioned, there is a difference between the perceived fitness, S_d, and the actual fitness. Varying D_h represents changing actual fitness. Using the assumption that fitter predators are more likely to catch prey, increases in D_h indicate increases in actual predator fitness. This is more desirable than changing S_d, as changing perceived fitness alters the number of mobbing agents.

5   Simulation Results

The simulation data was analyzed for the aforementioned values of parameters S_b, f_t, and D_h. Figures 3a, 3b, and 3c show the mortality rate for each combination of mob sizes and deception rates present in the group, when D_h was held constant at .05; while f_t=100 in 3a, 125 in 3b, and 150 in 3c. Figures 9a, 9b, and 9c (from [5]) demonstrate the same combinations but where $D_h = .10$, and figures 10a, 10b, and 10c (from [5]) show this data when $D_h = .15$.

For each frustration threshold, there exists a minimum number of mobbing agents (M_m), for which the predator's frustration always exceeded its f_t and fled. The minimum number of mobbers for which zero attacks occur across each f_t is shown in table 1 (from [5], for reference $M_m = 3$ for f_t=100). Attacks being reduced to 0 results in a 0% mortality rate. Deceiving in groups smaller than these minimum mob sizes is lethal. The deadliest conditions for lying, when f_t=125 and 150, was a mob formation consisting of 2 deceiving agents and a sentinel. Mobbing a predator with these frustration thresholds and only deceiving agents, resulted in a mortality rate of approximately 70%. When $f_t=100$, the highest mortality rate occurs when 1 deceiving agent and a sentinel participate.

It is desirable to discover if adding deceiving agents to a purely honest situation would result in fewer fatalities. Obviously when adding enough deceivers to exceed or equal M_m for each frustration threshold value, the mortality rate drops to zero. However it is more interesting to investigate critical mob sizes (M_c) that can result in both the predator attacking or fleeing. M_c for each frustration value is presented in table 1 found in [5] (for reference $M_c = 3$ for $f_t=100$). Figure 3 shows that a purely honest mob group has a higher survival rate than any group containing a deceiver, with two exceptions. Other results can be found in figures 9-11 of [5]. As evidenced in figure 9b in ($f_t=125$ $D_h=0.10$), a group of 3 honest mobbers yields a mortality rate of 0.16. Adding one deceiving babbler to this group reduces the mortality rate by 25%. Similarly, as seen in figure 10c ($f_t=150$ $D_h=0.15$), 3 honest mobbing babblers have a mortality rate of 0.20. Adding one deceiving babbler drops the mortality rate by 30%.

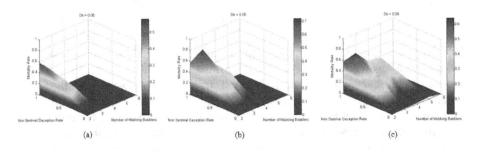

(a)   (b)   (c)

Fig. 3. Surface plot of number of agents, deception rate in non-sentinel group members, and the mortality rate from the group makeup. The sentinel is always an honest mobber. $D_h=.05$ and the probability that a lying agent is killed, D_l , is 95% for all above figures. A, B, and C simulate values of 100, 125, and 150 for f_t respectively.

Since these are the only two incidents in the entire data set in which the addition of a single deceiver decreases the mortality rate, it can be concluded that lying with $D_l = .95$, is not a strategic decision in mob groups less than M_m. Figure 11, found in [5], shows the result of reducing D_l to 50% and increasing D_h to 30% while f_t was 150. Under these new conditions, deception improves survivability in group sizes of M_c. Adding one deceiving member to mob size of 3 with any deception rate decreased the mortality rate by an average of 16%. While this may not be realistic, it proves that there is a set of conditions in which deceiving can improve survival rate consistently.

6   Conclusion

Mobbing behavior, in nature, has clearly proven to be an effective method of predator deterrence. Our research shows the ability to transfer this biologically inspired behavior to robotic behavior in simulation, where the robotic agents emulate the ethology of mobbing birds. The addition of deception to the handicap principle returns mixed results. For this simulation, deception is the best strategy when adding a single agent pushes the mob size to M_m. In this case, the predator is driven away and no member is attacked. For mob sizes smaller than M_m, complete honesty yields the lowest mortality rate. This is because the punishment for bluffing is high. If the price of bluffing is reduced, adding deception can reduce motrality rates.Mobbing permits the agents working in teams to create multiple formations and allows them to group in specific areas. Future work will investigate the impact of varying D_l on mortality rate and implementing this simulation on physical robotic systems. Understanding how many honest and dishonest prey agents are required to successfully drive a predator away has value in the hope of understanding the effectiveness in making this defensive strategy effective for relevant robotic applications when agent survival is at stake.

Acknowledgements. This research was supported by the Office of Naval Research under MURI Grant #N00014-08-1-0696.

References

1. Arkin, R.C.: Behavior–based Robotics. MIT Press, Boston (1998)
2. Army, U.: Field manual 90-2, battlefield deception (1998), http://www.enlisted. info/field-manuals/fm-90-2-battlefield-deception.shtml/
3. Balch, T., Arkin, R.C.: Behavior–based formation control for multi–robot teams. IEEE Transactions on Robotics and Automation 14(6), 926–939 (1998)
4. Bond, C.F., Ronbinson, M.: The evolution of deception. Journal of Nonverbal Behavior 12(4), 295–307 (1988)
5. Davis, J.E., Arkin, R.C.: Mobbing behavior and deceit and its role in bio-inspired autonomous robotic agents (long form technical report). Tech. Rep. GIT–MRL– 12–02, Georgia Institute of Technology, Atlanta, GA, USA (2012)
6. Duncan, B., Ulam, P., Arkin, R.C.: Lek behavior as a model for multi-robot systems. In: Proc. IEEE International Symposium on Computational Intelligence in Robotics and Automation, pp. 25–32. IEEE Press, Piscataway (2009)
7. Graw, B., Manser, M.B.: The function of mobbing cooperative meerkats. Animal Behaviour 73(3), 507–517 (2007)
8. Johnstone, R.A., Grafen, A.: Dishonesty and the handicap principle. Animal Behaviour 46(4), 759–764 (1993)
9. Lorenz, K.: On Agression. Harcourt, Brace and World Inc., New York (1966)
10. Owings, D.H., Coss, R.G.: Snake mobbing by california ground squirrels: Adaptive variation and ontogeny. Behaviour 62(1-2), 50–68 (1977)
11. Wagner, A.R., Arkin, R.C.: Acting deceptively: Providing robots with the capacity for deception. International Journal of Social Robotics 3(1), 5–26 (2011)
12. Wright, J., Berg, E., De Kort, S.R., Khazin, V., Maklakov, A.A.: Cooperative sentinel behaviour in the arabian babbler. Animal Behaviour 62(5), 973–979 (2001)
13. Zahavi, A., Zahavi, A.: The Handicap Principle:A Missing Piece of Darwin's Puzzle, pp. 125–175. Oxford University Press, Oxford (1997)

Performance of Bacterial Foraging Optimization in Dynamic Environments

Jade Abbott and Andries P. Engelbrecht

CIRG, Department of Computer Science
University of Pretoria, South Africa
{jabbott,engel}@cs.up.ac.za

Abstract. The bacterial foraging optimization (BFO) algorithm is a new complex, swarm-based optimization algorithm. The algorithm has shown to be successful in static environments; however there is little research available on analysis of its performance in dynamic environments. The aim of this article is to conduct an elaborate empirical analysis of BFO in a number of dynamic environments. Additionally, a modification to BFO is proposed to improve BFO's performance in dynamic environments.

1 Introduction

Bacterial foraging optimization (BFO) is a stochastic, swarm-based optimization method based on the foraging behaviour of E-coli bacteria [12] which has been successfully applied to a wide range of problems in [9,8,4], mostly in stationary environments. BFO's nature suggests that it is designed to perform well in dynamic environments. However, little substantial research has been performed to evaluate the performance of BFO in dynamic environments.

This paper examines the performance of BFO in a range of dynamic environments and modifies the BFO algorithm to improve BFO's performance in dynamic environments. The modified BFO, dynamic BFO (DBFO), is benchmarked against a number of swarm-based algorithms developed for dynamic optimization.

The remainder of the paper is organized as follows: BFO is described in Section 2, and background on dynamic environments is given in Section 3. Section 4 describes the PSO algorithms used to benchmark against, and issues with BFO in static environments and the new DBFO algorithm is discussed in Section 5. The experimental procedure is described in Section 6, while Section 7 presents and discusses results.

2 Bacterial Foraging

Passino [11] developed BFO which models the foraging behaviour of E coli. bacteria. BFO is a complex algorithm and thus for brevity a summary of the algorithm is provided. Full details of BFO are in [11]. BFO consists of 3 phases organized in

M. Dorigo et al. (Eds.): ANTS 2012, LNCS 7461, pp. 284–291, 2012.

a triple nested loop: chemotaxis, reproduction and elimination/dispersal, where chemotaxis occurs in the innermost loop, reproduction occurs in the middle loop and elimination dispersal occurs in the outermost loop. The following aspects of the BFO algorithm are discussed:

- **Chemotactic Step.** Chemotaxis is the integral phase of the algorithm, modelling how bacteria move up the nutrient gradient. It consists of two parts: (i) tumble and (ii) swim. A tumble is simply a reorientation of the bacteria to a random direction. A swim is a movement of the bacterium in the tumble direction of a specific step size C_i for each bacteria i. Chemotaxis consists of a tumble, then repetition of the swim step until a decrease in the nutrient gradient is observed. Included as part of the nutrient gradient calculation is the effect of cell-to-cell attractant that occurs between bacteria. Bacteria are attracted to other bacteria based on proximity but also repel each other at short range, resulting in bacterial swarming behaviour.
- **Reproductive Step.** Bacteria are sorted by health and the unhealthy half of the bacteria is removed and the remaining half of the bacteria is copied to create a population of original size.
- **Elimination-dispersal Step.** With a certain probability bacteria are reinitialized to a new position modelling the natural disturbances in the environment of E. coli. bacteria.

3   BFO for Dynamic Environments

This section analyses BFO's weaknesses and a new dynamic BFO algorithm is proposed.

3.1   Issues of BFO in Dynamic Environments

Due to the triple nested loop structure of BFO, the frequency each operation occurs is inconveniently dependant to the frequency of the outermost operation loops. For example, the frequency of reproduction is dependant on frequency that reproduction occurs but also on frequency that elimination-dispersal occurs. Since the frequency of each operation effects behaviour of the algorithm, three simple running time control variables have the bad side effect of changing the behaviour of the algorithm.

Also, if a large environmental change occurs, the optimum may move outside the bounds of the area covered by bacteria. Finding the optimum may be slow as the bacteria are concentrated in one area of the search space, increasing chances of getting stuck in local optima.

Lastly, BFO is unable to fine tune good solutions due to the constant step size for each bacterium.

3.2 Related Work on BFO in Dynamic Environments

The performance of BFO in dynamic environments has been explored by [13], focussing on a technique for maintaining diversity in the reproductive step of the algorithm. The results were not reproducible, given the description in [13], and thus were not compared to the algorithm proposed in this paper.

3.3 Structure for Dynamic BFO Algorithm

To solve the structural problems of BFO, the algorithm is factored out into a single loop with three sequential operational steps. Chemotaxis, reproduction, and elimination-dispersal operations are set specific frequency parameters: F_c, F_{re}, and F_{ed}, allowing for fine-grained management of operations. For example, the reproduction operation will occur once each only F_{re} iterations. In terms of the original BFO, chemotaxis should occur every iteration with a frequency of 1.

3.4 Diversity of DBFO

Section 2 states that elimination-dispersal of bacteria is caused as a response to disturbances to the environment. When a large environmental change is detected in BFO, it is appropriate for an elimination-dispersal event to occur. An elimination-dispersal event would spread the bacteria across the search space, allowing for improved search abilities. In DBFO, if a substantial change in the environment is detected, then an elimination-dispersal event occurs. A substantial change is any operation which causes an abrupt decrease in average health of the bacteria by ϵ. The best value of ϵ requires further research.

3.5 Change in Step Sizes

In order to improve exploitation of good solutions, DBFO includes a step size modification, such that step size, C_i, is changed over time, allowing the bacterium to initially explore but exploit good solutions. The change will occur as follows for each bacterium s_i

$$C_i(t) = \begin{cases} \mu & \text{if } C_i(t-1) \geq \tau \\ C_i(t-1) & \text{if } C_i(t-1) < \tau \end{cases} \tag{1}$$

where $\mu = 0.9$ and $\tau = 0.01$. These values were empirically chosen to work well over a variety of problems, but further research needs to be done to determine their behaviour. In DBFO, the step size is reset to the initial value of 1, to enable the bacteria to explore more after an environmental change. The elimination-dispersal event is extended with this reset step. The modified BFO algorithm is given in Algorithm 1.

Algorithm 1. DBFO

Initialize parameters
Initialize bacteria
for $t = 1, ..., max_{it}$ **do**
   chemotaxis step
   if t mod $F_{re} = 0$ **then**
      reproduction step
   end if
   if environmental change is detected **then**
      elimination-dispersal step
      for all bacterium $s_i \in S$ **do**
         Calculate $C_i(t)$ as in equation (1)
      end for
   end if
end for

4 Experimental Procedure

This section gives configurations for the moving peaks dynamic environment generator, the bacterial foraging algorithms BFO and DBFO, and the PSO benchmark algorithms used.

4.1 Algorithm Setup

The collective mean error (CME), which is the average of the error measurement over all iterations performed, is measured [10]. For both BFO and DBFO, the swarm size S is 50, δ =1 and $P_{ed} = 0.75$, the cell-to-cell attractant parameters $d_{attract}$, $w_{attract}$, h_{repel}, and w_{repel} were set to 0.1, 0.2, 0.1 and 10 respectively and N_s was set to 8. For BFO, N_c, N_{re} and N_{ed} were set to 500, 2 and 2 respectively. The frequency of reproduction, F_{re}, was set to 1000 and $\epsilon = 25\%$, for DBFO. The total number of iterations for each algorithm was calculated to be 2000. The configurations for BFO were shown to work well on a variety of problems as in [11].

The BFO algorithms were compared with PSO algorithms using 50 particles and acceleration constants, c_1 and c_2, were set to 1.496180. The dynamic PSO algorithms used were:

- **Charged PSO** (CPSO)[2]: Swarms consisted of 50% charged and 50% neutral particles with a charge magnitude of 16 [3]. The lower cut off value p_{core} was set to 1 and p is set to 30.
- **Quantum PSO** (QPSO)[1]: Swarms consisted of 50% quantum and 50% standard particles. The radius of the cloud, ϕ_{cloud}, was set to 30.
- **Reinitializing PSO** (RPSO) [6]: 10% of particles reinitialize when an environmental change is detected.
- **Multi-swarm PSO** (MPSO) [2]: 5 sub-swarms of 10 particles of 50% quantum and 50% neutral particles were used.

4.2 Dynamic Environment Setup

Four classes of dynamic environments are used: quasi-static/static environments, progressively changing environments, abruptly changing environments and chaotic environments as proposed by [5]. The moving peaks dynamic environment generator [7] is used to generate the dynamic environments of the required classes for the purposes of this paper. The position, height, and shape (width) of the optima change at predetermined intervals

The width severity (w_s) and height severity (h_s) were set to 0.1 and 0.7 respectively. The peak heights fall in the range $[30, 70]$, while the peak width were in the range $[0.08, 1]$. Dimensionalities of $d = 2, 5, 10, 30$ where considered and the function domain for all functions was $[0, 100]^d$. The λ value was set to 0.75 and random seed was fixed for all algorithms ($seed = 1$). The algorithm was tested for a number of severities, s, and frequencies, f, specifically $s = 0, 1, 10, 20, 30, 40, 50$ and $f = 1, 5, 50, 100, 200, 2000$. Each algorithm was run for 2000 iterations. Each experiment was repeated on 30 generated environments for each setting combination. Figure 1a demonstrates how the environment types discussed in Section 3 relate to the grid layout in Figure 1b.

5 Results

Results are summarized using 3-dimensional plots of the CME after 2000 iterations for all algorithms. Additionally, tables are given to summarize performance after 2000 iterations for severity, frequency, and dimensionality.

Tables 1a to 1c shows BFO performed generally worse than all the PSOs. However, further examination shows BFO performance was within an acceptable range of the average PSO performance, indicating that BFO has inherent properties suitable to dynamic environments. However, the standard deviations of the CME for all experiments for BFO was high indicating instability of BFO. Instability may be attributed to the stochastic manner that search directions were chosen or that BFO performance was dependent on the initial bacteria positions. High standard deviation may show that BFO is sensitive to local minima.

Figure 1b shows that BFO performance improved in the progressive quadrant compared to other quadrants, demonstrating that BFO tracked optima better in highly progressive environments. BFO's improved ability to optimize in progressive environments may be because the cell-to-cell repellent force maintains a small amount of diversity around the optimum. If the optimum moves within the small area covered by the swarmed bacteria, bacteria are more likely to locate the new optimum position; thus, BFO has the ability to track small but frequent changes distinct to progressive environments.

Performance of BFO is worse in the abrupt quadrant. The BFO algorithm shows slow convergence, and thus if the optimum has moved significantly then BFO will take time to move the bacteria to the newly positioned optimum.

Figure 1c and Figure 1d indicate that, as dimensions increase, BFO performance decreased showing that BFO is highly sensitive to increases in

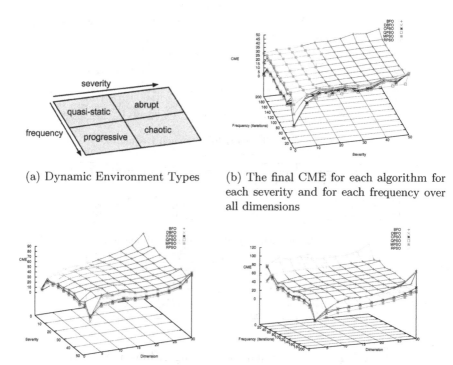

(a) Dynamic Environment Types

(b) The final CME for each algorithm for each severity and for each frequency over all dimensions

(c) The final CME for each algorithm for each severity and for each frequency over all dimensions

(d) The final CME for each algorithm for each dimension for each frequency over all dimensions

Fig. 1. 3-dimensional plots of the CME after 2000 iterations for all algorithms

dimensionality. BFO's lack of scalability may be the result of the bacterial position update strategy employed by BFO. The update strategy forces the bacteria to move the same distance in all dimensions, regardless of optimality of the specific dimension. Supposing a bacterium has located the optimal position in a single dimension, but has a sub-optimal position in the remaining dimensions, after the position update, the position will be moved in all dimensions, regardless of optimality of a single dimension.

Conclusively, BFO suffers from sensitivity to dimensionality, instability and slow convergence, but BFO has the ability to track optima in progressive environments, but requires further improvement.

Tables 1a to 1c show that DBFO generally performed better than BFO and is only outperformed by BFO in isolated circumstances. DBFO had greater ability to exploit good solutions as well as re-diversify in the event of an abrupt change, thus resulting in improved performance. Although it is evident that the changes made to BFO have improved performance, DBFO still suffered from sensitivity to dimensionality, instability and slower convergence.

Table 1. CME for each algorithm over all peaks

(a) CME for each algorithm for each severity

Algorithm	Severity					
	0	1	10	20	40	50
BFO	16.32(141)	27.72(240.2)	37.95(328.6)	43.068(372.1)	45.12(391.08)	45.26(392.1)
DBFO	15.87(137)	28.15(243.5)	39.2(338.7)	41.3(357.5)	42.84(370.34)	43.06(372.2)
CPSO	8.35(2.54)	18.5(4.54)	32.91(3.15)	36.7(4.583)	38.91(3.84)	39.60(3.56)
QPSO	8.86(2.74)	17.28(3.52)	32.48(5.71)	34.15(2.474)	36.83(5.21)	37.30(4.52)
MPSO	15.67(4.48)	22.62(4.27)	34.05(3.85)	37.04(4.796)	39.2(4.26)	40.145(3.88)
RPSO	18.59(3.63)	24.27(4.35)	34.45(3.46)	37.16(3.711)	38.94(2.77)	39.781(2.86)

(b) CME for each algorithm for each frequency

Algorithm	Frequency				
	1	5	50	100	200
BFO	48.405(418.18)	43.964(380.86)	37.296(322.99)	33.747(292.77)	30.214(261.24)
DBFO	47.325(409.81)	42.741(370.58)	36.006(311.69)	32.828(282.9)	28.286(244.48)
CPSO	48.263(7.9237)	38.504(2.206)	24.361(2.4297)	19.639(2.7402)	15.048(3.2196)
QPSO	47.602(8.3217)	37.512(3.26)	22.242(2.4406)	17.824(2.8246)	13.925(3.3217)
MPSO	49.377(7.5864)	40.292(3.3093)	26.386(3.0823)	22.213(3.3897)	19.032(3.9077)
RPSO	55.089(6.9221)	44.692(2.632)	25.668(2.1753)	20.267(2.5534)	15.277(3.0453)

(c) CME for each algorithm for each dimension

Algorithm	Dimensionality			
	2	5	10	30
BFO	17.966(155.48)	34.519(299.05)	43.306(374.8)	59.11(511.5)
DBFO	12.323(107.19)	34.169(296.01)	44.456(384.38)	58.801(507.99)
CPSO	14.339(3.0798)	24.988(4.4022)	32.787(4.5392)	44.539(2.7942)
QPSO	14.61(3.294)	24.439(4.1113)	29.724(4.2919)	42.51(4.4376)
MPSO	20.99(3.996)	27.398(3.9485)	32.999(4.2521)	44.453(4.8236)
RPSO	14.648(2.3923)	28.78(3.8114)	37.333(3.844)	48.034(3.8147)

Figure 1c and Figure 1d show that the PSO algorithms performed better than DBFO in all dimensions save for a few select configurations. It is evident in Figure 1c that, problems of low dimensions and low severity DBFO outperformed the PSO algorithms and Figure 1d shows that DBFO outperforms all PSO algorithms in low dimensions with extremely high severity. DBFO is therefore more suited to the highly progressive or quasi-static environments, and abrupt environments than the PSO algorithms, but only in problems of few dimensions. This implies DBFO must be modified to improve sensitivity to increases in dimensionality.

Figure 1b shows that all algorithms demonstrated decrease in performance in the chaotic quadrant, thus struggling to track the movements of optima in chaotic environments. It is difficult to track an optimum in chaotic environments and thus all algorithms performance chaotic environment was inconclusive.

6   Conclusion

This paper evaluated the performance of bacterial foraging optimization (BFO) on a variety of dynamic environments. A new dynamic BFO (DBFO) algorithm was proposed for dynamic environments and was included in the evaluation. The results were compared to that of dynamic PSO algorithms which have been developed specifically for dynamic environments. BFO appears, on an algorithmic level, to be suited towards dynamic environments with properties such as the ability to maintain diversity.

However, in practice, a number of flaws in the algorithm, such as sensitivity to dimensionality, instability and susceptibility to local optima, inhibit the algorithm, rather than assist it in dynamic environments. In an attempt to solve those problems, DBFO was proposed which attempts to solve the downfalls of the original BFO algorithm. DBFO is a slightly modified version of BFO, which increased the accuracy of solutions in certain types of dynamic environments and improved the flexibility and intuitiveness of the BFO structure. Although the DBFO improved on the BFO in many environments, it still did not entirely overcome the problems identified in BFO.

Although the PSO algorithms outperformed BFO and DBFO, BFO has shown potential in dynamic environments and further research needs to be done to further refine DBFO to overcome the identified problems.

References

1. Blackwell, T., Branke, J.: Multiswarms, exclusion, and anti-convergence in dynamic environments 10, 459–472 (2006)
2. Blackwell, T.M.: Swarms in Dynamic Environments. In: Cantú-Paz, E., Foster, J.A., Deb, K., Davis, L., Roy, R., O'Reilly, U.-M., Beyer, H.-G., Kendall, G., Wilson, S.W., Harman, M., Wegener, J., Dasgupta, D., Potter, M.A., Schultz, A., Dowsland, K.A., Jonoska, N., Miller, J., Standish, R.K. (eds.) GECCO 2003, Part I. LNCS, vol. 2723, pp. 1–12. Springer, Heidelberg (2003)
3. Blackwell, T., Branke, J.: Multi-swarm optimization in dynamic environments, pp. 489–500. Springer (2004)
4. Chatterje, A.: Bacterial foraging techniques for solving EKF-based slam problems. In: Control Conference
5. Duheim, J.: Particle Swarm Optimization in Dynamically Changing Environment An Empirical Study. Master's thesis, Department of Computer Science, University of Pretoria (2011)
6. Eberhart, R.C., Shi, Y.: Comparing inertia weights and constriction factors in particle swarm optimization, vol. 1, pp. 84–88. IEEE (2000)
7. Krink, T., Vesterstrom, J.S., Riget, J.: Particle swarm optimisation with spatial particle extension, vol. 2, pp. 1474–1479. IEEE (2002)
8. Majhi, B., Panda, G.: Recovery of Digital Information Using Bacterial Foraging Optimization Based Nonlinear Channel Equalizers, pp. 367–372 (2007)
9. Mishra, S., Bhende, C.N., Lai, L.L., Delhi, N., Group, E.S.: Optimization of a distribution static compensator by bacterial foraging technique, pp. 13–16 (August 2006)
10. Morrison, R.W.: Performance measurement in dynamic environments. Foundations and Trends in Accounting 2(3), 175–240 (2003)
11. Passino, K.M.: Biomimicry of bacterial foraging for distributed optimization and control, vol. 22, pp. 52–67. IEEE (2002)
12. Ramos, V., Fernandes, C., Rosa, A.C.: On ants, bacteria and dynamic environments (2005)
13. Tang, W.J., Wu, Q.H., Saunders, J.R.: Bacterial foraging algorithm for dynamic environments, pp. 1324–1330. IEEE (2006)

Piecewise Linear Approximation of n-Dimensional Parametric Curves Using Particle Swarms

Christopher Wesley Cleghorn and Andries P. Engelbrecht

Department of Computer Science
University of Pretoria
{ccleghorn,engel}@cs.up.ac.za

Abstract. This paper derives a new algorithm for piecewise linear approximation of n-dimensional parametric curves, specifically to be used with particle swarm optimization. The aim of the algorithm is to find the optimal piecewise linear approximation for a predefined number of segments. The performance of this algorithm is evaluated on a set of functions of varying dimensionality.

1 Introduction

In many real world situations functions are encountered that are not explicitly known, but it would still be useful to able to infer meaning from the analysis of said function. The first step is often to try and approximate the function. A common approach is that of piecewise linear approximation (PWLA) [1]. The main issue with PWLA when the explicit function is known is that explicit parameters for the linear segments can be obtained only if the ideal partitions of the independent variables of the PWLA are known. However, knowledge of the function and ideal partitions are usually not known.

This paper proposes a particle swarm optimization (PSO) approach to PWLA, without assuming knowledge of the function nor the ideal partitions. The PSO approach to PWLA used is to analytically solve for segment coefficients and then to utilize the PSO to find the ideal partitions. To the authors' knowledge this is the first population-based approach to PWLA of parametric curves.

Background is given in section 2. A derivation of the closed formulas for the algorithm is given in section 3. The algorithm is presented in section 4. The experimental set up is discussed in section 5, and the results in section 6.

2 Background

This section provides the reader with an overview of the techniques used throughout the paper. PWLA is defined in section 2.1. Section 2.2 overviews PSO, and Section 2.3 discusses related works.

M. Dorigo et al. (Eds.): ANTS 2012, LNCS 7461, pp. 292–299, 2012.

2.1   Piecewise Linear Approximation

In one dimension, PWLA can be formalized as, given the non-linear relationship, $y \approx f(x)$ for $i_0 \leq x \leq i_p$ to obtain an approximation of f using p segments of the form

$$y(x) = \begin{cases} a_1 + b_1 x & \text{for } i_0 \leq x \leq i_1 \\ a_2 + b_2 x & \text{for } i_1 \leq x \leq i_2 \\ \dots & \dots \\ a_p + b_p x & \text{for } i_{p-1} \leq x \leq i_p \end{cases} \tag{1}$$

where a_i and b_i are the y intersect and the gradient of the line segment on the interval $i_{i-1} \leq x \leq i_i$ respectively. The objective is to find a piecewise mapping that minimizes the least squares error (LSE) between the function f and y:

$$LSE = \int_{i_0}^{i_p} (f(x) - y(x))^2 dx = \sum_{j=1}^{p} (f(x) - (a_j + b_j x))^2 dx \tag{2}$$

The problem is solved by assigning optimal values to the coefficients $a_k, b_k \forall k : 1 \leq k \leq p$ and $i_k \forall k : 0 < k < p$. The dimensionality of the optimization problem is therefore $2p + p - 1$ (the end points i_0 and i_p are known quantities).

2.2   Particle Swarm Optimization

Particle Swarm Optimization (PSO)[2] is a population-based search algorithm, based on simple models of bird flocks. The fundamental principle of PSO is to update the position of a particle based on: the momentum of the particle, the cognitive component, and the social component. The momentum is a fraction of the current velocity. The cognitive component attracts a particle to it's best found solution. The social component attracts each particle to the best solution found by its neighbourhood.

PSO is formalised as follows: let $l_k(t)$ be particle k's position at discrete time step t (often called iteration t). A particle's position and velocity update using

$$l_k(t+1) = l_k(t) + v_k(t+1) \tag{3}$$

$$v_k(t+1) = wv_k(t) + c_1 r_1(t)(b_k - l_k(t)) + c_2 r_2(t)(nb_k - l_k(t)) \tag{4}$$

where w, c_1, and c_2 are the inertia weight, cognitive and social coefficients respectively; $r_1, r_2 : \forall i, r_{1,i}, r_{2,i} \in U(0,1)$; b_k is the best position obtained by particle k; and nb_k is best position obtained in the neighbourhood of k.

The neighbourhood of a particle is determined by a social network topology [3].This paper uses the Von Neumann topology, where particles are connected to form an multidimensional grid structure. The Von Neumann topology has been shown in a number of empirical studies [3,4] to outperform other neighbourhood topologies.

2.3   Related Work

Many non-population based approaches to linear approximation exist, primarily designed for application to digital curves [5,6]. Many of the classical approaches to PWLA [7,8] either place requirements on the form of the function being approximated, and/or require an explicit definition of the function. As a result, research is done on special cases. A recent example is the recursive descent approach of Imamoto and Tang [9], which, while highly efficient, requires knowledge of the explicit function that is being approximated (to enable the derivation of the actual derivative, not just an approximation of the derivative) in addition to the requirement that the function is convex.

This paper assumes that the explicit function is unknown, and that no knowledge of the function's form is available. Research that has similar assumptions is PWLA of digitized curves (DC). Some DC algorithms differ slightly from the definition in that the line segments of the approximation need not join, i.e the resulting PWL approximation is not guaranteed to be continuous on the function domain. A well known example is the algorithm of Manis et al[10]. In contrast, the objective of this paper is to obtain a continuous PWLA.

Some DC algorithms do closely match the assumption on the explicit function: Horst and Beichl [11] designed their DC algorithm for efficiency with respect to running time, and Pavlidis [12] and Dunham [13], focused on optimality of the PWLA. These algorithms share the general approach to finding the optimal PWLA: starting with a very high segment count and continually remove segments until a point is reached where any continued segment removal will push the error over an acceptable threshold. This is very different from the approach taken in this paper, where the number of segments must be specified by the user, while no error threshold need be given. This is due to the fact that the approach in this paper is to find an optimal segment arrangement, not to find the lowest segment count possible while remaining above an error threshold.

3   Derivations of Analytical Component

The problem to be solved is that of PWLA of a n-dimensional parametric function. Specifically, the area between the target (though explicitly unknown function) and the approximated function must be minimized. This paper uses the n-dimensional version of equation (2) to minimize the square of the area, MF, between the two functions.

$$MF = \int_{i_0}^{i_p} (\, \|\boldsymbol{f}(t) - \boldsymbol{x}(t)\|_2) \, ^2 dx \tag{5}$$

given

$$\overrightarrow{x}(t) = \begin{pmatrix} y_1(t) \\ y_2(t) \\ \vdots \\ y_n(t) \end{pmatrix}, y_j(t) = \begin{cases} a_{j,1} + b_{j,1}t & \text{for } i_0 \le t \le i_1 \\ a_{j,2} + b_{j,2}t & \text{for } i_1 \le t \le i_2 \\ \dots & \dots \\ a_{j,p} + b_{j,p}t & \text{for } i_{p-1} \le t \le i_p \end{cases} \tag{6}$$

Minimization of MF is done by finding optimal values for $a_{j,k}, b_{j,k} \forall k : 1 \leq k \leq p$, $\forall j : 1 \leq j \leq n$ and $i_k \forall k : 0 < k < p$. The minimum of the function MF is where all of its partial derivatives are zero.

It was shown by Stone [14] that, for equation (2), if the partition points are not fixed, a closed form solution does not exist in general, and more complicated techniques for approximating the solution that require the explicit function have to be used. Given that the closed form solution with non-fixed partition points cannot be analytically solved in general, it is assumed that the partition points are fixed. The system of partial derivatives can then be explicitly solved using an extension of Stones approach:

$$\frac{\partial MF}{\partial a_{j,k}} = 0 = -2 \int_{i_{k-1}}^{i_k} f_j(t)dt + 2a_{j,k}(i_k - i_{k-1}) + b_{j,k}(i_k^2 - i_{k-1}^2) \qquad (7)$$

$$\frac{\partial MF}{\partial b_{j,k}} = 0 = -2 \int_{i_{k-1}}^{i_k} t f_j(t)dt + a_{j,k}(i_k^2 - i_{k-1}^2) + \tfrac{2}{3}b_{j,k}(i_k - i_{k-1}) \qquad (8)$$

This results in nj simultaneous pairs of equations which are solved to obtain

$$a_{j,k} = \frac{3}{(i_k - i_{k-1})^3}\left(\tfrac{4}{3}(i_k^2 + i_k i_{k-1} + i_{k-1}^2)\int_{i_{k-1}}^{i_k} f_j(t)dt - 2(i_k + i_{k-1})\int_{i_{k-1}}^{i_k} t f_j(t)dt\right) \qquad (9)$$

$$b_{j,k} = \frac{6}{(i_k - i_{k-1})^3}\left(2\int_{i_{k-1}}^{i_k} t f_j(t)dt - (i_k + i_{k-1})\int_{i_{k-1}}^{i_k} f_j(t)dt\right) \qquad (10)$$

The above integrals are approximated using the composite Simpson rule[1]:

$$\int_a^b g(x)dx \approx \frac{h}{3}\left(g(a) + 2\sum_{j=1}^{\frac{n}{2}-1} g(x_{2j}) + 4\sum_{j=1}^{\frac{n}{2}} g(x_{2j-1}) + g(b)\right) \qquad (11)$$

$$h = \frac{b-a}{s}, \quad x_j = a + jh \qquad (12)$$

and s is the sample count.

4   Particle Swarm Algorithm for PWLA

The ideal partition points can be found quite naturally with the PSO algorithm. Using equation (9) and (10), only the values for the intervals are required, and since the only independent variable is t, regardless of the dimensionality of the space mapped to by the parametric function, the search space size remains unchanged under dimension alteration.

Each particle represents a set of partition points between the two end points i_0, i_p. If an approximation using N segments is required, then $N - 1$ dimensions are used. The particle's components are sorted in ascending order of value to ensure that the resulting PWLA is in fact a function (each element of the domain maps to only one element of the range). The update of a particle's position and velocity is different from the standard approach. Application of equation

(3) on a particle's position may alter the ordering of the particle's position's components. This is rectified by sorting the position's components after the completed application of equations (3) and (4).

Particles often leave the search space in the initial iterations, and later move back within the search space [15]. This behaviour results in the problem that, if a particle leaves the boundaries of the search space, the resulting PWLA is meaningless as the evaluation of equation (5) is potentially invalid as a distance measure cannot be defined if the values of the true function are unknown. To rectify this problem, components of a particle position that violate boundary constraints are removed. A new valid component is then randomly generated and inserted into the particle position vector in an order preserving manner.

The fitness function is MF as defined in equation (5), using the composite Simpson rule in equation (11) to approximate MF. The PWLA approximation for a given partition point set is calculated using equations (9) and (10). The stopping condition is to halt once a predefined number of iterations have elapsed.

5   Experimental Procedure

The algorithm is evaluated on the six functions in Table 1. For each function, the PSO was used to produce 5, 10, 20, and 30 line segments. The average fitness and standard deviation of fitness are displayed for each segment number. Results are given as average fitnesses over 30 independent runs of the PSO. The efficiency of the PSO is analysed by comparing the median sampled PWLA obtained against the actual function.

For each function, samples are computed as $\{x_j = a + jh, \ j \in \mathbb{R} : x_j \leq b\}$, $h = \frac{b-a}{s}$ where a, b are the left and right most end points respectively, and s is the sample density. For all simulations, $s = 1000$. The PSO control parameter values used on all runs for every function are population size=64, iterations used= 2000, w=0.7, c_1=0.6, c_2=0.5. These settings have been chosen after extensive testing, and performed well for all chosen functions.

Table 1. Test Functions

1	$x(t) = cos(t) + sin(t), \ t \in [-4, 4]$	(13)
2	$x(t) = sin(t) + tcos(t)sin(t), \ t \in [-10, 10]$	(14)
3	$x(t) = 20e - 20e^{-0.2\sqrt{t^2}} - e^{cos(2\pi t)}, \ t \in [-4, 4]$	(15)
4	$f(t) = \begin{pmatrix} x_1(t) \\ x_2(t) \end{pmatrix} = \begin{pmatrix} tcos(2t) \\ tsin(2t) \end{pmatrix}, \ t \in [-3, 3]$	(16)
5	$f(t) = \begin{pmatrix} x_1(t) \\ x_2(t) \end{pmatrix} = \begin{pmatrix} sin(t) \\ cos(t) \end{pmatrix} \left(e^{cos(t)} - 2cos(4t) - sin^5\left(\frac{t}{12}\right) \right), \ t \in [0, 2\pi]$	(17)
6	$f(t) = \begin{pmatrix} x_1(t) \\ x_2(t) \\ \vdots \\ x_n(t) \end{pmatrix} = \begin{pmatrix} x \\ x + x^2 \\ \vdots \\ \sum_{i=1}^n x^i \end{pmatrix}, \ t \in [-1, 1]$	(18)

6   Results

The PWLA obtained for function 1 to 5 are displayed in figure 1 to 5 respectively. Table 2 contains all the fitness evaluations and standard deviations. Functions 2 to 5 required a higher segment count than functions 1 did to obtain a good PWLA of the explicit function. Function 1 experienced negligible improvement with increased segment count. This is illustrated in figure 1(a) for function 1, where a good approximation was obtained using only 10 segments. No significant improvement was obtained with more segments(see 1(b)).

However, on functions 2, 3, 4 and 5, when given a sufficient number of segments, the approximation accuracy increased drastically as show in figures 2 to 5. Function 2, when only 5 segments were used, is of particular interest: it

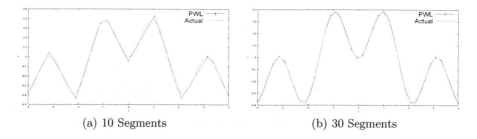

(a) 10 Segments   (b) 30 Segments

Fig. 1. Function 1

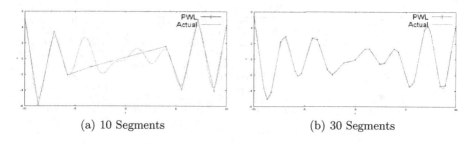

(a) 10 Segments   (b) 30 Segments

Fig. 2. Function 2

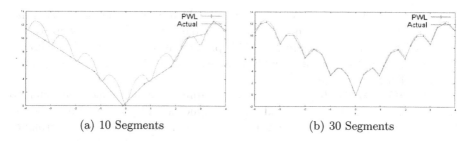

(a) 10 Segments   (b) 30 Segments

Fig. 3. Function 3

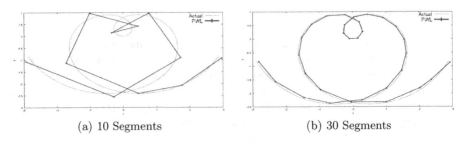

(a) 10 Segments   (b) 30 Segments

Fig. 4. Function 4

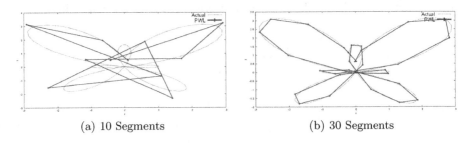

(a) 10 Segments   (b) 30 Segments

Fig. 5. Function 5

Table 2. Average fitness and deviations obtained using the PSO for PWLA

Segments	5	10	20	30
1	0.102738±0.0000710	0.003087±0.0000471	0.000408±0.0000283	0.000181±0.0000106
2	40.74514±3.0119749	7.209360±0.6965713	0.515423±0.0720595	0.143820±0.0095007
3	4.794305±0.0062657	2.450909±0.0935256	0.322576±0.0039322	0.128684±0.0042731
4	1.355459±0.0013390	0.082165±0.0001007	0.007494±0.0001478	0.007494±0.0000455
5	6.900478±0.0101289	0.535711±0.0081520	0.067585±0.0024342	0.017286±0.0009005
6(n=2)	0.000087±0.0000000	0.000067±0.0000000	0.000060±0.0000000	0.000058±0.0000015
6(n=3)	0.000874±0.0000000	0.000245±0.0000003	0.000223±0.0000008	0.000220±0.0000013
6(n=4)	0.002912±0.0000000	0.000600±0.0000006	0.000527±0.0000020	0.000521±0.0000023
6(n=5)	0.007547±0.0000002	0.001109±0.0000026	0.000926±0.0000032	0.000919±0.0000041
6(n=6)	0.014951±0.0000001	0.001872±0.0000053	0.001496±0.0000058	0.001486±0.0000056
6(n=7)	0.026646±0.0000011	0.002874±0.0000191	0.002179±0.0000073	0.002167±0.0000087
6(n=8)	0.041858±0.0000009	0.004162±0.0000274	0.003038±0.0000122	0.003013±0.0000098
6(n=9)	0.062087±0.0000013	0.005770±0.0000531	0.004022±0.0000157	0.003986±0.0000148
6(n=10)	0.083246±0.0000053	0.007678±0.0000696	0.005179±0.0000281	0.005129±0.0000232

illustrates a limitation in PWLA in general, which occurs when a function has substantially more turning points than available segments. A poor approximation results, as shown in figure 2(a). This problem is alleviated with an increase in segment count, specifically, doubling the segment count from 10 to 20 resulted in a 92.9% fitness improvement.

The PSO also handled the increase in dimensionality effectively(refer to table 2). The performance degradation on dimensionality increase on function 6 appears to be linearly. The PSO also exhibited small levels of performance deviation over the 30 runs, implying that the approach used in this paper to preform PWLA is quite robust.

7 Conclusion

The aim of this paper was to design a way of using a PSO algorithm to solve the problem of piecewise linear approximation of n-dimensional parametric curves. The problem of finding line segment parameters a_j, p and b_j, p as defined in equation (6) were solved analytically using the method described in section 3. The remaining task of finding optimal partition points was achieved using a PSO as described in section 4. The approach explained in this paper achieved this aim, by obtaining very accurate PWLAs of the test functions.

Future work can include approaches to optimize the number of segments. The approach can also be adapted to deal with multi-variate vector functions.

References

1. Burden, R.L. and Faires, J.D.: Numerical Analysis. Brooks Cole (2007)
2. Kennedy, J., Eberhart, R.C.: Particle Swarm Optimization. In: Proceedings of the IEEE International Joint Conference on Neural Networks, pp. 1942–1948 (1995)
3. Kennedy, J., Mendes, R.: Population Structure and Particle Performance. In: Proceedings of the IEEE Congress on Evolutionary Computation, pp. 1671–1676 (2002)
4. Peer, E.S., van den Bergh, F., Engelbrecht, A.P.: Using Neighborhoods with the Guaranteed Convergence PSO. In: Proceedings of the IEEE Swarm Intelligence Symposium, pp. 235–242 (2003)
5. Sklansky, J., Gonzalez, V.: Fast polygonal approximation of digitized curves. Pattern Recognition 12(5), 327–331 (1980)
6. Salotti, M.: An efficient algorithm for the optimal polygonal approximation of digitized curves. Pattern Recognition Letters 22(2), 215–221 (2001)
7. do Carmo, M.: Differential Geometry of Curves and Surfaces. Prentice-Hall (1976)
8. Velho, L., de Figueiredo, L.H., Gomes, J.: Journal of the Brazilian Computer Society 3(3), 1–14 (1997)
9. Imamoto, A., Tang, B.: A Recursive Descent Algorithm for Finding the Optimal Minimax Piecewise Linear Approximation of Convex Functions. In: Advances in Electrical and Electronics Engineering, pp. 287–289 (2008)
10. Manis, G., Papakonstantinou, G., Tsanakas, P.: Optimal Piecewise Linear Approximation of Digitized Curves. In: Proceedings of International Conference on Digital Signal Processing, pp. 1079–1081 (1997)
11. Horst, J.A., Beichl, I.: A Simple Algorithm for Eficient Piecewise Linear Approximation of Space Curves. In: Proceedings of International Conference on Image Processing, pp. 744–747 (1997)
12. Pavlidis, T.: Polygonal Approximations by Newton's Method. IEEE Transactions on Computers 25(8), 800–807 (1977)
13. Dunham, J.G.: Optimum uniform piecewise linear approximation of planar curves. IEEE Transactionson Pattern Analysis and Machine Intelligence PAMI-8(1), 67–75 (1986)
14. Stone, H.: Approximation of Curves by Line Segments. Mathematics of Computation 15(73), 40–47 (1961)
15. Engelbrecht, A.P.: Particle Swarm Optimization: Velocity Initialization. Accepted for IEEE Congress on Eevolutionary Computation (2012)

Probabilistic Stochastic Diffusion Search

Mahamed G.H. Omran[1] and Ayed Salman[2]

[1] Department of Computer Science,
Gulf University for Science and Technology, Kuwait
omran.m@gust.edu.kw
[2] Computer Engineering Department, Kuwait University, Kuwait
ayed.salman@ku.edu.kw

Abstract. Stochastic Diffusion Search (SDS) is a population-based, naturally inspired search and optimization algorithm. It belongs to a family of swarm intelligence (SI) methods. SDS is based on direct (one-to-one) communication between agents. SDS has been successfully applied to a wide range of optimization problems. In this paper we consider the SDS method in the context of unconstrained continuous optimization. The proposed approach uses concepts from probabilistic algorithms to enhance the performance of SDS. Hence, it is named the Probabilistic SDS (PSDS). PSDS is tested on 16 benchmark functions and is compared with two methods (a probabilistic method and a SI method). The results show that PSDS is a promising optimization method that deserves further investigation.

1 Introduction

Swarm Intelligence (SI) is the collective behavior of decentralized and self-organized systems. SI systems are typically made up of a population of agents or particles interacting with each other and with their environment. Interaction between agents yields collective intelligent behavior. Typical SI algorithms are ant colony optimization (ACO), particle swarm optimization (PSO) and stochastic diffusion search (SDS).

Stochastic Diffusion Search [2] is an efficient resource allocation algorithm that has been applied to a wide range of applications [4]. However, there is little work on using SDS to solve continuous nonlinear function optimization defined as follows,

$$Minimize \ (or \ maximize) f(\overrightarrow{x}) such \ that \ L_i \leq x_i \leq U_i, for \ i = 1, \ldots, D.$$

Where $f(\overrightarrow{x})$ is the objective function, $\overrightarrow{x}$ is a candidate solution consisting of D parameters (x_i), and L_i and U_i are the lower and upper bounds for each parameter, respectively.

A new class of optimization methods is Probabilistic algorithms. Probabilistic methods search a problem space using an explicit probabilistic model of candidate solutions. Thus, in probabilistic methods a population is approximated with a probability distribution and new potential solutions are generated by sampling

M. Dorigo et al. (Eds.): ANTS 2012, LNCS 7461, pp. 300–307, 2012.

this distribution. Two representative probabilistic algorithms are the Estimation of Distribution Algorithm (EDA) [6] and the more recent Cross-Entropy (CE) method [12]. Probabilistic algorithms have been successfully applied to a wide range of optimization problems (see [11]).

In this paper, we propose a probabilistic SDS (PSDS) method that explicitly uses a probability distribution to tackle unconstrained continuous function optimization. Several well-known benchmark functions are used to compare the proposed method against CE and PSO.

The remainder of the paper is organized as follows: Section 2 provides an overview of SDS. The proposed approach is presented in Section 3. Benchmark functions to measure the performance of the different approaches are provided in Section 4. Results of the experiments are presented and discussed in Section 5. Finally, Section 6 concludes the paper.

2   Stochastic Diffusion Search (SDS)

Stochastic Diffusion Search (SDS) [2] is a population-based, swarm intelligence optimization algorithm that is based on direct (one-to-one) communication between agents. The SDS algorithm consists of two phases, a test phase and a diffusion phase. In the test phase, each agent tests its hypothesis (a potential solution to the problem). In the diffusion phase, agents share information about hypotheses via one-to-one communication. The test and diffusion phases are repeated until a swarm of agents converge to the optimum hypothesis. SDS convergence to global optimum has already been studied by Nasuto and Bishop in [8] and its time complexity has been analyzed by Nasuto et al. in [7]. SDS has been successfully applied to a wide range of optimization problems (e.g. object recognition [3], site selection for wireless networks [14], amongst others [4]). Little work has been done in the context of continuous optimization. Two recent attempts have been made in this area but by hybridizing SDS with other methods (e.g. PSO [1], a local search method [10]).

3   The Proposed Method

In this paper, we propose a new variant of SDS that can be used as a continuous global optimizer. In the proposed approach, each agent has hypothesis and status. *Hypotheses* are defined as candidate solutions to a problem while *status* is a Boolean variable used to distinguish between active and inactive agents.

The general algorithm of the proposed method is shown in Alg. 1. The algorithm starts by initializing a population of N agents. The fitness of each agent is then determined. As in the CE method, The N^e best performing agents (representing an *elite sample*) are used to estimate the parameters of a probability distribution. In this study, normal distribution is used, hence, the parameters are μ and σ^2. These two parameters are estimated (i.e. $\hat{\mu}$ and $\hat{\sigma}^2$) using the sample mean and sample variance of the elite samples. In the test phase, each agent is compared against another randomly chosen agent. If it has a better fitness function than the selected agent, it is set as *active*, otherwise it is set as *inactive*.

In the diffusion phase, if an agent, $(\overrightarrow{x_i})$, is inactive, a random agent, $(\overrightarrow{x_r})$, is chosen. If $(\overrightarrow{x_r})$ is active, it communicates its hypothesis to $(\overrightarrow{x_i})$. This could be done in many ways. In this paper, $(\overrightarrow{x_i})$ is set to a solution in the neighborhood of $(\overrightarrow{x_r})$ as follows,

$$\overrightarrow{x_i} \sim N(\overrightarrow{x_r}, k_1.\hat{\sigma}^2)$$

Where k_1 is a user-defined constant.

On the other hand, if the selected agent, $(\overrightarrow{x_r})$, is inactive, $(\overrightarrow{x_i})$ is re-initialized. Re-initialization can be done at random or in a more intelligent way. In this paper, $(\overrightarrow{x_i})$ is set to a random sample from the $N(\hat{\mu}, k_2.\hat{\sigma}^2)$ distribution as follows,

$$\overrightarrow{x_i} \sim N(\hat{\mu}, k_2.\hat{\sigma}^2)$$

Where k_2 is another user-specified constant. Intuitively, k_1 should be less than or equal to 1 to intensify the search around an active (i.e. good) solution while k_2 should be greater than or equal to 1 to avoid premature convergence (i.e. to improve diversification). A good balance between intensification and diversification is needed for any search method and this balance is achieved by our PSDS. After a fixed number of iterations PSDS terminates.

4   Experimental Setup

To test the performance of the proposed PSDS method, we have chosen 16 functions (ten functions from the CEC 2005 benchmark set (namely, F1-F10) and six canonical test functions). The ten CEC functions have different characteristics (e.g. rotated, non-separable, shifted, unimodal, multimodal, etc.). For more details about these functions, the reader is referred to [13]. The six canonical functions are Rastrigin, Normalized Schwefel, Levy, Ackley, Shifted Griewank and Step. Rastrigin, Normalized Schwefel, Levy, Ackley and Shifted Griewank functions are difficult multimodal functions while the Step function is a discontinuous unimodal function. The definition of these functions could be found in many papers [9].

For the CEC functions we use 100,000 function evaluations (FEs), $D = 10$, admissible error is 10^{-6} for F1-F5 and 10^{-2} for F6-F10 and run each method for 25 independent simulations as suggested by Suganthan *et al.* in [13]. For the canonical functions we use 100,000 FEs, $D = 30$, admissible error is 10^{-4} and we use 50 runs (to get more accurate statistical results). To measure the *effectiveness* of a method we use two metrics:

1. The mean and the standard deviation of the best-of-run error which is defined as the absolute difference between the best-of-the-run $f(\overrightarrow{x}_{best})$ value and the actual optimum $f(\overrightarrow{x}^*)$ of a given function. Avg. err. $= f(\overrightarrow{x}_{best}) - f(\overrightarrow{x}^*)$
2. 2) Success rate (SR): The number of successful runs (a run is successful if avg. err. $\leq$ admissible error).

Initialize agents and calculate their fitness;
repeat
    /* Estimation of distribution */
    Let I be the indices of the N^e best performing agents;
    for $j=1$ to D **do**
$$\widehat{\mu_j} = \sum_{j \in I} \frac{x_{ij}}{N^e} \;;$$
$$\widehat{\sigma_j^2} = \sum_{j \in I} \frac{(x_{ij} - \mu_j)^2}{N^e} \;;$$
    end
    /*Test-phase */
    for $i=1$ to N **do**
        randomly choose an agent, $(\vec{x_r})$, from the swarm ;
        if $f(\vec{x_i}) \leq f(\vec{x_r})$ **then**
            $active_i = true$;
        else
            $active_i = false$;
        end
    end
    /* Diffusion-phase */
    for $i=1$ to N **do**
        if $active_i = false$ **then**
            randomly choose an agent, $(\vec{x_r})$, from the swarm;
            if $active_r = true$ **then**
                set $(\vec{x_i})$ to a solution randomly chosen from the neighborhood of $(\vec{x_r})$ as follows,;
$$\vec{x_i} \sim N(\vec{x_r}, k_1.\hat{\sigma}^2)$$
            else
                Set $(\vec{x_i})$ to a random sample generated from the $N(\hat{\mu}, k_2.\hat{\sigma}^2)$ distribution, i.e. ;
$$\vec{x_i} \sim N(\hat{\mu}, k_2.\hat{\sigma}^2)$$
            end
        end
    end
until Until a stopping criterion is met;

Algorithm 1. The proposed PSDS algorithm

5   Experimental Results

In this section, PSDS is compared with the CE method and Standard Particle Swarm Optimization 2011 (SPSO2011) (http://www.particleswarm.info). CE has been chosen as a recent example of probabilistic algorithms while SPSO as a representative of SI methods. For CE and SPSO2011 we use the recommended settings defined in [5] and (http://www.particleswarm.info), respectively. For

PSDS, we set $N = 100$, $N^e = 10$, $k_1 = 0.5$ and $k_2 = 1.5$. To be fair, we did not adjust each set of parameter to each problem.

All the tests are run on an Apple MacBook Pro computer with Intel Core i7 processor running at 2.7 GHz with 4GB of RAM. Mac OS X 10.7 (Lion) is the operating system used. All programs are implemented using MATLAB version 7.11.0.584 (R2010b) environment. The statistically significant best solutions have been shown in bold (using the non-parametric statistical test called Wilcoxon's rank sum test for independent samples [15] with $\alpha = 0.05$).

The effectiveness of CE, SPSO2011 and PSDS is shown on Table 1 and Table 2 for the CEC and canonical functions, respectively. Table 1 shows that PSDS performs better than CE and SPSO2011 on F4, F5, F6 and F9. SPSO2011 outperforms the other methods on F3, F8 and F10. While CE performs better on one function, F7. PSDS and SPSO2011 perform comparably on F1 and F2. An interesting observation regarding F10 is that F10 is actually a rotated F9. SPSO2011 is rotationally invariant ("almost" since there is no 100% rotationally invariant method unless the search space is a hyper-sphere), thus, its performance has not deteriorated when rotation occurs. This is not the case for CE and PSDS (actually many popular metaheuristics are not rotationally invariant, e.g. SPSO2007, GA, DE.) that treat each parameter independently. For the canonical functions, Table 2 shows that PSDS performs better than CE and SPSO2011 on two functions (i.e. Ackley and Step) while CE performs better on one function only (i.e. Normalized Schwefel). For the Levy function, although SPSO2011 achieves the smallest error, PSDS achieves the highest SR. Hence, the results of Tables 1 and 2 show that PSDS generally performs better than CE and performs comparably to SPSO2011. However, PSDS is relatively easier to code than SPSO2011.

Table 1. Comparing the effectiveness of CE, SPSO2011 and PSDS on the 10 CEC functions

	CE		SPSO2011		SDSP	
	Avg. Err.(SD)	SR(%)	Avg. Err.(SD)	SR(%)	Avg. Err.(SD)	SR(%)
F1	$1.20e + 00(3.68e - 01)$	0	$8.09e - 07(1.23e - 07)$	100	$7.89e - 07(1.83e - 07)$	100
F2	$6.95e + 01(2.00e + 01)$	0	$8.57e - 07(1.19e - 07)$	100	$8.81e - 07(1.20e - 07)$	100
F3	$2.00e + 07(1.11e + 07)$	0	$3.79e + 04(2.75e + 04)$	0	$1.15e + 05(9.69e + 04)$	0
F4	$1.05e + 02(3.07e + 01)$	0	$8.95e - 07(1.03e - 07)$	100	$7.92e - 07(1.48e - 07)$	100
F5	$6.21e + 02(1.57e + 02)$	0	$9.18e - 07(6.86e - 08)$	100	$8.52e - 07(8.73e - 08)$	100
F6	$9.05e + 02(3.17e + 02)$	0	$2.84e + 01(6.37e + 01)$	0	$9.93e + 00(1.87e + 01)$	0
F7	$8.30e - 01(8.34e - 02)$	0	$1.27e + 03(3.16e + 00)$	0	$1.27e + 03(3.97e - 02)$	0
F8	$2.03e + 01(8.03e - 02)$	0	$2.03e + 01(9.85e - 02)$	0	$2.04e + 01(5.44e - 02)$	0
F9	$2.25e + 01(3.07e + 00)$	0	$5.76e + 00(2.16e + 00)$	0	$2.31e + 00(1.37e + 00)$	4
F10	$2.37e + 01(2.95e + 00)$	0	$4.90e + 00(2.27e + 00)$	0	$2.40e + 01(7.69e + 00)$	0

Table 2. Comparing the effectiveness of CE, SPSO2011 and PSDS on the 6 canonical functions

	CE		SPSO2011		SDSP	
	Avg. Err.(SD)	SR(%)	Avg. Err.(SD)	SR(%)	Avg. Err.(SD)	SR(%)
Rastrigin	$2.92e + 02(1.66e + 01)$	0	$2.51e + 01(7.08e + 00)$	0	$4.16e + 01(3.68e + 01)$	0
Normalized Schwefel	$8.24e - 03(8.08e - 03)$	0	$1.75e + 02(2.22e + 01)$	0	$1.11e + 02(4.42e + 00)$	0
Levy	$1.63e + 02(2.92e + 01)$	0	$7.55e - 01(4.93e - 01)$	2	$1.54e + 00(1.68e + 00)$	8
Ackley	$2.10e + 01(4.44e - 02)$	0	$1.07e + 00(6.76e - 01)$	24	$9.55e - 05(4.34e - 06)$	100
Shifted Griewank	$1.69e + 02(2.04e + 01)$	0	$6.99e - 03(8.41e - 03)$	46	$1.36e + 00(9.50e + 00)$	48
Step	$1.84e + 04(2.14e + 03)$	0	$1.10e + 00(1.27e + 00)$	38	$0(0)$	100

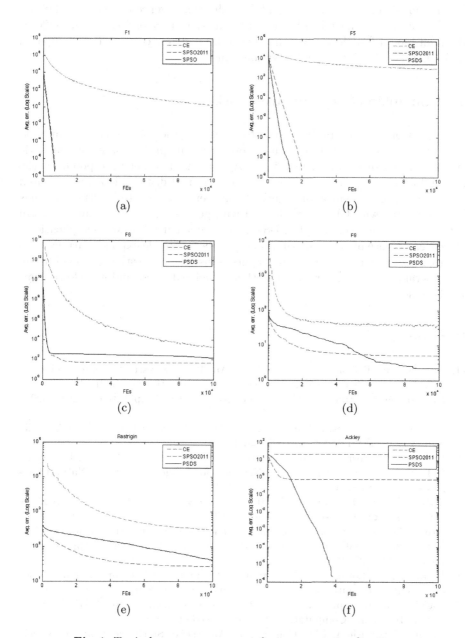

Fig. 1. Typical convergence curves for representative functions

The convergence characteristics of a set of representative functions are depicted in Fig. 1 in terms of the average error (in logarithmic scale) vs. FEs. For unimodal functions (i.e. F1 and F5), the convergence curves of PSDS descend much faster and reach better solutions than that of CE and SPSO2011. For multimodal function, PSDS has generally a slower convergence (compared to SPSO2011) and it reaches better solutions.

6   Conclusions and Future Work

This paper presented a probabilistic stochastic diffusion search (PSDS) method for solving unconstrained continuous optimization problems. A probabilistic model (normal distribution in this study) was used to generate points in the SDS diffusion phase. The parameters of the normal distribution were updated in each iteration. The proposed method has been tested on 16 functions and has been compared with CE and SPSO2011 with good results. Our future work will investigate the performance of PSDS on constrained and real-world applications. Moreover, the use of other distributions (e.g. beta, double exponential) needs to be investigated. The effect of k_1 and k_2 needs also to be investigated. In addition, the generalization of the proposed method to solve discrete and mixed problems will be studied.

References

1. Al-Rifaie, M., Bishop, M., Blackwell, M., An, T.: An investigation into the merger of stochastic diffusion search and particle swarm optimization. In: Proc. of the 13th Annual Conference on Genetic and Evolutionary Computation, GECCO 2011 (2011)
2. Bishop, J.M.: Stochastic Searching Networks. In: Proc. 1st IEE Conf. on Artificial Neural Networks, London, pp. 329–331 (1989)
3. Bishop, J.M., Torr, P.: The Stochastic Search Network. In: Linggard, R., Myers, D.J., Nightingale, C. (eds.) Neural Networks for Images, Speech and Natural Language, pp. 370–387. Chapman & Hall (1992)
4. SDS: Stochastic Diffusion Search (2011), http://www.doc.gold.ac.uk/~mas02mb/sdp/index.html (access date: August 9, 2011)
5. Kroese, D., Porotsky, S., Rubinstein, R.: The Cross-Entropy Method for Continuous Multi-extremal Optimization. Methodology and Computing in Applied Probability 8, 383–407 (2006)
6. Larranaga, P., Lozano, J.: Estimation of Distribution Algorithms: a new tool for evolutionary computation. Kluwer Academic editors (2002)
7. Nasuto, S.J., Bishop, J.M., Lauria, L.: Time Complexity of Stochastic Diffusion Search. In: Neural Computation, Vienna, Austria (1998)
8. Nasuto, S.J., Bishop, J.M.: Convergence Analysis of Stochastic Diffusion Search. Journal of Parallel Algorithms and Applications 14(2), 89–107 (1999)
9. Omran, M., Engelbrecht, A.: Free Search Differential Evolution. In: The Proc. of the IEEE Congress on Evolutionary Computation (CEC 2009), Norway, pp. 110–117 (2009)

10. Omran, M., Moukadem, I., Al-Sharhan, S., Kinawi, M.: Stochastic Diffusion Search for Continuous Global Optimization. In: The Proc. of the International Conference on Swarm Intelligence (ICSI 2011), Cergy, France (June 2011)
11. Pelikan, M., Sastry, K., Cantu-Paz, E.: Scalable Optimization via Probabilistic Modeling: From Algorithms to Applications. Springer (2006)
12. Robinstein, R., Kroese, D.: The cross-entropy method: a unified approach to combinatorial optimization. Monte-Carlo simulations and machine learning. Springer-Verlag (2004)
13. Suganthan, P., Hansen, N., Liang, J., Deb, K., Chen, Y., Auger, A., Tiwari, S.: Problem definitions and evaluation criteria for the CEC2005 special session on real-parameter optimization. Technical report, Nanyang Technology University, Singapore (2005)
14. Whitaker, R.M., Hurley, S.: An agent based approach to site selection for wireless networks. In: Proc. ACM Symposium on Applied Computing, Madrid, pp. 574–577 (2002)
15. Wilcoxon, F.: Individual comparisons by ranking methods. Biometrics 1, 80–83 (1945)

Self-organized Clustering of Square Objects
by Multiple Robots

Yong Song, Jung-Hwan Kim, and Dylan A. Shell

Dept. of Computer Science and Engineering, Texas A&M University
{porawn,jnk3355,dshell}@cse.tamu.edu

Abstract. Object clustering is a widely studied task in which self-organized robots form piles from dispersed objects. Although central clusters are usually desired, workspace boundaries can cause perimeter cluster formation to dominate. This research demonstrates successful clustering of square boxes—an especially challenging instance since flat edges exacerbate adhesion to boundaries—using simpler robots than previous published research. Our solution consists of two novel behaviors, *Twisting* and *Digging*, which exploit the objects' geometry to pry boxes free from boundaries. We empirically explored the significance of different divisions of labor by measuring the spatial distribution of robots and the system performance. Data from over 40 hours of physical robot experiments show that different divisions of labor have distinct features, *e.g.*, one is reliable while another is especially efficient.

1   Introduction

Object clustering involves gathering spatially distributed objects into a single central pile. This operation, akin to raking leaves, simplifies subsequent handling and is useful within a longer manipulation pipeline. The task is ideal for studying the role of physics and environmental interactions in producing complex collective behavior. This paper is concerned with clustering square objects, which is an important direction because (i) such objects have greater relevance for applications (specifically construction involving bricks), (ii) radically different packings result, which challenge existing geometry-based clustering theories, and (iii) sensitivity to environment boundaries, which may cause existing approaches to fail in forming central clusters, is exacerbated.

We introduce two simple behaviors *Twisting* and *Digging* exploiting objects' shape to pry boxes away from boundaries. A group of robots executing mixture of these two behaviors is able to repeatedly form central clusters. Through over 40 hours of experiments, we examined the effect of different numbers of twisters and diggers on the system's performance, empirically determining the most reliable and most efficient divisions of labor. This paper's primary contributions are:

- Assessment of Kazadi's cluster growth theory [1]: Experimental data verifies the theory, previously only validated with simulations of hypothetical robots.

- Division of labor: This is the first examination of the division of labor for clustering tasks; this paper illustrates that it can play an important role.

M. Dorigo et al. (Eds.): ANTS 2012, LNCS 7461, pp. 308–315, 2012.

- New way to address boundary effects: This paper describes an open-loop motion to limit cluster formation on the boundaries. The motion does not depend on the robot disambiguating particular circumstances, but rather it is the context within which the actions are executed that produces the desired outcome. From a self-organization perspective, this is a particularly satisfying solution to the boundary problem since it depends primarily on the physics of the robot-environment interaction for its success.

- Illustrating that spatial distribution matters: While existing techniques for dealing with boundaries, (e.g., using sophisticated rules for releasing objects [2]), our approach simply modifies the spatial distribution of robots. Thus far, analysis techniques (e.g., [1,3]) only consider spatially homogeneous distributions.

2   Motivation and Related Work

Multi-robot object clustering has been widely studied: Deneubourg et al. [4] presented an early distributed algorithm which achieved "sorting" with a local density sensor and no direct communication between agents. Inspired by biological models, Beckers et al. [5] carried out the first physical robot experiments and also demonstrated clustering without a density sensor. They gave an initial explanation for the emergence of clusters on the basis of the geometry of the piles. Martinoli [6] further quantified this geometric notion. Thereafter, Kazadi et al. [1] introduced a model which gives conditions for cluster formation to occur.

Holland and Melhuish [2] extended the clustering task to include spatial sorting. They conducted several experiments in which clusters formed at the edge of their arena, since flat boundaries have geometric properties similar to very large clusters. A similar "preference" for cluster formation along boundaries has been noted within a biological system [7]. Some authors [4,5,2] explained clustering through *stigmergy* [8], a process wherein the environment, modified by agents' previous actions, affects subsequent task performance. More recent connections between robot clustering and biological models have been published [9].

Almost all previously published work in robotic clustering considers cylindrical pucks. However, square objects have flat edges which exacerbate adhesion to boundary walls. It is particularly difficult for a cylindrical robot to move a box positioned against a wall into the center of the workspace. This is observable in the video posted by Vaughan's Autonomy Lab[1] in which 36 iRobot Creates successfully cluster square objects; most of the clusters form on the boundary.

Table 1 is a comparative summary of robots' capabilities and experimental environments in the most closely related literature. Our robots are much simpler than others, except for Vaughan's demo. They recognize the existence of an obstacle (via IR), but cannot ascertain its type. Interestingly, the rows in the table with the simplest robots either produced boundary clusters or have a special way of treating them, e.g., Maris and Boeckhorst [10] define objects to be "lost" once they were pushed against a wall.

---

[1] We thank Vaughan's Autonomy Lab at SFU for posting this video as it inspired this paper. The video can be seen at http://www.youtube.com/watch?v=b_kZmatqAaQ

Table 1. A comparison of robot capabilities for clustering tasks

Work	Pucks/Seeds/Cubes/Boxes		Environment	
	Sensing	Manipulation	Sensing	Boundary & Effects
Beckers et al. [5]	⋄ Detect circular pucks with force sensor in C-shaped scoop	⋄ Push circular objects ⋄ Control the number of carried pucks with a microswitch	⋄ Two IR sensors for obstacle avoidance	⋄ A square arena ⋄ Side-steps the effect of boundary by using a deformable boundary
	Note: The robots can push pucks trapped on the boundary due to a deformable wall.			
Martinoli [3]	⋄ Discriminate between circular seeds and obstacles with distinct IR sensor signatures	⋄ Grasp, carry and release seeds	⋄ Six IR proximity sensors for detecting obstacles	⋄ A square arena ⋄ Effect of the boundary ignored
	Note: The robots can recognize and access clusters geometrically.			
Holland & Melhuish [2]	⋄ Detect circular pucks by sensing backward force on gripper	⋄ Grip, retain, and release circular pucks with semicircular gripper	⋄ Four IR proximity sensors for sensing the boundary	⋄ An octagonal shaped arena with rigid boundary ⋄ Use the probability of detecting a wall
	Note: Robots cannot discriminate between other robots and the boundary. *The strategy of varying the wall probability introduces the false positive.* *The robots overcome the effect of boundary with sensors.*			
Maris et al. [10]	⋄ No sensing of the cubes	⋄ Cubes pushed until obstacle detected	⋄ Six IR proximity sensors for obstacle detection	⋄ A square arena ⋄ Consider pushed cubes against the boundary as "lost"
	Note: The robots manipulate cubes by only pushing behavior for clustering task. *Robots pass over cubes on the boundary.*			
Vaughan [unpubl.]	⋄ Detect square boxes with bumpers	⋄ Push and leave a box by a bumper's threshold	⋄ No sensor for detecting objects except for boxes	⋄ A rectangular arena ⋄ Effect of the boundary ignored
	Note: Several clusters formed on the boundary.			
This paper	⋄ Detect square boxes with bumpers	⋄ Push and leave a box by a bumper's threshold	⋄ A single IR proximity sensor for sensing the objects on the right side	⋄ An octagonal shaped arena with rigid boundary ⋄ Overcome the effect of boundary using motion strategies
	Note: No puck manipulator. *Limited sensor information (1-bit IR sensor, 1-bit bumper).* *Boundary effect overcome without explicit sensing of it (self-organization).*			

3   Materials and Methods

We used iRobot Creates robots having only two sensors: a bumper and a proximity sensor. We consider 35cm×35cm square boxes as the objects to cluster; although a box has an insufficient mass to activate the bump sensor, two or more boxes together have adequate mass. Similar to Melhuish and his group (*e.g.*, [2,9]), we used an octagonal shaped workplace (4.5m×4.5m). Figure 1 (left) shows the initial configuration. We used 5 robots and 20 boxes. Three trials, each lasting 90 minutes, were conducted for each condition. All experiments were videotaped and annotated by observing frames every 5 seconds. A cluster is a group of more than three boxes, each touching at least one other. We distinguish between boundary and central clusters, and the goal being to produce only the latter. A boundary cluster is a group which has at least one box touching a wall.

Fig. 1. (left) initial configuration, (center) an example final configuration using the basic strategy, and (right) an example final configuration using the mixed strategy (2 Twisters and 3 Diggers). Video clips are available at http://students.cse.tamu.edu/jnk3355/experiments.html.

4   The Basic Strategy

Based on the controllers in [5,2], we implemented the simple algorithm shown in Figure 2. The robots move straight but make a random turn when their bumpers are pressed. All operations depend only on local information. Figure 1 (center) shows the final configuration of the first trial of the basic strategy. In all three runs, the robots produced clusters of square boxes, but most clusters formed on the boundary (*cf.* Experiment 2 in

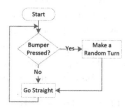

Fig. 2. Flowchart showing the basic behavior

[5]). The results underscore the earlier statement: the boundary influences cluster formation since walls have the properties comparable to a large cluster. The workspace walls buttress partial structures and the motion required to dislodge boxes only occurs infrequently.

5   The Mixed Strategy

We propose two new behaviors to overcome the effect of the boundary and to increase the formation of a single central cluster of boxes. Our approach exploits the mechanics of square objects. As shown in Figure 3 (left), striking the corner of a box can pry it loose from a tight packing. This reduces the area in contact with the wall and makes subsequent separation more likely when repeated. Using this prying motion, we introduce two complementary behaviors, *twisting* and *digging*. We call a robot executing the twisting behavior a *twister* (T) and a robot performing digging a *digger* (D). A group comprising both types of robots is said to employ a *mixed strategy*. We stress the simplicity of both operations: only one IR proximity sensor is added to the basic strategy's requirements. Figure 3 (right) shows trajectories of both behaviors on the boundary after a bump or time out (the latter, only for twisters). Diggers move along a curved arc to find a wall, while twisters go into the central region, potentially pushing a box. Intuitively, the twisters are more likely to convey objects, while the diggers form gaps between boxes and the boundary.

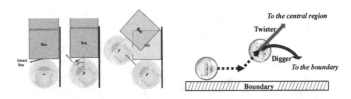

Fig. 3. (left) prying boxes away from the wall, and (right) trajectories of the twisters and diggers after the prying motion

Twisting Behavior. The prying motion shifts a box, and robots reaching the twisted box subsequently butt and bring it into the center, as shown in Figure 4a. To raise the probability of contact with boundary boxes, the robot operates in a wall following mode when its IR sensor detects an object on the robot's side. However, a robot will keep pushing it if one boundary box exists. Since it can be counter-productive to continue wall following, the robots only do so for 5 seconds, then perform a prying motion. The robot's motion in the center is the same as the basic strategy. Figure 4b shows the flowchart of the detailed algorithm.

Digging Behavior. The digging behavior was developed to improve overall performance, by increasing the chance to detecting a wall, and further separate twisted boxes from walls. Unlike twisters, the robot remains in a wall-following mode when its IR sensor detects an object. Also, the robot tries to find a boundary with the movement in a curved path instead of a straight trajectory. Apart from these two exceptions, the digging robots perform the same as the prying motion as twisters. The behavior is depicted in Figure 5b.

Resulting Cluster Dynamics. We carried out experimental trials under the condition identical to the basic strategy case in order to verify the clustering performance of the mixed strategy. Five robots were used, two twisters and three diggers. Although twisting and digging are complementary, the division of labor affects the overall performance; we present the details in Section 6.

Figure 1 (right) shows the final configuration of the first trial in the mixed strategy. Unlike to the basic strategy, a single large cluster emerged in the

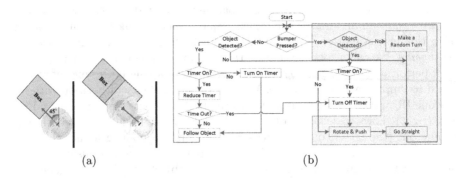

(a)   (b)

Fig. 4. (a) Motion on the boundary and (b) Flowchart of the digging behavior

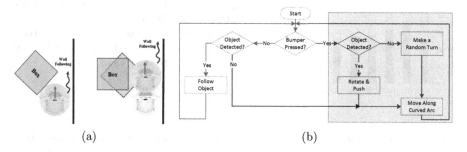

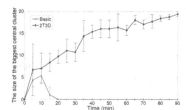

(a)   (b)

Fig. 5. (a) Motion on the boundary and (b) Flowchart of the digging behavior

middle of the arena in all three trials. Figure 6 shows the average size of the biggest central clusters and their standard deviations through the time for the basic and mixed strategies. The results verify that our proposed motion strategy can successfully overcome the boundary effect and collect spatially distributed objects into a single pile at the designated position, the center of the workspace.

Fig. 6. A comparison of clustering performance. Vertical axis is the size of the largest central cluster (essentially the same performance metric employed by [5]). The horizontal axis is time measured in minutes.

6   Analysis of Division of Labor

The most significant difference between twisting and digging behaviors is the spatial distribution of robots. Figure 7 shows the averaged spatial distributions of robots for particular divisions of labor (these data were collected without boxes as a baseline). The numbers of robots for each case are normalized by area (via basic case numbers). As the ratio of diggers increases, boxes on the boundary are more likely to be separated from the wall. However, it does not guarantee that the separated objects will be brought into central clusters since diggers will remain along the wall after the prying operation. From this analysis, we consider how differences in spatial distribution might affect clustering progress.

6.1   Clustering Performances of Differing Divisions of Labor

We conducted three trials for all possible combinations of the twister and the digger. Only few trials succeeded in forming a single central cluster having all

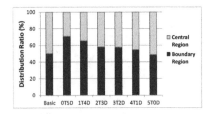

Fig. 7. Averaged spatial distribution of robots (central versus boundary regions) with respect to division of labor. Note: basic strategy robots are assumed to be uniformly distributed due to their random turn.

20 boxes within 90 minutes. Despite single central clusters not being completely formed in all cases, it appeared as if the robots could achieve the goal if given more time. We are interested in the question of whether, given unlimited time, all combinations would form a single central cluster. This question is examined using Cluster Growth Theory in the next section.

Figure 8 shows the averaged size of the largest central clusters for each case. As a summary, showing means of the three trials hides a few interesting facts. For example, the 1T4D case appears to perform poorly compared to 2T3D. In fact, it was a very capable division of labor and once formed a complete central cluster in the shortest observed time of 25 minutes. However, 1T4D also failed in one of its trials. This illustrates that while 2T3D is to be preferred for reliable clustering, 1T4D may be preferred for efficient clustering.

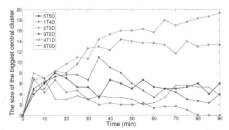

Fig. 8. Averaged performance of different Divisions of Labor

6.2   Cluster Dynamics under Differing Divisions of Labor

According to the theoretical dynamics of clustering systems, proposed by Kazadi et al. [1], a sufficient condition for the convergence of puck clustering systems is that the ratio of puck removal and puck deposit is monotonically decreasing. The cluster formation function was defined as below,

$$g(n) = \frac{Total\ number\ of\ box\ removal\ in\ cluster\ size,\ n}{Total\ number\ of\ box\ deposit\ in\ cluster\ size,\ n}. \tag{1}$$

To identify the effect of differing divisions of labor on generating a single central cluster, we examine g(n) for the central boxes here. Except for the 0T5D case, all values of g(n) for all cases are monotonically decreasing and are located below 1. On the basis of Kazadi et al.'s result, this would prove that each division of labor guarantees forming a single central cluster if sufficient time is allowed. The case of 0T5D can be explained by the spatial distribution of the robots: the diggers effectively generate gaps between boxes and boundaries, but the objects are rarely brought into the central region.

7 Conclusion

This paper described a multi-robot system in which agents employ simple local interaction rules to gather square objects into a single pile in the center of their workspace. As an existence proof, the work has two important aspects: First, we employ less capable robots than previous work. Secondly, the objects are square, making them more challenging to cluster and more functional than previous cases. We examined cluster growth properties through theoretical model of clustering of Kazadi et al. [1]. This work is the first empirical verification of cluster formation functions for physical robots we are aware of.

Through physical experiments, we demonstrated that the combination of two complementary behaviors, twisting and digging, allows robots to overcome the influence of the boundary. Our approach uses mechanical interactions with boxes on the perimeter, and emphasizes action rather than sensing. It is closer to the spirit underlying the self-organized clustering process itself than previous approaches to lessen formation of boundary clusters. This work also focuses on managing the spatial distribution of robots rather than specialized manipulation of the objects. In this regard, it is a departure from the focus within the literature, which assumes a uniform distribution of robots. It suggests that one way to direct such self-organized systems might be to influence where they spend their time.

References

1. Kazadi, S., Abdul-Khaliq, A., Goodman, R.: On the convergence of puck clustering systems. Robotics and Autonomous Systems 38(2), 93–117 (2002)
2. Holland, O., Melhuish, C.: Stigmergy, self-organization, and sorting in collective robotics. Artif. Life 5(2), 173–202 (1999)
3. Martinoli, A., Ijspeert, A.J., Mondada, F.: Understanding collective aggregation mechanisms: From probabilistic modelling to experiments with real robots. Robotics and Autonomous Systems 29(1), 51–63 (1999)
4. Deneubourg, J., Goss, S., Franks, N., Sendova-Franks, A., Detrain, C., Chrétien, L.: The dynamics of collective sorting robot-like ants and ant-like robots. In: Proc. of Simulation of Adaptive Behavior (SAB), pp. 356–363 (1991)
5. Beckers, R., Holland, O., Deneubourg, J.: From Local Actions to Global Tasks: Stigmergy and Collective Robotics. In: Proc. of Artificial Life IV, pp. 181–189 (1994)
6. Martinoli, A.: Swarm Intelligence in Autonomous Collective Robotics from Tools to the Analysis and Synthesis of Distributed Control Strategies. PhD thesis, École Polytechnique Fédérale de Lausanne (1999)
7. Bonabeau, E., Theraulaz, G., Fourcassié, V., Deneubourg, J.L.: Phase-ordering kinetics of cemetery organization in ants. Phys. Rev. E 57(4), 4568–4571 (1998)
8. Grassé, P.: La reconstruction du nid et les coordinations interindividuelles chez bellicositermes natalensis etcubitermes sp. la théorie de la stigmergie. Insectes sociaux 6(1), 41–80 (1959)
9. Scholes, S.R., Sendova-Franks, A.B., Swift, S.T., Melhuish, C.: Ants can sort their brood without a gaseous template. Behav. Ecology & Sociobiology 59, 531 (2005)
10. Maris, M., Boeckhorst, R.: Exploiting physical constraints: Heap formation through behavioral error in a group of robots. In: Proc. of Conference on Intelligent Robots and Systems (IROS), pp. 1655–1660 (1996)

Self-reproduction versus Transition Rules in Ant Colonies for Medical Volume Segmentation

Robert Haase[1], Hans-Joachim Böhme[2], Rosalind Perrin[1],
Klaus Zöphel[3], and Nasreddin Abolmaali[1,3]

[1] OncoRay, Medical Faculty Carl Gustav Carus, TU Dresden, Germany
{robert.haase,nasreddin.abolmaali}@oncoray.de,
[2] Faculty of Computer Science/Mathematics, HTW Dresden, Germany
[3] University Hospital Carl Gustav Carus, TU Dresden, Germany

Abstract. Target volume delineation in image stacks resulting from low contrast positron emission tomography (PET) remains a hot topic in the field of medical image processing. We propose an algorithm based on artificial ants moving in three dimensional image space controlled by transition rules which are able to self-reproduce. This investigation shows by variation of the transition rules that the impact on segmentation results is small because self-reproduction is the overwhelming effect in the simulation.

1 Introduction

Diagnostic imaging increasingly includes modern data processing techniques to support physicians in analysis of the resulting image data. In some specific areas, such as positron emission tomography (PET) development of specialized segmentation algorithms remains a hot topic. While there is a number of automatic segmentation algorithms available for PET in general, most of them were developed for standard high contrast PET and to solve specific tasks, such as target volume delineation in lung cancer [7] or head and neck cancer [6]. However especially for low contrast PET there is currently a lack of automatic routines for target volume delineation. Two example images of standard PET and low contrast PET are shown in Figure 1. For the automatic segmentation of such low contrast PET images we developed a segmentation algorithm based on virtual ant colonies. This investigation focuses on variation of the ants' transition rules to determine the effects on segmentation results.

2 Materials and Methods

2.1 Related Work

The first utilisation of virtual ant colonies for solving combinatorical problems [1] appeared in the early ninetees. Lately ant-based medical image processing

M. Dorigo et al. (Eds.): ANTS 2012, LNCS 7461, pp. 316–323, 2012.
© Springer-Verlag Berlin Heidelberg 2012

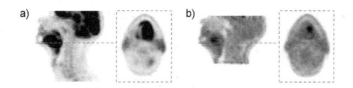

Fig. 1. Exemplary PET images of a head and neck cancer patient: a) [^{18}F]fluorodeoxyglucose (FDG) PET shows increased glucose metabolism in tumour and brain in black. b) In the same spatial position as in the tumour in the FDG PET image there is increased hypoxia expressed in black in a low contrast [^{18}F]fluoromisonidazole (FMISO) PET image.

was proposed for example to detect microcalcifications in digital mammograms [5]. Another ant-based approach to image segmentation used self-reproduction to automatically vary the colony population [3]. Our proposed algorithm, called PETACS, is based on the same principle: ants in regions with high signal intensity reproduce and thus ants accumulate inside the target object.

2.2 Proposed Algorithm

The proposed segmentation algorithm consists of two main procedures, shown in figure 2. The ant colony of PETACS is separated in two castes: scout ants for locating the target object in the PET volume (exploration) and worker ants for segmenting the target object from the background (exploitation). At the beginning of every iteration scout ants are seeded randomly on 4% of the voxels of a spherical region of interest (ROI) manually defined by an experienced radiologist. Worker ants only appear through self-reproduction. After the simulation, only the distribution of worker ants is analysed to determine the segmentation of the target object. The randomly seeded scout ants do not influence the result directly. For a detailed report on how to extract the binary image from ant distribution and pheromone field, the reader is referred to [4].

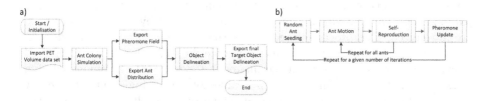

Fig. 2. Schematic overview of the proposed algorithm: Figure a) Shows the embedding of PETACS in an image processing pipeline leading from the original PET image to the target object delineation. Figure b) shows the sub procedures of the simulation comprising of two loops.

Ant Motion The motion of the ants is based on the transition rule proposed for Ant Colony based systems [1] adapted to handle voxels of three dimensional imaging data instead of edges and vertices in graphs:

$$p_{ij} = \frac{[A_j]^\alpha \cdot [\tau_j]^\beta}{\sum_{k/M(i)} [A_k]^\alpha \cdot [\tau_k]^\beta} \tag{1}$$

The probability p_{ij} that an ant moves from voxel i to j is calculated using grey values A (a PET scanner measures activity A) and pheromone intensities τ of voxels. The term $\sum_{k/M(i)}$ expresses the fact, that the sum is calculated over all voxels k in the Moore-neighbourhood of voxel i. If the sum is zero, the ant is constrained to stay at its current location. The weighting exponents α and β are used to make ants more attracted by either activity A or pheromone τ. Both ant castes are algorithmically identical, but α and β may differ allowing to give ants a different behaviour. Thus α_{scout}, β_{scout}, α_{worker} and β_{worker} are defined to induce different behavior of the ants belonging to both castes. An example for this implementation of division of labour is shown in figure 3.

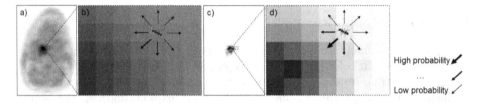

Fig. 3. Division of labour: Figure a) shows an image with the target object in black. Figure c) shows the corresponding pheromone field. Zoomed views in b) and d) show an ant and its transition probabilities to neighbouring voxels expressed as thickness of the arrows. If the ant only perceives activity ($\alpha = 1$, $\beta = 0$) as implied in b) transition probabilites to all directions are mostly uniform. If the ant only perceives the pheromone ($\alpha = 0$, $\beta = 1$) as implied in d) the ant is more attracted by the target object.

Self-Reproduction As an approach for filling target objects with ants the paradigms of ageing and self-reproduction as proposed by Fernandez et al. [3] are introduced. The process of ageing describes the limitation of the life span of ants. Every ant has an initial survival probability $p_S = 1$, which is decreased after every iteration by a given parameter $0 \leq \Delta p_S \leq 1$. In our simulation is $\Delta p_S = 0.33$. Respecting current p_S values of every single ant, after every iteration a number of ants are eliminated. The process of self-reproduction is the only chance for the colony to grow. This effect seems to be decisive for image segmentation by filling an object with ants. If the number of ants is defined a priori, the size of the object that can be filled is limited. Thus the colony needs a way to control the population size autonomously. Furthermore self-reproduction is an alternate approach for ant motion, because descendants are deposited in neighbouring voxels and thus the relative position of the colony changes. An exemplary simulation showing how an ant colony moves in space only by self-reproduction is shown in figure 4. In PETACS self-reproduction is allowed for ants occupying voxels i fullfilling the conditions

$$A_i - \bar{A}_{\max(1..t)} > 0, \text{ with } \bar{A}_{\max(1..t)} = \max(\bar{A}_1, ..., \bar{A}_t) \tag{2}$$

$$\tau_i > P \cdot t_{A,\max} \cdot \tau_{\max}. \tag{3}$$

Condition (2) ensures that only ants on voxels with activity above a threshold $\bar{A}_{\max(1..t)}$ are allowed to seed descendants. This threshold is calculated by determining the maximum of the average activity $\bar{A}_t$ of all voxels occupied by ants after any previous iteration t. Condition (3) further restricts the group of self-reproducing ants to ants occupying voxels with pheromone intensity above a certain threshold. This threshold depends on a constant $P = 0.015$, the number $t_{A,\max}$ of iterations passed by until the maximum average activity was reached and the current maximum pheromone intensity $\tau_{\max}$. This threshold ensures that the ants can not spread over the whole ROI at the end of the simulation.

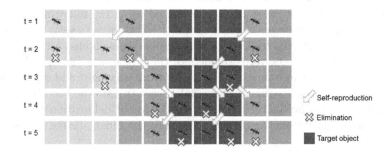

Fig. 4. Visualization of self-reproducing ants on a one-dimensional image during five iterations ($t = 1...5$): Ants occupying voxels with activity above average seed descendants (arrow). After two iterations every ant is eliminated (cross). In this example the ant-density inside the target object stabilizes in iteration $t = 4$ and $t = 5$. Note that none of the shown ants moves, the 'colony motion' is a result of self-reproduction.

Pheromone Update The pheromone field, which is used for the transition rule given above, is sampled onto a matrix of the same size as the processed PET volume data set (512 x 512 x 50 voxels) and initialized with zeros. After every iteration t all ants emit pheromone $\Delta\tau_{i,t}$ to the voxel i where it is located. The amount of pheromone is calculated from activity A_i in the voxel and the average activity $\bar{A}_t$ of all voxels being occupied by ants after iteration t:

$$\Delta\tau_{i,t} = \max(0, A_i - \bar{A}_t) \tag{4}$$

$$\tau'_{i,t} = (1 - \rho)\tau_{i,t} + \rho\Delta\tau_{i,t} \tag{5}$$

$$\tau_{i,t+1} = \sum_{k/N(i)} \tau'_{k,t}/7 \tag{6}$$

Equation 4 ensures that only ants on voxels with activity above the average emit pheromone. The pheromone intensity τ' of voxel i after iteration t is then calculated using the evaporation constant $\rho = 0.1$ in equation 5. This so called local pheromone update is well established in Ant Colony System-based algorithms [2]. Afterwards in equation 6 the pheromone intensity $\tau_{i,t+1}$ of the next iteration is calculated by blurring the pheromone field using a mean filter on the von-Neumann-neighbourhood $N(i)$ of voxel i including voxel i. Thus, after several iterations all voxels in the pheromone field are assigned non-zero values even if no ant has ever emitted pheromone on them. The result is a pheromone field with a gradient in almost all voxels aiding the ant in finding regions with high activity.

2.3   Experimental Setup

A collection of low contrast [^{18}F]fluoromisonidazole PET images from 46 head and neck cancer patients were further processed using the following procedure. Three experienced observers delineated the PET data sets searching for presumptive positive regions. In 35 data sets all observers defined a target object. The remaining 11 data sets were excluded for the further analysis. The PET data sets were segmented three times by PETACS using varying α and β parameters. Automatic and manual segmentation results were transformed to binary image stacks afterwards. The Jaccard Index J, a degree of delineation overlap, was then used as similarity metric for comparison of the binary image stacks:

$$J(A, B) = \frac{|A \cap B|}{|A \cup B|} \tag{7}$$

A and B represent the binary image stacks as sets. A is the set of all positive segmented voxels of one segmentation result, B represents the set of positive voxels of the other result. If $J = 0$, there is no overlap, if $J = 1$ the contours match perfectly in three dimensions.

After segmentation, there were three manually generated contours for every patient data set. These contours were compared to each other pair wise resulting in three J_{IOV} measurements of inter-observer-variability. The average of these measures is denoted as $\bar{J}_{IOV}$. Comparing the three automatically generated contours of every single α-β-configuration pair wise with each other resulted in a measure of reproducibility $\bar{J}_R$. Segmentation quality $\bar{J}_{SQ}$ is retrieved from comparison of automatically generated delineations with manually generated delineation. Analogously the symmetrical mean contour distance $\bar{D}$ is determined. Assuming the set $C(A) \subseteq A$ contains all voxels on the boundary of A and the Euclidean distance $d(a, b)$ of two contour elements a and b is given in millimeters, the mean contour distance $\bar{d}$ between sets A and B is given. Because this measure is not commutative, the symmetrical mean contour distance $\bar{D}$ is defined:

$$\bar{d}(A, B) = \frac{\sum_{\forall a \in C(A)} \min(d(a, b))}{|C(A)|}, b \in C(B) \tag{8}$$

$$\bar{D}(A, B) = \frac{1}{2}(\bar{d}(A, B) + \bar{d}(B, A)) \tag{9}$$

Seven different α-β-configurations for scout and worker ants were tested to simulate ant colonies with scouts and workers following the same transition rules ($\alpha_{Scout} = \alpha_{Worker}$ and $\beta_{Scout} = \beta_{Worker}$), ant colonies where ants used different transition rules depending on which caste they belonged to, ants moving randomly ($\alpha_{Scout} = \alpha_{Worker} = \beta_{Scout} = \beta_{Worker} = 0$) and ants which were not allowed to move.

The Wilcoxon Matched Pairs Test was applied to the J_{SQ} and D_{SQ} values of the tests pair wise. For example J_{SQ} values of all data sets of test 1 were compared to the corresponding values of test 2. The criterion for significant differences between these values was $p < 0.05$.

3   Results

After execution of 735 simulations (35 patients, 3 times, 7 configurations) and 3045 contour comparisons the average $\bar{J}$ and $\bar{D}$ values were calculated. Comparing the manually generated delineations resulted in $\bar{J}_{IOV} = 0.46$ and $\bar{D}_{IOV} = 6.39$ mm. Exemplary contours from PETACS and observers is shown in figure 5. The resulting $\bar{J}$ and $\bar{D}$ measures of contour comparisons and corresponding α and β values are shown in table 1. Firstly $\bar{J}_{SQ}$ and $\bar{D}_{SQ}$ values suggest that the automatic segmentation results match the manual delineations slightly worse than manual delineations match each other. Test 1 yielded the highest segmentation quality ($\bar{J}_{SQ} = 0.43$ and $\bar{D}_{SQ} = 7.40$ mm) even though the ants are moving randomly in image space ($\alpha_{Scout} = \alpha_{Worker} = \beta_{Scout} = \beta_{Worker} = 0$). The highest reproducibility measures were observed in test 2 ($\bar{D}_R = 1.16$ mm) and test 3 ($\bar{J}_R = 0.70$). Disabling ant motion (test 7) led to segmentation results that were worst reproducible ($\bar{J}_R = 0.72$ and $\bar{D}_R = 1.82$ mm) compared to all other tests. Figure 6 shows exemplary simulations of test 6 and 7 in comparison. In both cases ants accumulated inside the target objects even though ants were not allowed to move in test 7.

The Wilcoxon Matched Pairs Test on J_{SQ} showed significant differences ($p < 0.05$) for test 3 versus 4 and test 7 versus 2, 3 and 6. The corresponding analysis on D_{SQ} values showed significant differences in the same cases and additionally in tests 1 versus 2 and 3 and test 3 versus 4. In all other cases differences are not significant ($p \geq 0.05$), even though α and β vary.

4   Discussion

The presentend algorithm delineated target objects with a segmentation quality comparable to experienced observers, but did not outperform them in any

Table 1. List of performed tests: Varied α and β parameters are given as well as the resulting segmentation quality $\bar{J}_{SQ}$, $\bar{D}_{SQ}$ and reproducibility $\bar{J}_R$, $\bar{D}_R$ measures. Underlined measures highlight the best value of the corresponding metric in all experiments. *In test 7 ant motion was disabled. Thus α and β are not given.

Test	α_{Scout}	β_{Scout}	α_{Worker}	β_{Worker}	$\bar{J}_{SQ}$	$\bar{D}_{SQ}$ [mm]	$\bar{J}_R$	$\bar{D}_R$ [mm]
1	0	0	0	0	<u>0.43</u>	<u>7.40</u>	0.76	1.60
2	1	0	0	1	0.40	7.61	0.79	<u>1.16</u>
3	1	1	1	1	0.40	7.65	<u>0.80</u>	1.17
4	1	0	1	0	0.41	7.54	0.75	1.52
5	0	1	0	1	0.40	7.64	0.78	1.31
6	0	1	1	0	0.41	7.55	0.79	1.21
7*	-	-	-	-	0.42	7.52	0.72	1.82

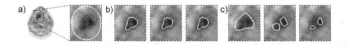

Fig. 5. ROI shown in a) was segmented. The resulting delineations of PETACS shown in b) are compared to target object delineations of observers in c). The PETACS based delineations match the manually generated delineations better ($\bar{J}_{SQ} = 0.46$) than the manually generated contours match each other ($\bar{J}_{IOV} = 0.43$).

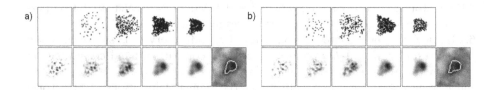

Fig. 6. Observing PETACS during a) test 6 and b) test 7 after 1, 3, 5, 10 and 20 iterations (from left to right) shows no obvious differences in development of worker ant distribution (upper row) or pheromone field (lower row). Even though ant motion was disabled in b), segmentation results (right) appear very similar.

case. Nevertheless, further improvement is needed before it can be applied in clinical routine. Segmentation results of randomly moving ants compared to ants controlled by transition rules show slightly increased segmentation quality. This fact poses the question as to whether transition rules are needed in this algorithm. The reason for the higher $\bar{J}_{SQ}$ and $\bar{D}_{SQ}$ values may be seen in the gap-filling purpose of ant motion. Through elimination of ants after every iteration, unoccupied voxels appear inside the target object. These voxels can be occupied again by reproduction or by ant motion. If the algorithm provides both, the probability of a gap being filled is higher and thus $\bar{J}_{SQ}$ and $\bar{D}_{SQ}$ may be higher.

5 Conclusion

The proposed ant based segmentation algorithm was able to delineate target objects in low contrast FMISO PET data. Variation of the transition rules influenced the segmentation results only to a small degree. Ants using transition rules induced the best reproducible results and randomly moving ants induced results best matching to experienced observers. However removing the transition rules from the algorithm is not worthwhile, because an increase of segmentation quality should not be achieved by a method decreasing segmentation reproducibility.

Acknowledgements. The authors RH and NA are supported by grants from the Sächsische Landesexzellenzinitiative (Project 100066308) and the Federal Ministry of Education and Research of Germany (BMBF-03ZIK042).

References

1. Colorni, A., Dorigo, M., Maniezzo, V.: Distributed Optimization by Ant Colonies. In: European Conference on Artificial Life, pp. 134–142. MIT Press, Cambridge (1992)
2. Dorigo, M., Birattari, M., Stützle, T.: Ant Colony Optimization - Artificial Ants as a Computational Intelligence Technique. IEEE Computational Intelligence Magazine, 28–39 (2006)
3. Fernandes, C., Ramos, V., Rosa, A.C.: Varying the Population Size of Artificial Foraging Swarms on Time Varying Landscapes. In: Duch, W., Kacprzyk, J., Oja, E., Zadrożny, S. (eds.) ICANN 2005. LNCS, vol. 3696, pp. 311–316. Springer, Heidelberg (2005)
4. Haase, R., Böhme, H.-J., Hietschold, V., Andreeff, M., Abolmaali, N.: A New Segmentation Algorithm for Low Contrast Positron Emission Tomography based on Ant Colony Optimization. In: Proceedings of the 55th IWK Crossing the Borders with ABC, Automation, Biomedical Engineering and Computer Science, pp. 505–510. TU Ilmenau (2010)
5. Jevtić, A., Quintanilla-Domínguez, J., Barrón-Adame, J.M., Andina, D.: Image Segmentation Using Ant System-Based Clustering Algorithm. In: Corchado, E., Snášel, V., Sedano, J., Hassanien, A.E., Calvo, J.L., Ślęzak, D. (eds.) SOCO 2011. AISC, vol. 87, pp. 35–45. Springer, Heidelberg (2011)
6. Nehmeh, S.A., El-Zeftawy, H., Greco, C., Schwartz, J., Erdi, Y.E., Kirov, A., Schmidtlein, C.R., Gyau, A.B., Larson, S.M., Humm, J.L.: An iterative technique to segment PET lesions using a Monte Carlo based mathematical model. Med. Phys. 38, 4803–4809 (2009)
7. Schaefer, A., Kremp, S., Helbig, D., Rübe, C., Kirsch, C.-M., Nestle, U.: A contrast-oriented algorithm for FDG-PET based delineation of tumour volumes for the radiotherapy of lung cancer: derivation from phantom measurements and validation in patient data. Eur. J. Nucl. Med. Mol. Imaging 35, 1989–1999 (2008)

Swarm Interpolation Using
an Approximate Chebyshev Distribution

Joshua Kirby[1], Marco A. Montes de Oca[2], Steven Senger[2], Louis F. Rossi[2],
and Chien-Chung Shen[1]

[1] Department of Computer and Information Sciences,
University of Delaware, Newark, USA
[2] Department of Mathematical Sciences, University of Delaware, Newark, USA
jothki@udel.edu, {mmontes,senger,rossi}@math.udel.edu,
cshen@mail.eecis.udel.edu

Abstract. In this paper, we describe a novel swarming framework that
guides autonomous mobile sensors into a flexible arrangement to interpolate values of a field in an unknown region. The algorithm is devised
so that the sensor distribution will behave like a Chebyshev distribution,
which can be optimal for certain ideal geometries. The framework is designed to dynamically adjust to changes in the region of interest, and
operates well with very little a priori knowledge of the given region.

For comparison, we interpolate a variety of nontrivial fields using a
standard swarming algorithm that produces a uniform distribution and
our new algorithm. We find that our new algorithm interpolates fields
with greater accuracy.

1 Introduction

The capability for a swarm of robots for tracking the location of a contamina-
tion or other hazard has been well understood for some time [6] [4], but once a
primary body has been identified, or if its location is obvious from the start as
for a large oil spill, mapping out the distribution of the field, the *swarm interpolation problem* is a different matter. Bertozzi et. al. presented a system for edge
tracking, using a linked chain of robots that shape themselves to the outside contours of the region [2]. This method is sufficient for gathering information about
the shape of a contaminated region, but not about the distribution of contaminants within it. Turduev et. al. developed a system for coordinating movement
towards areas of higher concentration, but is designed more for identifing locations of maximum concentrations than for complete coverage of the region [10].
Cortes et. al. put forth a system for coverage via managing the configuration of
Voronoi partitions, but it is optimized to detect events rather than gather data
[3] . Finally, Krause et. al. presented an algorithm using the concept of mutual
information to optimize placement, but assumes a fixed network rather than a
mobile swarm [8] .

Kalentar et. al. proposed a solution involving dividing the robots present into
two mutually exclusive groups [7] . One group acts to orient itself with the edge

M. Dorigo et al. (Eds.): ANTS 2012, LNCS 7461, pp. 324–331, 2012.
© Springer-Verlag Berlin Heidelberg 2012

of the region, in a manner similar to Bertozzi's work. The second group acts to fill out the middle of the group, using a more conventional swarming algorithm to maintain a uniform distribution. The goal of this paper is to demonstrate a technique for improvement upon the distribution of robots within such a region.

When interpolating fields with a large number of measurements, the distribution of interpolating nodes is crucial for minimizing error. An effective distribution for this is based on the roots of a Chebyshev polynomial. (See [1], [9], and the references contained therein for a general discussion.) The following system yields the roots of the desired Chebyshev polynomial.

$$T_0(x) = 1, \quad T_1(x) = x, \quad T_{n+1}(x) = 2xT_n(x) - T_{n-1}(x) \quad (n \geq 1) \qquad (1)$$

Restricting the domain to [-1,1], for instance, Chebyshev polynomials can be specified by

$$T_n(x) = \cos(n \cos^{-1} x) \quad (n \geq 0) \qquad (2)$$

where n is the desired number of roots for the polynomial. Using the positions of the roots of a Chebyshev polynomial as interpolation nodes for a 1D field leads to an error formula of

$$|f(x) - p(x)| \leq \frac{1}{2^n(n+1)!} \max_{|t| \leq 1} |f^{(n+1)}(t)|, \qquad (3)$$

where $f(x)$ is the function being interpolated and $p(x)$ is the interpolation polynomial based on the Chebyshev roots. This distribution is optimal for polynomial interpolation. The distribution can be further extended from 1D into a 2D circle by applying the Chebyshev distribution along the radial axis while distributing points uniformly along the angular axis.

Aligning a swarm to a grid is a difficult problem when the area to be covered is not known in advance, but generating a similar but meshless distribution is a simpler matter. Typical swarming algorithms will produce meshless uniform distributions of robots, so we finesse a standard swarming algorithm by altering the distances measured between robots. If the perceived positions of the robots are transformed such that a Chebyshev distribution appears to the robots to be a uniform distribution, then the robots will naturally settle into an arrangement which is extremely close to an appropriate Chebyshev distribution as they swarm. In this paper, we present a model for achieving this distribution.

2 Force-Based Swarming Model

The simulation is carried out by a modified version of the Qualnet simulation platform, which handles actions and communications as discrete events, and simulates delay and signal loss in communications.

The algorithm utilizes a force-based model, where each robot has attractive or repulsive forces exerted on it by other nearby robots. In order to simulate a more realistic environment with limited communication ranges, and to limit the amount of computation required, a cutoff based on physical distance is applied, with robots that fall outside that distance being ignored by each other when forces are calculated. The overall force for a robot is given by

$$F_n = \sum_{j \in r_{near}} \text{Force}(n, j) \tag{4}$$

where F_n is the total force vector for robot n, r_{near} is the set of nearby robots, and $\text{Force}(n, j)$ is a function giving the force vector felt between two robots n and j.

In order to allow the robots to rapidly spread across a region while being constrained by its edge, we used an algorithm that alters the behavior of robots based on the difference between their current sensor readings and a set field strength, with the force felt by the robots directly proportional to that difference. Robots within the region thus feel repulsive forces and robots outside the region feel attractice forces, which approach zero as robots approach the edges of the region. In addition, a small field-independent repulsive force is included. This serves both to prevent robots on the outside from overly converging, and to prevent robots directly on the edge from becoming completely locked into position. The equation for the forces is

$$\text{Force}(n, j) = (\text{Fscale}_n e^{-F_{\text{factor}}\sqrt{(x_n - x_j)^2}} + R_{\text{scale}} e^{-R_{\text{factor}}\sqrt{(x_n - x_j)^2}})$$
$$\times (\cos(\arg(x_n - x_j)), \sin(\arg(x_n - x_j))) \tag{5}$$

where F_{factor}, R_{scale}, and R_{factor} are scaling factors, and Fscale_n is given by

$$\text{Fscale}_n = a(\phi_n - \text{edgevalue}) \tag{6}$$

where a is a scaling factor, ϕ_n is the value sensed by robot n at its current position, and edgevalue is the value that is sensed on the boundary of the region.

Unlike for physical forces, the net force does not indicate an acceleration, but rather a target velocity. The equation for acceleration is

$$A_n = \kappa(F_n - V_n) \tag{7}$$

where V_n is the current velocity of robot n as measured at the time of computation and κ is a factor determining the rate at which acceleration occurs.

This model will yield a uniform spread across the region of interest. The modifications necessary to produce a Chebyshev distribution are described in the next section.

3   Applying Chebyshev Distribution

In order to move from a uniform distribution to a Chebyshev distribution, the coordinates can be remapped in such a way that they appear uniform when the nodes are properly distributed. The equation for forces then becomes

$$\text{Force}(n, j) = (\text{Fscale}_n e^{-F_{\text{factor}}\sqrt{(vx_n - vx_j)^2}} + R_{\text{scale}} e^{-R_{\text{factor}}\sqrt{(x_n - x_j)^2}})$$
$$\times (\cos(\arg(x_n - x_j)), \sin(\arg(x_n - x_j))) \tag{8}$$

while the formula for $\overline{vx}$, assuming that the points lie along the x axis, is

$$\overline{vx} = \frac{x_{max} - x_{min}}{2}(\pi - \cos^{-1}(\overline{x} - \frac{x_{max} + x_{min}}{2})) \tag{9}$$

where x_{max} is the high endpoint of the region, x_{min} is the low endpoint of the region, $\overline{x}$ is the set of true positions of the robots, and $\overline{vx}$ is the set of virtual positions of the robots, which will be used for generating forces.

The concept of a Chebyshev distribution can be extended to a circular region, with a dense outer edge and a sparse middle. An example of such a distribution is given in Figure 1. Extending a Chebyshev distribution in such a manner requires a shift in the way coordinates are handled, above and beyond simply adding an additional dimension. The same basic density distribution is present, but rather than simply remapping both the x and y axes, the coordinates need to be remapped along every line passing through the midpoint of the region.

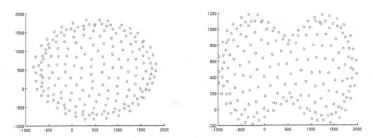

(a) Circular Chebyshev Distribution (b) Starlike Chebyshev Distribution

Fig. 1. 2D Chebyshev Distributions

This can be accomplished by converting the coordinates of the robots from Cartesian to polar, centered on the midpoint of the region. Once this is done, the necessary coordinate shifts will all be parallel to the radial axis, and the magnitude of the shifts will be based solely on the radial positions. The equations for the shifts are

$$\overline{r} = \sqrt{(\overline{x} - x_{mid})^2 + (\overline{y} - y_{mid})^2} \tag{10}$$

$$\overline{\theta} = \tan^{-1}((\overline{y} - y_{mid}), (\overline{x} - x_{mid})) \tag{11}$$

$$\overline{vr} = r_{edge} \cos^{-1}(\frac{\overline{r}}{r_{edge}}) \tag{12}$$

$$\overline{v\theta} = \overline{\theta}, \overline{vx} = \overline{vr}\cos(\overline{v\theta}), \overline{vy} = \overline{vr}\sin(\overline{v\theta}) \tag{13}$$

where x_{mid} is the x coordinate of the midpoint of the region, y_{mid} is the y coordinate of the midpoint of the region, and r_{edge} is the radius of the region.

Perfectly circular regions are unlikely to exist under realistic conditions, but the concept of a Chebyshev-like distribution can be extended by allowing the value of $\overline{r_{edge}}$ to vary across the region. As a result, each robot will have its own idea of how its distribution should work based on its angular position. The formula for this is

$$\overline{vr} = \overline{r_{localedge}} \cos^{-1}\left(\frac{\overline{r}}{\overline{r_{localedge}}}\right) \tag{14}$$

where $\overline{r_{localedge}}$ is an array containing the local edge distances for each node. An example of such a distribution is given in Figure 1.

Ideally, $\overline{r_{localedge}}$ would contain the exact values for the edge distances, but in this algorithm, the only information available is the reported positions and sensor readings of the other nodes. In order to approximate the true distance to the nearest edge, the nodes on the outside of the region are self-selected to act as representatives for a section of the edge, based on whether there is at least a 90 degree arc between any of the node's neighbors. Nodes on the inside look for the edge representative with the closest angular distance, and base their value for $\overline{r_{localedge}}$ on the distance between the representative node and the swarm, while nodes on the outside adopt their own distance, canceling out any shift in position.

4   Experiment Design

Four sets of experiments were performed with the algorithm, each based on a different sensed field. The equations for the four fields are given below, with (15) generating a circular level set, (16) generating a square, (17) generating a perturbed circle, and (18) generating a concave level set.

$$\phi(x, y) = e^{-8((x-.5)^2+(y-.5)^2)} \tag{15}$$

$$\phi(x, y) = e^{(-8\max(|x-.5|,|y-.5|)^2)} \tag{16}$$

$$\phi(x, y) = (.05 * (\sin(15(x - .5)) + \sin(15(y - .5))))$$
$$\times e^{(-8((x-.5)^2+(y-.5)^2))} \tag{17}$$

$$\phi(x, y) = e^{(-8((x-.15)^2+(y-.5)^2))}$$
$$+ e^{(-8((x-.85)^2+(y-.5)^2))} \tag{18}$$

Each set consisted of multiple experiments, across which the number of nodes varied, with each experiment run using 50, 100, 200, or 400. In addition, the same configurations were used for a version of the algorithm with the virtual coordinate remapping, yielding uniform distributions of robots across the region, with the same exterior edge but different interior node density. Each set therefore contained four Chebyshev runs and four corresponding uniform runs.

For all of the runs, the robots were initially placed in a uniform rectangular grid spanning from the coordinates [0,0] to [1000,1000], though they flowed beyond those boundaries during the runs. The parameters used for the swarming algorithm were $F_{factor} = .01$, $a = 200$, $R_{scale} = .02$, and $R_{factor} = 100$. The target edge strength for all fields was edgevalue $= .5$. The scaling factor for acceleration was $\kappa = 1$.

5   Interpolation

In the kinds of applications we are envisioning, all the data we will have at our disposal are measurements at the robots' locations. Thus, our input is a set $\{(\boldsymbol{x}_1, \phi_1), (\boldsymbol{x}_2, \phi_2)), \ldots, (\boldsymbol{x}_N, \phi_N))\}$, where N is the number of robots, $\boldsymbol{x}_n \in \mathbb{R}^2$ represents the location of the nth robot, and $\phi_n = f(\boldsymbol{x}_n)$ is the nth robot's measurement of the variable of interest (represented by the evaluation of the function f, whose definition is not known). Our goal is to find a function g such that $g(\boldsymbol{x}) = \phi$ and that the difference between g and f at locations different from $\boldsymbol{x}_n$, $n = 1, \ldots, N$ is as small as possible. This problem is known as *scattered data interpolation* [5].

In this paper, we tackle this problem using radial basis function interpolation. The goal is to find the values of the coefficients c_k, $k = 1, \ldots, N$ such that

$$g(\boldsymbol{x}) = \sum_{i=1}^{N} c_i \varphi(||\boldsymbol{x} - \boldsymbol{x}_i||_2), \tag{19}$$

where φ is a radial basis function, and $||\cdot||_2$ is the Euclidean norm. The radial basis functions used in our experiments are Gaussians of the form

$$\varphi(r) = e^{-(ar)^2}, \tag{20}$$

where a is a parameter called *shape parameter*. By enforcing the condition $g(\boldsymbol{x}_i) = y_i$, the coefficients c_i, $i = 1, \ldots, N$ can be found by solving the linear system $Ac = \phi$ where the entries A_{jk} of the matrix A are equal to $\varphi(||\boldsymbol{x}_j - \boldsymbol{x}_k||_2)$, $j, k = 1, \ldots, N$, $\boldsymbol{c} = [c_1, c_2 \ldots, c_N]^T$, and $\phi = [\phi_1, \phi_2 \ldots, \phi_N]^T$.

We use two error measures. The first measure is the root-mean-square error (RMS-error) and is computed as follows

$$\text{RMS-error} = \sqrt{\frac{1}{M} \sum_{j=1}^{M} (g(\boldsymbol{\mathcal{E}}_j) - f(\boldsymbol{\mathcal{E}}_j))^2}, \tag{21}$$

where $\boldsymbol{\mathcal{E}}_j$, $j = 1, \ldots, M$ are the evaluation points. The second measure is the maximum error (MAX-error) and is given by

$$\text{MAX-error} = \max\{|g(\boldsymbol{\mathcal{E}}_j) - f(\boldsymbol{\mathcal{E}}_j)|\}. \tag{22}$$

6   Results and Conclusions

We generated a rectangular grid of 500×500 points to sample a function f, which represents the fields described in Section 4, in the region $[-0.2, 1.2]^2$ and selected the points where $\boldsymbol{x} \in [-0.2, 1.2]^2$ to compute the RMS and MAX errors.

The positions of the robots were rescaled so that the boundary of the swarm matched the level curves corresponding to $f(\boldsymbol{x}) = 0.5$ in all the tested fields, resulting in a slightly smaller evaluation domain. The shape parameter of the radial

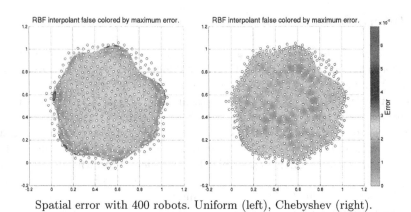

Spatial error with 400 robots. Uniform (left), Chebyshev (right).

Fig. 2. Spatial distribution of the error on the irregular field (Eq. 17)

Table 1. Error Ratios

Robots	RMS Error				MAX Error			
	Circular field	Rectilinear field	Perturbed field	Concave field	Circular field	Rectilinear field	Perturbed field	Concave field
50	6.28e−01	8.35e−01	7.78e−01	7.20e−01	7.36e−01	5.68e−01	**1.15e+00**	**1.17e+00**
100	**1.21e+00**	9.65e−01	**1.29e+00**	9.81e−01	**1.47e+00**	3.76e−01	**2.30e+00**	**2.04e+00**
200	7.00e−01	5.79e−01	**1.08e+00**	**1.38e+00**	8.59e−01	5.39e−01	**2.36e+00**	**3.82e+00**
400	**1.11e+00**	8.37e−01	**2.36e+00**	**2.31e+00**	**2.06e+00**	5.80e−01	**2.98e+00**	**3.60e+00**

basis function used in our experiments was set to 7. Videos and results of the experiments can be found at http://degas.cis.udel.edu/SwarmInterpolation/.

Fig. 2, shows the spatial distributions of the error on the perturbed field with 400 robots. While the uniform distribution shows high error regions close to the edges of the evaluation domain, which confirms the observation made in Section 1 about the tendency of the error to grow near the boundaries of the domain, the Chebyshev-like distribution of robots results in the error being more evenly distributed across the domain.

In Table 1, we report the ratio of the errors obtained with the uniform distribution to the Chebyshev-like distribution using RMS and maximum metics. A ratio greater than one (highlighted in boldface) means that the error obtained with the uniform distribution is greater than the error obtained with the Chebyshev-like distribution.

In the majority of test cases, the RMS and MAX errors were greater than one, meaning that the Chebyshev-like distribution outperformed the uniform distribution. This effect was particularly pronounced for the more complex perturbed and concave fields, and with greater numbers of robots within the fields. The primary exception to this was the rectilinear field, which we assume is due to issues our swarming algorithm has with reaching the corners of the level curves.

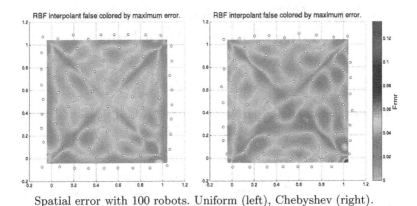

Spatial error with 100 robots. Uniform (left), Chebyshev (right).

Fig. 3. Spatial distribution of the error on the rectilinear field

Acknowledgments. The authors thank Sherry Vaughan for her contributions to this project. This material is based upon work supported by the National Science Foundation under grant CCF-0916035.

References

1. Battles, Z., Trefethen, L.N.: An extension of matlab to continuous functions and operators. SIAM J. Sci. Comput. 25(5) (May 2004),
http://dx.doi.org/10.1137/S1064827503430126
2. Bertozzi, A., Kemp, M., Marthaler, D.: Determining environmental boundaries: Asynchronous communication and physical scales. LNCIS, vol. 309, pp. 403–405 (2005)
3. Cortes, J., Martinez, S., Karatas, T., Bullo, F.: Coverage control for mobile sensing networks. IEEE Trans. on Robotics and Automation 20(2), 243–255 (2004)
4. Cui, X., Hardin, T., Ragade, R.K., Elmaghraby, A.S.: A swarm-based fuzzy logic control mobile sensor network for hazardous contaminants localization. In: 2004 IEEE Int. Conf. on Mobile Ad-hoc and Sensor Systems, pp. 194–203 (October 2004)
5. Fasshauer, G.E.: Meshfree Approximation Methods with MATLAB. Interdisciplinary Math. Sci., vol. 6. World Scientific Publishing, Singapore (2007)
6. Kadrovach, B.A., Lamont, G.B.: A particle swarm model for swarm-based networked sensor systems. ACM, New York (2002)
7. Kalantar, S., Zimmer, U.: Distributed shape control of homogeneous swarms of autonomous underwater vehicles. Autonomous Robots 22(1), 37–53 (2007)
8. Krause, A., Singh, A., Guestrin, C.: Near-optimal sensor placements in gaussian processes: Theory, efficient algorithms and empirical studies. J. Mach. Learn. Res. 9, 235–284 (2008), http://dl.acm.org/citation.cfm?id=1390681.1390689
9. Trefethen, L.: Spectral Methods in MATLAB. SIAM, Philadelphia (2000)
10. Turduev, M., Atas, Y., Sousa, P., Gazi, V., Marques, L.: Cooperative chemical concentration map building using decentralized asynchronous particle swarm optimization based search by mobile robots. In: 2010 IEEE/RSJ International Conference on Intelligent Robots and Systems (IROS), pp. 4175–4180 (October 2010)

Using MOPSO to Solve Multiobjective Bilevel Linear Problems

Maria João Alves

Faculty of Economics, University of Coimbra / INESC Coimbra, Portugal
mjalves@fe.uc.pt

Abstract. In this paper we propose a multiobjective particle swarm optimization (MOPSO) algorithm to solve bilevel linear programming problems with multiple objective functions at the upper level. A strategy based on an *achievement scalarizing function* is proposed for the *global best* selection and its performance is compared with other selection techniques. The outcomes of the algorithm on some bi-objective instances are compared with those obtained by an exact procedure that we developed before. The results indicate that the algorithm seems to be effective in solving this type of problems. In particular, the proposed selection technique provides a good convergence towards the Pareto front.

1 Introduction

Bilevel programming is useful to model decentralized planning problems with two levels in a hierarchy. In bilevel programs there are two decision makers, the *leader* (in the upper level) and the *follower* (in the lower level), which pursue different objectives in a non-cooperative manner and control different sets of variables subject to interdependent constraints. Thus, the decision of each part affects the decision space and the objective value of the other. A bilevel program is very difficult to solve, even the linear case. Multiple objectives at one or both levels add further complexities, thus posing new challenges in handling such problems.

Although the bilevel programming problem has been widely studied, little research has been conducted on multiobjective bilevel problems, either using classical methods, evolutionary algorithms, swarm intelligence or other types of approaches. Recent work on this field includes the developments of Eichfelder [6] on the nonlinear multiobjective bilevel problem. Interactive algorithms have been proposed, e.g. by Shi and Xia [13] and Alves et. al [2]. The latter is devoted to bilevel linear problems with multiple objectives at the upper level and is based on the reformulation of the problem as a multiobjective mixed 0-1 linear programming problem. It can be used in an interactive way and can also determine the whole Pareto front for bi-objective problems. A few evolutionary algorithms have also been proposed, e.g. the co-evolutionary algorithm of Deb and Sinha [4] and the genetic algorithm of Osman et al. [10]. In the context of bilevel multiobjective optimization using particle swarm optimizers, a study of a real-world application problem was carried out by Halter and Mostaghim [7].

M. Dorigo et al. (Eds.): ANTS 2012, LNCS 7461, pp. 332–339, 2012.

In this paper we propose a Multi-Objective Particle Swarm Optimization (MOPSO) algorithm to solve bilevel linear problems with multiple objectives at the upper level and a single objective function at the lower level. This MOPSO algorithm is intended to generate a good approximation set of the Pareto front of the problem. We test and compare different techniques to select the *global best* guides, which are used (together with the *personal best* guides) to define the direction of movement of the particles of the swarm, at each generation. This is a crucial step in a MOPSO algorithm as it affects both the convergence and the diversity of solutions yielded by the algorithm [11]. We consider random selection, selection based on crowding distance values using binary tournaments [12] and a new selection scheme based on an *achievement scalarizing function*. The results of the algorithm considering the different selection techniques are compared with the exact Pareto optimal solutions yielded by the procedure of Alves et al. [2] applied on bi-objective problems.

The remainder of this paper is organized as follows. In Section 2 we state the problem, introduce the notation and some basic concepts. The proposed MOPSO algorithm is described in Section 3. Computational tests and a discussion of the results are presented in Section 4. In Section 5 we draw some conclusions.

2 Problem Formulation, Basic Concepts and Notation

Consider the following formulation of the bilevel linear programming problem with k objective functions at the upper level:

$$\underset{x,y}{Maximize}\ F(x,y) = (F_1(x,y), ..., F_k(x,y)) = Cx + Dy \qquad (1)$$

$$\text{Subject to } x \in X$$

$$y \in \underset{y}{\arg\max}\ \{f(y) = dy : Ax + By \le b, y \in Y\}$$

where $x \in \mathbb{R}^{n_1}$ and $y \in \mathbb{R}^{n_2}$ are the variables controlled by the *leader* and by the *follower*, respectively. $C \in \mathbb{R}^{k \times n_1}$, $D \in \mathbb{R}^{k \times n_2}$, $d \in \mathbb{R}^{n_2}$, $A \in \mathbb{R}^{m \times n_1}$, $B \in \mathbb{R}^{m \times n_2}$ and $b \in \mathbb{R}^m$. The sets X and Y place additional linear constraints on x and y, in particular upper and lower bounds such that $x^L \le x \le x^U$ and $y^L \le y \le y^U$.

Let w represent a solution (x, y) to (1). A solution w' dominates w'' if $F_j(w') \ge F_j(w'')$ for all $j=1,...,k$ and $F_j(w') > F_j(w'')$ for at least one $j=1,...,k$. A feasible solution w is called *Pareto optimal* if there is no other feasible solution w' that dominates it. The set of all objective vectors $F(w)$ corresponding to the Pareto optimal solutions is called the *Pareto front* (P^*). In this paper we refer to as nondominated solution any potentially nondominated solution found by the algorithm and we denote by Q the corresponding set.

3 The Proposed MOPSO Algorithm

The MOPSO algorithm we propose herein is intended to approximate the Pareto front of the multiobjective bilevel problem (1). A particularity of the algorithm stems from the fact that each particle of the swarm is composed by two different parts: x and y. For each $w^i = (x^i, y^i)$, the position of x^i is updated according to the principles of particle swarm optimization, while y is given afterwards through the resolution of the lower-level optimization problem with x fixed to x^i.

The algorithm can be described in the following steps, where the nondominated archive Q is the final output of the algorithm. Different techniques for the *global best* selection are discussed below.

Step 1. *Initialization*

$t = 0$
Initialize the swarm P_t: for each particle $i=1,\dots,N$, randomly generate $x_t^i \in X$ and solve the linear program (2) to obtain y_t^i

$$\max \left\{ f(y) = dy : By \le b - Ax_t^i, y \in Y \right\} \qquad (2)$$

If (2) is unfeasible, generate another $x_t^i \in X$ and repeat the computation of y_t^i. Let $w_t^i = (x_t^i, y_t^i)$, $i=1,\dots,N$
Initialize *velocity* vectors and the *personal bests* for all particles: $v_t^i = 0$ and $p_t^i = w_t^i$, $i = 1,\dots,N$.
Initialize the external archive Q with the nondominated solutions of P_t.

Step 2. *New generation (generate P_{t+1} and update Q)*

For each $w_t^i \in P_t$ ($i = 1,\dots,N$) do:
- Select a *global best* among the particles in Q
  $g_t^i = Select\_gbest(Q, w_t^i)$
- Update velocity (which only concerns part x of the particle)
  $v_{j,t+1}^i = w.v_{j,t}^i + r_1 c_1 (p_{j,t}^i - x_{j,t}^i) + r_2 c_2 (g_{j,t}^i - x_{j,t}^i), \quad j = 1,\dots,n_1$
  with r_1, r_2 random values in [0,1] and w, c_1 and c_2 constants.
- Update position of the particle i, first part x and then part y
  Part x:
  $x_{t+1}^i = x_t^i + v_{t+1}^i$
  Apply turbulence (mutation) to x_{t+1}^i with a given probability
  Push x up/down to limits, if necessary: for each $j = 1,\dots,n_1$, if $x_{j,t+1}^i < x_j^L$ then $x_{j,t+1}^i = x_j^L$, and if $x_{j,t+1}^i > x_j^U$ then $x_{j,t+1}^i = x_j^U$
  Part y:
  Solve (2) with x_{t+1}^i to obtain y_{t+1}^i
  If (2) is unfeasible, then $x_{t+1}^i = x_t^i$, $y_{t+1}^i = y_t^i$ and $v_{t+1}^i = 0$.
  Let $w_{t+1}^i = (x_{t+1}^i, y_{t+1}^i)$.
- Update p^i: if w_{t+1}^i dominates p_t^i then $p_{t+1}^i = w_{t+1}^i$; else if p_t^i dominates w_{t+1}^i then $p_{t+1}^i = p_t^i$; else randomly select p_t^i or w_{t+1}^i to assign to p_{t+1}^i.
Update Q with P_{t+1}

Step 3. $t = t + 1$
If $t = T$, stop. Else, go to Step 2.
Return archive Q.

We adopt a mutation rate (in step 2) of $1/n_1$ [12], with a maximum of 0.1. Uniform mutation is applied, in which a random value for the variable is chosen within its range of values.

At each generation, the archive Q is updated. The procedure to update Q aims to meet a principal goal of maintaining a diverse nondominated solution set, while controlling the size of the archive. Archive size control is important because the number of nondominated solutions can grow very fast, in particular in multiobjective bilevel linear problems whose Pareto fronts are composed by continuous solutions often distributed across disconnected regions. The technique adopted herein to filter Q is based on the crowding distance in the objective space [3], which has already been used in other MOPSO algorithms with good results (e.g. [11]). Accordingly, after Q has been updated by inserting the new nondominated particles of the swarm and removing the elements that became dominated, if the size of Q exceeds a maximum size M, then the crowding distances of all solutions in Q are computed. Then the most crowded solution (the one with the lowest value) is eliminated until the limit size M of the archive is reached.

During the algorithm, the maximum and the minimum values taken by each objective function ($F_j^{\max}$ and $F_j^{\min}$, $j=1,\ldots,k$) are also kept and updated. They are used for normalization purposes in the computation of the crowding distances and in the scalarizing function described below.

3.1   Selecting the Global Best for Each Particle

The procedure $Select\_gbest(Q, w_t^i)$ selects a member of Q to be the global best g_t^i for particle i with current position w_t^i. The selection of global best guides may have a strong impact on both convergence and diversity of the solutions yielded by the algorithm, thus a careful option must be taken. For this purpose, we try three alternative techniques, which we call *gRand*, *gCrowd* and *gScalarf*.

- *gRand*: randomly choose a point from Q. Random selection is the simplest strategy to select a *global best* and can provide some diversity.
- *gCrowd*: first, the crowding distances according to [3] are computed for all solutions in Q; then, for each particle i, a binary tournament is run and the least crowded solution is assigned to g_t^i [12]. Crowding distance has been extensively applied in evolutionary multiobjective algorithms and also in some MOPSO algorithms to promote diversity. The *gCrowd* scheme follows the one used by [12] (one of the best MOPSO algorithms according to [5]).
- *gScalarf*: choose a point of Q according to the function (3) that uses $F(w_t^i)$ as reference point. This does not minimize a Tchebycheff distance but rather optimizes an *achievement scalarizing function* (in the sense of Wierzbicki [14]) that aims at improving the reference point. Function (3) selects an $a' \in Q$ that dominates w_t^i, or is nondominated in relation to w_t^i if the former does not exist.

$$g_t^i \in \underset{\forall a' \in Q}{\arg\min} \left\{ \max_{j=1,\ldots,k} \left(F_j(w_t^i) - F_j(a') \right) \right\} \tag{3}$$

In order to use equalized ranges, normalized objective values are used in (3), so $F_j(\cdot)$ is replaced with $F_j(\cdot)/\left(F_j^{\max} - F_j^{\min}\right)$.

This new selection technique is intended to promote convergence. Note that solutions in Q that dominate the current particle w_t^i are always preferred to solutions that are nondominated in relation to w_t^i (a property already supported by [1]). In our case, this preference exists because the operator $max(.)$ in function (3) gives negative value for any a' that strictly dominates w_t^i, zero for a' that weakly dominates (or is equal to) w_t^i, and positive value otherwise. Then, the operator $min(.)$ selects the minimum among them. Figure 1 illustrates this technique: a_1 is chosen to be the global best for particle w because it dominates w and a_2 does not, although the latter is 'closer' to w. Note that it may happen that $g_t^i = w_t^i$ more often than with the other selection techniques, and specially at the beginning of the algorithm. However, a throughout monitoring of this situation during experiences indicated that this did not happen too often. In addition, excluding $a' = w_t^i$ from consideration in function (3) did not lead to improved results, so the formulation in (3) was kept. Finally, it should be remarked that minimax (or maximin) functions have already been used in MOPSO, but in a different way (e.g. [8]).

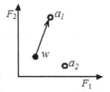

Fig. 1. Illustration of the *gScalarf* technique

The impact of these strategies is tested and compared in the computational experiment reported in section 4.

4   Computational Experiment

The proposed MOPSO algorithm was implemented and tested on multiobjective bilevel problems with formulation (1). It was implemented in Delphi for Windows using the revised simplex method (by calling the free *lpsolve*) to solve the lower level linear programs. To our knowledge, there is no standard set of test problems for multiobjective bilevel linear optimization, so randomly generated instances were used. The rules of [9] were applied to construct a bounded constraint region. Rational numbers with one decimal place were considered. The elements of the matrices C, D, A and B were randomly generated in $[-10, 10]$, except the last row of the constraint matrices whose elements were required to be positive, being generated in $(0, 10]$; the elements of d were also generated in $(0, 10]$; $b_i = \sum_{j=1}^{n_1} A_{ij} + \sum_{j=1}^{n_2} B_{ij} + 2\mu_i$, $i=1,\ldots,m$ with $\mu_i \in [0,n_1]$ random values. In addition, sets X and Y impose that $0 \leq x_j \leq 1$, $j=1,\ldots,n_1$ and $y_j \geq 0$, $j=1,\ldots,n_2$.

In this experiment we considered only bi-objective instances in order to compare the algorithm's outcomes with the true Pareto fronts obtained by the exact procedure in [2]. That procedure can fully determine the Pareto front of bi-objective problems, except for a gap (in objective space) between continuous solutions, which can be set as small as the user wishes. Since we wanted to produce a thorough representation of the whole Pareto front ($P*$), and the exact procedure is computationally expensive, we did not consider large problems. We generated 7 instances (called P1 to P7) with 20 to 40 variables and 10 to 20 constraints. Information on the problem size of each instance is included in table 1 in the format $n_1 - n_2 - m$. For each instance we performed two scans (directional searches) with the procedure of Alves et al. [2], one from the optimum of F_1 to the optimum of F_2, and the reverse scan, both with a maximum gap of 1%. The number of Pareto optimal solutions obtained for each instance varied from about 200 to more than 1000.

To assess the performance of the MOPSO algorithm and the techniques for the global best selection we considered two unary and one binary measures of quality: *Inverted Generational Distance (IGD)*, *Hypervolume (HV)* [15], which can assess both convergence and spread of solutions, and *Coverage of two sets (C)* [15] which compares two approximation sets. The IGD from $P*$ to Q is defined as in [12]: $IGD(P*,Q) = \frac{1}{|P*|} \sum_{p \in P*} d(p,Q)$, where $d(p, Q)$ is the Euclidean distance (measured in the objective space) between p and the nearest element in Q. Lower values of IGD are preferred. The HV measure considers the volume of the region of the objective space that is dominated by the approximation set Q. It was computed using the code from http://iridia.ulb.ac.be/~manuel/hypervolume, setting the reference point to the true nadir point (which was determined by the algorithm [2]). The higher the HV value, the better the approximation set is. The set coverage measure $C(Q^a, Q^b)$ gives the fraction of points in Q^b that are dominated or equal to points in Q^a.

For each each problem, we made 30 runs of the MOPSO algorithm with each selection technique (*gRand*, *gCrowd* and *gScalarf*). We chose parameter values for the swarm size (N), archive size (M) and number of iterations (T) similar to those chosen by Durillo et al. [5] in their comparison study of MOPSOs: $N = M = 100$, $T = 250$. We considered $c_1 = c_2 = 1$ and $\omega = 0.4$ (as in other MOPSOs, e.g. [11]).

For each quality indicator, IGD, HV and C, the median and interquartile range were computed, as measures of central tendency and statistical dispersion. These values are presented in Table 1. For a better assessment of the quality of the approximation sets, the HV of $P*$ is also included. Table 1 only shows set coverage values (C) between the approximations obtained with *gScalarf* and *gCrowd*, the two variants that revealed better performance according to the previous indicators. The best median value of each indicator in each problem is in bold face. In addition, a best median value that is also better than 75% of the values of that indicator in the other variants has gray background.

We believe that the MOPSO algorithm showed an overall good performance in this set of problems. Although the indicator values do not differ very much

Table 1. Median and interquartile range (in subscript) of the IGD, HV and C indicators

		Problem						
		10-10-10 P1	10-15-10 P2	15-10-10 P3	15-15-15 P4	15-20-15 P5	20-15-15 P6	20-20-20 P7
IGD	gRand	$2.34_{0.52}$	$0.72_{0.22}$	$0.28_{0.08}$	$4.18_{0.73}$	$14.15_{7.14}$	$4.26_{1.71}$	$10.19_{3.49}$
	gCrowd	$1.88_{0.44}$	$0.52_{0.05}$	$0.29_{0.11}$	$3.84_{0.86}$	$11.32_{6.13}$	$\mathbf{2.50_{1.31}}$	$7.60_{2.20}$
	gScalarf	$1.94_{0.58}$	$\mathbf{0.43_{0.07}}$	$\mathbf{0.19_{0.05}}$	$\mathbf{3.79_{0.56}}$	$15.94_{6.43}$	$3.25_{1.19}$	$\mathbf{6.34_{1.62}}$
HV	P^*	5866	3517	580	8295	6401	1758	8094
	gRand	$5782_{13.1}$	$3470_{10.5}$	$576_{0.6}$	$7314_{133.9}$	$5663_{164.2}$	$1582_{44.7}$	$7383_{102.3}$
	gCrowd	$5790_{12.5}$	$3480_{6.9}$	$576_{0.7}$	$7362_{221.2}$	$\mathbf{5779_{79.3}}$	$1627_{20.8}$	$7543_{139.1}$
	gScalarf	$5790_{14.6}$	$\mathbf{3489_{2.7}}$	$\mathbf{577_{0.7}}$	$\mathbf{7450_{157.8}}$	$5500_{174.5}$	$\mathbf{1642_{28.6}}$	$\mathbf{7655_{132.5}}$
C	(gCrowd,gScalarf)	$0.13_{0.05}$	$0.13_{0.04}$	$0.13_{0.06}$	$0.10_{0.05}$	$\mathbf{0.49_{0.16}}$	$0.03_{0.04}$	$0.07_{0.08}$
	((gScalarf,gCrowd)	$\mathbf{0.29_{0.07}}$	$\mathbf{0.27_{0.07}}$	$\mathbf{0.19_{0.06}}$	$\mathbf{0.39_{0.08}}$	$0.16_{0.09}$	$\mathbf{0.79_{0.14}}$	$\mathbf{0.82_{0.12}}$

among the selection techniques, we can conclude that *gRand* was outperformed by the other variants. In addition, *gScalarf* provided a particularly good convergence to the Pareto front in most cases. *gScalarf* presented the best coverage measure in all problems except in P5, with a great distinction in P6 and P7. However, some IGD and HV values were better with *gCrowd* than with *gScalarf*. Actually, we could better understand these values by observing the graphical representations of the solutions in the objective space (omitted herein for space reasons). They showed that the approximation sets were generally very close to P^* in a vast area of the Pareto front, but the algorithm sometimes had difficulty to reach the extreme parts of the Pareto front. *gScalarf* could not overcome this weakness better than the others, being still slightly worse in a few cases. The worst performance case for *gScalarf* was problem P5. Nevertheless, it was the only variant that could get very close to the extreme part of P^* near the optimum of F_1.

5   Conclusions and Future work

In this paper we presented a specific MOPSO algorithm for bilevel linear programming problems with multiple objectives at the upper level. A new technique for the *global best* selection was proposed. This selection mechanism revealed a good performance when compared with two other techniques usually used in MOPSO algorithms (random selection and a crowding-based selection). It is very promising because it showed better convergence features than the other techniques. However, in some cases the algorithm had difficulty in reaching the extreme parts of the Pareto front. As future work we intend to address this issue, by exploring the combination of different selection techniques in order to provide more diversity without destroying convergence. Properties of the linear constraints will also be exploited and computational experiments will be performed on problems with more than two objective functions.

Acknowledgements. This work has been partially supported by FCT under project grant Pest-C/EEI/UI0308/2011.

References

1. Alvarez-Benitez, J.E., Everson, R.M., Fieldsend, J.E.: A MOPSO Algorithm Based Exclusively on Pareto Dominance Concepts. In: Coello Coello, C.A., Hernández Aguirre, A., Zitzler, E. (eds.) EMO 2005. LNCS, vol. 3410, pp. 459–473. Springer, Heidelberg (2005)
2. Alves, M.J., Dempe, S., Júdice, J.J.: Computing the Pareto frontier of a bi-objective bilevel linear problem using a multiobjective mixed-integer programming algorithm. Optimization 61(3), 335–358 (2012)
3. Deb, K., Pratap, A., Agarwal, S., Meyarivan, T.: A fast and elitist multiobjective genetic algorithm: NSGA-II. IEEE Trans. Evolut. Comput. 6(2), 182–197 (2002)
4. Deb, K., Sinha, A.: An efficient and accurate solution methodology for bilevel multi-objective programming problems using a hybrid evolutionary-local-search-algorithm. Evol. Comput. J. 18(3), 403–449 (2010)
5. Durillo, J.J., García-Nieto, J., Nebro, A.J., Coello Coello, C.A., Luna, F., Alba, E.: Multi-Objective Particle Swarm Optimizers: An Experimental Comparison. In: Ehrgott, M., Fonseca, C.M., Gandibleux, X., Hao, J.-K., Sevaux, M. (eds.) EMO 2009. LNCS, vol. 5467, pp. 495–509. Springer, Heidelberg (2009)
6. Eichfelder, G.: Multiobjective bilevel optimization. Math. Program. 123(2), 419–449 (2010)
7. Halter, W., Mostaghim, S.: Bilevel optimization of multi-component chemical systems using particle swarm optimization. In: Proc. of the 2006 Congress on Evolutionary Computation (CEC 2006), pp. 1240–1247. IEEE Press (2006)
8. Li, X.: Better Spread and Convergence: Particle Swarm Multiobjective Optimization Using the Maximin Fitness Function. In: Deb, K., et al. (eds.) GECCO 2004. LNCS, vol. 3102, pp. 117–128. Springer, Heidelberg (2004)
9. Moshirvaziri, K., Amouzegar, M.A., Jacobsen, S.E.: Test problem construction for linear bilevel programming problems. J. Global Optim. 8, 235–243 (1996)
10. Osman, M.S., Abd El-Wahed, W.F., El Shafei, M.M., Abd El Wahab, H.B.: An approach for solving multi-objective bi-level linear programming based on genetic algorithm. J. Appl. Sci. Res. 6(4), 336–344 (2010)
11. Raquel, C.R., Naval Jr., P.C.: An effective use of crowding distance in multiobjective particle swarm optimization. In: Beyer, H.-G., Reilly, U.-M.O. (eds.) GECCO 2005, pp. 257–264. ACM Press (2005)
12. Reyes-Sierra, M., Coello Coello, C.A.: Improving PSO-Based Multi-objective Optimization Using Crowding, Mutation and ε-Dominance. In: Coello Coello, C.A., Hernández Aguirre, A., Zitzler, E. (eds.) EMO 2005. LNCS, vol. 3410, pp. 505–519. Springer, Heidelberg (2005)
13. Shi, X., Xia, H.: Model and interactive algorithm of bi-level multi-objective decision-making with multiple interconnected decision makers. J. Multi-Criteria Decsion Analysis 10, 27–34 (2001)
14. Wierzbicki, A.: Reference points in vector optimization and decision support. Tech. Rep. IR-98-017, IIASA, Laxenburg, Austria (1998)
15. Zitzler, E., Thiele, L.: Multiobjective evolutionary algorithms: A comparative case study and the strength Pareto approach. IEEE Trans. Evolut. Comput. 3(4), 257–271 (1999)

Clustering Moodle Data
via Ant Colony Optimization

Päivi Suomalainen

Department of Mathematics and Statistics, Faculty of Science,
University of Helsinki, Finland
paivi.suomalainen@gmail.com

Moodle[1] is a virtual learning environment that keeps track of the activities of students in the learning environment. The amount of data in Moodle is vast and it contains, for example, the whole learning material, information on completed assignments, and records of when a student accesses the learning material. By clustering the students based on the material we can learn to understand the different learning strategies of students in the virtual Moodle environment.

The idea of this article is to study the clustering problem via ant colony optimization (ACO) [2]. ACO has been used before in the context of clustering (see eg. [4], [1]). In this article, we present a novel ACO approach to clustering based on a probabilistic clustering model. That is, we decided to choose a probabilistic clustering framework based on the well-known naive Bayes model. In order to avoid overfitting and underfitting, we use the minimum description length (MDL) principle [3] as our model selection scheme.

Ant Colony Optimization

We try to minimize the MDL code length [3]. At each iteration, the ants build solutions by adding one cluster label at a time to the data items. The local probability models are learned from the previous solution of the ant and used as heuristic information of the current iteration. After an ant has completed the solution, an optimization step is performed: local probability models are learned from the current solution and cluster labels are set again so that they maximize the total probability of the data and the clustering. We use Bayesian predictive probabilities as our probability models with all Dirichlet hyperparameters equal unity. After the optimization steps the ants update the pheromone trails, and after that the pheromones are evaporated. Only the three best scoring ants of the iteration and the all-time best scoring ant are allowed to update the pheromones.

Experiments

We tested our algorithm with the Moodle data. The number of observation vectors to be clustered was 178. We experimented with ten and twenty ants, and we compared the results (see Table 1) with several alternative optimization methods: Expectation-Maximization (EM), Markov Chain Monte Carlo (MCMC),

---

[1] http://moodle.org.

M. Dorigo et al. (Eds.): ANTS 2012, LNCS 7461, pp. 340–341, 2012.

Table 1. Comparison of our ACO algorithm with several different optimization methods. The code lengths are measured in bits.

Method	2 clusters	3 clusters	4 clusters	5 clusters
ACO 10	**2797.25**	2771.71	**2791.58**	**2816.01**
ACO 20	**2797.25**	**2770.92**	2796.28	2824.52
EM	2801.15	2822.03	2878.93	2928.46
MCMC	2817.21	2991.20	3034.74	3101.19
GA	2852.46	2898.56	3067.43	3060.77
TS	2798.29	2771.54	2794.39	2824.32
SA	**2797.25**	2771.53	2813.09	2919.66

genetic algorithms (GA), Tabu search (TS), and simulated annealing (SA). In the light of the results the optimal number of clusters was three and the MDL cost kept on increasing after three clusters. The numbers in the table are bits, and they represent the total code length with uniform code length for the models. We present only the results for the cluster numbers from two to five. The code length for a one cluster model was 2933.98 bits.

When we examined the best clustering found we noticed that the students had divided into the three clusters based on the following: the first cluster included students who had not performed well according to their grade and were inactive, the second cluster included mostly students who had performed mediocre and vere moderately active, and the third cluster included students who had performed well and were active.

Conclusions

The results show that the ant-based approach can compete with other optimization methods. In fact, the ant-based approach achieved the best results with the Moodle data compared to other optimization methods in terms of minimizing the code length. Next, we will test our algorithm with artificial data and with some existing databases. In addition, some more complex models and a factored NML cost are worth examining.

References

1. Chen, L., Xu, X.-H., Chen, Y.-X.: An adaptive ant colony clustering algorithm. In: Proc. 3rd Int. Conf. Machine Learning and Cybernetics (2004)
2. Dorigo, M., Stützle, T.: Ant Colony Optimization. The MIT Press (2004)
3. Grünwald, P.D.: The Minimum Description Length Principle. The MIT Press (2007)
4. Runkler, T.A.: Ant colony optimization of clustering models. Int. J. Intelligent Systems 20 (2005)

Continuous Trait-Based Particle Swarm Optimisation (CTB-PSO)

Ed Keedwell, Mark Morley, and Darren Croft

University of Exeter, UK
{e.c.keedwell,m.s.morley,d.p.croft}@exeter.ac.uk

In natural flocks, individuals are often of the same species, but there exists considerable variation in the traits possessed by each individual. In much the same way as humans display varied levels of aggression, gregariousness and inquisitiveness, so do the animals on which PSO is based [1]. Recent research has shown that this disparity of behaviour is very important in the ability of the flock to solve problems effectively, which might have profound implications for PSO. One of the key aspects is that although certain behaviour types (e.g. more adventurous individuals) might individually be better at problem solving; selecting for a group that all have adventurous traits has been shown to reduce the performance of the flock as a whole [1]. Therefore a flock that has a variety of behaviours leads to better performance in natural systems and it is this that motivates the work here. This paper explores a variant of PSO known as Continuous Trait-Based PSO (CTB-PSO) where individuals within a swarm have traits based on a continuous scale as opposed to discrete behaviour groupings.

There is a considerable body of work that explores behaviour variation through the use of multiple species, but the most relevant single-species work is that of Andries Engelbrecht [2] and the Heterogenous PSO algorithm(HPSO). HPSO is similar in motivation to CTB-PSO but exploits intra-species variation via a discrete 'behaviour' pool. CTB-PSO differs from HPSO as it achieves heterogeneity through the generation of $c1$ and $c2$ coefficient values from a Gaussian distribution with known mean and standard deviation to determine different behaviours for each of the particles in the initialisation stage, in line with what is known about behavioural traits in animals. Once determined, these coefficient selections remain constant for each particle for the duration of the optimisation and the remainder of the PSO algorithm is then run in a standard fashion.

Method

CTB modifies standard PSO by varying the extent to which each particle is influenced by the global and personal best positions within the group.

1. Generate a random population of particles.
2. For each particle, randomly select $c1$ and $c2$ coefficient values drawn from a Gaussian distribution with a specified mean and standard deviation.
3. Execute remainder of PSO as normal.

M. Dorigo et al. (Eds.): ANTS 2012, LNCS 7461, pp. 342–343, 2012.

Experimental Setup and Results

The algorithm was run for 1000 generations with a swarm size of 50, and for 30 repeated trials to account for the effect of the random seed. CTB-PSO was tested on four test functions taken from the literature: *Absolute Value, Spherical, Griewank and Ackley* and results for 2 functions are shown below. For further information on the functions see [2]. Experiments were conducted on problem sizes from 10 to 100 dimensions. The mean and standard deviation of the Gaussian applied to $c1$ and $c2$ was modified, with best performance observed with mean=2.0 and stddev=0.5. The standard PSO operates with fixed $c1$ and $c2$ coefficients of 2.0 and HPSO results are taken from [2].

Table 1. Comparison with HPSO on Two Test Functions From the Literature

Dimensions	HPSO-Griewank	CTB-PSO-Griewank	HPSO-Ackley	CTB-PSO-Ackley
10	**0.0782**	0.130	3.99E-15	**2.01E-18**
30	0.0407	**0.0085**	1.20	**0.27**
50	0.154	**0.0048**	2.87	**1.94**
100	3.61	**0.02**	**2.87**	3.58

The results for all four functions (not shown) show that CTB-PSO improves on our standard PSO formulation at smaller dimensionalities. The comparison in Table 1 shows that in the majority of cases, CTB-PSO also improves on the performance of HPSO in both functions indicating that trait-based PSO could offer improved performance over homogeneous and discrete-heterogeneous PSO.

Acknowledgements. This work was funded by the 'Bridging the Gaps: Exeter Science Exchange' project funded by the EPSRC (EP/I001433/1).

References

1. Croft, D.P., Krause, J., Darden, S.K., Ramnarine, I.W., Faria, J.J., James, R.: Behavioural trait assortment in a social network: patterns and implications. Behavioral Ecology and Sociobiology 63, 1495–1503 (2009)
2. Engelbrecht, A.P.: Heterogeneous Particle Swarm Optimization. In: Dorigo, M., Birattari, M., Di Caro, G.A., Doursat, R., Engelbrecht, A.P., Floreano, D., Gambardella, L.M., Groß, R., Şahin, E., Sayama, H., Stützle, T. (eds.) ANTS 2010. LNCS, vol. 6234, pp. 191–202. Springer, Heidelberg (2010)

Exploring Different Functions for Heuristics, Discretization, and Rule Quality Evaluation in Ant-Miner

Khalid M. Salama and Fernando E.B. Otero

School of Computing, University of Kent, Canterbury, UK
{kms39@kent.ac.uk,f.e.b.otero}@kent.ac.uk

Data mining is a process that supports knowledge discovery by finding hidden patterns, associations and constructing analytical models from databases. Classification is one of the widely studied data mining tasks in which the aim is to discover, from labelled cases, a model that can be used to predict the class of unlabelled cases. Ant-Miner, proposed by Parpinelli et al. [3], is the first ACO algorithm for discovering classification rules. Ant-Miner has been shown to be competitive with well-known classification algorithms, in terms of producing comprehensible model with high predictive accuracy. Therefore, there has been an increasing interest in improving the Ant-Miner algorithm [1].

Otero et al. [2] presented cAnt-Miner as a variation of the original Ant-Miner algorithm, which is able to cope with continuous-valued attributes during the rule construction process through the creation of discrete intervals on-the-fly. Salama et al. recently introduced an efficient version of the algorithm, μAnt-Miner [4], based on selecting the consequent class of the rule before constructing its antecedent and utilizing multiple pheromone types, one for each permitted rule class. This idea gives the motivation of utilizing the pre-selected class in term heuristic information calculation and continuous attribute discretization using different measure functions.

In this paper, we utilize the μAnt-Miner idea of selecting the class before the rule construction to extend cAnt-Miner in three essential aspects. First, we use a class-based measure function to compute heuristic information for a term. Second, we use this function as criteria to carry out the dynamic discretization of the continuous attributes and select the best created interval with respect to the pre-selected class. Third, we use the same measure function used for both previous operations to evaluate the quality of the constructed rule for the sake of pheromone update.

Since we evaluate the quality of a constructed rule with a given function f_x, there is no need to select terms that maximize another function f_y. Intuitively, the selection of terms that maximize f_x should lead to construct a high quality rule with respect to f_x. Moreover, using class-based evaluation function for heuristic information and discretization leads to the selection of terms that are relevant to the prediction of a specific class, rather than selecting terms simply to reduce the entropy among the class distribution on the dataset as in the original cAnt-Miner. Therefore, we use a unified quality evaluation function QEF to compute the heuristic information of a term, to create intervals from continuous

M. Dorigo et al. (Eds.): ANTS 2012, LNCS 7461, pp. 344–345, 2012.

attributes in the discretization, with respect to the pre-selected class value, and to evaluate the quality constructed rule as well.

First, in order to compute heuristic value for $term_{ij}$ given class k, we construct a temporary rule with only $term_{ij}$ in its antecedent and labelled with class k, and we evaluate the quality of this rule using the unified QEF.

Unlike cAnt-Miner, where the threshold value is selected only to minimize the entropy among the classes, we aim to select a threshold value that generates partitions with more relevance for predicting that class by taking the advantage of the class pre-selection. In essence, we calculate the absolute difference in quality (measured in terms of QEF) between the upper and the lower intervals for each candidate value v_i. The idea is to select the threshold value v_{best} that maximizes the quality discrimination—with respect to the current selected class value—between the two intervals.

Finally, the QEF function is used to evaluate the constructed rules, where the best rule created in the colony is used to update the pheromone.

We explore the use of 10 different functions—for heuristics information calculation, continuous attributes discretization and rule quality evaluation. The set of functions is {Certainty Factor, Collective Strength, f-Measure, Jaccard, Kappa, klosgen, m-Estimate, R-Cost, Sensitivity × Specificity, Support + Confidence}.

Concerning the predictive accuracy, there is no algorithm that performs absolutely best. Our results show a great diversity amongst the performance of different quality evaluation functions. This suggests that combining the measures of multiple quality evaluation functions can lead to improvements in the search of the algorithm, since the use of different measures can capture different aspects of the performance of a candidate rule and provide a more robust measure of quality across multiple datasets. Moreover, different quality evaluation functions can be used for each component of the algorithm—i.e., for heuristic, dynamic discretization and rule evaluation. These ideas present research directions worth further exploration.

References

1. Martens, D., Baesens, B., Fawcett, T.: Editorial survey: swarm intelligence for data mining. Machine Learning 82(1), 1–42 (2011)
2. Otero, F.E.B., Freitas, A.A., Johnson, C.G.: cAnt-Miner: An Ant Colony Classification Algorithm to Cope with Continuous Attributes. In: Dorigo, M., Birattari, M., Blum, C., Clerc, M., Stützle, T., Winfield, A.F.T. (eds.) ANTS 2008. LNCS, vol. 5217, pp. 48–59. Springer, Heidelberg (2008)
3. Parpinelli, R., Lopes, H., Freitas, A.: Data mining with an ant colony optimization algorithm. IEEE Transactions on Evolutionary Computation 6(4), 321–332 (2002)
4. Salama, K., Abdelbar, A., Freitas, A.: Multiple pheromone types and other extensions to the ant-miner classification rule discovery algorithm. Swarm Intelligence 5(3-4), 149–182 (2011)

Fuzzy-Based Aggregation
with a Mobile Robot Swarm

Farshad Arvin[1], Ali Emre Turgut[2], and Shigang Yue[1]

[1] School of Computer Science, University of Lincoln, UK
{farvin,syue}@lincoln.ac.uk
[2] IRIDIA, Université Libre de Bruxelles, Belgium
aturgut@iridia.ulb.ac.be

Aggregation is a widely observed phenomenon in social insects and animals such as cockroaches, honeybees and birds. From swarm robotics perspective [3], aggregation can be defined as gathering randomly distributed robots to form an aggregate. Honeybee aggregation is an example of cue-based aggregation method that was studied in [4]. In that study, micro robots were deployed in a gradually lighted environment to mimic the behavior of honeybees which aggregate around a zone that has the optimal temperature (BEECLUST). In our previous study [2], two modifications on BEECLUST – *dynamic velocity* and *comparative waiting time* – were applied to increase the performance of aggregation.

In this paper, we proposed a fuzzy-based aggregation algorithm for cue-based aggregation with a mobile robot swarm (AMiR [1] and simulation software [6]). We compared the performance of our fuzzy-based aggregation algorithm with the state-of-the-art cue-based aggregation strategy BEECLUST and an extension of BEECLUST algorithm that we called the naïve method. BEECLUST aggregation [4] follows a simple algorithm. When a robot detects another robot in the environment, it stops and measures the magnitude of the ambient audio signal and waits based on this magnitude. The higher the magnitude is the longer the waiting time becomes. When the waiting time is over, the robot rotates ϕ degree, which is a random variable drawn uniformly within $[-180°, 180°]$. In the naïve aggregation method [5], we employ a deterministic decision making mechanism based on both the intensity and the direction of the sound signal. In the fuzzy method [5], which is the main contribution of the paper, we calculate the waiting time using the same way as in the BEECLUST and the naïve algorithms, whereas ϕ is estimated using the intensity of the sound signals using a fuzzy logic controller. The fuzzy logic controller has four inputs that are connected to the microphones and one output to estimate the direction of the sound source, hence the turning angle of the robot.

Fig. 1 illustrates the results of experiments with real and simulated robots. In general, when the number of robots increases, the aggregation time reduces significantly, since increasing the population size increases the number of collisions eventually causing faster aggregation. Results show that, fuzzy aggregation is faster than naïve and BEECLUST owing to more precise estimates ϕ values after each collision, which increases the performance of the aggregation. In addition, the fuzzy algorithm is more robust to noise than naïve algorithm.

M. Dorigo et al. (Eds.): ANTS 2012, LNCS 7461, pp. 346–347, 2012.
© Springer-Verlag Berlin Heidelberg 2012

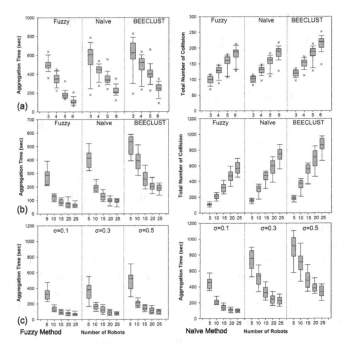

Fig. 1. Aggregation time and total number of inter-robot collisions as functions of population size for fuzzy, naïve, and BEECLUST methods with (a) real robot and (b) simulated robot experiments. (c) Effects of different noise values in different populations for (left) fuzzy and (right) naïve algorithms. Noise is modeled as a uniformly distributed random variable within range $[-\sigma, \sigma]$.

Acknowledgments. This work is supported by EU FP7-IRSES project EYE2E (269118) and LIVCODE (295151).

References

1. Arvin, F., Samsudin, K., Ramli, A.R.: Development of a Miniature Robot for Swarm Robotic Application. International Journal of Computer and Electrical Engineering 1, 436–442 (2009)
2. Arvin, F., Samsudin, K., Ramli, A.R., Bekravi, M.: Imitation of Honeybee Aggregation with Collective Behavior of Swarm Robots. International Journal of Computational Intelligence Systems 4(4), 739–748 (2011)
3. Şahin, E., Girgin, S., Bayındır, L., Turgut, A.E.: Swarm Robotics. In: Blum, C., Merkle, D. (eds.) Swarm Intelligence, vol. 1, pp. 87–100. Springer, Heidelberg (2008)
4. Schmickl, T., Thenius, R., Moeslinger, C., Radspieler, G., Kernbach, S., Szymanski, M., Crailsheim, K.: Get in touch: cooperative decision making based on robot-to-robot collisions. Autonomous Agents and Multi-Agent Systems 18(1), 133–155 (2009)
5. Supplementary Data,
   http://webpages.lincoln.ac.uk/farvin/Supplementary.htm
6. Vaughan, R.: Massively multi-robot simulation in stage. Swarm Intelligence 2(2), 189–208 (2008)

Maturity of the Particle Swarm as a Metric for Measuring the Particle Swarm Intelligence

Zdenka Winklerová

Brno University of Technology, Dept. of Intelligent Systems, Brno, Czech Republic
iwin@fit.vutbr.cz

The *PSO* (*Particle Swarm Optimization*) algorithm is known primarily as a stochastic algorithm which shows signs of intelligent behaviour. In this paper, a maturity model of the particle swarm operational space as a metric for the swarm intelligence is introduced and then, the swarm intelligence is assessed according to this model.

The model is proposed as a combination of the *Maturity Model* of the *C2* (*Command and Control*) operational space and the model of *Collaborating Software*. The swarm particles are considered for a system's software modules, and the *PSO* algorithm for the system. Then, the whole particle swarm is assessed according to generic characteristics of the collaborative behaviour. These attributes are: (i) an appropriate *representation* of information, (ii) the existence of *awareness*, (iii) *investigation*, (iv) *interaction*, (v) *integration*, and (vi) *coordination*.

A three-dimensional *maturity vector* determines the resulting maturity of the swarm operational space. The coordinates of the maturity vector determine the degrees of *allocation of decision rights, information sharing*, and *social interaction* among particles. Depending on the values of the coordinates, the resulting *maturity of the operational space* then takes one of the values (*conflicted, de-conflicted, coordinated, collaborative, agile*).

While analyzing the maturity of the swarm, the cooperative swarming strategies directly derived from the original version of the algorithm published in 1995 were examined. The subject of discussion was to determine what values should take the coordinates in the maturity model so that the swarm could be considered as *coordinated* or *collaborative*.

The highest achieved level of *information sharing* has been evaluated as *shared projection*: While conducting its activity, each particle has an opportunity to learn the accessible information about the global best position, to estimate the situation and to update the shared information if it becomes the global best particle, and to move in the estimated direction. The swarm particles control their activities according to the best position yet discovered, i.e. they *project* this global information into their activities.

In terms of *social interaction* as the particle's ability to combine its own results with the results of the other swarm particles, the swarm can be considered as an *integrated system*, since the swarm particles in all examined variants of the *PSO* algorithm are able to operate simultaneously and react continuously on the intermediate results.

M. Dorigo et al. (Eds.): ANTS 2012, LNCS 7461, pp. 348–349, 2012.

In terms of *allocation of decision rights*, the particles are not completely autonomous, since the particle's velocity during its flight through the hyperspace is artificially regulated from outside the system. It follows from the discussion that the method of the particles' coordination based on the application of tuning parameters *established externally*, namely by *external* inertia weight and *external* acceleration coefficients, is a way of control which is inconsistent with the principle of self-organization as an *autonomous activity* of the individual entities that deal with their own individual tasks and communicate in order to coordinate their activities while solving a common task.

The conclusion from the maturity assessment of the particle swarm is that the swarm system as a whole is not mature enough: A swarm particle does not have the ability of learning from its own experience or from the experience of the other particles, or from some observer inside the search space, to get all the information needed to update its velocity, and if a particle has a problem, the other particles do not know about it. Lack of the system's awareness seems to be the main cause of the persistent unreliability of the *PSO* algorithm and its variants in optimization of multimodal functions with many local optima. In order to improve the system's awareness, the *decision making autonomy of individual particles should be enhanced* so that the swarm could be considered as coordinated or collaborative, eventually.

A solution would be a continual adjustment of the particle's velocity as a function of its level of confidence in its actual direction. However, such approach involves adaptation of behavioural rules so that the particle could use only the coefficients whose value would be provided *from inside the system*, without external control. It means to understand the meaning of the coefficients and the objective function through the swarm operation. Stochastic stability analysis has become a method to understand the *PSO* convergence properties from this point of view. A study has been published in 2009 referring to previous studies in this area showing that the *PSO* algorithm performs well in certain areas of coefficient space. These regions are similar for different objective functions and are dependent on the number of dimensions of the objective function. Given the stochastic nature of the swarm, a more precise adjustment of particle's velocity according to the actual influence of the objective function in a particular location of the search space thus requires continuing research for a deeper understanding, from which the swarm derives its intelligent behaviour.

Multi-objective Firefly Algorithm for Energy Optimization in Grid Environments

María Arsuaga-Ríos[1] and Miguel A. Vega-Rodríguez[2]

[1] Beams Department, European Organization for Nuclear Research, CERN,
Geneva, Switzerland
maria.arsuaga.rios@cern.ch
[2] ARCO Research Group, University of Extremadura, Dept. Technologies
of Computers and Communications, Escuela Politecnica, Cáceres, Spain
mavega@unex.es

Current researches are focusing on optimizing energy consumption in Grid computing [1], being the job scheduling a challenging task. These researches reduce the energy consumption by heuristics or greedy algorithms and some of them try to balance this reduction regarding the execution time using weights for evaluating these objectives. In this work, a new approach is studied related to the multi-objective optimization for these two conflictive objectives, considering them with the same importance. The obtained solutions show the suitable resources for each job and their order of execution. This new approach is called MO-FA (Multi-Objective Firefly Algorithm) and it is based on the recent FA (Firefly Algorithm)[2] adding multi-objective properties to the preceding versions. The scheduler is implemented in the well-known grid simulator, GridSim to recreate the performance of grid infrastructures and compare MO-FA with other schedulers like *Workload Management System* (WMS) from the most used European middleware Lightweight Middleware for Grid Computing (gLite) and also the well-known *Deadline Budget Constraint* (DBC) from Nimrod-G.

MO-FA: Multi-Objective Firefly Algorithm

This multi-objective approach is defined as the minimization of two objective functions. These functions represent criteria that are in conflict each other - execution time and energy consumption-. Because of that, MO-FA returns not only one solution, but a set of them, called *non-dominated solutions*. When this set of solutions are represented in the objective function value space, they form a *Pareto front*. MO-FA is an adaptation of FA designed to solve multi-objective problems. FA is based on the fireflies behaviour which its location represents a solution. The main feature is the attraction among fireflies due to their brightness. Fireflies with more intensity of brightness attract with more force other fireflies with less brightness, causing their movement to the first ones. Fireflies with major brightness represent the best solutions for the problem and their location is represented by the union of two vectors, indicating the job allocation in the available grid resources and the order of their execution. Execution time and energy consumption compose the main firefly properties. In the adaptation of FA to MO-FA, fireflies need to be compared each other

M. Dorigo et al. (Eds.): ANTS 2012, LNCS 7461, pp. 350–351, 2012.

according to the dominance. Once all the fireflies are compared and the updated movements are carried out, a stagnation checking method is applied to the new firefly population. This method is an improvement with respect to the original FA in order to avoid the population stagnation in case that MO-FA suffered it along several iterations. Finally, when the time limit comes the fireflies are classified per Pareto fronts and the first Pareto front is returned as the set of best solutions for the tackled problem.

Results and Conclusions

The obtained results are divided into two complementary studies. On the one hand, the behavior of MO-FA, as a multi-objective algorithm, is studied. Reference point, average hypervolume and its standard deviation [3] are calculated in order to consider them in future improvements from this algorithm or others. These results show that hypervolume percent arises more than 50%, thus it is a good point with respect to the solutions found. Standard deviation also presents a minimum value, so it might be considered that the solutions are quite reliable. On the other hand, MO-FA, WMS and DBC are compared and evaluated. The results prove that MO-FA solutions always dominate the solutions offered by the WMS and DBC reducing their energy consumption around a 50% and 30% respectively, obtaining MO-FA always better response time than the real schedulers. In addition, WMS and DBC algorithm reports unsuccessful jobs when the deadline is more restrictive. While, MO-FA always executes all the jobs required. In conclusion, it might be said that MO-FA is a good competitor respect to WMS and DBC in all the cases. Also, due to their multi-objective qualities, MO-FA offers a good range of solutions for decision support.

References

1. Lee, Y.C., Zomaya, A.Y.: Energy conscious scheduling for distributed computing systems under different operating conditions. IEEE Trans. Parallel Distrib. Syst. 22(8), 1374–1381 (2011)
2. Yang, X.-S.: Firefly Algorithms for Multimodal Optimization. In: Watanabe, O., Zeugmann, T. (eds.) SAGA 2009. LNCS, vol. 5792, pp. 169–178. Springer, Heidelberg (2009)
3. Zitzler, E., Thiele, L.: Multiobjective Optimization Using Evolutionary Algorithms - A Comparative Case Study. In: Eiben, A.E., Bäck, T., Schoenauer, M., Schwefel, H.-P. (eds.) PPSN 1998. LNCS, vol. 1498, pp. 292–304. Springer, Heidelberg (1998)

Particle Swarm Optimization with Random Sampling in Variable Neighbourhoods for Solving Global Minimization Problems

Gonzalo Nápoles, Isel Grau, and Rafael Bello

Centro de Estudios de Informática
Universidad Central "Marta Abreu" de Las Villas, Santa Clara, Cuba
{gnapoles,igrau,rbellop}@uclv.edu.cu

Particle Swarm Optimization (PSO) is a bio-inspired evolutionary meta-heuristic that simulates the social behaviour observed in groups of biological individuals [4]. In standard PSO, the particle swarm is often attracted by sub-optimal solutions when solving complex multimodal problems, causing premature convergence of the algorithm and swarm stagnation [5]. Once particles have converged prematurely, they continue converging to within extremely close proximity of one another so that the global best and all personal bests are within one minuscule region of the search space, limiting the algorithm exploration. This paper presents a modified variant of constricted PSO [1] that uses random samples in variable neighbourhoods for dispersing the swarm whenever a premature convergence state is detected, offering an escaping alternative from local optima.

PSO-RSVN Algorithm

The Variable Neighbourhood Search (VNS) is a simple and effective meta-heuristic for combinatorial problems and global optimization [2] which is based on the systematic change of the neighbourhood in the search process. Inspired by this idea, we present a procedure called Random Sampling in Variable Neighbourhoods (RSVN) which aims to disperse the swarm when it detects the premature convergence state. The main idea of this procedure is to restructure the particle swarm from the selection of random samples uniformly distributed in several neighbourhoods generated around the global best particle of the swarm. In this procedure m neighbourhoods with parameters $\xi_j \in (0,1]$ are computed; where the neighbourhood factor ξ_j is used for controlling the j-th neighbourhood proportion to the size of the search space. After collecting the samples in each partition, a selection process of the particles takes place. These agents will form the new swarm as shown below:

$$\beta = \Phi_1 \cup \Phi_2 \cup ... \cup \Phi_m = \bigcup_{j=1}^{m} \Phi_j | \Phi_j \subseteq \Psi_j, \forall j \ . \tag{1}$$

where β represents the particle swarm and Φ_j is a subset of good enough particles compared to all samples Ψ_j using an elitist criterion. In this procedure each generated particle is a candidate to replace the best global particle, which

M. Dorigo et al. (Eds.): ANTS 2012, LNCS 7461, pp. 352–353, 2012.

complements the swarm dispersion process. The diversity introduced by the dispersion mechanism ensures the exploration of new areas of the solution space, increasing the possibility of escape from sub-optimal solutions. Moreover, due to the elitist replacement, simplicity and low computational cost the RSVN procedure could be adapted and integrated into several evolutionary paradigms.

Performance Study

We compared PSO-RSVN against five approaches evaluated in [3]: constricted PSO, Gaussian Mutation based PSO (GMPSO), Hybrid PSO and Simulated Annealing (HPSO-SA), Quadratic Interpolation based PSO (QIPSO), and Attraction Repulsion based PSO (ATREPSO) by using nine well-known benchmark function taken from [3]. These functions are minimization problems including unimodal, multimodal and noisy functions that helps in deciding the credibility of an optimization algorithm. In each simulation we used 30 particles and 300.000 objective function evaluations in a 20-dimensional search space. In addition, we used two variable neighbourhoods with factors $\xi_1 = 0.05$ and $\xi_2 = 0.1$. Finally, the fitness value for each algorithm was averaged over 30 independent trials.

From the numerical results of the experiments some conclusions came out: PSO-RSVN always finds the global optimum satisfactorily for Sphere, Rastrigin, Griewank, Himmelblau and Shubert functions, whereas for Rosenbrock and Quartic it provides acceptable estimations. For Schwefel function, HPSO-SA locates the best solutions; however, PSO-RSVN finds better approximations than the others. Finally, QIPSO has the best results reported for Ackley function, followed by PSO-RSVN. These results reveal that PSO-RSVN is a competitive and very promising approach for solving global optimization problems. Future work will incorporate a more rigorous statistical analysis to explore significantly differences among these approaches and there will be studied the algorithm performance using other well-known benchmark functions.

References

1. Clerc, M., Kennedy, J.: The particle swarm - explosion, stability, and convergence in a multidimensional complex space. IEEE Transactions on Evolutionary Computation 6, 58–73 (2002)
2. Hansen, P., Mladenovic, N.: Variable neighbourhood search: Principles and applications. European Journal of Operations Research 130, 449–467 (2001)
3. Idoumghar, L., et al.: Hybrid PSO-SA type algorithms for multimodal function optimization and reducing energy consumption in embedded systems. Applied Computational Intelligence and Soft Computing 2011, 12 pages (2011)
4. Kennedy, J., Eberhart, R.: Particle swarm optimization. In: Proceedings of the 1995 IEEE International Conference on Neural Networks, pp. 1942–1948 (1995)
5. Kennedy, J., Russell, C.E.: Swarm Intelligence. Morgan Kaufmann (2001)

Author Index